The Jewish Guards

Supervision in the Dutch Gateway to Hell

Frank van Riet
The Jewish guards
Supervision in the Dutch Gateway to Hell

© 2016, 2022 Frank van Riet

© 2022 English translation: Nedvision Publishing
Translated by: Aylin Kluver
Proofed by: Brian Lissette

 **Nedvision**

Nedvision Publishing, Assen, Netherlands
nedvision.com   info@nedvision.com
ISBN 978 908 308 6088

Cover design & insert layout by: Dick van der Zee

FRANK VAN RIET

The Jewish Guards

Supervision in the Dutch Gateway to Hell

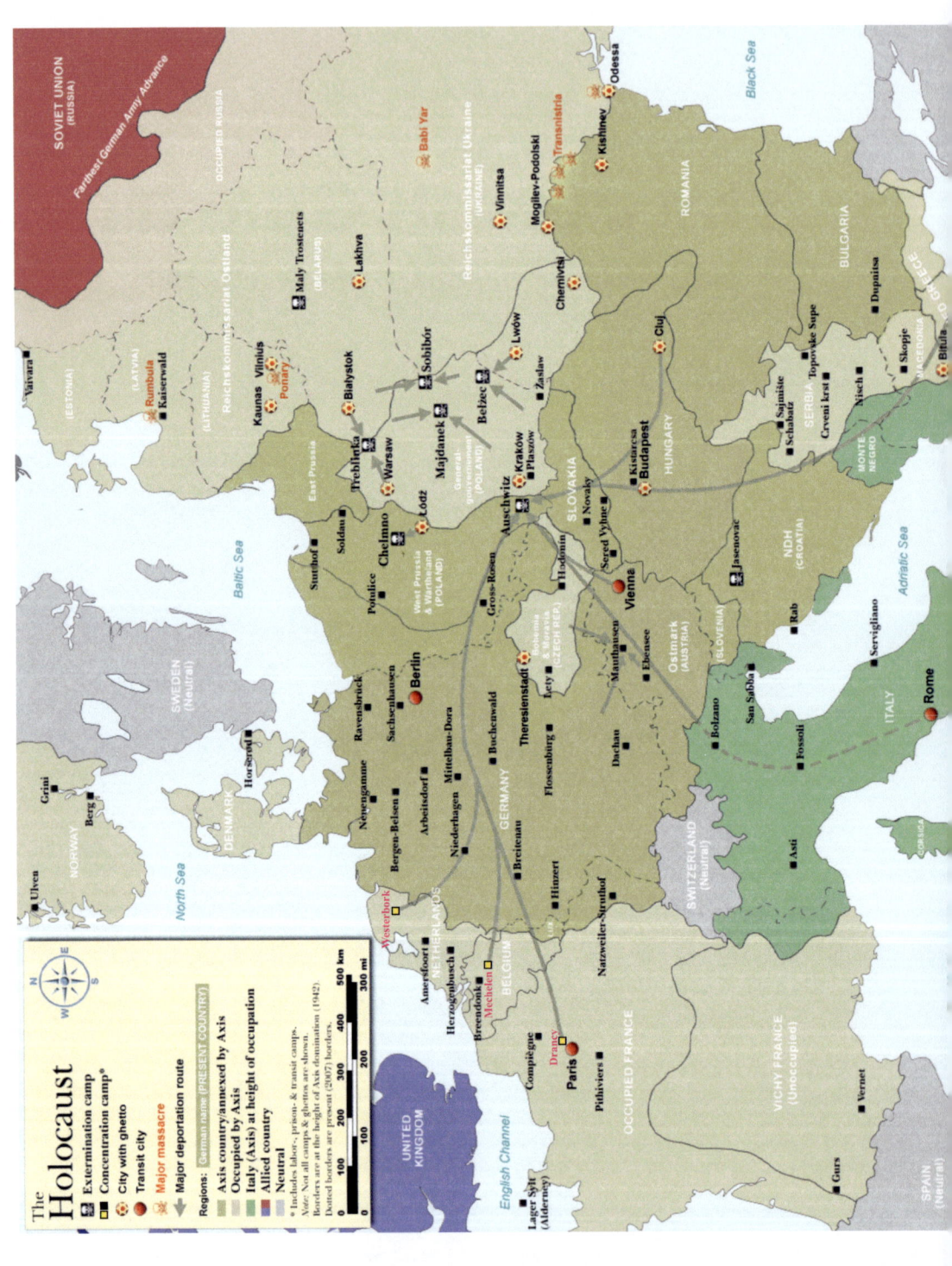

CONTENTS.

INTRODUCTION

In 1939 the construction of a central refugee camp was started on the heath in Drenthe, near the Municipality of Westerbork. The camp, consisting generally of wooden barracks, was destined for the Jews who had fled from the Nazi regime. When the occupier took over the camp on 1 July 1942 and changed its function from a facility for Jewish refugees to a transit camp, order and discipline became even more important than before. The deportation machine had to be started and kept running at full speed. Every hitch could potentially jeopardise the solution of the Jewish question in the Netherlands. From mid-July 1942 onwards, the first trains left for the (extermination) camps. Nearly 107,000 Jews and several hundred Sinti and Roma were deported to these camps, largely via Westerbork.

Apart from a visit to the memorial centre and the camp site, my first more or less direct confrontation with the past of Camp Westerbork took place during an interview with J.J. (Jacobus) Bombergen in early December 1997. This former Sergeant of the State Police was part of a Dutch Police Battalion during the occupation. According to Bombergen, this Amsterdam based battalion was in charge of the outdoor surveillance of the transit camp from 1 June 1944 onwards. He stressed that he and his colleagues had nothing to do with internal affairs and that they were not allowed to maintain contact with the Jews.

The former Policeman was still struggling with the past, even after so many years. He reacted not only fiercely but also emotionally to some (scientific) publications, in which 'his' Police unit was generally depicted very negatively. This did not apply directly to the standard works of Jacob Presser and Loe de Jong[1], since both historians did not include a comprehensive analysis or value assessment of the Dutch guards of Camp Westerbork in their publications. In later studies, the opinion of Bombergen's Battalion is less nuanced and far from positive. Willy Lindwer, for example, wrote in his book *Kamp van hoop en wanhoop (Camp of Hope and Despair)* that most of the Battalion consisted of Schalkhaarders. According to him, these were greatly feared Police Officers who had followed an SS based training course at the Police Training Battalion in Schalkhaar.[2]

Because Lindwer did not criticise the Gendarmerie Detachment that had been in charge of the surveillance of the camp for much longer before the Battalion arrived, Bombergen did not understand Lindwer's negative attitude towards 'his' Battalion. After all, he knew that when the railway line to Westerbork had not yet been finished, the Jews had been escorted from Hooghalen station to the camp by the gendarmes. In addition, Lindwer's book contains a photo in which it is clearly visible that the gendarmes celebrated the Germanic Yule festival in the camp together with the Schutzstaffel, or SS. Bombergen said that it left a bad taste in his mouth, because the Police Battalion did not maintain any contact with the SS Officers in the camp.[3] By saying this, he tried to confirm that he and his colleagues had played a different and much more limited role during the German occupation of the Netherlands.

The Jewish journalist Philip Mechanicus, who had kept a diary during his stay at the camp, admitted that there were some bad men among the gendarmes, but he also ruled that the majority was friendly and mild. According to Mechanicus, the Dutch guards, originating mainly from the three northern provinces, looked surly and strict, but were generally mild in their actions. They were even said to pity the Jews they were supposed to guard and they were far from positive about the task imposed on them by the occupier.[4]

It is not possible to immediately be able to create a unanimous judgment on the various Dutch Surveillance Units of Camp Westerbork. It should also be borne in mind that these units were only responsible for outdoor surveillance from January 1943 onwards. For the supervision of the barbed wire fence, a specific service group was formed that consisted of Jewish men from the camp's population. In Dutch it was called the Ordedienst (OD). This term will be used in the rest of the book to refer to this service group. Mechanicus' view on this service was anything but mild. Among other things, he wrote that the worst people among the Jews, both German and Dutch, had been chosen as OD members. They were rude men, without civilisation, without feeling, without compassion; who lived solely for a cigarette and an easy adventure with women of their own kind. According to Mechanicus, the Jews in the camp had labelled the OD members as 'the Jewish SS'.[5] Presser and De Jong took over this term.

Another historian, Jacob Boas, concluded that the tasks of the OD corresponded to those of the regular SS in other camps. He further described these tasks as misdeeds and because the camp residents witnessed these on a daily basis, they feared and despised the OD members with an 'unprecedented ferocity'.[6] Other statements and literature show that the guards of Camp Westerbork were both hated, loved and feared. If it could be said that the Amsterdam Police Battalion was not made up solely of highly feared Policemen, that the gendarmes were good to a large extent and that the term 'Jewish SS' was too harsh for the OD, why did the occupying forces not deem it necessary to employ many of their own men instead? It would have been much more in line with their usual approach to send a number of sadistic and brutal guards from their men to Westerbork, as they did to many other camps and to the Extermination Camps, the final destination of the packed trains. However, the presence of only a dozen SS men, most of whom had suffered grave injuries on the Eastern Front, proved sufficient to run Camp Westerbork like a well-oiled deportation machine. In addition to answering the question of how the organisation and the monitoring of the camp could have been so effective, the background and motivation of the individual guard is explored for the first time.

Thank you to all who helped make this book possible. Dirk Mulder, former director of the Memorial Centre Camp Westerbork, for facilitating the research, and curator Guido Abuys for his help. I would also like to thank those who have contributed as a reader or in another way: Herman and Willem Brinkman, Johannes Houwink ten Cate, Coen Cornelissen, Libbe T. Henstra, Bram Hoeijenbos, Bas Kortholt, Ton Rappa and Douwe van der Werf.

1. FLEEING THE NAZI REGIME

On the morning of Saturday 1 April 1933, uniformed and partially armed National Socialists, including members of the *Sturmabteilung* (SA), marched through the streets of many German villages and cities. Linnich, near the Dutch border, was one of them. Around 10:00 AM a number of National Socialists who came from the village were on their way to the shops and businesses of Jewish owners. Linnich, with a total of 2,248 residents, had a Jewish community of 138 people.[1] A few SA men had chosen the Department Store of the Jewish businessman Albert Moses, located at Rurdorfer Straße 40, as a target. They stood guard in front of the entrance to scare off customers. They likely also had pamphlets with them on which stood: *Deutsche! Wehrt euch! Kauft nicht bei Juden!* A photograph was taken of customers leaving the shop and they were warned that they were in the process of supporting a Jewish business.

Born and raised in Linnich[2], Albert married Henriëtte Samuel Baum in 1920. The couple had a son and a daughter. Albert was actively involved in

Members of the SA in front of a Jewish store with a warning sign.

the village community as a member of the Voluntary Fire Brigade and the carnival association. He even served in the German Army during the First World War. Back then, the fact that he was of Jewish origin was not considered a problem. For his actions on the front, Albert was awarded the Iron Cross.[3]

Boycott Campaign

At the end of January 1933, after the appointment of Adolf Hitler as chancellor, many Jews noticed that there was more and more hatred and aggression towards them. The new rulers blamed the Jews for all problems and considered them the inferior race. From the end of February onwards, many 'wild actions' took place, of which mainly Jewish merchants and traders were victims. They were abused, threatened, imprisoned and in some cases even murdered. In addition, their businesses and shops were plundered and destroyed or closed by order of the National Socialists. Several countries, including Great Britain and the United States, protested against these actions and some (Jewish) organisations proceeded to ban German wares and services.

The new National Socialist rulers saw in this so-called *Greuelhetze* from abroad an opportunity to take large scale measures against the German Jews for the first time. Dr. Joseph Goebbels, Reich Minister of Propaganda, was partially responsible for the national boycott action, which then took place on Saturday 1 April. The action had been announced in the newspapers. The Jewish people would find out who they were dealing with that Saturday. However, the organisers had probably hardly taken into account the Sabbath, because they found many shops and businesses closed. That is why the National Socialists began bashing windows and looting.[4]

For many Jews, the boycott action and the increasing anti Semitism were signs that there was no future for them anymore in Germany. As a result, the first major emigration wave began in 1933. They hoped to be able to build up a better life elsewhere. Approximately 51,000 men, women and children were able to leave Germany quite simply. Of this group, 4,000 people chose the Netherlands as their (temporary) destination, including Albert Moses. He saw his expectations of the future fall apart as well because of these events, so he went to Sittard with his family. Here the businessman opened a furniture store, which he named 'De Limburgsche Meubelcentrale'.[5] Albert's wife followed his example and became an entrepreneur. She opened a fashion house called 'De Dame' at Limbrichterstraat 30 in Sittard.[6]

Initially, the first group of foreigners was able to settle in the Netherlands without having to deal with legal regulations. According to the Act of 1849 regarding the admittance of aliens, foreigners who had sufficient means of livelihood and who were in possession of valid documents would be granted access to the Netherlands. The second major exodus started after the introduction of the so-called Nuremberg Laws on 15 September 1935. These particularly racist laws, which are also referred to as 'racial laws', banned non-Jewish Germans from marrying Jews or having sexual relations with them. Furthermore, the Jews lost all civil rights.[7]

Because many of the Jews who had emigrated to the Netherlands found work, the chances of anti Semitism developing among the Dutch population increased significantly. Partly because of the already existing crisis, there were not many jobs available, which led to a large number of families having to live on Government support. As in Germany, there was the possibility that Jews who had been allowed into the Netherlands would be blamed for the increasing unemployment and poor conditions. The Government considered it of vital importance to prevent further escalation. One of the measures taken to prevent this was the continuous tightening of refugee policy. By introducing a permit system in 1934, refugees already had a smaller chance at finding work. The result of this measure was that those who did not have their own funds were less likely to meet the requirement of having sufficient means of livelihood.[8] In addition to more stringent measures in the Netherlands, the persecution of Jews in Germany began to take on greater forms. As a result, the Jews' escape from the Nazi regime was increasingly hasty and often difficult.

When Albert Sachs[9] wanted to leave Germany with his wife Emma and their daughter Friedl, they faced the stricter refugee policy. In May 1938 they asked permission from the Dutch authorities to move to Borne. It was no coincidence that they chose this village in Overijssel, as Emma was born there and several of her relatives, including her brother, still lived there. Mid July 1938, the family received a message via the Mayor of Borne that the Minister of Justice had decided to allow them a temporary stay. However, certain conditions were attached to this: they had to be in possession of valid residence documents and their stay in the Netherlands could not be paid for by the public purse. For the latter, the family could count on the support of the church council of the Dutch Israeli Municipality of Borne if necessary. In a letter, the church council let the Sachs family know that they would never have to use public or private charity. If this should prove to be necessary, the church would take care of them. But the family did not need help, because Emma got a job as a teacher at the Jewish school in Almelo.[10]

Novemberpogrom - Kristallnacht (Night of Broken Glass)

In early November 1938, Ernst vom Rath, Secretary of the German Embassy, was shot down in Paris by the 17 year old Herschel Feibel Grynszpan, a Jewish Polish immigrant. The Secretary lived for another few days, but died of his injuries on 9 November. This incident led the German authorities to announce a national retaliation campaign immediately.[11] Thus, on the night of 9 to 10 November, many Jewish properties fell prey to the vindictive National Socialists. A large number of synagogues went up in flames. Furthermore, Jewish shops were destroyed and plundered, while the windows of many of the Jews' residences were smashed. Because of all the broken glass, this night went into history as the *Reichskristallnacht*.

Another retaliatory measure involved arresting a great number of Jewish men, including Siegfried Frank.[12] Siegfried worked in his father's butcher's workshop in his hometown Velen, but after the number of customers and sales dropped as a result of the boycott, there was nothing more to do than to rent out the business. Siegfried lost his job, but was given a job by a Jewish businessman in nearby Gemen. There he was arrested during the *Kristall-nacht* and locked up in the local fire station with a number of other Jewish men. A few days later, it was decided at the headquarters of the *Geheime Staatspolizei* (Gestapo) in Münster that those who had visas for another country could be released immediately. Since Siegfried did not have these papers, this did not apply to him. On 15 November 1938, he received a message from the Mayor that he would be transferred to a Concentration Camp two days later, together with six other Jewish men. It was not yet known which camp this would be.

In the meantime, family members of his 18-year-old fellow inmate, Werner Romann, were feverishly working to get him and the others visas that would allow them to go to the Netherlands. For this they called on acquaintances and friends from Winterswijk. On 17 November, the day of transport, the telegram came which showed that Werner Romann, Moritz Neumann, Richard Wolff and Siegfried had permission to settle in the Netherlands. The men left Germany as soon as possible on the day of their release.[13] Siegfried reported directly at the crossing point in Winterswijk. There he was allowed in on the grounds of a so-called family visit by order of the border inspector.[14]

Hermann Anspacher[15] owned a horse and cattle trade at Kornstraße 37 in Bremen. Because of the trade ban imposed in 1937, he could hardly keep his business running. In the *Kristallnacht*, Hermann was arrested and taken to Sachsenhausen. This camp, together with Buchenwald and Dachau, was one of the Concentration Camps where 30,000 mainly Jewish men were imprisoned in mid-November. Hermann and his wife had managed to send their son Bernhard and daughter Rosemarie abroad safely. Bernhard left in November 1938 with a so-called *'Kindertransport'* (children's transport) to England. There he joined the *Manchester Regiment in 1940*. Rosemarie was placed with family members in Antwerp.

After a few weeks, Hermann was allowed to leave Sachsenhausen, provided that he did not tell anything about his experiences, would strictly comply with the trade ban and would leave Germany as soon as possible. Because there was a possibility that he could emigrate via the Netherlands to the United States, he moved to Groningen in early April 1939, where some family members let him move in. His wife remained alone in Bremen because she had not yet been given permission to settle in the Netherlands. The formalities were not completed until 8 May 1940. Since the German Army was on the verge of invading the Netherlands by then, it was impossible for her to travel to her husband. The family members with whom Rosemarie had been staying fled and left her in Antwerp; an aunt living in Brussels took her in. After a while, her mother managed to bring Rosemarie to Bremen. However, family reunification in the Netherlands would no longer take place, because mother and daughter were deported to Poland in November 1941. Sometime later, both women ended up in the Minsk ghetto. There they were killed at the end of July 1942, during a purge by the SS or the German Police.[16]

Initially, it did not seem that the victims of the November pogrom could easily settle in the Netherlands, because the Government had drastically tightened the admission policy in May 1938 once again. After Austria was annexed by Germany several months before, it was expected that a large number of refugees would come to the Netherlands.[17] Via a widely spread letter, the Minister of Justice, Mr. C.M.J.F. Goseling, announced that the influx of refugees would be restricted. New refugees received the label 'undesirable alien'. People who had entered the Netherlands after 1 March 1938 and were arrested were sent across the border and those who reported at the border were not allowed to enter the country. Border surveillance was extended and the local Police were given a broader task.

Even if a person had sufficient financial resources, this was no longer a criterion for admission. The Inspector of the Royal Gendarmerie or the relevant Attorney General could only consult the Minister if the refugee's life was in any real danger if they were not admitted or sent back.[18] It will not surprise anyone that the number of applications for a visa increased significantly after the *Kristallnacht*. More than 40,000 people tried to leave Germany in this legal way. At first, it seemed that the Dutch Government would stick to the stricter admission policy and actually keep the borders closed. After articles about appalling incidents at the border appeared in the newspapers and the Dutch population strongly criticised the refugee policy, the Government allowed about 10,000 refugees until May 1939. Persons who were not eligible and therefore did not receive a visa could only attempt to cross the border illegally. This was not easy because of the border control. Still, thousands of refugees managed to enter the Netherlands in an unofficial way in the end.

The brothers Hans[19] and Peter Margules[20] belonged to the group of refugees who wanted to cross the border without the necessary papers. The brothers had been in a Jewish orphanage from 1931, when their father had passed away, until 1936. After the November night of 1938, Hans lost his job as a window dresser in a Berlin fashion store, after which he decided to leave with his brother to the Netherlands. An attempt to cross the border at Kleve seemed initially to fail because a Dutch Customs Officer refused to let them in. After there had been telephone contact with The Hague several times, they still got access to the Netherlands and thus obtained the legal status.[21]

The trip Werner Bloch[22] made to the Netherlands went a little less smoothly. Although Werner was able to hold his own for some time and as Jewish boy even participated in events with a National Socialist touch, he too was not allowed to go to school anymore in the long run. He left his familiar environment to work at his uncle's wholesale business in Essen. Werner rented a room, where he did not notice what was happening during the November night in question, because he was in a quiet part of the city. When he took the tram to work in the morning, he saw what horrible things had happened that night. Shop windows had been smashed everywhere and his uncle's business had been turned into a mess.

Partly because of the many warnings, Werner soon figured out that there was no future for him in Germany. From his aunt he received the address of a man in Osnabrück who could put him in contact with someone who could help him cross the Dutch border against payment of 150 marks. Relatively speaking, this was probably a reasonable amount, because there were also refugees who were offered assistance only in exchange for large sums of money or valuable goods and were then handed over to the German Police anyway. Yet the trip seemed to come to an early end for Werner as well. The person who was going to help him with the crossing had become scared. Eventually, this person decided to drop Werner a few kilometres away from the border on the night of 17 to 18 November.

He was instructed on the spot to try to get around the now reinforced border surveillance in the dark. If he succeeded in reaching the Netherlands in this way, he had to go to a pub near Nieuw Schoonebeek. Hours later than expected, Werner arrived at the agreed location. The next day he was transferred to Groenlo by bus and train. The journey was not without danger, because patrols of the Gendarmerie were actively looking in the border area for refugees who, if they were found, would be sent back across the border immediately. Despite these patrols, Werner managed to reach Groenlo, where he was given shelter by the Jewish family Heijmans on the Mattelierstraat. There he was safe for a while.[23] Every Jewish emigrant or refugee, whether legal or illegal, had his own history, but had come to the Netherlands with the same ideals: a safe future in a free country. The first groups of emigrants/refugees who moved to the Netherlands between 1933 and 1938 were generally likely to adapt to a greater or lesser extent to the new situation. Many of them found a job despite the problematic job market. At first, it seemed that those who had crossed the border, often illegally, since the beginning of November 1938 also quickly acquired a place in Dutch society. For example, Hans Margules, together with his brother Peter, could turn to private individuals in The Hague. Here Hans received a scholarship for the Hague Academy of Fine Arts and was able to further develop his creativity.[24]

Werner Bloch initially thought he was safe with the family in Groenlo; the application for a temporary residence permit seemed like a formality. However, when he had to go to the town hall sometime later to retrieve the relevant document, he was sorely disappointed. Instead of a residence permit, Werner received a form stating that as an illegal refugee, he had to leave the Netherlands within 24 hours. The Jewish community of Groenlo did not agree with this decision and contacted influential acquaintances directly. They were successful, because Werner was informed shortly after that he could still retrieve his temporary residence permit. His foster parents took care of him and had him enrolled as a pupil of the vocational school in nearby Winterswijk.[25]

Besides Werner, more young refugees living in Groenlo had received a temporary residence permit from the local Police. This was true at least for Siegfried Frank and Sigmund Keller.[26] They received the coveted paper from the Police on 19 November.[27] Nevertheless, the situation for them and many other refugees soon changed.

Refuge In The Netherlands

Mid December 1938 the Legal Secretary at the Second Department of the Ministry of Justice, Mr. J.C. Tenkink, wrote in a note to the Secretary General of Justice, Mr. J.R.M. van Angeren, that the number of illegal refugees in Amsterdam had increased to 400 and that strong measures had to be taken. According to Tenkink, the Jews residing illegally in Amsterdam should be housed in a camp where it was less pleasant to stay than it was in the residences of those who had entered the country with the permission of the Ministry of Justice.[28]

Minister Goseling sent a letter to the Attorney General the next day. In this he indicated that despite the tightened border control, a significant number of refugees had been able to enter the Netherlands without his permission. In his view, this uncontrolled entry was unacceptable in connection with public order. That is why he decided to place all male refugees who had been staying in the Netherlands since 10 November in a separate camp.[29] For this purpose, various places of residence were sought all over the country. The legal and illegal refugees had to be taken care of separately. For the legal refugees, for which the Ministry of the Interior was responsible, the quarantine establishments at the Zeeburgerdijk in Amsterdam and Beneden Heijplaat near Rotterdam, the houses 'Cromvliet' and 'Overvoorde' in Rijswijk Z.H., the 'Zeehuis' in Bergen aan Zee, the Israeli Health Colony in Ter Heide and the 'Noorderhuis' in Hoogeveen were used. In total, there were about 50 locations that served as residences for Jewish refugees.

At the beginning of 1939, the brothers Margules had to exchange the busy The Hague for the quarantine facility in Beneden Heijplaat, which had been completed in 1933 and had hardly been used. A high fence with barbed wire had been placed around it and there was a guardhouse at the entrance, from which a guard with a shepherd dog supervised.[30] Initially, the conditions were far from optimal and there was little entertainment, but this changed over time. The composition of the group, which usually consisted of 200 to 300 people, changed regularly because refugees were allowed to leave abroad or were transferred to other shelters.

The latter was true for the Margules brothers. A few months after their arrival at the Heijplaat facility, they moved to the former emigrant hotel of the Holland America Line on the Wilhelminakade in Rotterdam. This building had been put into use at the beginning of January 1939 and there was room for 250 mainly legal refugees. Due to their legal status, residents were allowed to move outside the hotel premises. They could apply for the necessary permits they needed from the Detectives of the Rotterdam Police present at the hotel.[31] This measure allowed Hans Margules to continue his training at the Rotterdam art academy.[32]

The shelters for the illegal people were supervised by the Ministry of Justice and were less numerous than those for legal refugees. The 'Rotterdamsch Vakantiekamp' in Hook of Holland, the Norg labour camp in Veenhuizen and the 'Roomsch Katholieke Kweekschool' of the Heilige Hart convent in Reuver were the most important locations. The refugees were mainly housed in vacant buildings.[33] At the building in Reuver, where there was room for about 150 people, three buses with Jewish refugees from Germany and Austria arrived from Amsterdam on 20 December 1938 under Police supervision.[34] A few days before, the Jewish men in Amsterdam had to report to the *Comité voor Bijzondere Joodsche Belangen* (Committee for

Special Jewish Affairs). Those who did so were detained and handed over to the immigration Police.

After being locked up for a few nights, a journey to an unknown destination followed. Women and children stayed behind in Amsterdam and were generally placed there with private individuals. At first, the men were afraid that they would be returned to Germany, but eventually their journey ended in Reuver near the German border.[35] In addition to the Amsterdam group, a number of Jewish refugees residing elsewhere in the country were brought to Reuver.[36] One of them was Werner Bloch. After spending a quiet period of about three months with the family in Groenlo, the situation changed on 13 February 1939. That day, two Policemen appeared at the house with a letter from the Minister of Justice. This showed that they had been ordered to transfer Werner to a place for illegal Jewish refugees in Limburg. Protesting would no longer help. Werner had one hour to pack his things and say goodbye. Under the guidance of the two Policemen, he went on a journey, with Reuver as final destination.[37]

Siegfried Frank and Sigmund Keller also had to exchange Groenlo for this facility. The entry in their passports that related to their residence permit was deleted. According to a questionnaire sent to Reuver, Siegfried intended to emigrate to Canada or Palestine. Sometime later, he received a message from the Canadian Government that he would not receive a possible Landing Permit before 1940. The Committee for Jewish Refugees in Amsterdam then tried to make his emigration to Palestine possible. Meanwhile, as he awaited the outcome of this attempt, he stayed in Reuver.[38]

In the beginning, the men were allowed to walk through Reuver once or twice a week, together and under the guidance of Policemen. They gradually gained more and more freedom of movement. First they were allowed to go out a few hours a week, provided with a special pass, and they were later given permission to leave the building for 24 hours.[39] Despite the increase in the number of privileges, the mood dropped due to the horrors that took place in Germany. The men were allowed to write letters, read newspapers and listen to the radio, so they were aware of the situation in Germany.[40]

This knowledge and the previous experiences with the Nazis increased the tension among the refugees. Among other things, they were afraid that they would be too close to the border in the event of a possible raid and would therefore not be safe. By writing letters to the Government and Queen Wilhelmina, the refugees tried to gain sympathy and understanding for their situation, with the aim of being transferred to facilities farther away from the border. Eventually, the Government complied with their request. At the end of August 1939, the men left by boat to a destination unknown to them. It was certainly far enough away from the border, because the journey ended in Hook of Holland. In this coastal town, the former export slaughterhouse 'Vianda' became the new home of Werner Bloch, Sigmund Keller, Siegfried Frank and the other refugees from Reuver. Since the Second World War had now begun, Hook of Holland had an important role in connection with the coastal defence. This resulted in the need for the creation of barriers on the beaches, for which volunteers were sought. Werner signed up for this. The advantage of this work was that there was more freedom of movement on the beach, so that he felt more like a free man.[41]

The feeling of having sufficient freedom was certainly not experienced at first by Ernst Rosendorff[42], who, together with 218 male refugees, came from Amsterdam and was transferred to the Norg labour camp of the state labour institution in Veenhuizen. Two sections of this establishment were set up as a facility for illegal Jewish refugees. Like the men who had been brought to Reuver, Ernst's group departed by bus and was supervised by Policemen, and they too feared that the trip would end in Germany.

Although this was not the case, the stay in Veenhuizen was described as shocking and degrading.[43] It is said that refugees were treated there as prisoners, while sanitation and heating were shockingly inadequate. There was also too little food. Ernst slept in a hammock made of burlap hanging in a steel cage. At night the cage was locked. Perhaps this was because the Military leadership, which itself was struggling with the circumstances, was afraid that the refugees would flee again and thus took out their frustrations on them.[44] News of this undesirable situation soon reached the Government in The Hague. The Government decided on 3 January 1939 to transfer the 182 refugees still present in Veenhuizen, including Ernst, to the buildings that had been abandoned by the Navy in Hellevoetsluis in South Holland.[45]

Limited Freedom

Because they were placed in a shelter, the refugees had to surrender a substantial share of their freedom. For some men, it was the second time that they had to deal with these kinds of circumstances in a short period of time. Because of their Jewish background, they had previously been in a German Concentration Camp. One of the measures limiting their freedom was censorship of incoming and outgoing letters. A request from the Committee for Special Jewish Affairs to the Government to abolish this measure did not directly produce the desired result. According to an official of the Ministry of Justice, this decision was taken in the best interest of both the refugee himself and the Netherlands in general. Certain communications could cause problems for relatives still residing in Germany. In addition, it was possible that certain texts were detrimental to the relationship between the Netherlands and Germany, since it was assumed that the German authorities read the letters. It was feared that they would take offence at judgments less favourable to them.[46] Over time, the control over correspondence became less strict, particularly over the communications of the legal refugees.[47]

Especially the married men whose spouses and children generally had not been transferred to the shelters had to deal with another measure. In most occasions, women were allowed to visit, but they often had to make a long journey by public transport. In Hook of Holland the journey for the women ended in a deception at the end of December 1938. In connection with a few escape attempts, all visits were prohibited. In order to prevent new escape attempts, a barbed wire barrier was created and lamps were placed on the rear side. On the outside, guards with dogs were supervising and Police Officers of the Municipal Police also kept an eye on the barrier. Speaking with the guards outside, which at times included relatives, was forbidden.

Despite these intensified measures, the women still came to visit. They would wait outside the barrier, while the men inside gathered in front of the gate. As a result, a threatening situation arose, so that a guard had to break up the group of men.[48] Partly because of this incident, the refugees decided to go on a hunger strike a few months later. Another reason was the poor quality of the food. The Camp's Director, Reserve Captain Jacob Schol, responded directly by banning eating from deep plates, which limited the use of too much gravy. The already bad mood in the camp dropped to a new low due to these measures. A newspaper article even mentioned the Concentration Camp regime which had to be put to an end soon. After all, the German Jews had not fled from Nazi Germany only to find themselves in another Concentration Camp. The hunger strike led to a debate in the

Marechaussee supervises the construction of Camp Westerbork.

'Tweede Kamer' (House of Representatives). The protest and attention in the media were successful, because the situation improved.[49]

The Minister of Justice agreed to more freedom of movement for the refugees. Under certain conditions, they were allowed to leave the camp for some time. Married men were allowed to meet their wives in some houses outside the camp. A prerequisite for these freedoms was that they had to keep an eye on each other, because unwanted behaviour was not allowed to occur. They were warned that violating the rules could have serious consequences for those responsible. For one, the freedom of movement could be taken away from the other refugees wholly or partly.[50] It was not necessary to specify what the other and most severe consequences for those who had violated the rules were, because the refugees knew that this meant returning to Germany, and this was one of the worst nightmares for many.

In some shelters, minor offences were immediately punished. For example, someone who came in five minutes late was grounded for fourteen days.[51] In combination with censorship of correspondence and limited freedom of

Ernst Kruit with the guard of the Gendarmerie in the camp.

movement, this meant that the refugees knew what they could expect. One of the few advantages was that they were safe from the Nazi regime.

Centralisation

On 10 March 1939, the Minister of the Interior, Hendrik van Boeijen, addressed the circumstances in the 25 remaining facilities in a letter to Queen Wilhelmina. In addition to a major economic disadvantage, he said, there were even more negative aspects to these decentralised facilities. Because most of the sites could only be used for a short period of time and were certainly not suitable for the longterm housing of large numbers of refugees, serious moral dangers were lying in wait. In addition, according to the Minister, Police supervision was not sufficiently guaranteed. The solution would be to accommodate all refugees in a central camp.

The location of this camp had to meet a number of requirements and wishes. From a financial point of view, the price of the land should not be too high. Furthermore, it was desirable for mental and medical care to be present in the vicinity of the camp, although it should not be too close to the border either. A suitable location that met most of the requirements was the Elspeeterveld in Elspeet, in the Municipality of Ermelo. According to the Municipality of Ermelo, there would certainly be sufficient Police supervision.

The reason why the Minister shared information about the location with the Queen had to do with the fact that the Queen had property in the vicinity of the intended terrain. It is therefore not surprising that Queen Wilhelmina said in her response that it would be appreciated if they could find a different location.[52] Queen Wilhelmina was not the only one to object to the plan to set up the central refugee camp on the Veluwe. Some organisations with a general or partial recreational purpose, such as the

Algemeene Nederlandsche Wielrijders Bond (ANWB), also expressed their displeasure about the location of the intended camp. They feared that it would have adverse effects on tourism. After the people of Elspeet had protested massively against the plan as well, the minister decided to abandon it and he immediately went looking for a new location for the establishment of a refugee camp.[53]

Within one week, the minister could already report that he had found a location in Drenthe. There was an area of *Staatsbosbeheer* between Hooghalen, Amen and the Oranjekanaal, in the vicinity of the Municipality of Westerbork. This place was accepted. Objections from the Jewish community, partly because they had to pay for the costs of the camp themselves, could no longer stop the decision.[54] On 19 July 1939 the order was given to start building the camp. Construction of the first barracks began shortly thereafter.[55]

2. CENTRAL REFUGEE CAMP

Before the first refugees were able to enter the new camp, some things had to be organised. At an early stage, on 8 May 1939, Dirk Arie Syswerda[1] was appointed Director of the Camp by Royal Decree. Before his appointment, Syswerda worked as an Administrator at the Dutch Reformed Association for Neuropsychiatry, *Zon en Schild*, in Amersfoort. His extraordinary managerial skills led the Minister of the Interior to appoint him for five years. As Director of the Refugee Camp, Syswerda received a significantly higher salary than for the position in Amersfoort. The task he was given was seen as extremely difficult and important. Not only was he responsible for the general leadership; the authorities also expected that he would be an outstanding organiser with a great social impact.[2]

The instructions drawn up by the Minister of the Interior clearly showed what he expected from the director and the residents of the new camp. Syswerda was also given limited opportunities to interfere with the development of the camp. For example, the creation of house rules, a work plan for the camp residents and a visit arrangement was left to him. The other instructions mainly concerned restrictions on freedom of movement, censorship of correspondence and the maintenance of public order. Camp residents were allowed to move freely in an area designated by the director and approved by the Minister. Only with a valid reason and with the permission of the director could a resident leave this area. Travelling by public transport was only allowed under supervision. For violating the rules, Syswerda himself was able to impose penalties, ranging from withholding allowances and prohibiting the attendance at celebrations and performances to prohibiting the lingering on certain parts of the premises or in buildings.[3]

When Westerbork was put into use as refugee camp on 9 October 1939 and the first 22 refugees arrived, it had already largely been determined what rules they would have to follow. Five of the new residents came from the Rotterdam emigrant hotel of the Holland America Line, eleven came from a facility at the 'Oostelijke Handelskade' in Amsterdam and six boys came from the 'Dommelhuis' in Eindhoven. Syswerda accompanied them from Zwolle to the camp, which was still under construction.

Tomorrow, Things Will Be Better

On the evening of the arrival, Syswerda gave a speech, which he ended with the words 'tomorrow, things will be better'. The circumstances were not all that great yet. For example, if it rained, the terrain would turn into a mud pool, making it barely passable. Furthermore, besides the daily work, there was little entertainment. Nevertheless, according to Syswerda's first report on October, the mood was good from the start. An incident in which two people were slightly injured was one of the exceptions. After an investigation initiated by Syswerda and a serious talk with those involved, order was restored quickly. Syswerda paid extra attention to the boys who had been transferred from the Eindhoven 'Dommelhuis' to Westerbork, as they were not accustomed to leadership and discipline.

In general, the first group of refugees assumed that the accommodation would become more pleasant once everything was ready. Mainly positive messages were sent from Westerbork to other facilities, which would have removed the fear and prejudice.[4] This was an important point for the refugee policy, because more and more facilities closed their doors and the refugees residing there were transferred to Westerbork. Bad news about the new camp could cause fear and negative feelings among the refugees, making them less likely to want to move to the central camp. However, new residents continued to arrive. At the end of November 1939, the population had increased to 125 people.

Ernst Rosendorff arrived on 8 November 1939. He would later be the first to join the Jewish Camp Police (*Ordedienst*). The next day Siegfried Frank arrived.[5] The Amsterdam Refugee Committee's attempt to arrange for him to emigrate to Palestine had still not yielded any results. Fourteen days later, the men of the Hook of Holland Camp were given the opportunity to volunteer to participate in the construction of Camp Westerbork. No one volunteered. The Commander of Hook of Holland mentioned the reason in his weekly report: the refugees were afraid to go to this camp because it was so close to the German border.[6] Because no one volunteered, a number of men were appointed. Hans Dieter Blume[7] and Werner Bloch were among those who were obliged to go to the camp in Drenthe.[8]

Despite the positive reports regarding the circumstances, those who arrived as new residents in Westerbork were often not happy with what they found there. The camp had not yet been completed and was far away from civilisation, which would not have been conducive to a good mood. Syswerda did his best to make the camp residents happy. It would be beneficial to him if the residents were not dissatisfied and would not oppose policy. This could have detrimental consequences for the peace and order within the camp.

Peace and order were subjects that also occupied the responsible authorities. At the end of October 1939, the Minister of the Interior sent a message to his colleague with the subject: 'The prevention of escapes or disturbances, and Police facilities in the vicinity of Westerbork.' According to the Minister, the intention was to take measures within the camp that were aimed at maintaining order and preventing any residents from fleeing. In order to achieve this, civilian guards would be appointed. These guards would also be in charge of the night watch in the camp. However, the civilian guards promised by the Interior were never appointed to Westerbork.

In order to guarantee sufficient supervision anyway, the existing Police surveillance in Hooghalen and possibly in other villages near the camp had to be strengthened.[9] The reinforcement was in any case meant for the Brigade of the Royal Gendarmerie in the Municipality of Westerbork. There the number of Gendarmes, which under normal conditions was five, was now increased to nine. From this Brigade, two Gendarmes came to the camp every night and every Sunday to supervise the camp. In addition, Gendarmes of the same Brigade patrolled around the camp from time to time. If supervision during the construction of the barracks is not included, this was the first period in which the Gendarmerie played a role in the surveillance of the camp.

In addition, a number of doormen were appointed who also got a small supervisory task. According to the instructions, they were responsible for the visit arrangements and the supervision of all persons entering or leaving the camp, among other things. Each visitor received a registration certificate, which had to be returned to the doorman upon departure. On departure and return, persons on leave also had to report to the doorman for registration in the record of persons on leave. As a supervisor, the doorman walked around the camp every hour, using a time clock.[10]

At the end of March 1940, the number of residents had risen to about 500 refugees. Despite this increase, the camp's management and the Government did not immediately consider it necessary to adjust the security measures. Even after the circumstances changed in Europe as a result of the threat of war and after the Dutch Army was mobilised, it was desirable that the Gendarmerie should remain in charge of guarding the camp, according to the inspector of the rural Police Force. The Attorney General in Leeuwarden stated in a message to the Minister of Justice that it was not desirable to accommodate more illegal refugees in Westerbork in connection with the peace and quiet. In the same message, he also wrote that the surveillance met the requirements of that time. Syswerda had previously indicated that he was afraid of attacks by NSB people or anti Semites on the refugee camp. In his opinion, if such an incident had occurred, Syswerda would have been able to control the situation with the help of the Gendarmerie and the Dutch, non-Jewish administrative staff of the camp. If necessary, he could also have called for reinforcement of the Policemen and Gendarmes stationed in the surrounding villages. Syswerda felt that he could not have counted on the male Jewish residents, as they were afraid, which was worsened by the physical and mental abuse that they had suffered in Germany.[11]

That the Government considered transferring the surveillance activities of the Gendarmerie during the mobilisation to the rural Police Force was entirely in line with the organisational structure of both Police units. After all, the Gendarmerie was a Military Police Force whose troops were generally collectively garrisoned. The rural Police Force, on the other hand, consisted of small Brigades, often one man posts, stationed in the villages amidst the population.[12] Therefore, if the Gendarmerie had to perform Military duties during the war, the rural Police Force would take over its duties at Westerbork.

This change did not take place. Partly due to the growing number of refugees, it was necessary to intensify Police surveillance especially within the camp. At the end of April 1940, Barteld Lukas Knol, born in Zwolle on 2 July 1883, was temporarily placed in the camp as a Municipal Police Officer. Knol knew the Police profession not only as the son of a Policeman, but also from his own experience. Before his appointment in Westerbork, he had already had a Police career. After a career in the 4th Division of the Royal Gendarmerie, he ended up as a Municipal Police Officer in the village of Buinerveer in 1910. There he was also appointed as an unpaid Policeman. The advantage was that this allowed him to act outside the Municipality.

Five years later, he transferred to the Municipality of Borger. That it was not a busy job is evidenced by the fact that shortly afterwards, he was also appointed supervisor of the general cemetery in Borger and messenger of the water boards Buiner Noordvenen and Bronneger. After Knol had applied in vain for the position of chief Police Officer in Emmen in 1918, he received a permit to act as debt collector and later also as a janitor of the town hall. In 1924 he was promoted to Chief Police Officer of Borger. At the age of 53, Knol could no longer function properly due to illness and physical health issues, so he retired on 1 March 1937 and was honourably discharged. At the official farewell, the Mayor expressed the wish that the man would be able to enjoy his retirement for a long time.

When a guard was searched for among the retired Police Officers for Camp Westerbork, shortly before the occupation, Knol applied for the position.[13] Right after the appointment of Knol, Syswerda notified the Minister of the Interior that the guard could not come live in the camp for the time being. According to Syswerda, it would be problematic to house him in one of the barracks, because then no more refugees could be accommodated. Knol did get to have barracks 51 at his disposal. This barracks had been furnished as a Prison with waiting room and could thus serve as a Police Station.[14]

Meanwhile, the criticism on Syswerda got worse. Because he did not comply with the instructions, he even received a warning from the Minister of the Interior in mid-January 1940 in the form of a written reprimand. According to the Minister, the bad name Westerbork already had would be further contaminated by Syswerda's weak behaviour.[15] For example, Syswerda had not yet drafted any house rules, work plan or a well-functioning visit scheme. As he showed no initiative and had no organisational capacity, he had failed as leader of the camp, resulting in a lack of order and discipline among the camp residents. Moreover, the camp seemed to be getting more and more dirty.[16]

The increased tensions in Europe caused other concerns, so there would have been less attention for Syswerda's bad job performance. The Government had been urged by various people, including the camp's residents themselves, to draw up an evacuation plan in case the Germans invaded the country. Shortly before the German Army actually crossed the Dutch borders on 10 May and started the attack, a plan was ready just in time to evacuate the approximately 700 residents of Camp Westerbork. This was meant to prevent them from falling directly into the hands of the Germans.

The May Days Of 1940

According to the evacuation plan, the camp residents were supposed to leave for the train in Hooghalen after the sound of the alarm bell, under the guidance of the Dutch staff. The train would then take them to Zeeuws Vlaanderen via Zwolle. On 10 May the residents left the camp. However, they had to deviate from the original plan quickly, because Dutch Soldiers had blown up the IJsselbrug near Zwolle. As a result, the train traffic stagnated in the direction of Zeeland, so the train moved north instead. The plan to bring the refugees from Harlingen to England by boat could not continue, as Harlingen had already been occupied. The final destination of the train was eventually Leeuwarden. The refugees were received by an evacuation committee at the 'Beurs'. With the help of the Mayor, they were soon taken in by families.[17]

After the capitulation of the Dutch Army, reporting on the reception of the refugees in Leeuwarden and the situation in Westerbork quickly began. On 18 May the Secretary General of the Department of Internal Affairs, K.J. (Karel) Frederiks, sent a message to the Acting Commander in Chief of the Army and the Navy, in which he indicated that the shelters were not sufficient and something needed to change. The families were no longer prepared to provide shelter for the refugees. Frederiks wondered what to do with the group. Returning to Westerbork was the most obvious option. According to Frederiks, if the choice was indeed made to return the refugees to Westerbork, some things had to be taken into account.

First of all, there was a chance that the Germans would use the camp for other purposes. If this was not the case, the location of the camp and the nature of the population could be detrimental to people's safety as well as public order. That is why Frederiks advised to accommodate the Jewish refugees in Amsterdam instead of Westerbork, because of the large Jewish community in that city. Of course, in Amsterdam, as in Westerbork, there had to be a strict internment.[18] The chairman of the Committee for Jewish Refugees, David Cohen, later one of the chairmen of the Jewish Council, spoke about this with Tenkink, who had by then been appointed Acting Secretary General of Justice. During this conversation, Tenkink urged Cohen to distribute the refugees to different places in the Netherlands. According to Cohen, Tenkink was afraid that the refugees who had migrated to Leeuwarden would attract the attention of the Germans and that this could have adverse consequences for all Jews living in the Netherlands. Cohen was pleased afterwards that he and his employees had allowed the period in which everything should have been arranged to pass by due to certain circumstances. The result was that the refugees were gathered on 27 May 1940 at Leeuwarden station and were then returned to Westerbork.[19]

Due to the changed circumstances and possibly also because of some incidents during the May days, such as food theft, the Police surveillance in the camp turned out to be inadequate. It was therefore decided that apart from Knol, who was in charge of guarding the Camp Prison, a Detachment of the Rural Police force would be placed in the camp as well. This Detachment, consisting of four Policemen led by Sergeant J. Geluk from Hoogkerk, arrived in mid-June 1940. The District Commander of this Police Force concluded from the information of his men that the camp's leadership was weak. Therefore, and because no cooperation was expected from director Syswerda, he instructed the inspector of his corps to personally interfere with this matter.[20] According to the reports, due to the extraordinary circumstances, it was desirable to transfer the management of the camp to the Department of Justice. The desired change took place on 16 July 1940. The circumstances also led to the need for a stricter policy. Syswerda was considered unable to implement this strict policy and was therefore honourably discharged on 15 September 1940.[21]

Commander J. Schol

The one who was found fit for the position of Camp Commander was Reserve Captain Jacob Schol. As Commander of the camp in Hook of Holland, he had already proven this. Schol was born on 9 September 1890 in Amsterdam. His Military career began in 1910 when he voluntarily joined the Military reserve. Five years later, he was sworn in as a Reserve Second Lieutenant of the 21st Infantry Regiment. During the First World War, Schol was mobilised. Repetition exercises followed every year after this, until he entered active service in early January 1939. Initially, Schol was supposed to become Commander of Texel. However, he ended up as captain in the Department of Justice and was then seconded to the immigration Police. His first assignment was to reorganise the refugee camp in Hook of Holland. He did this with gusto and he was not hesitant to take harsh measures. Because of the increased tensions in Europe, Schol still had to go to Texel in mid-June 1939 to defend the island as Commander of the troops.

A few weeks after the unequal battle and the subsequent capitulation, Schol was ordered to report to Tenkink in The Hague. According to a statement made by Schol after the liberation, he had to try to prevent the German refugees present in Westerbork from being sent back to Germany. If he accomplished this task, he would be appointed Commander of the camp.[22] If the fear of returning to Germany was the motivation for a more stringent policy, then Schol has certainly succeeded. Immediately after Syswerda left the leadership of the camp to Schol, new regulations were introduced. One of the first weekly reports drawn up by Schol immediately shows that something had changed with regard to the discipline in the camp. He personally checked if the residents were complying with the regulations.

Jacob Schol and his wife.

The occupier knew, partly because of the weekly reports, what was happening in Camp Westerbork. In the weekly report of 12 to 18 August 1940, Schol wrote that *SS-Obersturmführer König of the Sicherheitspolizei und des Sicherheitsdienst (Sipo und SD)* from Assen had visited the camp on 13 August to investigate an incident that had occurred on the night of 31 July. Schol had been conducting an investigation that night in the barracks, as he did often. When he wanted to check on a sleeping resident in room 2 of barracks 4, a struggle arose in which he got a black eye. One witness stated that Schol had aimed his flashlight at the resident's face and that the resident had hit him because he thought it was a joke, while another witness said that Schol wanted to pull him out of bed. Whether the other residents interfered is unknown. One of the witnesses stated that a Sergeant of the rural Police Force had fired some warning shots.

König interviewed all the residents of the barracks and decided that they would be placed in a separate group as punishment. This meant that for six weeks, they had to cut peat daily from 8:00 to 20:00 hours under the supervision of Policemen. This work was interrupted only by a lunch break of half an hour. The food had to be consumed on the spot. The punished ones marched to and from their work under the guidance of a Policeman. In addition, they were not allowed to have contact with other camp residents and had to stay in their dormitory outside of working hours. This dormitory was located in an empty barracks and was guarded, isolating the group completely. This barracks, number 35, would be used as a punishment barracks in the future. To prevent contact with the other residents, it was fenced with barbed wire.

Initially, the group consisted of 14 men, but König added Hans Weissman to the group because a letter from him had been intercepted which, according to the weekly report, was filled with hatred towards the Dutch and German Governments.[23] According to a witness, Schol struggled with this situation, because he gave these inmates more to eat and provided them with appropriate work clothing.[24] The camp residents immediately noticed that the situation in the camp had changed, that unwanted behaviour could be punished and that the occupier began to interfere more and more in certain matters. At the end of August 1940, Schol announced in a decree which penalties he could impose and how he would inform the ones that were punished. The penalties varied from a warning to house arrest and imprisonment in the punishment barracks or in the detention ward. He personally warned the parties concerned. All other penalties were announced during the roll call, in the presence of the entire camp population. Schol did give those who were punished the opportunity to tell their side of the story.[25]

The decree shows that in August 1940 there were already daily roll calls. It also shows what penalties had already been imposed. For example, during that same month, Dr. Abraham Windmüller[26] had been punished with one day in Prison for crossing the camp border. In addition, he had to report to the Police guard every two hours for 14 days.[27] The camp border was intended to limit the freedom of movement of the camp residents. Initially, this boundary was indicated by signs placed around the camp. Later there was an inner and outer ring. The built up part belonged to the inner ring.

The outer ring was marked with a white line. According to the guidelines, it was forbidden to leave the inner ring half an hour before the onset of darkness. If that happened, it would result in severe penalties.[28]

The camp border could only be crossed with permission or under supervision. This permission was granted to residents when they worked on the land outside the camp or participated in mining activities, among other things. All camp residents had to participate in the labour process. Failure to perform an assigned task could have consequences. This was experienced by eight camp residents at the end of September 1940. Because they had not carried out their work satisfactorily, they had to work for four days under the supervision of the rural Police Force. In addition, they were imprisoned during these days.[29]

The camp border was indicated by signs.

The instructions of January 1941 show that the commander, or his replacement, had been given the authority to impose a wide range of disciplinary penalties. He could withhold allowances and forbid the offender to attend performances and the like; he could also forbid the person to go to certain parts of the camp site or in certain buildings. Furthermore, he could forbid the offender to be outside the barracks where they slept after work for a maximum of 30 days. He could also order the offender to repeatedly report at certain times and at a specific location, and he could lock people in a cell, fully isolated, for a maximum of 10 days after work.

Schol was also instructed to keep a record of the penalties imposed. He had to send an extract from this register every week to the head of the immigration service and the Secretary General of Justice. In addition, the penalties imposed were added to the personal card of the offenders. Because of the rules and instructions, the camp residents knew what was expected of them. Life in the camp was to some extent controlled this way. In addition to the obligations they had, camp residents could also benefit from a limited number of privileges at specific times. An example of this is the visit arrangement, which also came with certain guidelines. The camp residents were allowed to receive visitors once a month and sometimes also on public holidays, from 14:00 to 17:00 hours.

In general, the visitors had to make a long journey. If they were early, they had to wait outside the camp until it was time. Before visitors were allowed to enter the camp, a check of the necessary documents was carried out. Then the bags and packages they had taken with them were examined. For example, uncensored letters were not allowed to enter or leave the camp. If a visitor nevertheless brought unwanted objects or objects, then apart from any criminal prosecution the visitor was no longer allowed into the camp. In addition, the receiving party was prohibited from receiving visits for a period to be determined by the Commander (up to six months). When it turned out that the camp resident had ordered or encouraged the bringing of the unauthorised objects, more severe penalties could follow.[30]

That they were not empty threats was revealed at the end of July 1941. After a Jewish woman who had visited a camp resident had tried to smuggle three letters and four postcards out of the camp that were not in line with the censorship rules, Schol immediately took action. The sending and receiving of letters was prohibited for one month. Furthermore, Schol decided to limit the normal frequency of postal dispatch after that month. Camp residents were allowed to send a letter or postcard once every 14 days, instead of once a week. The Jewish woman got banned from the camp. The four people whose letters or postcards would have been smuggled out were also punished: they were isolated in the punishment barracks and had to work on the land during the day. Sigmund Keller and Sandor Salmagne[31], two of these four people, later found no disadvantage of this incident, because they were able to join the Ordedienst that had yet to be formed without any trouble. The imposition of penalties at that time did not yet affect the chances of survival or a future career in the camp.[32]

Although the camp residents were given more duties than rights, there was still some freedom of movement within the borders of the camp and outside working hours. Residents could visit each other and there was even opportunity to apply for leave. One of the things the camp residents were less positive about was the food supply. Especially in the first years of the occupation, the camp residents received insufficient and monotonous food. They did not receive additional food packages yet, as was the case later when the Dutch Jews came to Westerbork. Especially those who worked outside the camp on the land tried to take something extra with them at times.[33] This was against the rules and violations were immediately punished. A 15-year-old boy had to deal with this when he was caught red handed trying to take five kilos of carrots and two kilos of black radishes from the field. Schol punished the boy by imprisoning him in a cell for a week from 18:15 to 7:15 and on Saturday and Sunday also during the day.[34] Partly because of the stricter enforcement of the rules, Schol laid a good basis for the further development of the camp.

Changing Of The Guard

The occupier had started reorganising the Dutch Police. This intervention was considered necessary because in the eyes of the occupier, the Police Department was severely fragmented and therefore failed to function properly. Five different Police units, including the rural Police Force and the Royal Gendarmerie, were engaged in maintaining order. The formation of a State Police was the ultimate goal of the occupying forces. In order to achieve this, there was a need to cut drastically into the number of parts. The rural Police Force was the first to be cut. This corps was disbanded on 1 March 1941.[35] After this organisational change, the camp's surveillance was transferred to the Gendarmerie. This Military Police Corps was not demobilised after the capitulation in the May days of 1940, but did lose the title of 'Royal'.[36]

Men in front of the Detachment Barracks, 12 June 1941. The men wearing caps are dressed in the uniform of the rural Police Force. The other three are wearing the uniform of the Gendarmerie.

According to a message of 15 October 1941, addressed to the Inspector of the Gendarmerie in The Hague, the strength of the Surveillance Detachment at that time consisted of two Sergeants and 13 Gendarmes. The two Sergeants performed the function of Detachment Commander and Deputy Detachment Commander. The rest of the men had to be sent by the entire VIIIth Division of the Gendarmerie. This was necessary because the district of Emmen, to which Camp Westerbork belonged, was unable to provide the necessary personnel. The report to the inspector also stated that the Detachment supervised 52 barracks, with a total camp population of about 1,200 Jewish refugees.[37]

The period of secondment to the camp was short: only one month. On the first day of each month, a Petty Officer and six Gendarmes were relieved of their duties. On the 15th day of the same month, the remaining seven gendarmes and the other Petty Officer were replaced as well.[38] Due to this system, the men hardly knew what was expected of them. By the time they figured that out, they were already exchanged for Gendarmes who were just as unfamiliar with the situation in the camp. The same was true for the Detachment Commanders. They were only able to act as independent Commander for 14 days because of the system. Furthermore, due to the reorganisation of the Police, very young Petty Officers were occasionally sent to Westerbork, who had insufficient control over the men and were therefore unable to lead them. According to the staff, in order to maintain the good name of the Gendarmerie, it was desirable to send an older Officer to Westerbork who, considering the composition of the camp population, was also somewhat adept at the German language.[39]

In addition to complaints about the short period of secondment, there were also complaints about the number of men in the Detachment. Schol was the first to complain about this. At the end of August 1941, he requested that the Detachment be extended by at least ten Gendarmes. This was necessary to prevent camp residents outside the camp from coming into contact with the ones cutting peat and other people from the surrounding area. Moreover, stricter surveillance had to prevent the smuggling of food and letters.

Barracks of the Gendarmerie.

Several months later, the inspector of the Gendarmerie rejected Schol's request. He stated that the staff for the Detachment came from several districts. The delivery and regular replacement did not benefit Police supervision in these districts. He also took the opportunity to complain about the many tasks that the Gendarmerie had to carry out that had nothing to do with the Police task. The inspector therefore requested for the camp to no longer be entrusted to the Gendarmerie. According to him, the camp residents had been brought together for political reasons, so the surveillance should not be assigned to a Dutch Police Force.[40] The inspector's request was not honoured; the Gendarmerie remained in charge of the surveillance of Camp Westerbork.

A few months later, the staff of the VIIIth Division supported Schol's request for more men. On paper the work schedule was correct, but in reality it turned out that there was insufficient staff available to carry out all the work properly. According to the schedule, two Gendarmes were required during the day and evening shifts to supervise the punishment barracks and to occupy the guardhouse. Anyone wishing to enter the camp had to report there to obtain an admission ticket and have the luggage checked.

Guard Detachment of the Gendarmerie, 1941.

In connection with the presence of a telephone, there always had to be someone at the guardhouse. As a result, during the change of the guard that had to take place every two hours, there was no supervision in the punishment barracks for about ten minutes. The use of the two man reserve service as a temporary instalment would have been a solution, but this was hardly possible because of the supervision of transports. To ensure that peace and order prevailed and that no one entered or left the camp without permission, the guards had to permanently patrol in and around the camp. According to the schedule, four Gendarmes were supposed to be available for this purpose.

Because the guidance tasks were numerous and consumed many hours of duty, these patrols were not carried out in most cases. Gendarmes had to escort camp residents to the Hospital in Groningen for treatment or for visiting patients, to Assen to buy much needed aids such as glasses, shoes or hearing aids, and to German authorities in Assen for questioning or to some judicial authority. They had to escort vehicles to Hooghalen, drop off school children or pick up mail and cargo. Four Gendarmes had been assigned the night shifts. Two of them surveyed the camp, while a third one remained in the guardhouse. The last one was responsible for the punishment barracks. This work was exchanged every two hours. Those who had done night shifts were given the opportunity to sleep in the morning from 7:00 to 12:00. They were supposed to patrol the camp again from 14:00 to 23:00 hours, but because of the transports, this was usually cancelled. In addition, not all work could be carried out according to the schedule. All this made the service in the camp quite tough. The staff therefore considered it necessary to increase the strength by ten men.[41]

At the end of November 1941, the Detachment still had not gotten the much needed extra men, which led Schol to make a request for the second time. In addition to the aforementioned points, such as unwanted contact with the environment and the smuggling of letters, he listed a number of other things that necessitated reinforcement. Due to problems with the capacity in the Dutch youth institutions, the German authorities placed a few young people in the camp to spend their time in custody there. The young people were placed in the punishment barracks and had to work under surveillance during the day. Schol indicated that an undesirable situation had arisen because one of those boys had managed to escape at a time when there were no Gendarmes available for surveillance. According to Schol, this had

Inge Winter (1931) with Gendarme J. van de Berg, 16 April 1941. Inge ended up in Westerbork in July 1940 and was dismissed on 14 July 1942. Her mother was non-Jewish and the family was baptised Lutheran. For her role in the piece Der Fidele Bauer, she received one and a half kilos of chocolates from the Gendarmerie.

left a painful impression on the occupier. He once again raised the problem of monitoring residents outside the camp. In mid-February 1942, Schol received the message from the person authorised to deal with the reorganisation of the Dutch Police, Mr. L.J. Broersen, that the request could again not be complied with due to lack of staff.[42]

Representatives of the German authorities regularly visited the camp. These visits in combination with the data from the reports meant that the occupier was well aware of the internal affairs and the trials and tribulations of the day-to-day management. In August 1941, the Drenthe *Beauftragte* of *Reichskommissar* Dr. Arthur Seyss-Inquart criticised the treatment of the Jewish camp residents and the role of Schol. The *Beauftragte* was of the opinion that the Jews in Westerbork were treated far too humanely. In addition, Schol's attitude would have made the Jews feel comfortable in the camp. In order to change this, according to the *Beauftragte*, another Camp Commander had to be appointed.[43]

Despite the criticism on his performance and the allegedly humane treatment of the residents, Schol remained in charge of the camp. The criticism is understandable; the anti-Jewish measures caused more and more restrictions to be imposed on the Jews in the rest of the Netherlands. While preparing his report, the *Beauftragte* probably forgot that the camp still served as a refugee shelter and not as a Prison or Concentration Camp. Not only Schol but the Gendarmes as well could have been criticised for their positive attitude towards the Jewish camp residents, because they generally maintained good contacts with them.[44]

Gendarme Reint Middel[45] was prepared, long after the liberation, to be one of the few to talk about his experiences in the refugee camp and how they dealt with the refugees. His interview also shows how he came to join the Gendarmerie at an early age. Reint spent his childhood in the Drenthe countryside. When he was 16, his father died of pneumonia. Two years later, his mother remarried, after which she and her husband had another three children. Because of the poor economic situation and partly on the advice of his stepfather, Reint decided to fulfil his Military Service. This went differently than expected, because he contracted jaundice and was Hospitalised for some time.

After he returned, it turned out that his superior had been told to pass on names of Soldiers who would then receive further training and because he had not been able to judge Reint, he had missed this opportunity. With the prospect of having a rank as a Corporal, Reint joined the Police Force after getting a call about a position. For this he received a training that lasted for four months at the Sarphatistraat in Amsterdam. When he had almost completed this training, the German Army invaded the Netherlands. Because his group had not yet been assigned to anything, they did not participate in combat operations. They were used to guard a large grass field outside Amsterdam. Because Schiphol could no longer be used due to bombing by the German Air Force, the field served as a runway for Dutch fighters. Reint experienced the capitulation there, remaining unharmed and without seeing a single German Soldier, after which he returned to the Sarphatistraat. Not much later he left with the others to the training depot of the Police in Nieuwersluis, where he was briefly deployed to guard Dutch draft dodgers who were still kept in custody there.

In order to avoid a sharp increase in the number of unemployed people, the demobilised Military could opt for a job in one of the Dutch Police Departments or in the Fire Brigade. Reint chose the Gendarmerie. In mid-August 1940 he had to report to their barracks at the Helperbrink in Groningen. From there the newcomers were sent to the various Brigades. His request to be placed close to his family home was accepted and so he ended up in Winschoten. His work here consisted, among other things, of patrolling with older colleagues and assisting the Municipal Police. After that, several secondments followed, such as in Brabant near the Belgian border because of smugglers, and in Veenhuizen to guard the prisoners.

After working in Groningen as well, Reint finally ended up in Veendam. A few months later, probably in the first half of 1942, he was told by his Commander that he had to report in Camp Westerbork for his next secondment. Reint knew where the village of Westerbork was located, but was not aware of the existence of the camp. After having travelled several tens of kilometers by bike, he entered the camp via the back. He was able to get through without any problems, because there was no entrance gate or security check at that time. After reporting to the Detachment Commander, Reint was referred to the barracks in which the Gendarmerie was housed. This barracks was in the camp. Initially, the work consisted of patrol services. When asked if someone had served in the liaison troops and could therefore handle the telephone switchboard, Reint signed up. During his service, he had been taught how to operate the phone and work with signal lights.

According to him, the contact between the Gendarmes and the camp residents was good. The Gendarmes were allowed to walk freely through the camp and they were sometimes invited by camp residents for a cup of coffee. Reint himself at times accepted such an invitation. He then went to visit people who were staying in residences and could therefore take care of themselves. He also visited a few football matches as a spectator, in which a team from the Gendarmerie took on a team of the residents. Contacts and visits that were no longer allowed outside the camp, such as the visiting of Jewish Doctors by non-Jews, took place within it. During his detachment in Westerbork, Reint visited a dentist for the first time in his life. This was a Jewish dentist from Amsterdam, who had established his practice in the camp. However, Reint could not remember his name. He knew that the man was very nice and that he had agreed with him to have his teeth cleaned free of charge by this dentist after the liberation.[46]

New Camp Organisation

The increasing interest of the occupier in the camp most likely had to do with its future destination, because at the end of 1941 the decision would already have been made to set it up as a transit camp for all Dutch Jews and Jews residing in the Netherlands. In early 1942, contractors were commissioned to build 24 large wooden barracks, in which a total of between 5,000 and 7,000 people could be housed. In connection with this expansion, Schol announced the modified camp organisation on 19 February 1942. The residents were more closely involved in the management of the camp. 13 service groups were established that took over all parts of the camp organisation. At the head of each service group was a service leader and his replacement. Because of this 'divide and rule' strategy, the residents were to a certain extent responsible for the day-to-day management of the camp.[47]

Shortly before the new organisation became a fact, Schol set out a number of rules. One of these rules related to order within the barracks. At the head of a barracks stood a barracks leader and his replacement. They were responsible for the peace and order within the barracks. Furthermore, they had to keep things under control when the food was handed out. Picking up and distributing the mail and checking the darkening of the barracks and the heating were also part of the duties of the barracks leaders. In addition, there was a so-called 'Police hour' (curfew). This meant that the residents had to be inside at a certain time. At the first signal of the bell, they had to go to the barracks and at the second signal, they actually had to be inside. The light in the barracks was allowed to stay on until half an hour after the specified time. Schol also explained the visit arrangement once again. Visits could now only be received on Saturdays from 13:00 to 16:00 and on Sundays from 11:00 to 16:00. Only family members up to the second degree and finances could benefit from this arrangement. An application had to be submitted to the administration five days before the day of the visit. A visitor was only allowed to visit once a month.

One part that had already been formed at an earlier stage and became part of the new camp organisation was the Fire Brigade. After all, the prevention and extinction of fires was important for safety. The surrounding moors and wooden barracks were a willing prey for the flames. When the fire hose was delivered to the camp at the beginning of October 1939, no personnel had yet been assigned to the Fire Brigade.[48] The formation of a Fire Department took place in the first months of 1940. 16 young men volunteered for the position of firefighter.

Werner Bloch was one of the volunteers. Together with a few friends, he belonged to the camp's initially largely inexperienced Fire Brigade. A large number of practical exercises had to change this. The exercises included the placing and connecting of hoses. The firefighters were also taught how to provide first aid. These lessons were taught by Dr. M. Schlesinger. Occasionally, the exercises could be used in real life. On 11 April 1942, the Fire Brigade had to turn out for a fire outside the camp. When the fire was extinguished after an hour, the men were able to return to the camp. Less than a month later, on 6 May, the Fire Brigade had to do a job outside the camp: a heather and forest fire had formed near the station Hooghalen. Together with the Fire Brigade of Beilen, the Fire Brigade of the camp extinguished the fire and after two and a half hours, they could return to the camp once again.[49] The Fire Department was classified as a service group with the number 11a in the camp organisation.

During the presentation of the new organisation, Schol took the opportunity to reiterate that Westerbork was a Military led labour camp with strict discipline. This strict discipline would be achieved mainly by introducing more and more rules. According to a statement from Schol, any offence would be severely punished. In order to check whether the many rules were actually complied with and whether order was guaranteed within the camp and in the day-to-day work, there was a need for adequate supervision. In any case, the Gendarmerie Detachment was still not large enough for this purpose. Therefore, this was taken into account in the new organisation. In addition to the Gendarmerie, a new Surveillance Group was assembled from camp residents, which started to operate as an 'Ordedienst' within the camp. With the establishment of this service group, Camp Westerbork got its own Camp Police at its disposal.

The men of the Ordedienst doing a firefighting exercise in the camp.

Origin Jewish Ordedienst (OD)

The Ordedienst as service group 10 initially consisted of 13 former firefighters. Although the strength of the Fire Brigade decreased to six men, it continued to exist. This service group later took over the remaining staff as well as all Fire Brigade duties.[50] The OD officially started performing its task on 1 March 1942: ensuring the order and discipline within the camp.[51] Arthur Pisk, born on 22 April 1891 in Vienna, was appointed service leader. His replacement was F. Frost. The appointment of Pisk did not come as a surprise, since he was head of the Fire Department and therefore knew the men of the OD.

Little is known about Pisk's background. After the so-called *Anschluss*, the Austrian Jews also had to deal with the persecution. Because of the many restrictive measures, it had become impossible for Pisk to sell his products as a trader in women's hats. He did not wait and when he got the opportunity to travel to the still unoccupied Netherlands, he took it. There he was housed in the quarantine establishments in Heijplaat in March 1939. After spending a short period in a similar establishment in Amsterdam, he was transferred to Camp Westerbork at the end of February 1940.

Schol may have appointed Pisk because of some similarities between them. He was almost the same age as Schol and had a Military background as a former Officer in the Austrian Army. The camp residents generally did not judge Pisk positively because he snapped and shouted at them and beat people. Philip Mechanicus called him 'the Chief of the Jewish Gestapo' or 'the Chief of the OD of Walt Disney' in his diary. Other names for the service leader of the OD were 'small dictator' or 'brute of Westerbork'. He was said to have been the most hated person in the camp.[52] The description of his appearance did not work to his advantage either. Because of his roughly built face, Hitler esque moustache and jet black hair and eyes, he looked like a kind of pirate or robber chief.[53]

Arthur Pisk.

The statements in Pisk's file are not in agreement. One witness saw his parents get kicked into the train by him. Another witness claimed to have seen that the service leader hit people at any place of the body he could reach, prior to a transport to Bergen-Belsen in the roll call area. In addition, he saw Pisk do the Hitler salute every time the Camp Commander spoke to him. When the witness made this statement in July 1945, he was ten year old.[54] The documentary *Kamp van Hoop en Wanhoop* (*Camp of Hope and Despair*), which was shown on Dutch television in 1990 and in which a picture of Pisk was shown, triggered old fears and forgotten anger in a former camp resident. According to her, Pisk was infected with the violence of the oppressors and had turned some subordinates into an extension of the occupier.[55]

One of these subordinates, Hans Margules, had a more positive view of the performance of his superior. Hans thought he was a nice and sensitive man who, unlike most other Service Leaders, never used his position to his own advantage. Maybe he snapped at someone sometimes, but according to Hans, that was because of the difficult and emotional situation. Hans understood that Pisk's appearance, along with the work carried out under his responsibility, evoked resistance among the people. However, disobedience could have adverse consequences for everyone.[56]

One person who had stayed in the camp for three years never actually saw Pisk act aggressively. In the eyes of this witness, he was honest and trustworthy.[57] As leader of the central distribution office, Aad van As, one of the Dutch civil servants, was able to work very well with Pisk. Because of his position, Pisk was able to help Aad rescue camp residents who were going to be transported. According to Aad, Pisk did not do the work to save himself, but the Germans simply had the dirty work of the transports carried out by the camp residents themselves.[58] That there were such different opinions on the actions of Pisk is understandable in connection with his function. Together with his men, he did indeed do the dirty work of the occupier. They had to perform this work in such a way that the occupier had no reason to act themselves. Correcting disobedient and troublesome camp residents was therefore part of the OD's work. Pisk had the authority to call to order the person who had committed a particular offence.

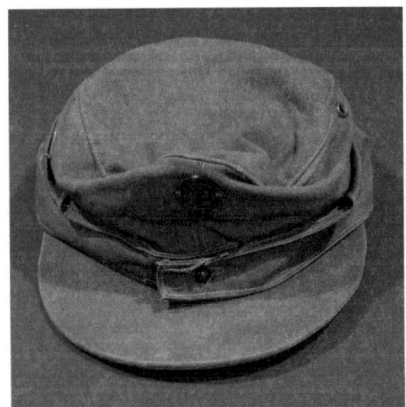

Cap OD with emblem.

From 12 March 1942 onwards, the OD wrote a daily report. This handwritten report shows what the work consisted of. Until around the beginning of July 1942, the report records which member of the OD, designated by a service number, had carried out the work. The amount of service numbers shows that the OD had quickly grown to 20 men whose average age was between 20 and 25 years. Most of the OD members, with the exception of a few Austrian refugees, were from Germany. The members of the OD wore brown overalls as uniform. The outfit also included a pair of (riding) boots. By wearing the overalls, it was clear to everyone who was part of the Camp Police.

One task with which OD members were frequently burdened was guiding people who had committed an offence from the punishment barracks to other places within the camp, such as the dentist or the Camp Hospital. Supervision at this barracks, guiding the inmates to their workplace in the field and supervising the work of this group were often recurring tasks. Previously, these Surveillance Services were carried out by the Gendarmes. Now the Gendarmerie could give the OD orders without Schol's intervention. An example of an assignment given to the OD by an Officer of the Gendarmerie at the beginning of April 1942 was to guard the camp border. On that day, two OD members had to monitor the border according to a fixed schedule from the moor on the northern side of the camp. If residents crossed that border anyway, it had to be reported to the Gendarme. Werner Bloch and Sandor Salmagne were ordered to supervise the camp border from 11:00 to 12:30. These patrol services were cancelled the next day. In most cases, the reason for the assignments was not mentioned in the report.

For some tasks, the entire OD was alerted. This happened on 12 March 1942 at 22:35 hours due to increased activity of allied aircraft. The four pre-

The OD moves out.

established double posts had to be in their assigned position at barracks 1, 21, 34 and 50. Around 23:45, the alarm was lifted, which meant that they could leave their posts again. Two days later, the entire OD was called into service from 11:00 to 13:50, now on the order of Schol. This call would have had to do with an unexpected gathering of residents in the camp. OD members had to take over the posts of the Gendarmerie in the waiting room and the punishment barracks. The barracks leaders were instructed to announce that the camp residents were not allowed to leave the inner part of the camp and should remain in the barracks as much as possible. They were not allowed to gather and stand still on the roads in the camp either. After no further incidents had occurred, the OD members were withdrawn from the posts at 14:00.[59]

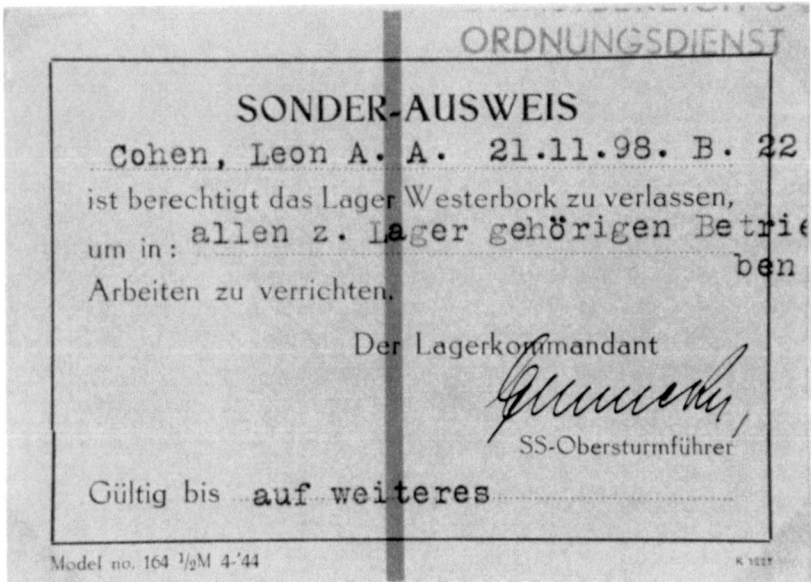

All OD members were given a special card.

The reports show that the OD received many different kinds of orders regarding law enforcement and supervision, especially within the camp. Because of this, the relatively small service group had become a well-functioning and usable part of the camp organisation in a short period of time. In the runup to the new position that the camp would be given in the foreseeable future, this was not an insignificant development.

The Pressure Gets Worse

At the beginning of the occupation, there was no reason to think that the camp would be given a new purpose two years later. Initially, it seemed that the Jewish population in the Netherlands had nothing to fear. However, the high ranking representatives of the German authorities who had proclaimed that the Dutch Jews would be left alone because there was no 'Jewish question' for them had been consciously or unconsciously insincere.

In June 1941 Special *Einsatzgruppen* in Russia began with the *Ausrottung der jüdisch-bolschewistischen Intelligenz* behind the lines. At the Wannsee conference on 20 January 1942, the technical details for the 'final solution to the Jewish question' were discussed. The first measures against the Jewish population, such as no longer allowing the appointment of Jewish officials and the obligation for all persons of all or partly Jewish blood to get registered, were relatively innocent in the view of many.[60] The residents of Camp Westerbork also had to deal with these first measures. At the end of 1941, each resident was obliged to go to Amsterdam to be registered at the *Zentralstelle für jüdische Auswanderung.* The reason given for this obligatory registration was that it would make voluntary emigration simpler.[61]

Despite the promise of the occupying force to leave the Jewish population alone, more and more restrictive measures were introduced, gradually bringing about economic and social isolation. One of the most confrontational measures was the introduction of the Star of David that the Jews had to wear. With this distinguishing sign on all garments, it was immediately clear to everyone who belonged to the Jewish race.[62] Wearing the star was an obligation for all Jews, including the residents of Camp Westerbork. During the morning roll call of 3 May 1942, Schol would have informed the residents that wearing a star was also obligatory for them while being visibly emotional about it.[63]

That a change was coming was indicated in several ways. Representatives of the occupier not only increasingly visited the camp, but they also interfered with the organisation and supervision more and more. In the weekly report from 24 to 30 May 1942, Schol wrote that on 25 May a Lieutenant of the *Ordnungspolizei*, an Officer of the *Sipo* and an employee of the *Beauftragte* office, all from Assen, had visited the camp. Their aim was to check whether the persons who visited relatives in the camp had a valid travel permit, as well as how many people visited the camp.[64]

The reports soon revealed why the occupier was increasingly interested. In the first half of 1942, on the order of the Germans, the construction of larger barracks was started without any explanation as to why this was done. Documents prove that they waited until the last moment to do this. The Immigration Police learned what the occupier was planning to do with the camp a few days before it was taken over. A senior official of the Immigration Police, C.G. van Dalfsen, heard on 29 June 1942 during a conversation with *SS-Sturmbannführer* Dr. Erich Deppner, head of Division IV at the *Befehlshaber der Sipo und SD* (BdS) in The Hague, that Deppner's service would take over Westerbork on 1 July. From that date onwards, the camp would be used as a transit camp for all Jews, including the Dutch ones.

In the camp, inspections would take place to see if the residents were fit to go to work. In case of proven suitability, they were transported to the German eastern border. In a note addressed to the head of the Criminal Investigation Department, Van Dalfsen wrote that the people who were found unsuitable would probably remain in the camp. After the takeover, the Department of Justice lost control over the camp. However, Deppner did want the camp staff to remain in the service of the Department of Justice. The recruitment of new personnel, which was necessary because of the expansion, was also left to this Department.[65] This in combination with the Jewish self-government meant that the occupying forces were given a well-functioning and fully equipped barracks village, which had largely been paid for by the Jewish community itself.

Map Camp Westerbork.

3. THE FIRST TRAINS DEPART FOR THE EAST

On 1 July 1942 the Dutch Government handed over Camp Westerbork to the Germans. The term refugee camp was dropped. After all, a new function required a new name. *Polizeiliches Durchgangslager Westerbork* became the official name, but in general *Judendurchgangslager* or *Lager Westerbork* was used. At the time of the transfer, 1,527 Jews were staying in the camp, including 270 children.[1]

Murderer With Officer's Attitude

After the takeover, Schol remained largely in charge of the daily management. The BdS, Dr. Wilhelm Harster, appointed Erich Deppner as the first German Commander of the camp. When Schol heard about the takeover, he informed Deppner that he was resigning from his duties immediately. Deppner then ordered him to remain because he did not have enough staff at his disposal to take over the camp as a whole.[2] Schol, according to his own words, gave in not because of the order, but because he had received requests and even pleas from inside and outside the camp to stay. One of these pleas came from the Jewish Council in Amsterdam, who would have asked him not to leave so that they had someone else in the camp who could defend the Jews. The camp residents would also have urged Schol to stay. Schol stated after the liberation that his role was limited to the management of the household part of the camp, making him responsible only for food, clothing and warehouse management.[3]

Whether Schol's role was indeed so small is doubtful. Until mid-January 1943, he signed all camp orders as commander.[4] It is not likely that the occupier had plans to change the existing chain of command immediately after the takeover. It was much more important to them that Westerbork continued to function and that peace and order prevailed. Deppner was mainly in control as responsible representative of the occupying forces, but let Schol carry out the work, assisted by the Jewish self-government. Meanwhile, Deppner was able to quickly transform the refugee camp into the gateway to the murder factories.

Deppner, son of a businessman, was born in Neuhaldensleben on 8 August 1910. It looked like he was headed for a legal career, because after studying law in Marburg, München and Halle, he obtained the doctoral degree in law in 1937. Deppner was attracted to National Socialism early on. In 1933 he became a member of the NSDAP during his studies and he became a member of the SS a year later. In 1937 he joined the SD. In early 1940, after training at the *Reichssicherheitshauptamt* in Berlin, Deppner was charged with leading the *Referat III C 1*, which dealt with the food problem. After the German Army had overwhelmed the Netherlands in May 1940, Deppner was transferred to the headquarters of the BdS in The Hague. There, as head of *Abteilung IV*, he was in charge of fighting the resistance and organising measures against the Jews.[5]

The text on the board indicates that the situation had changed.

In March 1941, Deppner was promoted in the SS rank to *SS-Sturmbannführer*. He was described as a Nazi at heart.[6] At the beginning of April 1942, he had to show that he was willing to carry out the most extreme orders. He was instructed by his chief, Harster, to act as leader of a firing squad. This squad had to shoot 77 Russian prisoners of war, just outside the camp site on the Leusderheide, who had been imprisoned in Camp Amersfoort.[7] Deppner accomplished this assignment and even personally

The camp was surrounded by a fence of barbed wire, canal and watchtower.

shot some of the victims. As a result, he would have been considered a suitable candidate by his superiors for taking over the command of Camp Westerbork. Presser described Deppner as a 'type of an SS leader, ice cold, ruthless, murderer with Officer's attitude'.[8]

Because of the new physical security measures, it was immediately clear that the camp had been given a different function after the takeover. One of

One of the seven watchtowers.

the most striking changes was the two metre high barbed wire fence. On the inside of the fence, camp residents had to dig a ditch of about 4 metres wide. Next to that was a 5 metre wide piece of ground, before which a wire of 40 centimetres high was strung: the so-called forbidden zone. Large signs were placed on both sides of the fence, bearing warnings in German and Dutch, such as *'Gefahrenzone'* and 'Entering this section is prohibited. You will be shot without warning'.[9] In order to check that the forbidden zone was indeed not entered, seven watchtowers were placed around the entire camp. Although these security measures were supposedly meant to keep out unwanted visitors, they were, of course, mainly intended to keep those who were staying in the camp inside. Although at an earlier stage, there had been limited freedom of movement, Camp Westerbork was now completely shut off from the outside world due to the visible changes. In order to make it a fully-fledged 'Prison', the surveillance groups had to be considerably expanded. The Gendarmes already present in the camp were ordered to deal with the security inside the camp. They were assisted by the members of the Ordedienst. Outdoor surveillance was transferred to a Security Unit of the SS.

SS Wachbataillon Nordwest

In mid-1942 the *SS-Wachbataillon Nordwest* was founded. Through advertisements and slogans such as 'Show yourself to be a true Dutchman' or 'Listen to the voice of your conscience. Register with the *Waffen SS*, *'t Legioen* or the *Wachbataillon* in the Netherlands', the Germans tried to reach men who were willing to volunteer for the SS units. According to an article published in the newspapers on 12 October 1942, men aged 17 to 40 years could not only apply to be sent to the front, but could also join the security forces in the Netherlands. The volunteers were hired on the same favourable terms as the men of the other SS units, such as pay, household allowance, clothing and food. They were also given the uniform and the distinctive badges of the *Waffen SS*.[10] The willingness to apply left much to be desired.

Although *'Volksdeutsche'* (ethnic Germans) from Ukraine and rejected frontline Soldiers were accepted into the Battalion, the desired number of men was not reached. That is why half a year later, a newspaper article explained what kind of unit the *Wachbataillon* was. It would have been established exclusively for those who, for certain reasons, objected to Military Service outside the borders of the Netherlands. Each Soldier would receive full infantry training and, after proven suitability, could reach an Officer's rank. Former education was not important in this respect. Only character, behaviour and performance were decisive factors for promotion. The age limit had now been changed from 40 to 45 years and married men could also apply. Since there was no strict admission policy and there were not a lot of requirements for approval either, the men of the *Wachbataillon* cannot be seen as part of the elite Soldiers of the SS. The few Dutch people who did volunteer did not do so because they were so motivated and also not because of a political conviction. It was usually the benefits, such as a job in the Netherlands, sufficient food, drinks and cigarettes, that made them choose to volunteer.

Because the recruitment campaign did not result in enough applications, other ways of getting volunteers had to be looked for. Searching for people in Psychiatric Institutions and prisons seems to have been such a way. That the *SS-Wachbataillon Nordwest* became an 'unruly troop of misfits' because of this is no surprise.[11] Even the occupying forces would have considered the men to be the 'worst conceivable elements of a very low level in every way'.[12] The most important task given to the *Wachbataillon* was the surveillance of all camps in the Netherlands, such as Amersfoort, Vught and Westerbork. This only meant outdoor surveillance; the men were not allowed to interfere with internal affairs and they were not allowed to enter the camps. The troops of the *SS-Wachbataillon* came to Westerbork during or shortly after the takeover. This was probably the second *Wach-Kompanie*. According to a communication from Major Ynto de Boer, Commander of the Gendarmerie in Groningen, the Westerbork *Wachbataillon* consisted of 70 to 80 SS members.[13]

That the camp residents also knew about the bad reputation and background of these men, which led to them not taking the men too seriously, is shown among other things by a *Lagerbefehl* signed by Schol in mid-December 1942. In this *Lagerbefehl*, it is claimed that camp residents made mocking remarks and gestures in the direction of the 'wachen der SS-kompanie' on multiple occasions. Furthermore, there was a warning that the *kompanie-Führer* had ordered his men to shoot without warning in such cases.[14] As far as we know, the SS never actually shot at the Jews, although opportunities to shoot were quickly found. Getting too close to the gate could already be regarded as an attempt to escape, which allowed the SS member on duty to shoot. This expression of a sense of duty was encouraged, because the one who had fired was given three days leave as a reward, and sometimes extra cigarettes and drinks.[15] The Battalion stayed in the so-called 'SS Lager Hooghalen'. This camp, later known mainly as Camp Heidelager, had been built for the provision of jobs, but for this purpose it was never used. It was just over a kilometre from Camp Westerbork.

Indoor Surveillance

After the function of the camp had been changed, the second period began for the Gendarmerie Detachment. A few days after the transfer, Major De Boer informed the person authorised to deal with the reorganisation of the Dutch Police about the arrival of the first Dutch Jews. According to him, this group would only stay in the camp for a short time, because it would be transported elsewhere for the purpose of carrying out work. According to De Boer, the role of the Gendarmerie was limited to the surveillance inside the camp. There the men were entrusted with maintaining order, while in addition they had to prevent the residents from leaving the camp without permission. The tasks of the Detachment appeared to have been less extensive than before. Nevertheless, during a conversation with the German authorities, the expansion of the Detachment was one of the subjects. They considered adding another four Gendarmes to the Detachment, so that it was made up of 19 men. This expansion had to do with the future of the camp, as the camp population was expected to grow from 1,500 to somewhere between 6,000 and 7,000 residents within two weeks.[16]

Guiding food transports was one of the tasks of the Gendarmerie.

De Boer had probably not been made fully aware of the actual situation in the camp. More than two weeks after his message to this person, Warrant Officer R. Toering, Commander of the Emmen Division, was informed by the Commander of the Westerbork Department of the fact that the number of tasks had increased significantly, so that reinforcement was urgently needed. To get a good idea of the situation, Toering decided to visit the camp. During this visit, it became clear that the tasks of the Gendarmerie Detachment were much more extensive than De Boer had indicated. According to a list, the Detachment was responsible for the guidance of Jews who had arrived at station Hooghalen from the transports to the camp and vice versa. They were also responsible for the supervision of the luggage, the guarding of the barracks and the taking of other measures in the camp to maintain order, the operation of the telephone switchboard during the night, the supervision of the Jews who worked outside the camp, providing transport services to Assen, Groningen or other places, and for occupying posts at the entrances to the camp. Especially for the large transports, many Gendarmes were needed. Because of the many tasks, the Commander of the Westerbork Department proposed reinforcing the Detachment not by four but by 20 men, which more than doubled the original strength. Toering agreed with this proposal and contacted De Boer directly by telephone. Whether Toering had to convince De Boer with many words is not known, but the desired expansion did come. Meanwhile, the duration of the secondment had also been extended from one to two months.

On 12 July 1942 the number of OD men changed for the first time. That day five OD members were allowed to leave the camp for good, because they were in mixed marriages. The next day the group was already supplemented with seven new and two reserve OD members. Of the total number of OD staff, two members had the Dutch nationality. The remaining 18 were former

OD in front of the service barracks.

refugees.[17] In order to ensure proper supervision in the camp, new camp orders appeared more frequently, which resulted in a broader task area. This started right after the takeover. For example, on 2 July 1942 it was announced that from that day onwards, no one was allowed to be outside the barracks after 22:00 without specific permission. The inner ring should not be left after half an hour before the specified curfew.[18] That evening three patrols of the OD had to check whether the camp residents complied with this measure after 21:30. On 14 July the OD was assigned barracks 22. These and other measures were not taken without reason, because the first transport departed the next day from Westerbork to Auschwitz. In addition to the Gendarmerie, the entire OD was regularly deployed in the handling of incoming or departing transports.[19]

The First Transports

That there was indeed a 'Jewish Question' for the occupier in the Netherlands had gradually become more and more apparent. After first isolating the Jews, the final and most horrible phase of the persecution began: the deportation of the Jews. As a gathering place, Camp Westerbork undoubtedly became the gateway to the Extermination Camps. On Friday evening 26 June 1942, representatives of the Jewish Council, including one of the two Presidents, David Cohen, had to report to the *Zentralstelle für jüdische Auswanderung* in Amsterdam. There they received from the head of this Department, Ferdinand aus der Fünten, the important announcement that a *polizeilicher Arbeitseinsatz* would take place for Jews. The Jewish Council was instructed to provide upon request the names for the final part of the persecution of the Jews.[20] Jewish residents from various Dutch places received a written call in the following months to 'go to transit Camp Westerbork, station Hooghalen, for personal examination and medical inspection for possible participation in a work group in Germany under Police supervision'. In general, those who were summoned had to report to specially designated gathering places first, such as the Hollandsche Schouwburg in Amsterdam and Loods 24 in Rotterdam. Under the supervision of the German Police, fully packed trains left for Westerbork.

In addition to these large organised transports, there were also mostly smaller groups of Jews who were brought directly to Hooghalen or Westerbork under the guidance of Dutch Police Officers. Some agents volunteered to accompany these transports, because this had a number of benefits for them. Afterwards, for example, they were allowed to visit their families in the east or north of the country, while all travel expenses were reimbursed. The corps declared these costs to the Government, because the cash flow statement had to be correct. Because the accompanying Police Officers would receive a decent income afterwards as a reward, some Policemen voluntarily signed up for this unpopular task.[21]

Some of the Police Officers took advantage of the circumstances. Agents of the Hague Police Force, for example, would have advised Jews on the train to give their money and valuable objects to them for safekeeping, because everything was going to be taken away in the camp. The 'loot' could be up to 100 Dutch guilders per cop. Sometimes agents wrote down the names of the owners, with the promise that they would send food packages in exchange for the money. They probably never kept this promise. A telex from the later Camp Commander Gemmeker to the BdS in The Hague shows that some accompanying agents indeed crossed the line.

On the night of 6 to 7 August 1943, a transport from Amsterdam arrived in Westerbork. After emptying the wagons, chief Policeman Albert de Jong found a Jewish woman hiding under a bench when he was checking one of the wagons. During the interrogation, she told them that she had tried to return to Amsterdam in this way. Furthermore, it turned out that one of the Supervisors, Willem van der Veen, who was part of The Second Company of the Amsterdam Police Battalion, was aware of this flight attempt. In exchange for his cooperation, the supervisor had received a diamond ring from this woman. The Policeman had not known that this ring was worth only 100 Dutch guilders. By order of Gemmeker, De Jong had to arrest Van der Veen at the station of Assen. In addition, the ring was confiscated as evidence. Van der Veen stated that his superior, Sergeant Van Duivenbode, was aware of the whole thing. Together they would share the proceeds of the ring.

According to Van der Veen, another incident occurred during transport. During the entire ride, there were two Jewish women in the compartment of the guards. Three of the guards had probably had intercourse with these women on the way, including Van Duivenbode and Van Leeuwen, who acted as transport leader. Because of the darkness, Van der Veen had not been able to see enough, so he did not know the details. When the train stopped in Hooghalen, the guards would have let the two women escape. Van der Veen was handed over to the German authorities after questioning. His actions will certainly have resulted in his dismissal, as well as imprisonment in a Concentration Camp as punishment. Van der Veen died on 4 April 1945 in the East German town of Nordhausen. He had probably been employed in the 'Mittelbau-Dora' Concentration Camp located a few kilometres from the centre. In the rocks just outside the camp, tunnels were cut out in which prisoners had to work on the new German retaliatory weapons under bad conditions.[22]

The first time the OD report mentions an incoming transport of arrested Jews was on 28 May 1942. This transport, which came from Amsterdam, would not have been large, because the deployment of seven OD members was sufficient for shielding the main hall, where the registration took place, and other strategic points. To accompany the new camp residents to the Hospital and the barracks, only two OD members were needed. When the camp was given a new function a month later, the influx increased, so that all OD members were needed to manage the transports. On 10 July, during the arrival of a transport containing 160 Jews, the entire OD was ordered to occupy all pre-established posts. By order of the commander, two OD men had to spend the night in the barracks where the newcomers were housed. It was probably a special group, because this last assignment is not mentioned elsewhere in the report.[23]

In order to prevent the camp from becoming crowded, the deportation of the Jews had to begin. Therefore, it did not take long for the first transport to leave. Deppner was ordered in the second week of July 1942 to prepare the first transport, which would consist of 2,000 Jews. Initially it seemed that Deppner would easily be able to get the required number together, because this transport would be filled with Jews who should have reported in Amsterdam. In the capital city, 1,400 Jews received a call, stating that they had to go to the central station on Tuesday 14 July in the evening. The next evening, an equal number of Amsterdam Jews received a similar summons.[24] More Jews had been summoned than was required by the order. Despite this, Deppner probably did not believe that everyone would respond to the call. He therefore selected 100 men from Camp Westerbork to add to the first transport. Deppner made this selection himself and he chose mainly the men who were not immediately needed in Westerbork.[25] It soon became clear that a large part of the Jews summoned in Amsterdam had indeed not shown up. As a result, there was a shortage instead of a surplus, so Deppner decided that 50 orphans present in Westerbork, as well as the 100 selected men, would join the first train.[26]

On 15 July the OD was ready at 5:30, together with the Gendarmerie, to guide the first group of Jews that came from Amsterdam from Hooghalen station to the camp more than 5 kilometers farther.[27] Because the journey to and from the station was made on foot, it took more than two hours before the men returned with the group of Jews. The stay in the camp was short, because after the group was registered and had had something to eat, they were brought to Hooghalen, together with the selected men and orphans.[28] At the station they were put in freight wagons 'like animals'[29], according to Presser. The train, containing more than 1,100 Jews, left the same day from Hooghalen to a destination unknown to them. Somewhere in Germany they had to wait for another train that departed from the Netherlands a day later, because on 15 July the second group had to come forward in Amsterdam. With an increase of about 600 Jews, Deppner had another problem. The solution was Camp Amersfoort. The 300 Jews who were there were quickly transferred to Hooghalen on 16 July and joined the second transport after registration on the platform. After that, this train could also leave for Germany. There the wagons were linked together. As one transport, more than 2,000 Jews reached their final destination on the night of 17 to 18 July: extermination camp Auschwitz-Birkenau.[30]

One of the departing transports from Hooghalen where the Gendarmerie was present, autumn 1942.

The OD members and Gendarmes who were present during the first transports would no doubt have witnessed harrowing scenes, such as the rough way the Jews were forced into the freight wagons. The Jews who had been brought to Hooghalen from Amersfoort, without luggage, hungry and dirty, must have left a horrible impression.[31] In addition, Deppner's choice to fill the first transport with the orphans in Westerbork caused a lot of commotion. In fact, it almost caused a riot. A chaotic situation was the last thing the German authorities wanted. Due to the increasing number of incoming and outgoing transports, they benefited from peace and order within the camp.

On Saturday 18 July the OD had to be ready once again in the early morning to receive an incoming transport from Amsterdam. In contrast to the two previous transports, this group was temporarily housed in the camp, so that the registration could take place in peace. However, this stay did not last long, because most of them left on 21 July with the third transport to Auschwitz. The incoming and outgoing transports followed each other at a rapid pace after that.

Sometimes it happened that a new group arrived the same day on which a transport left. This was the case on Friday 31 July. From 7:45 onwards, the OD was deployed to accompany the sixth outgoing transport, which consisted of just over a thousand Amsterdam Jews. Later that day, the OD members returned to the camp with about 1,100 Jews from Rotterdam.[32] Although the supply of Jews from all over the country continued, it became increasingly difficult to achieve the number required by the occupier due to the declining willingness to answer the calls in large cities. New measures had to be taken to prevent the shutdown of the deportation machine.[33]

A Rough SS Man Without A Brain
After more than 12,000 Jews had been transported to Auschwitz in 15 trains at the end of August, Deppner was replaced. According to Harster, Deppner had been told in advance that he would only temporarily fulfil the position of commander.[34] The successor of Deppner, *SS-Obersturmführer* Josef Hugo Dischner, born on 31 January 1902 in Munich, took over command on 1 September 1942. According to Presser, Dischner was a 'type of a rough SS man, with no brains and almost always under the influence of alcohol'.[35] A later assessment made by Harster shows that, according to him, Dischner was not suited for the position of Commander of such a camp in any way[36]. After completing an education to become a merchant, Dischner joined the *vaterländischen Hilfsdienst* and the *Freikorps Epp* until July 1921. Until he was appointed as decorator in the textile industry in 1927, he was out of work. Dischner's career was difficult, because he was dismissed three years later by the Karstadt group because of his political preference. Joining the SS in July 1932 ensured that he was no longer welcome at Grohag, where he worked as a merchant.

His membership also had a positive effect, because it gave him a job within the SS. After following an education at the SS Officer's School in Bad Tölz, he was given a position among the personal staff of the *Reichsführer SS*. From April 1937 onwards, Dischner as *Verwaltungs und Unterkunftsführer* was part of the *III. SS-Standarte 'Germania'*, which was housed in the SS barracks in Radolfzell. At the end of October 1939 he had to leave the service because of anxiety issues. In June 1940 he had sufficiently recovered to take up an administrative position within the SS: first with the *Stadthauptmann* in Warsaw and later at the *Polizeiverwaltung* in Lemberg, where he was in charge of the construction of the *Strassenverkehrsamt*. Lemberg had a rich Jewish history and had one of Poland's largest Jewish communities. Immediately after Germany had taken the city, actions against the Jewish population began. Together with members of *Einsatzgruppe C*, Ukrainian nationalists had begun to rid the city of Jews. According to Loe de Jong, Dischner must have known that the Jews were being exterminated and it is very likely that De Jong was right about that. Even though Dischner was on the side lines because of his function, he will have heard and seen enough in Lemberg to draw this conclusion. This may have been the reason why he requested a transfer to the Netherlands in July 1942.[37]

After the change of command, the transports continued. In September 1942, nine trains departed from Hooghalen, bringing a total of about 6,700 Jews to Auschwitz.[38] The OD and the Gendarmerie sometimes spent day and night escorting the Jews.[39] Meanwhile, from August onwards, service regulations were published somewhat regularly in the OD report. These regulations were mainly intended to increase discipline within the camp. For example, the OD divided the summoned Jews and supervised them. The members of the Jewish Council were no longer allowed to enter the barbed wire area and bring Jews who had been put on transport back into the camp. The OD members themselves also got stricter rules. They had to focus only on their duties when they had to work in the Women's Department and they were not allowed to engage with female residents of the camp even when not on duty. In addition, the OD members who had to go to Hooghalen to do work there were not allowed to carry any money or letters with them. The fear remained that letters with negative messages about Westerbork would get out and that this would cause the Jewish people to panic.[40] The stricter rules were necessary, because Westerbork was about to enter a very busy period.

October 1942

On 24 September 1942, Hans Albin Rauter, who was in charge of the armed SS and the German Police as *Höhere SS und Polizeiführer* in the Netherlands, wrote a letter to his chief, *Reichsführer SS* Heinrich Himmler. In this he described the plans for the *Endlösung der Judenfrage* in the Netherlands. According to Rauter, a large number of unemployed Jewish men were employed in several closed companies and camps. The employment of these men was one of the anti-Jewish measures, because after the first dismissal of Jewish officials, the majority of the Jewish male labour force was expelled from the labour market. A large number of these men had to go to one of the 40 labour camps, mainly in the north and east of the Netherlands.[41] On 9 January 1942, 2,600 Jewish men from Amsterdam received a call to come for an inspection to see if they would be suitable for work in the labour camps. The next day, about a third of them left for these camps. The group of Jewish men who were forced to go became ever larger. In the long run, all Jewish men between the ages of 18 and 65, including the Dutch, were considered eligible for the employment.[42]

Group of Jewish men in the Geesbrug Labour Camp.

Some men from Assen were housed in the Orvelte labour Lin Drenthe. One of them was the Austrian born merchant Waldemar Ochs[43], who, together with his wife and daughter, had fled from Saarlauteren from the Nazi regime and ended up in Assen. The family lived there at Alteveerstraat 47. His Jewish neighbour of number 45, Karl Hecht[44], had also fled from Germany with his wife.[45] Both men had to help with the reclamation of the heathland and with harvesting potatoes in Orvelte.[46] Albert Sachs from Borne was transferred in August 1942 with a number of fellow Jewish townsmen to the labour camp 'Het Overbroek' between Ochten and Kesteren.[47] With about 140 other men, he had to do groundwork near the camp. The purpose of this heavy work was to demolish part of the *Grebbe line*, which Dutch Soldiers had built before the May days of 1940.[48]

The occupier deliberately left the labour camps alone for some time, so that even more Jews would 'flee' there, because working in the Netherlands was still better than being transported. At the time when Rauter wrote the letter to Himmler, about 7,000 Jewish workers remained in the labour camps, but he hoped that this number would increase to 8,000 by 1 October. According to Rauter's calculation, these workers had about 22,000 relatives. These figures do not correspond to the numbers Presser used in his work. Rauter may have painted a slightly rosier picture of reality to please his chief.[49] According to Presser, 5,242 Jewish men were housed in 42 camps on 25 September and these men had 8,877 family members[50]. These figures were not of any particular relevance for Rauter's plans. In his letter he wrote that German troops would occupy all labour camps on 1 October and that the family members had to be arrested on the same day. The Jewish men, women and children who came into the hands of the occupiers as a result of these actions went on transport to Camp Westerbork.[51] Rauter had a well thought out plan, which was a cunning move, because this way there was more or less forced family reunification.

It soon became clear that the planned action was actually implemented. Between 1 and 4 October 1942, German Soldiers and members of the *Ordnungspolizei* appeared at the labour camps and took the Jewish men with them. David Chajes[52] was staying at Camp 't Schut in Ede. Together with the other workers, he was transported on foot to Arnhem by the *Ordnungspolizei* on Saturday morning, 3 October, where the group arrived around noon. The transport did not continue directly; the men were brought to a courtyard somewhere in Arnhem. There they had to spend the night on a stone floor, probably without food. The next day the group continued. The journey ended hours later in Westerbork.

David had moved to Hungary from Poland around 1920. Before he came to the Netherlands, he had been living in Vienna for two more years. In Apeldoorn David found a job, with room and board, in a brush factory. Later he also worked for some time as a nurse in the Psychiatric Hospital *'Het Apeldoornsche Bosch'*. Because David was more suited for entrepreneurship, he entered the textile trade. In the meantime, he got married and had twin daughters. David's Company grew into one of the best textile stores in Apeldoorn and the surrounding area. On the night of 2 to 3 October a raid took place in Apeldoorn, as in other cities. David's wife had by then heard from the neighbour, who was stationmaster, that trains had arrived to take away the captured Jews. That night the Police went to David's apartment too. Since both daughters were ill because of bronchitis, David's wife left them with her parents and went to the Police Station alone. The registration of the Jews was arranged so well that they soon found out that the daughters had not come and David's wife was ordered to pick them up under the guidance of the Police. She was told that if she did not do this quickly enough, both girls would be thrown out the window.

When they arrived in the house, the accompanying Policemen saw David's in laws. Since his mother in law was terminally ill, she was allowed to stay behind, but his father in law had to come. The Chajes family was then escorted to a school, where they had to spend the night on the floor with other arrested Jews. The next day they were brought to the train early. This train stopped around noon in Arnhem. There everyone had to get off and after a long walk through the city, the group arrived at a Prison in the afternoon. This stop had probably been added because pick up operations were taking place in other cities and villages and it was not possible to send all transports simultaneously to Hooghalen.

The treatment of the Jews in the Arnhem Prison was inhumane. Each time they were instructed to get up and then sit down again, while they still had their backpacks on. By the evening the group had to go to the train again, with Hooghalen as their final destination. After a long walk, the camp was reached. There was still no opportunity to rest here, because formalities, such as registration, had to be dealt with first. When this was finally done, David's family was assigned a barracks. This too did not end all the misery, because the arrival of the many thousands of newcomers resulted in a chaotic situation in the camp. There was insufficient food and a lack of beds, meaning that several people had to spend the night in one bed together. When David arrived at the camp, he heard that his family was already there.[53]

Little was written in the OD report about the first days of October 1942. The reports of 3 and 4 October relate to the deployment of the OD and the number of Jews who had arrived. On both days, the OD was working day and night to handle all of the transports. The camp population grew within a few days from 3,000 to more than 15,000 Jews.[54] Due to the crowds, the Gendarmes also received 24 hour shifts. That not everyone could cope with that pressure is evidenced by a statement made by Gendarme Dirk Knol, who was seconded to the camp at that time. On 3 October he and the other staff of the secondment were ordered to place the newly arrived Jews in the designated barracks. One of the Gendarmes would have been overworked while he was in one of the barracks around midnight. He was ordered to remove all Jewish men from the beds in this barracks, because they were destined for the female camp residents. At one point, the man came to a bed on which a Jewish man was sleeping. This man was exhausted because he had not slept and eaten for three days, while his feet hurt from the amount of walking. The moment the Gendarme wanted to remove the man from his bed, the man hit him in his sleep, assuming that a co-resident was harassing him. The Gendarme, who according to Knol was very nervous, grabbed the man by his clothes and dragged him off the bed.

At the same time, Policeman Albert de Jong entered the barracks and shouted: 'Well, goddamned ugly jew, are you trying to hit my staff?! If there's hitting to be done, I'll do it!' While De Jong said this, he took his baton out of his pocket, grabbed the man by the chest and then pressed him into a corner of the barracks. After this, he hit the man on the head with his baton, causing him to fall to the floor with a gaping wound in the front of his head. The wound required stitching at the camp Hospital. The Gendarme who was involved in the incident was relieved of his secondment a few days later.

After the liberation, De Jong made a statement about this event. According to him, he came into a barracks on that particular night and found that a Gendarme was fighting with a Jewish man. De Jong stated that the man did not listen to the Gendarme and was hiding under an iron bed. This had led the Gendarme to remove the man by force. By grabbing him by the chest and slapping him with one of his hands, De Jong took over the situation. He considered this to be his duty and he claimed any Policeman would have done so. As far as De Jong could remember, he did not strike a blow with the baton and the man was not injured either. What is striking about De Jong's statement is that his memory abandoned him at certain times. At that time, he was still staying at the camp as a seconded Policeman. A few months later, he received a provisional appointment as acting Detachment Commander.[55] This incident shows that at the beginning of October, much was required of the OD and Gendarmerie, both physically and mentally. Not only did the many hours of service take their toll; seeing a lot of suffering must have had great impact. That things could be worse was proved by an event on Monday 5 October.

The Day Of Terror

On 5 October 1942 the 25th and largest train transport departed from the camp to the east. As usual, it was likely determined beforehand how many people had to go to Auschwitz that day. The OD report indicates that approximately 2,000 Jews were taken away. They were selected the night before and placed in the transport barracks. The guarding of these barracks probably did not count for much, because the group that left the camp in the morning and arrived in Hooghalen on foot appeared to be made up of 'only' 1,700 Jews. Although enough Jews were present in the camp to get the planned number on the train, Dischner opted for a different solution. He ordered the 200 to 300 women and children who had arrived in Westerbork the same morning and were waiting on a side road outside the camp to get on the train as well. As such, the quota was met much quicker. The women and children had been arrested during a raid in Amsterdam. In Westerbork they would be reunited with their husbands and fathers, who had previously been transferred from the labour camps elsewhere in the Netherlands to Westerbork. In many cases, they saw each other for the first time in months. Dischner ordered the newcomers to register immediately. This formality was completed at a rapid pace and did not arouse women's suspicion. They hoped that they could soon embrace their husbands after this.

However, when it turned out that the group was not allowed to go further into the camp but was led out again, they began to panic.[56] An employee of the Jewish Council happened to walk past the registration hall and, together with a number of other Jews from the camp, witnessed the tragedy that followed. The employee heard the women shout: 'We want to go to our men' and 'I will not let myself be slaughtered without my husband'. When the women came out of the registration hall, he saw that Schol also left the hall. He immediately began to whip the women and shouted: 'Order, I will teach you order.'[57] Another witness heard the noise as well. He saw that some Gendarmes, aided by OD men, were attempting to get the group moving by kicking and pushing them. A number of women opposed and tried, sometimes successfully, to enter the camp. Dischner had run to the group and started beating the women with his whip, with the aim of driving them out of the camp. According to the witness, it was a horrible sight.

Whether Dischner and Schol both hit the women with a whip is unknown. Schol declared after the liberation that he had been in possession of a whip for some time, but as far as he could remember he had never hit anyone. The numerous testimonies of witnesses prove that a whip was in fact used to control the defenceless and panicked women. The cries of help from the beaten women and the crying children made the horrific spectacle even worse. Eventually, the group started moving. The Jewish men who had to help with the construction of the railway link between the camp and Hooghalen station heard the screams and had come closer. When some men discovered that their wives were in line, they did not hesitate for a moment and joined them. At the station they voluntarily boarded the train.

Because the first group had been able to prepare for the journey, they had luggage with them. As a result, there was not enough space in the wagons to take everyone. By throwing a large part of the luggage out of the train, the transport could still leave. For the Jewish men who were in charge of handling the leftover luggage, the work was far from finished. They had to collect it all and make as good an inventory as they could of everything, based on the transport list. This task was carried out carefully and therefore took several days. To prevent the goods from being stolen, there had to be security. Since the Jewish men were not allowed to leave the camp after a certain time, the Gendarmerie was in charge of surveillance at night.

After an inventory had been made of all the suitcases and backpacks, they could be taken to the camp. Sometimes heartbreaking scenes took place there. Men whose wives and children should have been in the camp long ago feared that they had been put on transport. When they found the suitcases or backpacks of their loved ones between the goods that had been returned, a violent emotional reaction often followed.[58] The events surrounding the transport of 5 October and the brutal behaviour of Dischner were not conducive to the peace and order within the camp. As this could be detrimental to the next transports, the German authorities intervened. After only six weeks, Dischner was removed from office and transferred to the *Waffen SS*. In mid-June 1944 he was Commander of a *Kraftfahr-Kompagnie*.[59]

The 'Gentleman Commander'

As temporary successor to Dischner, *Polizei Inspektor* Bohrmann was pushed forward. Nothing is known about his performance as commander. This is not surprising, because after three days he was already gone. Presser described him as 'a useless man'. From 12 October onwards, the *SS Ober-sturmführer* Albert Konrad Gemmeker, born in Düsseldorf, was able to show whether he was fit to command Camp Westerbork. Gemmeker would have been walking around the camp for several days before he officially took up the position of Camp Commander.[60] It is likely that Bohrmann had deliberately been appointed as a temporary observer, so that Gemmeker could look at the camp without pressure and in peace.

On 27 September 1942, shortly before Gemmeker came to Westerbork, he had celebrated his 35th birthday. As the son of a stonemason, after having graduated from the *Volksschool*, he got a job at an Insurance Company at the age of eighteen. This career did not meet his expectations or did not go as planned, because Gemmeker went to the Police School in Bonn after having been unemployed for a short time at the beginning of April 1927. After the training, which lasted one year, he was appointed as a Policeman at the *Schutzpolizei* in Duisburg. Although he was promoted to *Oberwachtmeister* there, he probably did not like the operational Police work. He felt more drawn to an administrative job. Thanks to a friend who worked with the Police in the *Regierungsbezirk* Düsseldorf, he managed to return to his hometown in June 1933 as an administrative Police Officer. According to the guidelines of that time, a Police Officer had to decide how to continue his career after eight years of service. In 1935 Gemmeker had to make this choice. Because he preferred an administrative function, the possibilities were limited. The Police Force of Düsseldorf had no vacancies in this direction. Within the German Police Organisation, the *Geheime Staatspolizei* (Gestapo) was one of the parts where administrative staff members were still requested. Thus, according to Gemmeker, there was nothing else for him to do than accept the position of *Büroassistant-Anwärter*.[61]

Although this choice would have had nothing to do with any political conviction, Gemmeker wanted to join the National Socialists in early 1933.[62] However, he only officially joined the *NSDAP* in May 1937. He also voluntarily applied for membership of the SS. It is not clear whether this really was voluntary, since the *Gestapo* became part of the *Sipo* in 1936 and membership of the SS was therefore a prerequisite. After Gemmeker was initially admitted to the SS as *Hauptscharführer*, he was given the rank of *SS-Untersturmführer* after following a course. After the appointment as Commander of Camp Westerbork, or shortly before, he was promoted to Obersturmführer. Within the Gestapo he was also given the opportunity to further develop himself. The completion of an education resulted in him continuing his career as a *Büroassistent* at the end of 1936. The following year he was promoted to *Polizeisekretär*. At the end of August 1940, Gemmeker had to leave Düsseldorf, because he had been transferred to the BdS in The Hague as a *Personalreferent*. In early December 1940 he became *Ober-Sekretär*.[63]

Gemmeker got married for the first time in January 1934. The marriage lasted just over four years. One month after the divorce, Gemmeker got married for the second time. The relationship with his second wife had probably begun much earlier, because their first child was born before he married her. Later he had two more children with this woman. Despite that, this marriage did not last either. In 1944, Gemmeker filed for divorce, but because this claim was supposedly not *kriegswichtig*, it was not taken into consideration.[64] This did not prevent him from openly entering into a relationship with his Secretary, Elisabeth Helena Hassel-Mullender, who was also married. Frau Hassel, as she was later called in the camp, had already worked as a Secretary for Gemmeker for a few weeks in 1940. When he was working for some time in The Hague, he called Hassel and asked her if she wanted to work for him as a Secretary. She responded to that request and later followed Gemmeker to St. Michielsgestel and Westerbork.[65] In mid-August 1943 Hassel left for The Hague, because she had accepted an appointment as Second Secretary of the BdS. This transfer was not voluntary: BdS Harster had found out about the relationship between Gemmeker and Hassel and had therefore called her back to The Hague. A year later she was able to return to Westerbork, because Harster had been succeeded.[66]

Before Gemmeker went to Westerbork, he had been able to get used to the idea of acting as Camp Commander for several months. From June 1942 onwards, he was in charge of the management of the hostage camp which was located in the minor seminary Beekvliet in Sint-Michielsgestel. On 4 May 1942, in order to discourage acts of resistance as much as possible, the occupier arrested 460 prominent Dutch men who could be used for retaliatory actions if the resistance continued its activities. Because the regime in Beekvliet was not strict and the hostages had a lot of freedom of movement within the walls, the position of Commander there will not have been too taxing.[67]

After the departure of Gemmeker's incapable predecessor and after the turbulent October month, there was a need for a Commander who was confident and authoritative. Above all, he had to ensure that the correct numbers of Jews were put on the deportation trains without any commotion and that these transports left in time towards the (extermination) camps. Due to the proper functioning of the Jewish Camp Organisation, it took little effort for Gemmeker and the staff to fulfil this assignment. Because the unfortunate camp residents often let themselves be pushed into the train meekly and without opposition, the application of violence was hardly necessary. Therefore, few people judged negatively about Gemmeker. Because of his friendly and correct performance, he was nicknamed 'Gentleman Commander'.[68] According to a well-known quote, he did not kick 'his' camp people to Poland, like his predecessor, but laughed them to it. It was often wondered which one was actually worse.[69]

On 17 December 1943, Gemmeker gives a speech during the Yule Festival. To the left of him is Elisabeth Hassel and to the right is Ferdinand Aus der Fünten.

Residents, on the other hand, judged less positively about the behaviour of his mistress. According to them, more than Gemmeker, Elisabeth Hassel met the image of the typical camp executioner who developed into a ruthless Nazi.[70] Although she was not appointed as replacement of Gemmeker, Hassel did have certain powers. She especially made her presence felt during his absence and often acted in a harsh manner. She scolded the camp residents, punished them and did not take exemptions into account the way Gemmeker did.[71] Hassel admitted that Gemmeker had entrusted her with various tasks. However, these powers would only have consisted of signing internal documents. According to Hassel, it was entirely possible that there were penal orders or transport orders between these documents sometimes that caused a camp resident to end up in the camp Prison or to be deported.

However, she was not authorised to send someone on transport. Hassel denied hating Jews fanatically. She even claimed the opposite. During the occupation she always felt sorry for the Jewish people and where possible she claimed to have helped Jews. Because it was difficult for her to show her soft side, they had gotten a wrong impression of her.[72] No source shows that the mistress of Gemmeker had actually helped Jewish residents during her stay in Camp Westerbork or that she had difficulty expressing herself.[73]

At the time Gemmeker took command in Camp Westerbork, Schol was still present and in office. According to Schol, Gemmeker did not trust him from the start and for that reason he made several attempts to get Schol out of Westerbork. Schol mentioned some examples to show this. He was summoned to Gemmeker's desk fairly soon. There he was told that Gemmeker suspected that Schol's wife was Jewish. Schol refuted this and referred Gemmeker to the civil registry of the camp. Gemmeker had probably become suspicious because Schol's wife's first name was Sarah. A few days later, Schol had to appear again at the Camp Commander's Office. This time he was accused of hiding a Jewish child in his house. Schol did not deny that a child was staying with them, but they were not hiding him. It was a boy from a Jewish family that had fled Germany in 1939. His mother had died of tuberculosis. Sometime later, the father had also died of this disease and Schol had promised the man to take care of his son. Since the papers showed that the boy was born of a mixed marriage, he could fulfil his promise without problems. In order to arrange it officially, Schol had the boy registered in the civil registry and had himself appointed as guardian by a District Judge from Hilversum. As such, the child could not be considered hidden.

On 10 November 1942, a few months before Schol was forced to leave the camp, he personally interfered with public order. That day he announced that all camp residents, including those who were ill, had to take their luggage to the roll call area at 8:00 the next day. At the time indicated, many thousands of residents had shown up at the place in question. This action had to do with the capacity of the camp and the many incoming and outgoing transports. As a result, the camp administration had become completely mixed up. The redivision of the camp residents in the barracks had to ensure that the administration was reorganised. Together with Schol, Gemmeker took place on a small stage. One by one, the names were called out and the new arrangement was announced. Because people were walking in every direction, the action looked chaotic. It took until 22:00 at the very least before a big part of the camp residents actually knew which barrack they were supposed to be in. A small group would only be told the next day in which barracks they had been placed.

Many camp residents had to spend many hours at the roll call place during the redivision. Because of the long period of standing still, many got hungry and thirsty, but there was no possibility to eat or drink something. Some Jewish men decided to return to their barracks to get food there. The moment they returned to the area, Schol walked towards them and struck them in the face at eye level left and right with his riding whip, because they had left without permission. The men dropped the food and had to crawl back to the place where their luggage was standing because of the damage they had suffered to their eyes.

OD member Max Levy[74] witnessed the assault and saw the marks of the whip on the faces. At the end of December 1938, Max had fled with his family from the German town of Norden to the Netherlands and settled in The Hague. When all foreign Jews had to leave the coastal area, including The Hague, Max and his family moved to Hengelo in early September 1940. At the end of August 1942, he received a call for labour camp 'Het Overbroek' near Kesteren via the employment agency. Like many other Jewish men, Max arrived in Westerbork on 3 October 1942, where he was reunited with other family members.

From fellow residents Max had heard that Schol was sometimes very temperamental and had beaten Jews before, but he had never before witnessed this himself. Max made it clear in his statement that Schol acted more barbaric in many ways than Gemmeker, making all Jews more afraid of Schol than of the Camp Commander. At the beginning of December 1942, Gemmeker admitted he did not trust Schol and demanded that he leave the camp. However, since Schol was still employed by the Department of Justice, Gemmeker did not have the authority to send him away. The head of the immigration office deliberately did not fire Schol, because otherwise he would have no income. In any case, Schol signed several camp orders until mid-February 1943. Finally, under duress of Gemmeker, he left camp.[75]

In terms of supervision and surveillance, a greater change took place during the same period. In early 1943, the Company of the *SS-Wachbataillon Nordwest* was transferred from Westerbork to The Hague. From that moment on, mainly the OD was responsible for the order within the barbed wire fence. The Detachment of the Gendarmerie took care of the outdoor surveillance.

Gemmeker's Men

Because Gemmeker largely maintained the camp system and allowed the Jewish self-government to do its work, it was not necessary for the occupier to send men to Westerbork on a large scale again after the departure of the *SS Wachbataillon*. According to Elisabeth Hassel, Gemmeker had a staff with a total strength of eight to ten German Soldiers of the category C.[76] This designation would have been mainly related to the physical condition of the men, because most of them had fought on the Eastern Front and had gotten seriously injured there. Besides, they were not only German Soldiers, but both German and Dutch members of the SS or SD.[77] From early 1943 onwards, a group of them came to Westerbork at intervals. The names are known of at least 11 crews[78] that came to work in Westerbork. Four of them had the Dutch nationality. One SS man came from Austria and the rest came from Germany. Of the men in this group, which was likely not much bigger than the other one, six of them had sustained injuries on the Eastern Front. These injuries ranged from missing the right eye (two) and (lower) arm (two) to feet lost to frostbite. One of the SS men still had a bullet in one of his lungs.

Given these injuries, it cannot be said that Gemmeker had a fit elite unit. In fact, there was not really a staff, because most of them were not given a strategic position in the camp. The work initially consisted of operating the call centre, performing administrative tasks or working as a mechanic or driver.[79]

The German SS member Hans Georg Johann Reiser[80] came to the camp around February 1943 as one of the first. Before the outbreak of the war, Reiser had worked as a tanner. At the end of October 1939, he joined the *Waffen SS* in Munich as a Soldier. A month later, he was transferred to the *SS Polizei Division*. In June 1940 this Police Division took part in the campaign in France, where the German Army came out on top. Soon after that, Hitler had already made new plans, which were implemented in June 1941. On 22 June the attack on Russia began under the codename 'Operation Barbarossa'. This major offensive would ultimately turn out badly for the German Army, but they were initially successful. Reiser and his Police Division moved in the direction of Leningrad. Reiser did not participate in the siege of this city, because he was wounded during the fighting at the beginning of August 1941. The injuries were so serious that he lost his right forearm.

During the recovery period, which lasted more than one year, Reiser was nursed in Münster's Military Hospital. Because of the handicap, he was unable to return to the front. After being placed shortly with the *Genesungskompagnie* in Vught, he received a position at the end of September 1942 in The Hague as an assistant at the *IV B 4 Division*: the so-called *Judenreferat*.[81] It is possible that this function was the link to Camp Westerbork. After the liberation, Gemmeker and a number of residents, including OD members Hans Eisinger and Werner Bloch, gave their opinion on a large part of the SS people stationed in the camp. Reiser was described as a dumb and peculiar man. In his performance he was average at best as well, so he was not one of the feared figures. According to Gemmeker, Reiser did indeed have a poor mental development. He showed respect towards his superiors and got along well with his colleagues.[82]

The Dutch SS member Wilhelmus Severinus Antonie van Eck[83] was judged less favourably. He arrived a month after Reiser in Westerbork and soon became known as an unpleasant person who would develop into a real brute during his stay in the camp. Especially after Van Eck was appointed Commander of the punishment barracks in the second half of 1944, he developed into one of the most hated SS members, thus acquiring the nickname 'the terror of Camp Westerbork'. In 1940 Van Eck was trained to be a mechanic at a vocational school in Apeldoorn. Because of the poor economic and social conditions and because he was convinced that the Netherlands had to face the world as a single unit, he became a member of the NSB. When his fiancée broke off the relationship in March 1941, he seems to have been pretty upset. In order to forget his heartbreak, Van Eck volunteered for the *Nederlandsche SS* shortly thereafter. During the SS training in Hamburg, he was hit by a Military car. His shoulder was dislocated, so he had to be nursed in the Hospital room of the barracks. After his shoulder had healed several months later, Van Eck was sent to East Prussia to be trained as a driver.

In January 1942, a transfer to Russia followed. There he had to bring ammunition and food to the front by truck. On his way back, he took wounded Soldiers with him. Van Eck experienced that the profession of driver could be dangerous on 17 March 1942, when German artillery fired grenades in the direction of the front. One of these grenades exploded nearby, leaving some shards in Van Eck's left forearm and face. The facial injuries were so severe that he lost his right eye. After half a year, Van Eck had healed enough to be placed at the *Genesungskompagnie* in the Austrian city of Graz. Shortly thereafter, he was transferred to the *Kraftfahrtechnische Lehranstalt* of the *Waffen SS* in Vienna, where he was taught in vehicle engineering. This training must have lasted until March 1943, because then Van Eck, who had been promoted to *SS Rottenführer*, left for Camp Westerbork. There he was initially employed in the call centre. From a financial point of view and in connection with his injuries, Van Eck submitted a request to be promoted to *SS Unterscharführer*. This request was accepted.

A few months after arriving at the camp, Van Eck was given a position in the field force and others took over his work in the call centre. The new task consisted of checking the workshops. Because he had little knowledge of such work, he did not take his task too seriously. He had nothing to do with guarding the camp residents working in the field. This task was carried out by the Gendarmerie and members of the OD. Within the camp, Van Eck did not interfere with the surveillance either. This was also the case for the other SS members who had arrived in Westerbork after Reiser and Van Eck. One year after his arrival, Van Eck was given a position at the so-called 'Bauleitung'. At this institution he was engaged in checking repairs to the barracks and checking the inventory. According to the statement he made after the occupation, he was not actually allowed to be entrusted with this work. Nevertheless, he fulfilled this task in the titular rank of *Ober-scharführer* and in the uniform of the *Sipo*, because he was not given the official rank of *Oberscharführer*. According to Gemmeker, Van Eck could be weird sometimes. He was quick to anger and he had peculiarities. Gemmeker assumed that along with the loss of his eye, the mind of his subordinate had suffered a little as well.[84]

In September 1943, the number of SS members in the camp had risen to five: two Germans and three Dutchmen. In April 1943, the German Edmund Xaver Breil[85] was added to the 'staff' of Gemmeker, while Herman Benjamin van Laer[86] had already come to the camp in September 1942. When Van Laer lost his job as a kitchen chef in 1942, he reported to the employment agency in The Hague. There he was informed that he would be sent to a factory in Essen in connection with the war industry. It did not come to that, because his brother in law, who worked as a mechanic for the SD, made sure Van Laer got a job at the same service as a driver and mechanic. As the regular driver of architect Arthur Winne, who was in charge of the building of the barracks in Camp Westerbork, Van Laer arrived in the camp in September 1942. After the departure of Winne, in 1944, he stayed behind as a driver and mechanic.

Because of this function, he had no combat experience, so Van Laer was not one of the armed elites, nor would he have formed an opinion on the politics regarding the war. This is evidenced by the way he handled the people in the camp, for example. One of them stated that when they needed help, for example with smuggling letters and parcels, they could appeal to this Dutch SD man and he was always willing to help. Van Laer also regularly informed residents of the messages broadcast via the English channels and knew that these channels were being listened to illegally in 'his' workshop. Although this was part of the reason the residents' opinion of Van Laer was mostly positive, he abused his position in one case. In the second half of 1944, a resident approached Sandor Salmagne, who was employed by the OD, and asked him whether he could smuggle a sum of 5,000 Dutch guilders into the camp. This money was intended as a bribe to avoid deportation. Van Laer was said to be the one who could arrange it. Sandor knew from his own experience the reputation of this Dutchman dressed in SD uniform and agreed to mediate. After all, an OD member could make contact with a subordinate of the Camp Commander more easily than a resident could.

One of the evenings prior to the day he was going to Amsterdam, Van Laer received a letter which he had to deliver to a certain address, after which the money would be handed over to him. As thanks for the effort, he would get ten percent of it. A few days later, Van Laer returned. Despite several attempts, Sandor failed to get him to speak to him. It looked like the SD man was deliberately avoiding him. Only after a few days, the men met up. According to Van Laer, the mission had largely failed, because instead of the money, he had only received a package of food. This package was handed over by the OD man to the resident. After the liberation, Van Laer immediately confessed that he had received the full amount of money. He had treated three colleagues in Amsterdam and paid off his debts with them, leaving 4,000 Dutch guilders. He claimed that when he had returned to the camp, he gave 2,500 Dutch guilders to Sandor, announcing that he would pay back the rest later.

The resident, who became impatient, then contacted Van Laer himself and announced that the money was destined for him. Van Laer had told him that he had only received 500 guilders in Amsterdam and would later hand it over to him. He would have fulfilled this last promise by giving the resident 100 guilders a number of times, along with cigarettes and foodstuffs. At least he had to keep Sandor close because he knew too much about him. That is why he later gave the OD member a radio and a rifle with ammunition. Sandor denied receiving money. He did admit that he had received some radios, weapons, ammunition and hand grenades from Van Laer. These goods were paid for with alcohol and money.[87] This incident shows that there was (illegal) contact between camp residents and one or more SS members.

Having good contacts certainly did not apply to the Dutch SS man Hendrik van Dam[88], who had personally been brought to the camp by Gemmeker in September 1943. Just like Van Laer, Van Dam had not fought on the Eastern Front. Nevertheless, he did possess the right political colour, since he had been a member of the NSB since 1935. At that time, he was working at his father's business. Both of his parents had also joined National Socialism. In 1939, because of the mobilisation, Van Dam was summoned as a Sergeant at the 'Jagers' Regiment in Waalsdorp. After the capitulation and after working for a few months at the *Nederlandse Opbouwdienst* (a service which had to prevent more unemployment), he reported to an office in The Hague in hopes of getting a position in the Police Force. The training for this position would take place in Germany. In Germany, however, it turned out to be not a Police training, but a full Military training for the *SS-standarte 'Westland'.* Clearly, this strategy of recruiting young men under false pretences for the SS actually existed and was not just made up. After the liberation, several persons made a statement about similar recruitment practices.

Hendrik van Dam.

Van Dam stated that he had himself rejected when it became clear for what purpose he had been lured to Germany. In December 1940, he returned to the Netherlands at his own request, together with 30 'fellow refusers'. Despite the rejection, Van Dam's physical condition was apparently considered good enough to continue working for the SS, because in The Hague the group was told that they would be assigned to the Dutch SS. A few days later he had to report to the *Dienststelle* of the SD, located at the Binnenhof in The Hague. After he had been working as a doorman there for a short time, he was transferred to the administration. His daily work consisted of the arranging and storing of personnel files and the provision of ration stamps. In 1942, Van Dam was promoted to *SS Unterscharführer*, for which he also had to wear the uniform of the SD.

In The Hague, Gemmeker was his superior for a short period of time. According to him, Van Dam had returned to the Netherlands for another reason. He had gone to Germany with his brother and they had started the SS training in Munich. Because his Mother insisted that one of her sons should return to the Netherlands, the brothers decided among themselves that Hendrik would stop training and therefore would not have to go to the Eastern Front. Van Dam's statement about his placement at the SD is similar to that of Gemmeker, who got to know Van Dam during his period in The Hague as a fairly well developed person who had made a very good impression on him. After Gemmeker left, Van Dam stayed behind in The Hague. Once Gemmeker had become Commander of Westerbork and visited the *Dienststelle* sometime later, Van Dam submitted a request to him to be transferred to Westerbork, because he did not get along well with his chief. Gemmeker agreed to this and had him transferred.

Soon there was not enough administrative work left to be done, so Van Dam was appointed as General Guard. This function consisted partly of checking the incoming and outgoing mail items. In addition, he was tasked with guiding transports from Assen, Hooghalen and Beilen and with searching the Jews who were part of these transports. Furthermore, he was also involved in supervising the darkening of the windows in the barracks.[89] The OD members who had previously judged the other SS men in the camp considered Van Dam a sadist and a very peculiar person, one who acted brutally, like a real SS man would. Werner Bloch saw that during transports, Van Dam grabbed Jews roughly and pushed them aside on a regular basis. Such a thing occurred when Werner was in the waiting room of the OD at some point. Suddenly the door opened. Van Dam dragged in a Jewish man who he then proceeded to beat up. It later turned out that the man was punished for not having greeted him when he passed by him.

Sandor Salmagne got to know a different side of Van Dam. He saw him once in a completely drunken state, riding his bicycle into the waiting room of the OD. There he kept riding in circles around the heater for at least half an hour, after which he disappeared again.[90] Van Dam never denied that he had consumed a lot of alcohol. Before coming to Westerbork, he did not drink at all. This changed because of the situation in the camp. Because of its remoteness, he regularly felt shut off from the outside world, so he started trying to forget the feeling by drinking it away. Despite the distribution measures, it was not difficult to get liquor. More than enough liquor was found in the packages sent to the camp for residents. Van Dam admitted that he was often in a drunken state and it was therefore possible that he had done things he was ashamed of after the liberation. He did not specify what sorts of things he had done. However, he whole heartedly denied that he had abused Jews.

Several camp residents, including the then almost 70-year-old Salomon Praag, made an incriminating statement after the liberation. Salomon had come out of the laundry room of his barracks one night around 22:00. Van Dam and a colleague of his were already in the hall. He was screaming. When Salomon entered the hall, Van Dam ordered him to take off his hat. When he did not do so fast enough, Van Dam struck the cap off Salomon's head and had apparently slapped him across the face as well. That same evening, he brought Salomon to the punishment barracks, telling him that he had to stay there for three weeks. Luckily for Salomon, he was able to return to his barracks after twelve days. He knew that the people who had been placed in the punishment barracks as punishment were often put on transport faster than the rest of the camp.

A Jewish couple also witnessed Van Dam's brutal behaviour. After they were arrested at a safe house in Amsterdam, they were transported to Westerbork. In Hooghalen Van Dam took over the transport from the agents who had escorted it from Amsterdam. He immediately started counting, and everyone who did not move away quickly enough was brutally pushed away. The man got a slap in the face because he had been in the way. After arriving at the camp, the couple was taken directly to the punishment barracks. Here they came into contact with Van Dam again, because he was in charge of supervising the barracks at that time.

After an incident occurred in November 1943, Van Dam's position gradually began to weaken. He and Van Laer had driven a car from the German Army to Assen to pick up a transport that had arrived there. It probably involved a small group, because Van Dam brought the Jews to Westerbork on his own. Van Laer stayed behind in Assen. After the people were delivered, Van Dam was going to drive back to Assen to pick up Van Laer. He never got that far, because he ran into a tree at high speed on the way. The car was wrecked. Those who saw the pictures of the accident were of the opinion that the driver could never have gotten out alive. However, Van Dam was lucky: he only suffered a gaping head injury. For this he was Hospitalised in the Camp Hospital; in order to repair the damage to his head, he had to be operated on by Jewish Doctors. After a month, Van Dam had completely recovered.

Sometime later he was transferred to the SD in Zeist by Gemmeker because of another incident. A female resident gave the reason for this transfer after the liberation. Until she left for Theresienstadt in February 1944, this woman worked as a hairdresser in the camp and thus got to know Van Dam, because the SS men in the camp also came to the salon for a shaving and a haircut. According to the hairdresser, Van Dam's behaviour would have been revolting. One specific event came to her mind that had to serve as an example. During one of the evenings, a fellow resident of her barracks, a Jewish girl of fifteen year old, received a note from the barracks leader, stating that she would be picked up by the OD at 23:00. The reason for this was not in the note. When the girl later returned to the barracks, she told the hairdresser in tears that she had had to report to Van Dam and Van Laer. It turned out later that she had been delivered to the home of the first. Upon entering, the girl immediately noticed that both men were drunk. The things she had been forced to do with them had severely upset her.

Van Dam also made a statement about this event. He confessed that he and Van Laer had indeed been drunk one evening and that a Jewish woman had come to his apartment. According to him, this had been a married woman whose husband had died in the camp during an air strike. Because his wife would also have been present, Van Dam himself had done nothing with the Jewish woman, he said, but Van Laer did. He had locked himself in a room with her. Shortly after that, Gemmeker suddenly appeared in the house and saw what was happening there. Because this unwanted event took place in Van Dam's home, he was held responsible for this. That is why Gemmeker had him transferred to Zeist. The girl or woman was locked up in the punishment barracks and was put on transport shortly afterwards. The description of what took place on that evening largely corresponds to

Gemmeker's statement. While he was personally checking whether all the windows had been covered up, he found that in the home of Van Dam, in the company of friends and a Jewish woman, a drinking party was going on. Gemmeker could not remember the name of this Jewish woman. He did know she was unmarried.

That Van Dam had been transferred to the SD in Zeist also proved to be correct. Van Dam stated that he had deserted the Army when he was there, for which he was arrested during the occupation. During his detention in the Prison of Apeldoorn, the accident with the vehicle finally had its consequences. In early 1945 he had to appear before the *SS-und Polizei-gericht X* for driving a car under influence, speeding and destroying a vehicle belonging to the German Army. He was sentenced by this Court to eight months in Prison or enlisting with the *Waffen SS* and being transferred to the front. Van Dam refused the latter.[91] Gemmeker admitted in his statement that he had made a mistake by believing in Van Dam. He had brought the Dutchman to Westerbork, because he trusted him and saw something in him. That good impression changed, because partly due to all the incidents, Gemmeker described Van Dam after the liberation as a weak person for whom he had no respect whatsoever and who had never been worthy of his trust.

4. ORDER AND DISCIPLINE WITHIN THE BARBED WIRE

In order for the camp to function properly, order and discipline were extremely important. This was certainly true for the days when transports arrived and left. Through camp orders, announcements and regulations, it was made clear to everyone what their rights and, above all, their duties were.

Rules And Camp Orders

During the period in which Schol acted as Commander of the then refugee camp, over 200 regulations were introduced. These publications made the refugees aware of what was expected of them. Violation of the camp rules and unwanted behaviour were already punished at that time. When the occupier took over the camp on 1 July 1942, they were given a well-functioning and generally disciplined barracks village. Due to the growing number of residents and transports, discipline, peace and order became even more important. Disturbances in the camp and restlessness outside the camp could make the deportation machine falter or even come to a standstill, jeopardising the plans of the occupier. Residents were therefore expected to know the camp rules. For this purpose, a notice board was placed in each barracks, containing the most recent announcements (*Lagerbefehlen*). The people could ask the barracks leaders for the older announcements when they wanted to take a look at these. In addition, the same leaders were instructed to regularly re-highlight important regulations.[1] New residents at least had to be aware of some general obligations and prohibitions, such as the obligation to greet the camp officials and the prohibition of smoking[2]. The smoking ban was strictly supervised. The OD's normal patrol service was only allowed to check outside the barracks. A special smoke patrol was formed for checking inside them.[3]

At the beginning of January 1943 the numbering of the camp orders drawn up in German and Dutch began at one again. In the second order, attention was paid to the greeting obligation for residents. Male members of the *Lagerkommandantur* (regardless of what clothes they wore), the Camp Commander, Sub Commander and all uniformed German and Dutch civil servants had to be greeted.[4] The greeting obligation, which was only mandatory for male residents, was seen as a very serious subject. When a man was wearing winter headgear that was difficult to take off, it was allowed to stay on his head and the man in question could fulfil the obligation by standing at attention. For men who were at work and, for example, were pushing a wheelbarrow or carrying a heavy load and so were unable to greet, an exception was also made. If their work allowed it, they had to stand at attention.[5]

Failure to fulfil this greeting obligation was seen as a lack of discipline and could have consequences, which were experienced by Selig Goldstein, who was born in Poland. Selig had been working in the Apeldoorsche Bosch, a Jewish Psychiatric Institution, as certified nurse since September 1925.

He arrived in Westerbork with his wife on 2 February 1943.[6] Just like the other residents, Selig had to work. A few days after he had arrived, he was moving wood in the camp under the supervision of a foreman. The moment he was walking with a load of wood on his shoulder, Gemmeker, who was unknown to him, passed him from behind. Because Selig did not take his hat off in time, he had to hand over his camp card to Gemmeker. Many knew that once you had handed over this card, you would likely be put on transport shortly after, as was the case for Selig and his wife. In the night of 8 to 9 February, they were summoned for next day's transport. An attempt by a relative, who was working at the civil registry of the camp, to get the couple off the transport list failed. Selig and his wife were murdered in the gas chambers on 12 February, immediately after arrival in Auschwitz. After the liberation, Gemmeker could not remember the incident. Nevertheless, he tried to find an explanation for it. In all cases where camp cards were taken by him, he did so only when residents had deliberately broken the rules. According to Gemmeker, Selig must have been deliberately committing a disciplinary offence. He did not find it plausible that he had taken Selig's camp card because he did not greet Gemmeker.[7]

Gemmeker also used camp orders to warn residents against displaying unwanted behaviour, such as spreading rumours. Especially false and inflammatory messages could undermine the peace and order in the camp. For residents, however, rumours were important to maintain confidence in a successful outcome despite their often hopeless position. There were so many rumours in the camp that it even got its own name: the *Jüdische Presse Agentur* (JPA). Rumours about the cessation of transports and the positive course of the war for the Allies were particularly popular.[8]

On 27 July 1943 a message about the capitulation of the Italian Army circulated in the camp. When this was not confirmed later that day, the cheerful mood subsided.[9] Gemmeker also warned that the spreading of rumours could jeopardise the continuation of artistic performances, for example[10]. These threats apparently did little to impress the residents, because the spreading of rumours continued unabated.[11]

A little less than six months later, Gemmeker felt forced to announce penalties through a camp order. On Friday 17 December he celebrated the Germanic Yuletide in the main hall, together with his men and other prominent SS and SD Officers from The Hague and Amsterdam. Although the party had officially ended around 22:30, mainly the camp's SS members continued to party. Excessive alcohol consumption would have led to so much tension that the men began to fight each other. The medical service had to be called in to take care of the injured. News of this incident went through the camp like a wildfire. Gemmeker was not happy with this negative advertisement for his men and issued a camp order a few days later. According to this order, many rumours had been spread about Gemmeker and his guests as a result of the Yuletide celebrations hosted by the *Lager-kommandantur*. Because the threat of penalties did not help, Gemmeker held the entire camp population liable for this. He therefore forbade all celebrations around the Jewish and Christian holidays that would have taken place in the following days. Violations would be severely punished.

In addition, work had to be carried out on the public holidays covering the period from 22 December to 3 January. Sick leaves or other forms of refusal to work were punished even more by Gemmeker. Any object that could be associated with Christmas, such as twigs and candles, was prohibited. However, due to a power outage during this ban, they were still allowed to light the candles. The OD was ordered to check in barracks 73, where the baptised were staying, whether they were secretly celebrating Christmas. Gemmeker threatened that if rumours continued to circulate despite this warning, he would introduce a punishment which he knew for sure would prevent any more spreading of rumours.[12] They had clearly gone too far. Whether this stopped the rumours is doubtful.[13]

Gendarmes are celebrating Yuletide with the SS men, 17 December 1943.

The camp orders issued by or on behalf of Gemmeker were very diverse in nature. Sometimes they were meant to promote the greeting obligation; other times they were supposed to stop rumours. Some camp orders now seem somewhat extravagant or less important, such as an additional order related to the fight against flies and mosquitoes. There was even a period when every resident was obliged to catch 50 flies every day. They had to be wrapped in paper and handed over to the quarantine station.[14] This had a clear reason, because a fly and mosquito infestation was dangerous to the public health, since the insects could transmit contagious diseases such as diarrhoea and tuberculosis. Hygiene was important and a constant source of attention and care. The residents had to keep themselves as well as the sleeping, living and dining facilities clean. Despite these measures, diseases such as scarlet fever, diphtheria and jaundice broke out in October 1943. The quarantine state was activated with immediate effect, prohibiting entry into a particular area. At the entrances to this area there were warning signs with the text: 'Pay attention! Quarantine! Passage prohibited for pedestrians and vehicles due to contagious disease.' Since any contact between the camp and the outside world was prohibited, surveillance was tightened and posts were placed near the barrier. OD members had to guide labour groups to the barrier and back again. With a few exceptions, no work could be done outside the quarantine area. In the camp, however, the work continued as much as possible, because this was considered to be of great importance within the camp organisation.[15]

A few months before the quarantine was set up, Gemmeker had to issue a camp order with the subject of 'the refusal to work'. According to him, it had occurred repeatedly in the days before those new residents who had been assigned a job had not shown up. The order contained a clear warning, as Gemmeker would act with inexorable rigor against these non-working people from that moment on. Every case had to be reported to him, after which the resident in question was immediately put on transport. For those who were exempt from transport according to the regulations, a so-called *Schutzhaftantrag* was filed, meaning that after approval, they were locked up in a Concentration Camp. In the meantime, the exempted person who refused to work was placed under more stringent provisions in The Penal Company and isolated from others.[16]

As previously mentioned, the provisions in camp orders were often aimed at promoting discipline in the camp and improving hygiene. It can be concluded from the many warnings that these objectives were not understood by every resident. This also applies to the camp orders related to air protection. Due to increased activity of allied aircraft above the camp, the slightest bit of light could already be dangerous. The OD regularly came into action when they discovered during their rounds that someone somewhere in the camp had forgotten to turn off the light. They also had to be extra alert if there were a lot of aircraft.

It appears from camp order 79 of 27 May 1944 that Gemmeker had found significant violations of the regulations regarding hygiene and order when inspecting the barracks. According to him, if the residents were more disciplined, this would not have been the case. Since they were unable to maintain the necessary order on their own, he was forced to take some measures. The order also included a renewed warning regarding the air alarm behaviour. If the alarm went off at night, everyone had to get dressed completely and have a cloak and other necessities ready. Gemmeker expected everyone to check whether their neighbours were adhering to these policies. If the alarm went off during the day, those outside had to go to the nearest barracks.[17]

On 30 May 1944 an incident occurred that showed that the air alarm policies were not adequate and that staying in the barracks posed a danger. Fred Schwarz witnessed the incident and described what he observed in his book *Treinen op dood spoor* (*Trains on Dead Track*). During the lunch break, an allied aircraft flew low over the camp in the direction of Amen. Suddenly the plane made a sharp turn and flew back to the camp. Fred saw fire coming out of the on board machine guns and then heard glass shattering. When the aircraft was gone, it turned out that most of the bullets had ended up in barracks 85, the so-called Barneveld barracks. The OD immediately secured the surrounding area.[18] In this air strike, two residents were killed and some others were wounded and had to be admitted to the Camp Hospital.[19]

One of the wounded was the OD member Hans Dieter Blume. During the attack, Hans had been sitting behind the desk in the waiting room of the OD barracks. He had taken over his colleague Werner Bloch's shift that morning at his own request. A stray bullet flew through the wall of the barracks and ended up in Hans's leg. When he was finally found, he had lost a lot of blood. When he had arrived at the Hospital, there was an undesirable delay, because the only operating room was in use for the treatment of another injured person. When Hans finally got his turn, it turned out that his leg could no longer be saved. Amputation was the only solution. With the help of rehabilitation and the fitting of an artificial leg, Hans had to become somewhat mobile again. However, working as an OD member was no longer an option, which was why he got a job with the administration. On 4 September 1944 he went on transport to Theresienstadt. Shortly thereafter, he was transferred to Auschwitz, where he was murdered on October 26.[20]

Since a new attack from the air was not ruled out, the air protection measures were fully adapted and extended. Residents who had violated these modified rules or one of the many other rules were tracked down and punished. When the camp was still serving as a refugee camp, it was mainly the director who was authorised to punish people. In 1943 the OD was also allowed to impose penalties for smaller violations.

Penalties

In the annual report of the OD for 1943, Pisk included a list showing that in that year his service had found 561 violations of the camp rules. This list also indicated how the offenders were punished. The offence committed was not mentioned. In most cases, 418 times, it was a minor offence, for which a warning was given. Heavier penalties, such as a ban on cooking and barracks or compulsory cleaning of the toilets, were imposed 41 times. A small number of violations, 25 cases, were referred to the first service leader, Kurt Schlesinger[21], or to other Service Leaders. 13 cases were reported to Gemmeker.[22]

Philip Mechanicus belonged to the large group of offenders who received a warning for an 'offence'. On a Sunday evening in August 1943 Philip had visited a friend. As he walked to his own barracks, the signal that announced the curfew was sounded. At that time, a patrol from the OD stopped him. They indicated that it was now 22:00 and since the second signal had sounded, no one was allowed to be outside. Because Philip had broken the camp rules by being outside, he had to show them his camp card. One of the men wrote the data in his notebook. The OD member noted that he had no other choice, since Pisk had witnessed the offence. Philip's proposal to tear the relevant leaf with his details out of the booklet later fell on deaf ears. The next day Philip received a call to report to Pisk in the OD barracks at exactly 14:00. Philip was not the only offender who came to report at the specified time, because four or five other residents were present in the main hall of the barracks. To Pisk's question as to why he was found outside by the OD, Philip replied that he had been talking to a friend the other night and therefore had not heard the first signal. After the other offenders had also told their story, Pisk gave a brief speech. In this he argued that this time they got off with a warning. At a subsequent violation, they would have to deal with Gemmeker himself.[23]

This addition was correct, because the names of the offenders were recorded and collected in a card box. As a result, the OD could easily indicate at Gemmeker's request which camp resident had several violations to his or her name. In some cases, Gemmeker determined by an order signed by him which punishment the notorious offender would receive. The penalty imposed ranged from imprisonment to additional work or placement in the punishment barracks for a certain period of time. Sometimes even transport followed. This did not imply that the offender was put on a special transport. After leaving Westerbork, no distinction was made between them and the other Jews who were on the deportation list.[24]

Nevertheless, transport was the most severe sanction that Gemmeker could impose, because this meant that a longer stay in the camp was excluded and the offender would indeed be put on the next transport. Such a punishment was given to Leo van Messel[25] at the end of October 1943 for stealing wood. Camp order No. 54 was issued specifically for this offence committed by Leo. According to Gemmeker, it had been repeatedly pointed out that certain types of wood should not be used as firewood because that was not what the wood was for. Nevertheless, it appeared that lumber and parts of barracks had been removed and had disappeared as firewood in the fireplaces. Because Leo had committed this offence, he was transferred directly to the punishment barracks. He probably had to go on the next transport. Leo died on 11 March 1945 in Bergen-Belsen.[26] The camp order was mainly intended as a warning for the other residents.

The OD report also contains statements concerning the transfer to Prison of residents who had committed theft. Apart from the aforementioned sanctions, there were also other punishments for offences such as theft and abuse. Camp residents who, for example, did not leave the property of peers alone were given a special punishment. In a closed community like Westerbork, where the residents already owned little, theft could lead to fights and feuds. OD man Abraham Gudema[27] saw with his own eyes what punishment could be imposed for theft in addition to imprisonment. Probably at the beginning of 1943, while it was still winter, Abraham saw several residents standing next to the potato cellar near the barbed wire fence. Despite the bitter cold, these people had to stand at attention the whole day. In some cases, this punishment lasted several days.

The Amsterdam shopkeeper Salomon G. had to undergo this punishment as an offender at a different date and time. According to his statement, the sentence consisted of standing at the fence from 8:00 to 16:00 for three days and had been imposed by an OD man, possibly on behalf of Gemmeker. Salomon did not consider the punishment excessively severe. He took it more or less like a bit of fun. He did not have to stand at attention or suffer the cold, because he had limited freedom of movement, so he could move about a little. He did not even blame Gemmeker and even judged positively about the Camp Commander. Salomon had been in both Dutch and German camps and believed that Gemmeker was by far the best Commander he had experienced. According to Salomon, however, there was a possibility that other offenders had been placed at the fence under far more dire circumstances.[28]

After the liberation, Gemmeker was able to remember two cases in which he had sentenced one or more offenders from the punishment barracks to hours of standing at the fence. He thought one had to stand there for the duration of three hours and the other one for five hours. For what offences he had imposed these penalties, he had no idea. He considered it plausible that theft of property belonging to fellow residents was the reason. The punishment served as a deterrent. Gemmeker could remember another time he had punished a resident for committing theft. After the compulsory working time, he had the perpetrator walk through the camp for three days in a row with a sign on his front and back on which the following text was written in Dutch and German: 'I am a thief, because I robbed my fellow residents'. The OD had to accompany the man during his mandatory journey, because the other residents were so angry that they would not otherwise have left him alone. After this sentence, the man was put on transport.[29]

Because of the threat that one would be deported after violating the rules, it was hardly necessary to apply physical violence. The historian Eva Moraal believes that the threats can be regarded as psychological violence, which she said was certainly no less severe than physical violence.[30] The fear of deportation caused most residents to comply with the rules. Those who did not do this could also be locked up in the Camp Prison.

Camp Prison

The Prison was a small stone barracks with number 51. It had four cells and had already been used when the camp had still been serving as a refugee camp. According to Presser, barracks 51 was infamous. Especially the criminals who had committed 'major crimes' would have ended up in it, such as those who had tried to flee or were suspected of it. In the camp there were rumours that these people were treated badly, while no one was allowed to or even could do anything for them. Only the SS had access to the Prison.[31] The way Presser described the conditions in the Camp Prison does not correspond to the data from other sources. The Prison was not guarded by SS men for a long time. From the end of April 1939 until the beginning of 1943 it was under the supervision of Gendarme Barteld Lukas Knol. Because the Municipal Police was dismantled on 1 December 1942 and the Mayor found Knol redundant a few weeks later, it was decided in consultation with Gemmeker to terminate Knol's secondment with effect from 5 January 1943.[32] Knol did not agree with this and objected to this decision of the Mayor of Westerbork. This did not turn out well for him. He was assigned to the Police Force of the Municipality of Westerbork as Gendarme.

In the period in which Knol was in charge of supervision, no violent incidents occurred, according to him. His successor, Gendarme Berthrandus

Herman Paridaen[33], is said to have been viewed negatively by the 'good ones'. His fellow Gendarmes did not trust him. They thought Paridaen got along a little too well with both sides. Knol later heard that Paridaen had abused people in Prison. The indictment issued after the liberation supports Knol's declaration somewhat. It mentions four facts of which Paridaen would have been guilty during the occupation.

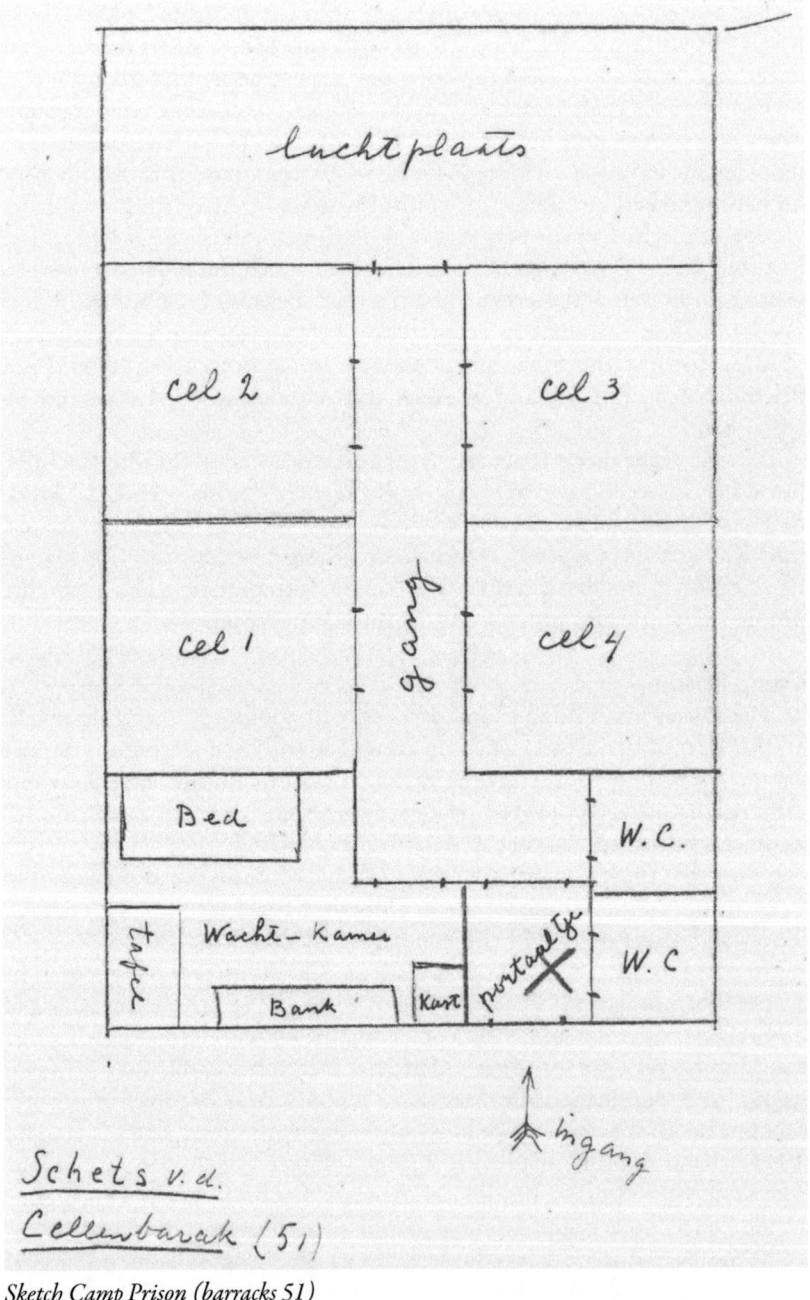

Sketch Camp Prison (barracks 51)

Only one of these facts concerns his work in the Camp Prison. He would have violently beaten and kicked several people detained there. The other three facts mainly related to his cooperation in the arrest of Jews who had fled from the camp and from a transport train. Paridaen was given the opportunity to tell his side of the story during the trial. Compared to other sources and testimonies, this statement contains some contradictions.

According to Paridaen, Knol was actually convinced of his trust-worthiness. Knol would have asked him to take over his good work for the prisoners, such as smuggling letters and parcels out of the camp and arranging for sufficient food. This statement was at odds with that of Knol. It is also plausible that the camp's management did not select the Prison Supervisors with a specific goal or background in mind. Knol, formerly a Patrolman, had started a second career. Paridaen, on the other hand, stood at the very beginning of his career and had not yet gained much experience as Policeman. He had joined the 1ˢᵗ Division of the Gendarmerie, Brigade Waalwijk, on 2 September 1940 as a so-called 'war Gendarme'. After initially having been placed in Baarle-Nassau, he was transferred to the 7th Division on 1 October 1941 at his own request, with Brigade Denekamp as his posting. He had made this request in order to live closer to his fiancée, who was living in Steenwijk. Because of the poor pay, he was barely able to pay for the costly train journey. After having been successively seconded to Denekamp, Apeldoorn, Assen, Veenhuizen and then Assen again, Camp Westerbork became his new workplace with effect from 13 January 1943. During the first two weeks, Paridaen's tasks consisted of monitoring the work crews and occupying the guard post at the entrance.

On 1 February Paridaen took over the role of Prison Guard. Compared to the other functions of the Gendarmerie Detachment, this task was special in certain ways. Of the entire Detachment, the Detachment Commander and the Prison Guard were the only ones living in the camp. The remaining men stayed in a residence outside the camp after service, the so-called Camp Heidelager. In addition, the tasks of the Detachment were mainly related to outdoor surveillance, while as a Prison Guard, Paridaen was mainly serving inside the camp. Because of these special circumstances, his colleagues had little contact with him. Nevertheless, some of them made an incriminating statement about him after the liberation. Paridaen would have been deliberately avoided by his colleagues, because he was known for abusing prisoners. Gendarme Paulus de Haan claimed to have witnessed such an incident. De Haan saw that while transferring a Jewish man, Paridaen was holding this man by the collar. Suddenly he let go of the man because the man had to go faster. According to De Haan, Paridaen unceremoniously kicked the man against his bottom twice. The man's reaction led De Haan to deduce that this hurt. This assault occurred at a time when there were no Germans nearby.

Other Gendarmes also reported abuses committed by Paridaen. In general, they had not witnessed these incidents themselves, but had received information from others. According to a Gendarme, the abused Jews could no longer make a statement because they had all died. Paridaen denied having been guilty of the abuse cited by De Haan. In this case, he would at most have faked the kicks. Paridaen also denied having committed the other offences of which he had been accused. On the contrary, he had deliberately played a certain role in front of the Germans, as his Lawyer described in the comprehensive written pleadings. His client belonged to a group of Policemen who had acted in a 'German manner' in front of the world during the occupation. As a result, they were at risk of being wrongly accused of being pro German, collaborators or even – as in Paridaen's case – being called a 'Jew torturer'.

Paridaen had developed a special attitude, making him appear very Militaristic. According to his Lawyer, he may therefore have shouted and roared louder than the other people in the camp. He acted this way only when there were Germans or colleagues nearby and his behaviour was intended to disguise his true attitude towards the Jews. Paridaen had played his harsh role with great conviction. He had even gone so far as to ask those who were in Prison to complain to others about his brutal actions. In reality, according to his Lawyer, he had felt sorry for the Jews and had been a support for the prisoners. More than 40 statements are quoted in the written pleadings, some of which were positive about Paridaen. These statements, coming mainly from Jews who were in the Camp Prison, show that he had provided extra food, fruit and cigarettes. In addition, he smuggled letters and parcels into and out of the camp and despite the rules, he allowed visitors. The prisoners were given the chance to listen to the English channel in his room. This proves that at certain times they were allowed to move freely within the Prison. Since the Prison was closed and unwanted visitors could be noticed in time if they paid careful attention, freedom of movement did not pose an unnecessary risk. If there were checks, the prisoners were warned in time. They then immediately returned to their cells and stood there neatly at attention.

To outsiders it may have seemed that Paridaen had his prisoners under control. He occasionally played cards with them. He let those who had no money win deliberately. With the money they had 'won', he bought things that the winner wanted. The husband of one of the prisoners had once visited and gave a statement about the role Paridaen played. One evening the visitor had been talking, playing cards and listening to the radio together with Paridaen and some prisoners. The next morning, he ran into the Prison Guard riding on his bike through the camp. As required, the visitor stepped aside and greeted. Paridaen did not greet back, almost hit the visitor and gave no sign of recognition. Although Paridaen had asked him not to come to the Prison during the day because this was too noticeable, the visitor went there that same afternoon, still angry, and criticised Paridaen's attitude. The man laughed and said: 'I don't know any of you when I run into you inside the camp. You guys are nothing but air to me. Next time I run into you again, I won't see you again.' Only then did the visitor understand Paridaen's attitude. This double role also had dangerous sides. The SD gratefully made use of Jews who turned in other Jews for money. If these traitors had done their job and had become useless, they would end up in Westerbork. Probably for their own safety, these people were usually stowed away in Prison. Paridaen was warned in such cases by his confidants in the camp. The traitors were given a different treatment than the other prisoners.

The Jewish witness Sylvia de Levier made an exculpatory statement. According to her, Paridaen had her taken off the transport list a few times. When this failed, he smuggled Sylvia out of the camp and brought her safely across the Belgian border. By doing this, he saved her life. They would not have been in a relationship. Paridaen explained this incident extensively. In the first half of 1943, two OD men brought the girl, who at that time was about 18 year old, from the punishment barracks to Prison. Sylvia ended up in there because the SD had arrested her while she had been hiding in Maastricht. In here, she asked her fellow inmates, whom she considered to be her companions, whether it was possible to flee from the camp.

Because ten residents would be put on the next transport if one person managed to escape, her fellow inmates reported Sylvia to the OD as suspicious. To prevent another attempt to escape, Gemmeker gave the order to lock her up in Prison. Sylvia claimed on arrival that she would kill herself if she had to go on transport. Paridaen probably took this claim very seriously, because he immediately got to work and investigated every possibility he had to get Sylvia out of the camp. When he asked her if there were any relatives of her still in hiding, Sylvia replied that her mother had found a safe house in Hasselt, Belgium, and that she knew this address. With this new information in mind, Paridaen formed a plan to get her across the Belgian boarder via his former place of secondment: Baarle-Nassau.

The requested leave for a visit to his former home and place of employment was allowed, but could not take effect until two weeks later. This was too late, because four days after he had submitted the request, Sylvia's name was on the transport list. According to Paridaen, it took him a lot of effort to get her name off the list. He would have received help from Kurt Schlesinger and the leader of the Jewish Council in the camp, Frits Grünberg. A week later, Sylvia's name was back on the list. Attempts to get her name off the list again failed, so he had to come up with another strategy. On the morning of the transport, he took Sylvia out of the cell at 5:00 AM and brought her to his own room, giving her very clear instructions to remain absolutely silent, since no one inside the Prison could know she was there. One hour later, two OD men came to pick up four prisoners, including Sylvia, for the upcoming transport. They took three prisoners, meaning they had not yet completed their mission. Paridaen told them that Sylvia had already been taken to the train via the Hospital.

Sometime later, the OD men reappeared at the Prison, because they had not found Sylvia, either in the Hospital or in or near the train. Paridaen said he would go check himself and cycled to the Hospital. There he asked a nurse he recognised to go with him. When asked why she had to come, he answered, 'Don't ask, nurse.' Paridaen then took the nurse to the train. To the OD members who had cordoned off the area, he said, 'Another one from 51.' Together with the nurse, he walked to the end of the train, left the cordoned off area there and escorted her back to the Hospital. He simply thanked her, told her never to mention the event again and said goodbye. The nurse shrugged and disappeared.

Upon returning to Prison, Paridaen locked Sylvia in cell 1 and put the key in his pocket. She had to hide in Prison until Paridaen's leave. If the situation allowed it, Sylvia could leave her cell. A few days after the transport, Paridaen saw Gemmeker and Detachment Commander Albert de Jong approach the Prison. Sylvia had to go to her cell right away. During the inspection, cell 1 also received its turn. Paridaen said it could not be opened because the key had broken inside the lock. The camp's smithy was currently working on the issue. According to Paridaen, both men had been satisfied with this answer and left the Prison after the inspection. Paridaen devised a plan to smuggle Sylvia out of the camp the night before his leave without putting the both of them in too much danger. Coach driver Kroon from Assen would bring Jews to the camp that evening who had arrived on the last train. Because the car usually drove back to Assen empty, this seemed to be the best option. Gendarme Jan Hoekema, who stood guard at the western entrance to the camp, was a colleague of Paridaen's and was reliable, but Paridaen still believed it would be better if he did not know the correct story. Paridaen asked Jan if he could remember the girl he had dated in Rolde. The previous month Paridaen had broken up with her, but because she could not forget him, she had come to the camp that night. He had secretly let her in and talked to her, or so he told Jan. When Kroon arrived, Paridaen took Sylvia out of Prison and brought her to the car. He told Kroon that it was his girl and that he had to take her to Assen because she did not have a bicycle.

There were no problems during the journey. Once they were in Assen, Paridaen brought Sylvia to the acquaintances who also regularly helped him send letters from prisoners. The next day, on the first day of his leave, Paridaen and Sylvia travelled by train to Tilburg. There they took the bus to Baarle-Nassau. Thanks to acquaintances, Sylvia was able to get to the other side of the border safely. She remained at the safe house in Belgium and got to experience the liberation.

Paridaen also helped the couple Schoenland (Schönland) Van Weerden to flee. They were in possession of false release documents, bearing the stamp of Aus der Fünten. However, they would not pass the check in Westerbork, because the documents there had to be marked with Gemmeker's stamp. The couple received new false release documents through Paridaen, which were produced on a typewriter in the Prison. The day the camp car left, Paridaen stood at the western entrance in civilian clothes. He told the Gendarme on duty, who was always particularly busy at such times, he would help him out for a while. This allowed the couple to get in the car after having been 'checked' by Paridaen. Paridaen drove to Assen with them and watched the couple get on the train. He sent over their luggage later on. After the liberation, the couple stated that he had fully cooperated in the escape.

Three of the four points in the indictment concerned the detection and arrest of three Jewish men. Two incidents had occurred during the escort of transports. Because of staff shortages, Paridaen had to go to Assen with colleagues several times to take over small groups of Jews in the second half of 1943. In mid-November, four Gendarmes, including Paridaen, were ordered to collect a transport of 85 Jews and escort them to Westerbork. The journey took longer than expected, because the train had to wait in Beilen for some time for another train to pass. When the train was about to leave, Paridaen saw a man climb out of a window and disappear on the train tracks. Since it had become dark, his colleagues and the other passengers had not noticed the escape. About 15 minutes after the train had left, chaos suddenly broke out in one of the carriages. Paridaen heard screams and the words, 'Flee! Run!' In an automatic reaction, he jumped off the train and shot in the air with his carbine. When the train continued its journey, he was unable to climb back into it, so he was forced to make the rest of the trip on foot.

Paridaen hoped to reach the railway crossing and the road to Hooghalen by following the train tracks. Suddenly he saw a silhouette close by and he almost bumped into the person. When he asked who was there, he received a fist to the face instead of an answer, after which a struggle arose. The man would have deliberately attacked Paridaen to give his son, who had also fled the train, a head start. When the attacker almost snatched the loaded carbine from Paridaen's hands during the struggle, Paridaen grabbed his revolver and shot in the direction of the unknown assailant. This shot probably hit the target, because the man let go of the carbine and stopped the attack. Two people who had been nearby and had heard the shot assisted Paridaen. The man declared he had fled the train. Paridaen managed to reach Westerbork via the nearest telephone. From there, a car with two Dutch SS members came to pick them up. In the camp, it turned out that the man who had fled had been hit in the shoulder.[34]

This act also had a very positive outcome for Paridaen, because on 17 February 1944 he was promoted to Sergeant Major of the Gendarmerie. During his speech, Major S.M. Oosterhoff, Commander of the Gendarmerie in Groningen and acting Regional Police Commander, stated that Paridaen fully understood his task in the camp. Oosterhoff called him a bold Policeman whose correct and courageous action had ensured that a resident who had fled from a large transport could be arrested in spite of heavy resistance.[35]

After the liberation, Gemmeker made a statement about Paridaen's actions and summarised why he had nominated him for promotion. Gemmeker believed that Paridaen was a real Military man. He knew how to act and was always very correct. He was loyal and cooperated, but was not *deutschfreundlich*. As a model Police Officer, he always performed his duty well. According to Gemmeker, it was possible that in his nomination for promotion, he had written that Paridaen was *deutschfreundlich*. He argued this had to be said, because the promotion would not have been possible otherwise; as far as Gemmeker knew, the *Ordnungspolizei* would not give permission for a person to be promoted unless they were said to be *deutschfreundlich*. Paridaen claimed that he was not happy with this promotion. Most of his colleagues did not congratulate him because they believed that Paridaen had forced the promotion through his actions. Because he was afraid he would suffer from this promotion later, he wanted to return to his original position. In his statement, he contradicted himself on this point. While he declared one moment that he wanted to leave the camp because of the difficult circumstances, he stated shortly afterwards that he could have alleviated the suffering and misery of some of the Jewish people and had become attached to his work because of their grateful attitude. He therefore never objected when his Detachment was extended.[36]

In addition to the Prison, there were other places in which the residents were locked up and so were prevented from moving freely. These so-called 'criminal cases' (also known as 'S-cases'; the 'S' is derived from the Dutch word 'straf', meaning punishment) could be locked up in three specially designed barracks at the end of 1942, after the completion of the camp.

Criminal Barracks And Penal Company

In September 1940, when the camp was still destined for refugees, residents who had committed less serious offences were already locked up in a separate barracks. Barracks 35, also referred to as the 'closed depot', was used for this purpose. A barbed wire barrier was installed around this barracks, because the offenders were not allowed to have contact with the other residents. Kurt Witrofski from Vienna ignored this order at the beginning of February 1942. He was found at the fence in the evening, talking to one of the people locked in the depot. Kurt was immediately imprisoned for three days as punishment. In general, the offenders had to work under the supervision of Policemen, and later Gendarmes or OD members, as additional punishment.[37]

The daily report of the OD shows that this service escorted offenders from barracks 35 several times, for example to the Doctor, Dentist or other places within the camp. They did this on an almost daily basis. The OD was once even commissioned by the Gendarmerie to escort a man from barracks 35 to the sports field. There they had to guard him during a football match.[38]

Even after July 1942, residents ended up in the Criminal Barracks for various reasons. Former Missionary Srul Tabaksblatt, born in Poland, was placed in the barracks at the beginning of March 1944 because of 'a serious offence against camp discipline'. Srul had been staying in the camp for almost a year and had still not been put on transport, because as a baptised Protestant he had been exempted from it. On Sunday 5 March, he went to the worship service that was held in the registration room. Although he was a preacher himself, this time he did not act as such. Because of a film recording, the service was special this time. Srul and a fellow believer were convinced that the recording was made for a clearly propagandistic goal. Because neither of them wanted to be part of this, they left the room in protest. Gemmeker had likely been informed of this action by the equally Protestant baptised Service Leader Heinz Todtmann, because the next Wednesday, both men had to explain their action to the Commander. According to Gemmeker, it was not a propagandistic film. The film was intended for internal use only and the entire camp life would be portrayed. Gemmeker regarded the action as a serious offence, because the men were in a leadership position. That is why he had them locked up in the Criminal Barracks and withdrew the exemption. After a few weeks, both men were allowed to leave the barracks and got their exemption back. Thanks to this exemption, they were not sent to Auschwitz later, but to Theresienstadt.[39]

In the second half of 1942, Jews who had violated one of the many anti-Jewish measures outside the camp were imprisoned in the barracks immediately upon arrival as 'S-Cases'. In the previous period, the Jews who had committed an offence were transported to the Mauthausen Concentration Camp in Austria via the camp in Amersfoort, among other ones. The majority of the 1,750 Jews who left the Netherlands in a healthy state died in Mauthausen.[40] According to the obituaries, heat stroke, dysentery or pneumonia was the cause of death every time. Because many families received the same sad message in a short time, doubts about the true cause of death arose. This was justified, as Mauthausen turned out to be one of the most horrific Concentration Camps. Prisoners had to climb up and down the 'stairs of death' in the nearby stone quarry while carrying heavy granite blocks. Those who did not soon die from this work were murdered in another way. Mauthausen quickly became a frightening concept among those who had been left behind in the camp. The occupiers reached their goal, because merely threatening the residents with deportation to that camp was in many cases enough to make the Jews do what they wanted them to.[41]

For example, on 7 August 1942 an additional edition of *Het Joodsche Weekblad*, the weekly magazine published by the Jewish Council, appeared. In the magazine, it was announced that all Jews who did not immediately comply with an appeal addressed to them for extra labour in Germany, who did not wear the Star of David, or who moved houses without the permission of the authorities would be sent to Mauthausen as punishment[42]. A few months later, Camp Westerbork became the gathering point for offenders, who were usually deported to Auschwitz or Sobibor after a short stop. Once they had arrived there, it did not matter whether one belonged to the offenders or to the other Jews deported from Westerbork, because most of them went to the gas chambers immediately upon arrival.[43]

In addition to Jewish offenders, in an unknown number of cases, non-Jewish people were also locked up in the Criminal Barracks of Camp Westerbork because they had helped Jews. The occupying forces called for strict action against those who had been arrested for hiding Jews or were otherwise helping them. According to the warning, there was a chance that the offender would receive the same treatment as the Jews. At the end of February 1943, the SD arrested Gijsbertus Petrus van Dalen for helping Jews. After a few days in Prison in Scheveningen, he was transferred to Camp Westerbork on 4 March. The compulsory stay in the Criminal Barracks lasted more than half a year. Gijsbertus then ended up via Bergen-Belsen in the German Concentration Camp Buchenwald. He returned after the liberation.[44]

The category 'S-cases' soon included the Jews who had gone into hiding but had been arrested. More and more Jews went into hiding once it became obligated to get registered, especially after the raids began and they were taken from their homes and sent to the camp. The occupier intervened and went hunting for this group. With the cooperation of traitors and fanatical Police Officers, they managed to get their hands on a large number of people who had been in hiding.[45] After the arrest, they were often at the mercy of the occupying forces and their loyal minions, while a large part had already been through a difficult period of time even before they arrived in Westerbork. There they were locked up in the barracks, just like the S-Cases who were already in the camp. Because of the many S-Cases, barracks 35 did not offer enough space in the long run. Before July 1942, the construction of new barracks had already started. In the northern part, nine large barracks were placed in rows of three. The three barracks in the northeast corner got the numbers 65, 66 and 67. In December 1942, barracks 66 could be put into use as a new Criminal Barracks. The layout shows that it had been taken into account that there would be a large number of offenders. In the separate men and women's sections, there were rows of single and double bunk beds of three levels each.[46]

The calculations on the influx of new S-Cases proved to be correct. Sometimes a few hundred new offenders came in a week. As a result, barracks 66 became overpopulated, so barracks 67 also regularly served as a Criminal Barracks. In the last week of 1943 and the first weeks of 1944, the barracks were particularly full, so the other two barracks were also used for this purpose. Since between 650 and 800 S-Cases had to have a place to sleep, several people would sleep in one bed at times.[47] This overpopulation was often short lived, because the people were generally on the next transport list. For example, the transport that left on 25 January 1944 took 950 people with it, including 550 S-Cases.[48]

In the second half of 1944, more offenders were still brought in. On 8 August, for example, a passenger train arrived from Amsterdam.[49] Among the newcomers there was a couple who, together with their two daughters, had been hiding in the back of a Company building on the Amsterdam Prinsengracht for over two years. Four days before arrival in Westerbork, German Soldiers had suddenly shown up in the building and arrested the family, as well as four other people who had been in hiding there. In this case, they had undoubtedly been betrayed, because the entrance to the shelter was well hidden behind a bookcase. There was nothing special about this family. In 1933, due to the emerging anti Semitism in Germany, they had moved from Frankfurt am Main to Amsterdam, where they built a new life. When the persecution of Jews began in the Netherlands, the family decided to hide in the shelter from July 1942 onwards. The shelter later became known as 'Het Achterhuis'. The youngest daughter of the family, Anne Frank, wrote letters to a fictional friend during this period. In these letters, she described what this life in 'Het Achterhuis' looked like. The diary was published after the liberation. It is titled Het Achterhuis (The Diary of Anne Frank) and has been translated many times. That her diary would one day become one of the most well-known books in the world, Anne could not have known. Her parents, her sister Margot and Anne herself were placed in the Criminal Barracks as ordinary 'S-Cases'.[50]

A double barbed wire fence was installed around the three barracks. As such, just like barracks 35, these barracks were separated from the other part of the camp. The entrance gate installed in the fence was under permanent surveillance of the OD. In addition to this security task, the OD also provided staff for work within the barracks. Salomon Sluijter[51], born in Amsterdam, had previously served in the rank of Sergeant Major as an instructor of the infantry in the Royal Dutch Indian Army. He was given the function of barracks leader. He was assigned the OD members Hermann Kirschen[52] and Ludwig Trier[53] as his assistants. L. Ehrlich-Cohn was responsible for the surveillance of the separate women's section inside the barracks. In addition to the supervisory functions, a kitchen chef and an administrator were added to the staff. Even for the medical care of the inmates, some Jewish Doctors were appointed. The entire thing was led by OD service leader Pisk. By regulating supervision and organisation in and around the barracks in this way, the German camp management did not have to employ its own personnel or those of the Gendarmerie for surveillance. Due to the extra barbed wire separation and separate organisation, a Sub Camp was created within the large transit camp.

For the Criminal Barracks – also referred to in official documents as OD punishment barracks – the camp's management created separate general rules. These rules were often more stringent and differed in various respects from those applicable to other residents. This gave the offenders a separate status during the period they stayed in the camp. Some rules concerned their appearance. From the beginning of August 1943, the men already had to have their hair shaved off by order of Gemmeker, something that was later included in these rules, which stated that this had to be done immediately upon entry. Each time on the first and fifteenth day of the month, this measure was repeated.[54] The hair of the women from these barracks did not have to be shaved off, but it did have to be short.[55] Their hair was not the only thing by which an S-Case could be identified. Since they were obligated to wear blue overalls with scarlet shoulder pads and a white armband with the letter 'S' on it, it was even more obvious to everyone who belonged to this unfortunate group.[56]

Until mid-November 1943, it was allowed to wear the overall over their own clothing. Due to some flight incidents, the permission to wear civilian clothing was changed. On 15 November, someone fled the barracks, and another person attempted to escape four days later. Between 18:00 and 19:00, two convicts had laid a board over the ditch and had fled in civilian clothing after cutting the barbed wire. Measures followed immediately. The convicts of the Criminal Barracks had to build an additional barbed wire barrier the next day and the day after, under the supervision of the OD. In addition, they were ordered to hand over all their civilian clothing, including those they were wearing but with the exception of their underwear, at the storage room of the OD barracks. The shoes were replaced by clogs, which obstructed mobility. Another response to the escapes was to tighten the general regulations. The OD members in charge of security were not allowed to talk to the convicts. The barracks leader and his replacement had to check this and also had to check the guard posts in the barracks. The use of the toilets in and outside barracks 67 was also strictly regulated. At some point, the use of the toilet while it was dark was allowed only for groups of up to five people. Two OD men were placed at the outdoor toilets.[57]

Willem Willing wrote in an illegal letter, dated 10 October 1943, that at 19:15 hours, shortly after returning from work, they were not allowed to leave their barracks to visit the toilet. For about 600 convicts from these barracks, only one toilet was available. However, the men had come up with an alternative: they peed in the sink and washed it away with tap water, so it was still somewhat hygienic.[58]

The additional measures were added to the already harsh approach to the inmates. The quantity and quality of the food was also worse, compared to what other residents received. Since they were not allowed to receive packages, the meagre ration could not be supplemented by family, friends or acquaintances who were staying outside the camp. Furthermore, they had to work harder and longer in the so-called 'Penal Company'.[59]

On 11 January 1943, Gemmeker announced through his first *Komman-danturbefehl* that a Penal Company had been compiled because of the frequent violations of the camp regulations. In addition to all S-Cases, residents who had committed an offence were placed in this Company. They were subject to a minimum sentence of one day. Gemmeker announced these sentences, probably as a warning, via a camp order. Richard K. was sentenced to eight weeks in the Penal Company at the beginning of June 1943, because he had deliberately provided incorrect data. During these eight weeks, he had to exchange barracks 57 for barracks 67. After serving his sentence, K. was allowed to leave barracks 67 and participate in the 'normal' camp life again.

This did not apply to the majority of the S-Cases: they remained in the barracks until their transport and worked in the Penal Company during that time. The working days of the Company were long and hard and initially started at 7:00 and lasted until 19:00. Between 12:00 and 12:30 they were allowed to eat. This meal was brought to the workplace by the OD and had to be consumed on the spot. During the winter time, working time was between sunrise and sunset. At the end of the working day, the Penal Company was not given an opportunity to rest. First they had to participate in exercises for one more hour. In mid-June 1943, the working hours of the Penal Company changed. After being awakened at 5:00, everyone was given the opportunity to prepare for the new working day, which began at 6:00. The lunch break lasted from 12:30 to 14:00. Because this break lasted longer than before, it was possible to eat in the barracks instead of at the workplace. After the break, the second part of the working day began, the end of which was fixed at 20:00.

The Penal Company was supervised by a *Kompanieführer*.[60] OD man and former Officer of the German Army, Mozes Benjamin Zimmern[61] was given this task. Zimmern had to ensure that the Company carried out the tasks assigned to it swiftly and meticulously. In addition, he was instructed to have the convicts perform 'special' feats. He had to teach those who were part of the Penal Company strict discipline, so that they would not break the rules in the future. A resident who was not among the convicts himself saw that Zimmern carried out his duties with verve. According to this witness, he could not get enough of snapping at people and harassing them. In addition, Zimmern would have been good at inventing the cruellest punishments and reporting persons to the Commander or to the Second Lieutenant of the Gendarmerie. Mechanicus supported the statements of this witness and even added to it. He wrote in his diary that Zimmern resembled an SS man and was known as a horrible man, a brute, who roared, mocked and cursed. He was hated so much that, according to Mechanicus, the people would have loved to beat him to death immediately. It never came to that. However, Zimmern was slapped in the face by a man from the punishment barracks.

The perpetrator had to stand still by the barbed wire for three days, eight hours a day, under the supervision of an OD member.[62] His function and behaviour did not or barely benefit Zimmern. Together with 30 other OD members, he was transported to Theresienstadt on 4 September 1944. From there he ended up in Auschwitz, where he died on 17 October.[63]

The female convicts of the punishment barracks and the men who did not work in the Penal Company were taken daily by the OD to the industrial barracks. There, under the supervision of the OD, they often had to do monotonous and dirty work, such as disassembling batteries or disassembling crashed aircraft.[64] Anne Frank and the rest of her family also had to work. Anne ended up having to disassemble batteries.[65]

Unlike the other residents, convicts also worked on Sundays from 7:30 to 12:30 from a certain period onwards. All the men of the Criminal Barracks, including those who worked outside the camp, had to exercise in advance. Gemmeker deliberately introduced this exercise duty because, according to him, the men from these barracks were not given enough physical activity because of their daily work in the industrial barracks. However, he would never have ordered them to do heavy and long exercises.[66] As such, Gemmeker did not consider himself responsible for the incidents that occurred in this area. A Dutch SS man, for example, had ordered the Penal Company to lie down in the mud and get up again in the autumn of 1943, simply because one of them did not take off his hat on time.[67] The women from these barracks took part in gymnastic exercises on Sunday morning between 8:00 and 9:00.[68]

In addition to having many duties, the convicts hardly had any rights. At regular intervals, family members from the camp were allowed to visit them. Because of the large number of people in the barracks, there were sometimes more than 200 visitors at a time, which called for a tightly organised visit scheme. Initially, visitors were only given access if they had filled out a form, which they had requested in advance at the OD barracks. From the beginning of August 1943, handing over the camp card was enough to gain access. The waiting time to be admitted sometimes lasted one hour or more, regardless of the weather.[69]

If visitors did not comply with the visiting hours and regulations, this could have consequences for the visitor themselves, or for the entire Criminal Barracks. On a Sunday evening in September 1943, a 50-year-old woman visited the barracks. In advance, she handed in her camp card to the guards. When she believed visiting hours had ended, she went outside and reported to the guards to get her card back. That is when the woman was told that she had broken the rules. The whistle that signalled the end of the visit had been blown five minutes earlier. The woman's statement that she had not heard the signal was not enough for the OD member. As punishment, the woman had to stand against a wall for 20 minutes.[70] More than a week later, a collective punishment for the inmates followed, because visitors deliberately did not respond to the signal of the OD. Because of this violation, the convicts were not allowed to receive visitors for a week. Talking to convicts outside visiting hours was not allowed. Residents who spoke with convicts on the street or in the workplace anyway could be severely punished.

According to Mechanicus, this particular order required almost superhuman powers because of the close relations between the people, which generally meant that they did not comply with the rules.[71]

The visiting arrangement was probably the only ray of light in the dark and stressful existence of the convicts, because they had little to no prospect of the future. The convicts tried to get rid of their 'S' by all means, so that they would be taken into the camp as a 'normal' resident. Sometimes they succeeded by paying large sums of money, diamonds or jewellery. Presser calculated that out of about 10,000 convicts, 1,750 Jews managed to lose their 'S'.[72] Mauritz Frankenhuis, together with his wife and two daughters, belonged to this group. Because they were arrested as people in hiding, the family came to Westerbork in early 1944 from the Scheveningen Prison as S-Cases. Through the Contact Committee, it was possible to obtain baptismal certificates. Although these may not have been original papers, the 'S' disappeared, followed by being released from the Criminal Barracks. For this change of position, the family would have paid 80,000 Dutch guilders.[73]

Most of the people were unable to pay off their 'S'. Because of the extra secure environment, the permanent surveillance by the OD and the difficult conditions, there was little else left for them to do but wait for what was to come. Only a small and brave, or perhaps reckless, group did not wait for that moment. These people tried to escape from the Criminal Barracks and the camp in an 'illegal' way.

Escapes
The flight incidents from the Criminal Barracks in November 1943, which caused the inmates to have to hand in their civilian clothing, were not isolated incidents. In the months before, some people had already fled or had attempted to do so. The first time the OD report mentioned an escape from the Criminal Barracks is on 7 June 1943. That day, around 4:20 AM, a transport from Vught arrived with more than 1,600 people. Of them, an unknown number were imprisoned. The processing lasted almost 12 hours.[74] At 19:00, visiting hours in the Hospital would have just begun, a whistle was blown, indicating that an unsafe situation had arisen in the camp. Visiting hours were immediately cancelled and everyone had to return to their barracks. Mechanicus initially thought that the signal was intended to frustrate the Jews from Vught, because they were now unable to visit the relatives they had sometimes been separated from for a long time. After a period of uncertainty, the real reason was announced an hour later: one of the newcomers from Vught, who was in barracks 67, had fled.[75] The whole OD had to come in to search the camp from east to west. In addition, all barracks were thoroughly searched. At about 22:00 the job was done and the signal could be given that everything was 'safe'. However, the massive manhunt had not produced the desired result, as the refugee remained lost without a trace. The unsuccessful action could have had unfavourable consequences for the OD, as there was the threat that ten OD members would be shot if the search failed.[76] This did not happen. The camp's management did try in a different way to prevent the camp population from attempting to escape in the future.

The next day, 8 June, the 65th transport left the camp, this time with Sobibor as final destination.[77] A large number of Jews from the group from Vught received a call for this transport. Since contact between family members had not been established, many voluntarily joined the transport, so that they were still together. As a result, the train was too crowded, so that not all the volunteers could join. While they were loading people into the train, the *Ordnungspolizei* was allegedly ordered by *SS Sturmscharführer* Franz Fischer to remove ten S-Cases from the wagon specially intended for this group. Fischer, who had been made responsible for the day-to-day management of the *Referat IV-B4* in The Hague by his chief Willy Zöpf, was present because of a visit to the camp. The ten men were taken away in a truck under the guidance of the *Ordnungspolizei*. The purpose of this action was to confuse the people who were left behind. They had to be given the impression that the men would be shot outside the camp as retaliation, so that residents would let go of any plans they might have had to escape.[78] However, the German Police did not actually carry out the retaliation action; the truck brought the ten men to Assen. There they were put on the train that had just arrived from Westerbork.[79] The flight incident had no consequences yet for the OD members on duty. However, another successful escape from the barracks did have consequences. Jacob Barzilay[80] had the bad luck that he was in charge of guarding the inmates at that very moment. In order to persuade the other OD members to continue to perform their duties meticulously, Jacob was held responsible for the escape and was placed on the transport list as punishment. He died in Auschwitz on 31 August 1944[81].

The threats and sanctions were successful. The OD began acting more stringently and tightened supervision. Saartje (Sonja) de Winter had to deal with one of these OD men who performed his task strictly according to the rules. On 20 January 1944 Sonja was taken from the Scheveningen Prison to Westerbork. She entered the camp as an S-Case, because from April 1943 she was hiding as a nurse in the Utrecht Deaconess Hospital. Sonja was put on the list for the next transport, which left a few days later. The organisation of the transport and loading into the wagons of about 950 people, including hundreds of convicts, went according to plan. Shortly before the train left from the station in the camp, which had been there since November 1942, Sonja saw a chance to escape from the train, after which she was able to hide in a barracks unnoticed.

After the train had left, she left her hiding place and walked to a nearby house. Because of her short stay in the camp, Sonja probably did not know this was a guardhouse. Inside, she found three men. She asked them if they could take her out of the camp. According to her, there was no risk because she had escaped from the train and was therefore no longer registered in the camp register. Her escape might not be discovered until the train was unloaded in Poland. After this request and the voluntarily addition, Sonja soon found out that she was in the wrong place. The house served as 'Post East' of the OD. At least two of the three men present there, Joël Granade[82], born in Amsterdam, and Sandor Salmagne, were employed by the OD. Joël would have been ordered by Sandor to bring Sonja to Pisk. Joël fulfilled this order. He grabbed Sonja and brought his 'arrestee' to the service leader of the OD, who immediately locked her in the Camp Prison. On 8 February 1944 Sonja was on the train again; escape was not possible this time. A few days later, she arrived in Auschwitz. At the end of January 1945, she was liberated by the Russians and in mid-August, Sonja returned to the

One of the guardhouses in the camp.

On 4 September 1944 Joël had to go with the second to last transport, which brought him to Theresienstadt. He also survived and came back to the Netherlands. His wife, whom he had married in Westerbork, and his 9-month-old-son were murdered in Auschwitz on 8 October 1944. Joël found work in a butcher shop on the Weesperstraat in Amsterdam and probably tried to leave behind the events that had taken place during the war as soon as possible. This attempt seemed to fail, because at the end of December 1945, Sonja's husband reported in writing to the *Bureau Nationale Veiligheid* (Dutch security agency founded after the war) in Amsterdam an incident which in his eyes had to be seen as a war crime. Her husband, who had escaped from Westerbork himself, found Sonja's arrest by a fellow Jew to be a disgrace and believed that Joël had to be punished.

A Detective from the *Dienst Politieke Misdrijven* (Political Crimes Service) started an investigation. Joël was tracked down and interrogated as a suspect of 'bringing a Jewish refugee into the hands of the enemy in Camp Westerbork'. Joël stated that he had not dared to take risks because of the presence of his fellow OD members and that if he had been alone, he would probably have acted differently. The former OD man hoped that when assessing his act, they would consider the plight in which he had found himself at that time, even though he knew he was guilty. According to his own words, he would have helped at least eight to ten Jews flee the train. No evidence of this has been found in his file, but it does contain a decision regarding the conditional dismissal of charges. Joël had to put himself under the supervision of the *Stichting Politieke Delinquenten* (Foundation for Political Delinquents) in Amsterdam and continue to behave as a good citizen. Joël's statement contains a passage in which he indicates that the arrest of Sonja was the only time he had behaved in such a highly disagreeable manner. There was probably no reason to doubt this remark, so nobody looked into any other facts possibly committed by Joël in the camp.[83]

If this had been done, the OD's report would have produced another questionable fact about Joël. On 19 September 1943, an OD member with service number 37 found two people outside the barracks near the main hall at around 23:00. They were transferred to the Camp Prison for being *Fluchtverdachtes*. The list of service numbers of the OD shows that number 37 was Joël's number. This case could likely not be built properly because, unlike Sonja, the victims did not return after the liberation. This was the case for most of the escape incidents in which the OD played a role. In many cases, both the victim and the perpetrator died shortly after their arrival in one of the (extermination) camps.

The OD report contains more records of escapes or attempts to do so. There were only a few cases in which the entire OD was deployed in order to search for a missing person. As a witness, Mechanicus was quite outspoken about the deployment of the Camp Police when there was an escape. He wrote: 'Like bloodhounds, OD men in their green uniforms were unleashed on the refugees with Police batons, which resembled table legs.' Mechanicus added with astonishment that the indignation of the residents was not directed at the pursuers, but at those who attempted to flee, since they were putting other residents at risk. Mechanicus's commentary continued as follows: 'Neither was the indignation aimed at the OD men, Jews who had gone after a Jew like wild dogs and had not given him the chance to flee. The mental degeneration has advanced so far here that they take out their indignation, not on the executioner and his servants, but on those who seek to get out of their hands.'[84]

Sometimes the men of the OD searched the camp several times a day, with varying success. In the other incidents, the deployment of one or a few OD members was sufficient. Some OD members were involved in several incidents, including Joël, but Sandor Salmagne as well. On the day of Sonja's arrest, Sandor was also confronted with another escape attempt. One of the convicts, a man who had to be put on transport, tried to flee from the laundry room of the punishment barracks in the morning. Together with two other OD men, Sandor foiled this attempt to flee. Sandor himself remained in the camp until the liberation.[85] The archives of the '*Bijzondere Rechtspleging*' (Special Court) do not show that after the liberation he made any statement about his function in the OD, nor as a witness in Sonja's case.

Not only convicts were looking for ways to get outside of the barbed wire barrier illegally. From the moment Camp Westerbork became a transit camp and the transports started, 'ordinary' residents also attempted to flee. The first escape would have taken place on 31 July 1942. That day the sixth transport left, with Auschwitz as final destination. The Russian Abraham Smoiro was on the transport list. With outside help, he managed to escape this transport. Abraham went into hiding, even participated in the resistance and witnessed the liberation.[86]

Many others tried with varying success to achieve the same as Abraham. Some attempts were successful, as they had been carefully prepared. In other cases, coincidence and luck were important elements. The latter was true for Avi Magid, born in Rotterdam, and his Mother. When Avi's Mother saw a gate open in the camp in the winter of 1942 and found that there was no guard nearby, she warned Avi. Together they snuck out through the gate and ran away. As they walked on the road, a car with two Gendarmes was approaching. Avi and his mother ran away, but this was pointless, because they had already been seen. Both had to sit in the car and their attempt to escape therefore seemed to have come to an end, but instead of returning to the camp, the Gendarmes continued their journey towards Assen. Along the way, they reassured Avi and his mother and promised to bring them to safety. Mother and son were brought to a house in Assen. Shortly thereafter, a safe return trip to Rotterdam followed, where both could later celebrate the liberation.[87]

Escapes and attempts to do so continued until the end of the occupation. The camp's management was not happy with this unauthorised departure and the measures they chose to take to prevent this from happening were already being carried out at a relatively early stage. On 11 February 1943, *Lagerbefehl* number 5 appeared. It was one of the most famous and important regulations. The barracks leaders were therefore obligated to read this order out loud regularly. According to the order, every attempt to escape had to be reported immediately to the guard on duty. Other services in the camp had to be informed about this only after this guard had been warned. It was not allowed to wait and see if a suspicion was confirmed. It was necessary to act immediately if a camp resident went missing during the meal or was not found in the barracks before curfew; a false alarm was still better than an investigation that was started too late. In the order, there was a clear warning about what would happen if an escape had been successful. In that case, ten residents from the same barracks would be put on transport. Moreover, Gemmeker created the possibility for himself to take special measures against the barracks leader.[88]

After the liberation, the issuing of the order was included in Gemmeker's trial. Although several escapes occurred during the period from 11 February to 12 December 1943, the retaliatory measure would have been applied only once, according to Gemmeker. He claimed that he actually played a positive role in the problems that arose around the escapes. By reporting every escape to the BdS, he fulfilled his obligation as he should. However, he managed each time to get the BdS to agree to his proposal not to go through with the retaliatory measure, except in one case. On 12 October 1943, Hartog van der Goen saw the opportunity to flee while he was part of a group of residents who worked in the so-called field service in Hooghalen. Measures followed immediately. The number of OD members accompanying the working groups to the jobs was increased. In addition, a camp order signed by Gemmeker appeared a day after the escape. In this he announced that he had determined that as punishment, the mother and sister of Van der Goen would be placed in the punishment barracks as S-Cases and would be put on the next transport. This order served as a warning and was intended to discourage residents with plans to flee. Gemmeker also stated that he had reported Van der Goen's escape to the BdS. The BdS proposed the deportation of relatives of the refugee, after which Gemmeker was forced to pass on the names of the mother and sister.

The Policeman responsible for questioning, Jan Schoenmaker, doubted Gemmeker's sincerity. According to Gemmeker, all the good measures concerning camp order number 5 would have come from him, whereas the bad measures had been taken at the initiative of the BdS. This statement was very illogical in the eyes of Schoenmaker. Although he pointed this out several times during the interrogation, Gemmeker stuck to his statement. Another point of discussion regarding Gemmeker's statement is the part in which he indicated that the retaliatory measure was applied only once in Westerbork. This does not match the data from the same report and other sources.[89] For example, on 13 October 1943, one day after the escape of Van der Goen, a Jewish man fled while travelling to Amsterdam to work there. His sister and brother-in-law, who had remained in the camp, were then transferred to the punishment barracks. Nothing else is known about the fate of the man and his relatives. There was only a short message in the OD report about this incident.[90]

An escape about which Gemmeker did make a statement, but which is also not included in the number of retaliatory measures taken by him, took place on or around 6 April 1943. Shortly before a transport left, two Jews who were on the transport list were missing. There was a suspicion that they had fled. These Jews had arrived in Westerbork with 500 others from Vught on 31 March. According to eyewitnesses, this group was in very bad shape. They were dirty, starving and covered in vermin. Some of them were also injured, because they had been bitten by guard dogs in Vught or on the way. After being deloused, the group was split up. The seriously ill and weak people ended up in the Hospital. The lighter cases were quarantined in barracks 57.

A few days after arrival, barracks leader Moses Kurt Löwenberg was handed a transport list. The night before the transport left, he had to read out the names of those on the list. When this group was ready to be taken to the train, it turned out that the two men were missing. Gemmeker was immediately informed of this, because Moses saw him storming into the barracks. Then he saw Gemmeker dragging sick Jews out of their beds, which he then selected for transport. The fact that these Jews had a provisional exemption did not stop Gemmeker; at that time, anger had most likely taken over. OD men brought the 20 unfortunate men in pyjamas to the train. Moses normally considered Gemmeker's behaviour to be mild, but found him extremely cruel in this case. Gemmeker was able to remember this incident somewhat during the interrogation. He believed he had gone to the OD after the escape was discovered. There he had also summoned Moses, after which Gemmeker ordered him to get 20 persons from the barracks of the missing people as retaliation for the escape. Moses would have pointed out the poor condition of these Jews. Gemmeker then contacted the Camp's

Doctor, Fritz Spanier, to learn from him in what state this group really was. According to Spanier, they were not doing that bad; he judged all residents of barracks 57 as slightly ill. Gemmeker admitted to having been angry when he went to the barracks. After this he would have checked the beds to appoint the least sick for transport, but he could not remember much of this. Because instead of 2,000 Jews, there were now 2,020 Jews who had to go on transport, Gemmeker assumed that it was a retaliatory measure. According to official figures, there were indeed 2,020 Jews deported to Sobibor that day.[91]

The figures show that during the period in which Westerbork served as a transit camp, between 230 and 300 persons fled. At the end of October 1943, Gemmeker himself made sure that an attempt to flee failed. One night, armed with a shotgun, he was walking along the fence with his girlfriend and Secretary Elisabeth Hassel. He had the shotgun with him to shoot wild rabbits, which were causing a lot of damage especially near the camp farm. Suddenly, Gemmeker saw someone walking in the forbidden area on the other side of the fence. When he got closer, it turned out to be a man who was carrying a briefcase with him and was dressed in an overcoat and hat. Gemmeker asked with a loud voice what the man was doing there and added that he had to leave because he was in the forbidden zone. The man turned around. Gemmeker got the impression that he was laughing while he just continued walking. Due to this, the distance between them became shorter. Gemmeker once again warned the man and in order to reinforce his words, he raised his shotgun. Because the man turned around again, Gemmeker concluded that he had heard the warning. Despite this, the man did not stop.

In this situation, fleeing was impossible and therefore useless. Since the man did not respond to the warnings and continued to walk in the forbidden area, Gemmeker deliberately shot in his direction. He purposefully aimed low, with a light hail pattern, which has little penetrating power. Elisabeth was frightened by the unexpected shot and snapped at Gemmeker that he had to warn her first when he was planning to shoot. Gemmeker saw the man jump and grab his leg, after which he disappeared. Further on, he was taken away by a few people who might have heard the shot and had come to see what was going on. Gemmeker later learned that the man he shot at was Frederik Lodewijk Spier. According to Doctor Spanier, the injuries were not too bad. Frederik's brother did not share this opinion, because when Frederik had to go on transport to Bergen-Belsen around January 1944, he was still not completely healed. Before Gemmeker returned to the *Kommandantur*, he first gave the Gendarme present on the watchtower a big earful, because he had not been vigilant enough. The Gendarme should at least have called out to the man suspected of trying to escape.[92] The man could not be blamed for anything else, since he was responsible for the outdoor surveillance.

Obedience and discipline were not only recurring subjects for residents. OD members were also regularly urged to behave in a disciplinary manner through new or amended service regulations. The camp's management took the opportunity to publish the guidelines among the men through the OD report, with the aim of improving discipline. Among other things, Gemmeker indicated that he also demanded a strict Military attitude and behaviour within the OD. According to him, the OD was a purely Military organisation and therefore had to set an example for the entire camp. If an OD man was caught for an offence, then he could expect a stricter punishment than the other residents who had committed similar offences would get. In addition, there was the threat of resignation from the OD, and everyone knew what this could mean: the loss of a safe status. The OD members were therefore not only expected to monitor surveillance in a Military manner as agents of the Camp Police, but also to have an exemplary function.

5. CAMP POLICE OR JEWISH SS

When the Dutch Jews also had to report from July 1942 onwards, the number of incoming and outgoing transports increased. Because the OD had to guide all of them to the camp, the strength of this service group had to be increased.

Expansion Ordedienst

In October 1942, 40 Jewish men, all of whom had the Dutch nationality, were placed in the OD.[1] As a result of this expansion, the total number of men increased to 60; the number of former refugees remained the same. This meant that after the expansion, 70% of the entire OD consisted of Dutch Jews. Although the old camp residents were in the minority within the service, they did retain the most important positions. Pisk remained responsible as a service leader. Some other 'old timers', including Werner Bloch, were given the position of Watch Commander. After the service leader and his replacement came the Watch Commanders, who were responsible for all the administrative tasks of the service. Based on the assignments they received from Gemmeker and other competent authorities within the camp, they divided the men into groups. In addition, the Watch Commander had to ensure that the day-to-day work was conducted properly.[2]

On 31 October a new arrangement of the OD was announced. From 1 November onwards, the service was made up of six groups. Each group consisted of eight men. In addition, there were four other groups of each four OD members who were in charge of the Fire Brigade.[3] The developments followed each other quickly. A few days later, a new message showed that the OD could be expanded by 60 people, almost doubling the strength. Among the new members was Leo Janowitz.[4]

Leo was born in Belarus. He married a Polish woman and built a life in Germany as a coffee manufacturer. When he got into trouble in Germany in 1936 because of his Jewish origin, he came to the Netherlands with his wife. He also brought his son and daughter, who had been housed with relatives in Zagreb just to be sure, to the Netherlands. In Amsterdam, Leo tried to build a new business. The family had been transferred to Westerbork at the end of September 1942 as S-Cases. What they were arrested for is unknown. Leo's wife realised on the way that the red 'S' on their papers would not be conducive to a long stay in the camp. That is why all family members, on her advice, destroyed their papers on the train. Upon arrival at the camp, they made themselves known at registration as Soviet citizens, whose passports were in Ankara for extension. The family was then housed in a barracks where English and American Jewish citizens were staying.

On 11 November, the day of resettlement, the family had to go to the roll call area. There they heard that the names of Jews who worked as a Doctor, nurse or in the kitchen of the camp were called. These groups were assigned a separate barracks. At some point, the names of their fellow barracks members were called. Leo did not hear his name or his family's. When they joined the group, they were told by the barracks leader that their names were not on his list. Usually, being on a list was a bad sign. Being a part of something meant you were assigned to a barracks. Leo's wife insisted that they had been called and belonged to this group.

In the meantime, Leo had gone out to investigate to see if there was anything he could arrange. At the roll call area, he saw Gemmeker sitting behind a table and at this table stood a row of men. When asked why these men were standing there, Leo was told that new members were needed for the OD. Leo decided to stand in line. When it was his turn, Gemmeker asked him if he had been in Military Service and when. Leo, who had picked up the German language because of his stay in Germany, said that he had served in the Army during the First World War. This information was correct, but he did not mention that he had fought against the German Army as a Russian Soldier. After proving that he could march, Leo got permission from Gemmeker to join the OD. With this news, he returned to his family with the message that they should go straight to the barracks in which the family members of the OD men were housed. Leo was housed in barracks 22 with the other OD men. Leo's daughter could remember that from that time on, the family had a special status in the camp.[5]

```
                                               1 Juli 1943.

     Geachte Heer Jellema,
                         U zult wel verwonderd zijn een brief van
     mij te ontvangen, doch vind ik het toch leuk eens iets va n
     mij te laten horen, gezien de lange gesprekken die in de loop
     der   laatste tijd bij U in de huiskamer heb gehad.
     Inmiddels ben ik reeds vanaf Aug. hier in het kamp en ma-
     ken zoowel mijn Vrouw als ik,het beiden prima alhoewel we
     al onze familie in dit jaar hebben zien vertrekken . Mijn
     Schoonvader(A. de Metz) en schoonmoeder zijn reeds maanden
     wegevenals de rest der famm., doch hopen we,dat we ze in
     gezondheid mogen terugzien. Uw voorspelling van een lange oor
     log is jammer genoeg uitgekomen en denk ik nog vaak aan Uw
     pessimistische voorspellingen!U zou me een plezier doen wanne
     heer U ons af en toe eens een pakje met fruit( tomaten, kom-
     kommers- enz) zouwillen zenden. Dit moet U als BRIEFPAKJE
     (gewicht tot 2Ko.) zonder afz. verzenden en is het na een
     dag reds in mijn bezit. Postpakketten mogen we alleen ontvang
     gen uit Amsterdam of uit andere plaatsen met als afz. de Jood
     sche Raad die
     sche Raad, die in Leeuwarden is Camminghastraat 57 . Het
     makkelijkste is dus een briefpakje.
     Bijgaand fl0.- voor de kosten en eidig ik met hartelijke groe
     ten,natuurlijk ook voor Uw vrouw,

                                            M. Cohen
                                            Kamppolitie
                                            Barrak 22 Zaal2
                                            Lager Westerbork.
        z.o.z.
```

OD man Max Cohen, born on 25 January 1918 in Amsterdam, stayed in the camp from the beginning of October 1942 onwards and got a position in the OD. He contacted an acquaintance in Leeuwarden to supplement his ration. Max was deported to Auschwitz on 8 February 1944 and died a few days later on 11 February.

David Chajes ended up in the OD the same way Leo did, possible even on the same date. When David saw the group of men at the roll call place, he asked a cousin of his wife who they were. The cousin said David had to try to join the line. If he was asked what his profession was, he had to say that he had been a truck driver. The moment a German who was near the group turned his back on him, David unobtrusively joined the line. Although he had no idea what they were going to do with them, he took the risk. After all, David's motto was: If I have to hang, I prefer to hang on the last tree. It worked out well for David and his family, because he was told that he had been admitted to the OD.[6]

Many newcomers actively started looking for a job within the camp organisation immediately after arrival, because they believed they would be able to stay longer in Westerbork that way. However, the attempts often failed, because those who already had a job remained in their position and there were not many jobs to begin with. Betty Loonstein's father also attempted to join the OD, but failed. He probably did not have enough 'vitamin R', because apart from being lucky, knowing the right people was important for getting a job.[7]

Maurits Beetz[8] did turn out to know the right people when he arrived at the camp in early October 1942. His contact person was none other than Schol. Maurits and Schol had known each other for a long time. Both had experienced the May days of 1940 on Texel as Military men. Schol had been the Chief of Maurits there as a reserve captain. Maurits hoped that the Commander could do something for him and contacted him. According to Schol, there were not many possibilities; a position in the OD was the only thing he could offer. Maurits took him up on it. His colleagues were not happy about this at first, because although he was one of the first Dutch people in the OD and got a low service number, he was already included in the group of new residents.[9]

The old residents saw formidable competitors in the newcomers, and they were afraid that they would lose their hard-earned position within the camp again. Werner Bloch wondered whether it was not logical that they defended the positions they had built up over the years in this dark society.[10] Many Dutch Jews did not understand that logic in any case when they too were eligible for deportation. Especially when they saw that the organisation and administration of the transports were carried out by their fellow Jews, who had previously taken care of them lovingly, envy could grow into hate.[11]

Still, some newcomers, including Louis de Wijze, understood the position of the old residents. Louis, who ended up in the camp on 2 October 1942 and had a lot of contact with the old camp population, could feel the difference between the old and the new residents very well. He considered it more or less obvious that former refugees had been given a position within this self-government. They had already been sent by the Dutch Government to Westerbork at an earlier stage and had therefore not voluntarily chosen this remote and desolate place. According to Louis, the old residents had suffered as much and often even more than the Dutch Jews. After the camp had been taken over by the occupying forces, they gratefully abused the existing camp system. By using residents more or less by force, the occupier only had to make the minimum number of staff available. Every day the residents experienced the fear of being sent on transport if they refused to do what was asked of them. Louis found this great inner struggle and the deployment of fellow members of the Jewish community in the deportation perhaps one of the most gruesome and refined cruelties of the occupier.[12]

In the last months of 1942, transports still came in that contained Jewish men who later joined the OD. On 21 November Jews were brought to Westerbork by three different transports. The first transport arrived early in the morning and consisted of nearly 600 Jews from Amsterdam. In the afternoon 20 Jews arrived from The Hague. The last group, consisting of 108 men, had left Ellecom in the afternoon and arrived at 19:20 hours. This transport was special. To the residents who saw the group entering, it must have been obvious that these men had been through a particularly difficult time. Most of them were visibly malnourished, abused and ill, and had to go straight to the camp Hospital. The 20-year-old Barend Scheffer[13] was one of those. He had been severely abused during his stay in Ellecom and had to be admitted to the Camp Hospital for treatment.

Barend had married Esther Appel on 20 July 1942. They moved into a house at Nieuwe Prinsengracht 52 in Amsterdam[14]. After a little over a month, the couple was separated again. Barend received a call regarding work expansion. Along with 48 other Jewish men from Amsterdam, he was brought to the Labour Camp Molengoot, north of Hardenberg in Overijssel, on 2 September. The final destination of the train was not Overijssel, however, but Dieren in Gelderland. On the platform, armed SS men were waiting for the group. They left Dieren by bus to their temporary destination: villa 'Irene' in Ellecom. That same day 45 Jewish men from The Hague were added to the group and a day later, another 45 men arrived from Rotterdam. After the morning roll call, the group, which had been divided into several labour groups, had to go on foot and under the guidance of the SS to the Avegoor estate, which was 800 meters away and was used as a training camp for the Dutch SS. On the estate, the men were forced to construct a sports field. The heavy work, combined with bad treatment and malnutrition, took its toll. Three men died and many others fell ill. When the work was finished after about 6 weeks, 108 men, including Barend, were barely able to travel to Westerbork.[15] Here he was reunited with his brother, Heiman Natan[16], who was part of the OD and had been staying in the camp since 18 July 1942. After Barend was discharged from the Hospital, he probably joined the OD with the help of his brother.

At the beginning of November 1942, there was some relief in the tasks of the OD and the Gendarmerie Detachment due to the completion of the work on the railway line outside the camp. This allowed the train to enter the camp, so that the escort of transports to and from the station in Hooghalen was no longer necessary.[17] This did not mean that less people were needed, because after the departure of the *SS Wachbataillon Nordwest* at the beginning of 1943, the indoor surveillance was virtually entirely left to the OD. The strength was probably adjusted for this purpose, since the number of men increased in January to 161.[18]

Via *Lagerbefehl* nr. 3 of 25 January 1943, Gemmeker announced the new Division of the Service Groups (*Dienstbereiche*). In doing so, he was able to build on the camp organisation set up by Schol, of which self-government remained an important part. The OD belonged to one of the twelve service groups.[19] In order to be aware of what was happening in the camp, every service group leader had to draw up a daily short report from 11 January onwards and submit it to the *Lagerkommandantur* before 10:00 AM. It included all the major events, achievements and incidents of the service group in question.[20]

In April 1943 the strength of the OD had increased to 182 men, but a month later this number declined again. In August Pisk still had 117 OD members.[21] The increase and decrease of the number of men available had several causes. Two of them had to do with the number of Jews residing in the camp and the frequency of incoming and departing transports. Supervising these transports was not the only task of the OD. In the annual report of 1943, Pisk summed up the tasks that the Camp Police had carried out that year:

- Fire Brigade inside and outside the camp
- Security at the canteen, the boiler room and the registration building, among others
- Patrol services in the camp
- Guiding the work groups outside the camp
- Checking the residents leaving and returning to the camp and managing the necessary passes
- Guarding and occupying four guard posts at the punishment barracks
- Guiding convicts to their workplaces
- Transferring sick people to and from the Camp Hospital on a stretcher
- Providing first aid
- Managing keys and found objects.[22]

Based on the listed responsibilities, it can be said that the OD functioned as a fully-fledged Police Force. Because both the Dutch and foreign OD members originally had traditionally Jewish professions, such as travelling salesman/representative, (market) merchant, butcher or diamond cutter, they had no experience in supervising or maintaining order. It was not because of these qualities that they had been placed in the OD. A logical conclusion is that the OD consisted of normal Jewish men who had the right contacts and/or qualities and thus managed to get a job within one of the most hated service groups. A longer stay in the camp was the reward they hoped to get for this.

Léon Albertus Alexander Cohen[23] was, as far as we know, the only OD man who had received actual Police training and had served as a Law Enforcement Officer before coming to Westerbork. Nevertheless, he joined the OD as an administrator of the Criminal Barracks, not because of this experience, but because he had the right contacts.

Léon was appointed to the Municipal Police of Amsterdam on 1 May 1919. His first workplace was the office on the Warmoesstraat. This was followed by transfers to a number of other agencies and the Traffic Police. By the time the Second World War began, he had been promoted to Detective First Grade. Shortly before the occupation, Léon had to go to

Card catalogue map Léon Cohen.

Amsterdam-Noord. This relocation was not carried out on a voluntary basis. The reason for it would have had something to do with the anti-Semitic attitude of his superior. All Jewish officials were first removed from office, honorary posts or service at the end of November 1940; they were fired a few months later. This measure was applied to 8 Jewish members of the Amsterdam Police Force, including Léon. However, because Léon was appointed to the Jewish Council as head of the Internal Department, he was able to stay in Amsterdam until he had to leave for Westerbork.[24] Léon would have arrived in Westerbork on 22 July 1943.

Initially, Léon was relatively safe in Westerbork, but when it looked like he too was going to be put on transport, he decided to make use of his contacts. Léon had already introduced himself to the Gendarmerie Detachment Commander, Albert de Jong, as a former Policeman. De Jong then told him that if there was anything he could do for Léon, he should turn to him. When the situation became difficult, De Jong arranged a job for him at the OD.[25]

Werner Bloch is wearing the overalls of the OD, including the insignia, star and emblem on the sleeve.

Although the OD did not consist of accomplished Law Enforcement Officers, the majority did have a Military background, which was more or less a requirement for this service group. After all, Military men had learned what order and discipline entailed. Just like Soldiers, the OD members were recognisable by a uniform that initially consisted of brown overalls with riding boots and a cap. Members of other service parts wore overalls of different colours. Via camp order 27, Gemmeker made a clear statement regarding the separation in the colours. As of 27 April 1943, the OD members began to perform their service in green overalls. They had to turn in the brown overalls. To complete the uniform, they were provided with a cap, boots and a belt. Members of other service units who were still in possession of green overalls had to exchange them for blue ones. The members of the OD no longer had to wear a red armband and were given an emblem with the letters 'OD' on it instead. According to Gemmeker's guidelines, it was mandatory to wear this emblem on the left breast pocket. On the same left side, the Star of David was also mandatory. The OD emblem was also visible on the cap and the left sleeve.[26]

As is customary within a Military unit, insignia indicated the ranks. The hierarchy within the OD was made visible with red stripes on the sleeves of the overalls. Pisk got three stripes as a service leader. The Watch Commanders were identified by two stripes and the other men had one stripe on the sleeve. Apart from the other characteristics, some overalls had a special sign with 'GA1' on it. This emblem indicated that the OD member in question belonged to the old residents.[27]

If the weather was bad, the members of the Camp Police could have a black or blue cape. Because of the boots, cap, belt and green overalls with red stripes and emblems, the OD members were clearly distinguishable from the other residents. The OD men abused this distinction and the privileges in the eyes of the camp's management. Therefore, a few months after the introduction of the green overalls, it was announced via a service notice that wearing the green overalls was not permitted when one was not working. In addition, they were not allowed to walk arm in arm with women through the camp during their shift.[28]

Several residents indicated that they were not pleased with the green overalls. They compared the outfits of the Camp Police with the green uniforms of the German Police. In addition to the uniform, the tasks of the OD were sometimes equated with those of the German Police. Especially because of this, the OD was seen as a crucial part of the refined German deportation system, which over time would even have been transformed into a cruel Military instrument.[29] It is therefore not surprising that a large proportion of residents could not respect the men of OD, because although the duties seemed relatively innocent at first, the group was soon considered the most hated service group within the Jewish self-government. In the judgment on the Jewish Camp Police of Camp Westerbork, there was little or no nuance. Especially the Dutch Jews who ended up in Westerbork as new residents were very critical.

Opinion Of The OD

One of these newcomers, who kept a diary during his stay in Westerbork and critically judged the OD, was the previously quoted journalist Philip Mechanicus, born in Amsterdam.[30] On Tuesday 1 June 1943, a few days after he had written his first words on paper, he wrote about the transport that left the camp that day. It was the 64th time a train left. According to the OD report, 3,010 Jews were brought to the Sobibor extermination camp.[31] It was the second largest departing transport.[32] Mechanicus paid particular attention to the role the OD played. The day began like most other transport days. After the names of those who had to go on transport had been announced, OD members gathered them outside the barracks and then escorted the group to the train. This train, 'a long mangy snake of old, dirty wagons,' was waiting at the 'Boulevard des Misères', as Mechanicus called the train and the station in the camp. The OD had cordoned off this place to keep away 'overly interested people'. Mechanicus's business report on the cooperation of the OD during this transport eventually turned into a merciless judgment. He described some of the OD members as crude and coarse men, without civilisation, without feeling and without compassion, who would live solely for a cigarette and an adventure with women of their own kind. Their behaviour was very similar to that of the German Police, so that the OD was referred to by the residents as the 'Jewish SS'.[33]

According to another eyewitness and writer, Jacob Boas, it was shocking to see how fellow Jews carried out the work of their enemy. In the absence of even more cruel Germans in the camp, the residents considered the OD members a greater evil than the SS itself. In Boas's opinion, the OD was a messy collection of wretched people, *Lumpen* and people with pathological issues, just like the SS. However, the transport days were the worst, because the uniformed minions of Pisk would bring the victims to the train with merciless zeal.[34]

Rudolf Breslauer, who made the famous *Westerbork film* commissioned by Gemmeker, filmed the entire ritual around the 'filling' of the wagons and the train departing on 19 May 1944.[35] The images clearly show that the troops of the OD were not only charged with escorting the Jews to the train, but also with closing the wagon doors. A wagon with number 9 written on it is closed and locked by the OD member Hans Margules. Because these actions were filmed, the work of the OD became a tangible concept. Willy Lindwer describes it as 'one of the unpleasant and dramatic tasks of the OD.'[36]

During transport days (Hooghalen) it was often extremely crowded and the supervision of the OD was necessary.

The fact that the OD clearly played a role in the transports was emphasised by the film. However, examples that support the allegations about the brutal actions of the OD are not all that numerous. Many eyewitnesses did not return. Paul Siegel was able to make a statement about such an incident. He was arrested while in hiding and came to Westerbork as a criminal case. Because he had the right contacts, Paul was released from the Criminal Barracks. He saw a chance to escape from the camp later. On 7 June 1943, a transport arrived from Vught. This transport, which contained more than 1,600 people, consisted largely of women and children.

According to Paul, the people had not had enough time to prepare for the journey, because this extremely unfortunate group had to leave Vught quite suddenly.

As a member of the Hachsjara youth group, Paul received a call to assist in handing out food packages, blankets and clothing. At one point, Paul saw that a woman with a baby on her arm dropped a small bag. Together with the woman, he picked up the contents that had been scattered on the ground, creating a congestion. This was an undesirable situation, because registering such a large group took a lot of time to begin with. Paul saw an OD man coming at them, who then pushed the woman away, causing her to fall down with her baby. Paul lost his self-control because of this action and attacked the man. He was immediately overpowered by other OD members and brought to the OD barracks. Pisk, described by Paul as a rude and power hungry man, yelled at him. He threatened to report Paul to the Camp Commander and claimed he would make sure that Paul was punished accordingly. It was clear to Paul what this 'punishment' would entail. Luckily for him, there was someone nearby who managed to save him from Pisk's 'clutches'.[37]

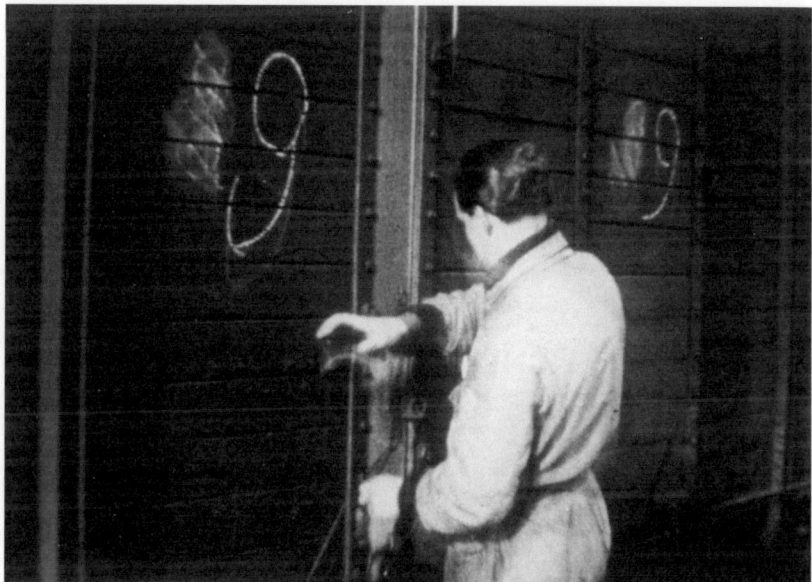

The closing of a wagon door by OD member Hans Margules.

According to Mechanicus, the OD would hunt those who had escaped like 'wild dogs' and cooperated in transports. They occasionally would push and/or scream people into the trains. Other tasks showed that the OD as a Camp Police also played a major role in maintaining order within the camp. Although not much information is available, the content of general service notices does provide greater clarity. At the beginning of May 1943, the OD was instructed via such a notice to keep the roads free of people, because nobody was allowed to walk on the main road of the camp during working hours. This had to be done vigorously, and passers-by had to leave quickly.

It was explicitly stated that no OD man should think that he could leave this to a colleague. Residents who remained on the road had to be sent away. According to the notice, the OD members were allowed to shout.[38]

ORDNUNGSDIENST   4.Februar 44

Uebersicht über den Stand des Ordnungsdienstes

Zeit	Gesamtzahl	ohne Nat.	holl.Nat.	Prozents. ohne	holl.
Juli 42	2o	18	2	90%	1o%
Oktober 42	6o	18	42	3o%	70%
Januar 43	161	76	85	47%	53%
April 43	182	76	1o6	42%	58%
Mai 43	15o	54	96	36%	64%
August 43	117	51	66	44%	56%
Januar 44	1o9	46	63	42%	58%
2o.1.44	76	39	37	51%	49%
4.2.44	72	37	35	51%	49%
9.2.44	67	35	32	53%	47%

Der Dienstleiter

gez. : Pisk

Strength of the OD per period, together with the figures on nationality.

On 20 September 1943 Mechanicus wrote in his diary that discipline in the camp had been weakened for several weeks. At that time, the OD no longer supervised the public road, allowing the residents to move freely through the camp. The men of the Camp Police were now only concerned with those who had been sent to the Criminal Barracks and kept a close eye on the visitors who went there.

Despite reports of reduced supervision and the fact that the strength of the OD was reduced from 182 to 76 (20 January 1944), it appears that checks were still being carried out in 1944. In mid-January, Pisk and his men surrounded barracks 64 in the middle of the day to check which men and women were still present while they should have been at work. The offenders were forced to hand over their camp card. Some men tried to dodge this check and quickly crawled under the covers, hoping they would be mistaken for luggage. Whether they outsmarted the inspectors, or whether there was no active search for them, the story does not tell.

A month later there was another action of the OD which was considered extremely unpleasant. The residents were told that there were fresh vegetables for sale in the cafeteria, which did not go unnoticed. Mechanicus was one of many who went to the cafeteria to score vegetables. In his diary he writes in detail about what he observed:

[...] So to the cafeteria. A stream of chaotic pushing each other in front of a narrow door, guarded by a few crooked OD members. [...] An OD man tries to bring some order in the chaos. Barking, he pushes back what is starting to stick out on the right side, tries to knead the human dough in such a way that it becomes neat rows of three or four. In vain: the people continue to stand stiffly together in the mud, which is what the ground here is made up of, numb from the cold. The procession is constantly expanding. More people are coming in than can be helped inside. [...] OD members keep trying to take action regularly, but it is in vain. They scold and curse, drag someone out of the group and chase him away, slap people here and there. People from the group report others who have pushed their way forward to the OD, but they remain deaf to complaints. 'You leave it to me; I know what I'm doing.' The people are powerless against the OD: they are the officially recognised guardians of order, but they understand nothing of keeping order and only take action when there is something to 'organise' and when it comes to getting girls. They are hated for their brutality and because they can get away with anything. A few days ago, another OD man in the cafeteria smashed the nasal bone of a young man who wanted to go in and used his foot to keep the door open. The OD man was not punished and still walks free with an arrogant air about him: am I not a hero?

The crowd is boiling internally: 'What a zoo!' 'What a *Wirtschaft*, what a society!' 'Wouldn't you just...' 'Just wait, our time will come too!' Etcetera, etcetera. The pushing continues, the complaining does not end. Old women are being squashed. Children disappear into the chaos: that they do not break, no one understands. OD members, with their stuffed faces, go along and around the heap like wolves around a bunch of horses: where can we drag one out? Eyes filled with hatred and disgust; the people are petrified. Sick people who come for their vegetables are likely to get even more sick thanks to the struggle for some vegetables. A shrill whistle. Pisk, the Basque pirate, the man in charcoal, appears on stage with a few ruffians. He roars a few orders with rolling r's, screams at the crowd; his OD men plunge into the masses, flatly chop the crowd in half at a certain point, chasing the severed part roughly against the wall of the adjacent theatre. Swearing in the crowd. Sighs. Curses.

There: Now the traffic for the cafeteria is taken care of. All those who were in the back are now in front of the door, the rest of them have been mixed up. The elderly, for whom the vegetables were primarily intended, and children who came for their sick parents have been pushed aside, have been trampled underfoot. Pisk oversees the battlefield with an unmoved face; OD men are making dirty jokes to young girls. The crowd waits patiently, powerless, loaded with annoyance, indignation, aversion. Would one still get their turn? Would there be enough vegetables? One waits patiently. One waits patiently leering in the direction of the door, where there seems to be no movement whatsoever. It is maddening how slowly it all goes. OD members are there in their khaki brown tunics or their long blue capes, watching it all in an excruciatingly provocative manner as the rulers of the moment. Untouchable, they are the ruffians of Pisk. By 11 o'clock, the OD announces: the cafeteria is closed until one. Curses. The crowd splits up. I waited exactly an hour and a half. [...][39]

The use of the Camp Police was not limited to the camp. From the beginning of 1943, OD members also had to provide assistance to the occupier far beyond the camp borders. Partly because they carried out this work, the OD was even more criticised.

OD Activities Outside The Camp

Amersfoort, Amsterdam, Apeldoorn and Barneveld are four locations outside the camp where the OD provided their services. The work in Amsterdam took longer than it did in the other cities. As opposed to Amersfoort, Apeldoorn and Barneveld, where the deployment of the OD usually took one day or a few days at most, OD members were sent to Amsterdam for several longer periods, spread over the course of a year. Nevertheless, it is the OD's deployment period in Apeldoorn that can be described as one of the darkest times of the existence of this service group.

Het Apeldoornsche Bosch

On the morning of Wednesday 20 January 1943 David Chajes discovered his service number, 116, on a list attached to a notice board. On this list were the numbers of a total of 102 OD members. This was about 63 percent of the group at the time. David was ordered with the other designated OD members to prepare himself for departure within half an hour. Never before had such a large group been summoned. At 10:00, under the guidance of some SS men and service leader Pisk, they took the train to a destination unknown to them. The purpose of this trip would not have been announced to them in advance either. The train stopped at the station of Apeldoorn, where David and his colleagues had to get out.[40]

After the group was set up in a column, they marched on. Eventually, after a journey of several kilometers, they arrived at the entrance of the Psychiatric Hospital 'Het Apeldoornsche Bosch', located on the Zutphensestraat in Apeldoorn. In addition, the Paedagogium Achisomog was also located here, which provided shelter to Jewish children who were simple minded or had educational problems. This was familiar territory for David, because not only had he lived in Apeldoorn, he had worked for some time as a nurse in the Hospital before the occupation.

Shortly after the OD had arrived, Gemmeker also appeared at the entrance to the facility. He had travelled separately from the group by car to Apeldoorn.[41] Gemmeker had known the purpose of the trip. He had been commissioned by Willy Zöpf to bring a hundred OD men to help with the emptying of the facility and putting on transport of patients and staff in

Apeldoorn.[42] Before Gemmeker arrived in Apeldoorn, he received a message that a mistake had been made with the date and that the train, which was supposed to transport the patients and staff, was not yet ready. The entire action had to be moved to the next day. After consultation with the head of the *Zentralstelle für jüdische Auswanderung*, Aus der Fünten, who was in charge of the evacuation, Gemmeker was able to return to Westerbork. Because the journey back and forth by train would have taken too much time for the group of OD members, the medical director of the establishment, Dr. J. Lobstein, was ordered by Gemmeker to place the group in the establishment and take care of them.

According to David, he and a number of his colleagues offered about a hundred staff members and patients the opportunity to flee that night.[43] Although the figures on the number of flights vary, it can be concluded with certainty that there were patients who actually left the establishment. One of them, the Jewish 21-year-old 'psychopath' Nathan Salomon de Leeuwe, born in Rotterdam, was brought from the building of the Jewish Council at Essenburgsingel 24b to the Police Station Oostervantstraat on 24 January by a Rotterdam Police Officer. He stated that he had been in *Het Apeldoornsche Bosch* for six years and that on Thursday 21 January 1943 he had left by train to Rotterdam without proof of identity and distribution documents. Since his father, who had been living in Rotterdam, turned out to have been deported and since Nathan had no money, he contacted the Jewish Council, which immediately informed the Police. Nathan was transferred to the political service, Group 10, at headquarters. He died on 30 April 1943 in Auschwitz.[44]

For the patients, staff and OD men who remained in Apeldoorn, there was nothing to do but wait for the inevitable evacuation. On Thursday 21 January, at 18:00, six trucks showed up on the premises of the facility. A hundred men from the *Ordnungs und Sicherheitspolizei* got out, hailing from Amsterdam and The Hague. A number of members of the *Ordnungspolizei* cordoned off the area of the Apeldoorn station, where the train with 40 freight wagons was now ready. Aus der Fünten, some staff members and Gemmeker also came to the facility. Preparation for the evacuation began immediately. The German troops closed off the entire area.[45]

The patients were separated from the nursing staff and locked in the pavilions. Pisk called the OD members together and informed them that the facility had to be evacuated and that the OD had to take the patients to the trucks. This instruction did not correspond to the statement made by Gemmeker after the liberation. In this he indicated that a Detachment of the *Schutzpolizei* was present to help with the transport and that 'his' OD 'Detachment was mainly responsible for blocking the area. According to Gemmeker, he and the Detachment had not interfered with loading the patients into the trucks.[46] Whether Gemmeker made this statement deliberately in order to protect the OD is not known. Jacob Boas was very clear about the role of the OD in Apeldoorn. He indicated that Pisk's men, according to testimonies, could have competed with the Nazis with how cruel they were. They would have stormed through the rooms, where they had dragged the patients out of their beds. These patients had not even been given any time to get dressed. They were then pushed into the cold night by the OD members.[47]

The statement by David Chajes partly corresponds to Boas's exposition. David admitted that the OD had been involved in the loading of the patients into the trucks. According to him, this had indeed happened in a brutal manner. Initially, he and his colleagues were able to carefully lay the bedridden patients on the sacks of straw present in the trucks. When the supervising Germans saw this, the OD members were beaten and told to stop it.[48]

Another OD man who wanted to cover a visibly seriously ill patient with a blanket was stopped and told that it was a shame to waste a blanket like this. Eyewitnesses saw that patients who had been carried to the trucks on mattresses were stacked on top of each other in order to save space in the trucks. Before the start of the evacuation, the men of the OD were allowed to disinfect their hands and forearms with a disinfectant. Among those who had to be transported were patients with infectious diseases, such as open TBC. It was clear that the OD had to provide assistance in Apeldoorn because the Germans were afraid of contracting such a contagious disease themselves.[49]

As with the bedridden patients, the 'healthy' patients had the most diverse mental illnesses. They also wore all kinds of clothes. Several patients wore night attire, one person was even completely undressed, while some of them were wearing a straitjacket. Most patients made a dazed impression on David, suggesting that they had been injected with a sedative. The Germans had benefited from this, because if panic had broken out, it would have delayed the entire operation. In addition, it was important that the loading of the 'mobile' patients was done as efficiently as possible, because the trucks had to be full before they left. This group was not treated gently either. The patients were forcibly pressed together, so that as many as possible could be stuffed into the trucks[50].

In addition to the patients from the Hospital, the children from the *Paedagogium Achisomog* also had to get in the trucks. An attempt by a Doctor to claim the children simply had to be raised better and that they were not patients did not change the plans of Aus der Fünten. He declared that the children were antisocial and therefore had to come along. Even a number of healthy Jewish men, women and children who belonged to the Jewish community of Apeldoorn and had been housed in the establishment after the city was 'freed of Jews' were placed between the patients in the trucks[51].

Once the trucks were full, they left for the train. According to David, OD members also had to go with these transports, because they had been ordered to transfer the patients to the wagons. At the train, David tried again to place a sick patient in a wagon with care and again, a German Soldier did not agree with this humane treatment. David was given a rough kick and was ordered to throw the man into the wagon without special treatment. He was later told by his colleagues that the sick patients were stacked on top of each other in the wagons. He himself never witnessed this, although he did see how the wagons were stuffed with people. This would not have been necessary, because there were empty wagons left. After all these observations, David got the impression that the patients were destined to die, because without food and (medical) supervision, and with the way in which they were forced into the train, many would not last long[52]. Nobody kept in mind the condition the patients were in. People with mild mental illnesses were put in cattle wagons among the serious psychopaths.

Around 5:00 AM all 1,069 patients were taken to the train and loaded into the wagons, making the operation almost complete. Only in the main building of the establishment, there were still staff members locked up. They had not been forgotten, because Aus der Fünten approached the group with the question whether the staff members would voluntarily join the patients. 20 people volunteered, but this was not enough. Aus der Fünten himself appointed 30 additional staff members. This group could sit in a passenger car, which was attached to the freight wagons.[53]

The Germans deliberately chose to allow the operation to take place in the middle of the night. Because there was a curfew, everyone was forbidden to go outside without permission. The chance that there were many witnesses to this degrading eviction was therefore nil. Around 7:00 AM, the packed train left and drove straight to Auschwitz. Shortly after the departure, an article already appeared in the illegal magazine *De Oranjekrant*. This short piece supports David's observations:

> [...] These freight wagons were loaded with Jewish lunatics who had been dragged out of their asylum by the Green Police and then simply thrown into the wagons as general goods, on top of, over and through one another. Among these people with mental illnesses, there were dangerous and harmless ones, and chronic and temporary lunatics. Because of the severe mistreatment they had just undergone, these poor souls became totally upset. A terrible scream rose from the wagons and in front of the small bars, the most hideous, distorted faces appeared. This final journey will have been unfathomably terrible for the unfortunate creatures. [...][54]

Unfortunately, the prediction about the consequences of these bad conditions turned out to be accurate, because a number of patients died during the journey. A Jewish group of workers and fanatical SS men were waiting for the survivors at the station in Auschwitz. One person tried to flee via the platform and was shot immediately. Guiding the patients to the gas chambers would have been one of the most obvious next steps, but that did not happen. The work crew had to throw the patients on tip carts and then load them into trucks. In order to make this work as smooth as possible, the SS men used their batons. The trucks drove directly to a pit in which the bodies of the Jews who had died in the gas chambers were burned. The crew, which included Dutch people, had to ensure that the horrific journey would end in the burning pit for the patients who were still alive.[55]

After the departure of the train, the work in Apeldoorn was not yet complete for the OD. The approximately 200 employees left behind in the establishment had to be escorted to Westerbork. Together with a large part of the OD, this transport arrived there on 22 January around 16:00. Some OD members, including David, stayed behind in Apeldoorn. They were instructed to collect all useful goods and bring them to certain classrooms.[56]

According to David, he and his colleagues destroyed these goods, including linen and medical equipment, in such a way that the Germans had no use for them whatsoever. Those Germans still present directly started to plunder the buildings. Then they, like the OD members, proceeded to destroy everything they could. When they were finished with this, it seemed as if a bomb had exploded in the facility.[58]

For those who were left behind, the work was done on 24 January. They returned to the camp in the evening. According to Werner Bloch, who did not participate in the evacuation, his colleagues who had experienced the 'inferno' needed a few days to regain their bearings. A part of the OD did not get much time to rest. Pretty soon after the evacuation, Quartermasters, including members of the *Waffen SS*, went to Apeldoorn to inspect the buildings, which they wanted to use as a recovery site. They will not have been happy with what they found there. On 25 January Pisk was ordered to travel to Apeldoorn again with 50 OD members. Two days later, another 30 OD members, led by the deputy service leader, had to go to Apeldoorn. In Westerbork, a number of stretcher bearers temporarily took over the task of the OD. Pisk and his men had to prevent new looting and prepare the upcoming cleanup.[60]

On 28 January, about 200 Jewish men had to report themselves in the evening in the main hall of Camp Westerbork, including some members of the *Fliegende Kolonne* (FK), who were providing their services for the transports. They got a blue overall and a yellow armband. The next day this group was brought to Apeldoorn. One of the men of the FK kept a diary, in which he described what he experienced in Apeldoorn. During a roll call, Pisk divided the group into teams and all teams received OD members as team leaders. In addition, an unknown number of Gendarmes were present, who had to guard the whole bunch. During the clean-up work, the destruction just continued. Everyone participated in the looting under the motto 'what you do not take, the SS will steal', including the OD men and Gendarmes.[61]

On 2 February 1943 the work in Apeldoorn was probably completed, because then the OD men returned to Westerbork.[62] In June the *Paedagogium Achisomog* was sufficiently renovated, because at that time the Police Officers' School opened its doors.[63]

The 'Kommando Amsterdam'

On 18 January 1943, two days before the first group of OD members travelled to Apeldoorn, 20 OD members left for Amsterdam with as many so-called 'OD stretcher bearers'. A few days before departure, the stretcher bearers had to exercise at the roll call place. In addition, they were taught how to transport sick people. Like the OD, they were given a *green overalls*, along with an OD armband, so that they went to Amsterdam as stretcher bearers of the OD.[64] Two OD members, Hans Eisinger[65] and Heinz Wolf[66], were in charge of this group, which largely consisted of Jewish men who were born and raised in Amsterdam. These men, like the so-called '*Kommando Amsterdam*', had to do the 'dirty' work for the *Zentralstelle für jüdische Auswanderung*, which was based in the city.[67]

Kurzfristige Reisegenehmigung No. 513

Der (die) Jude (Jüdin) **R o s e l a a r , Jechiël**
De Jood (Jodin)

geboren am   **14. August 1920**   in   **Amsterdam**

wohnhaft   **Lager Westerbork**
woonplaats

erhält die Genehmigung unter Mitführung des Passes - Kinderausweises - Arbeitsbuches - der Kennkarte (Bürgerlegitimation)
krijgt de vergunning, vergezeld van Paspoort - Kinderlegitimatie - Werkboek - Identiteitskaart (Burgerlegitimatie)

Nr. **A35/603362**   seinen (ihren) Wohnsitz in der Zeit
zijn (haar) woonplaats in den tijd

vom **18. Januar 1943**   bis   **19. Januar 1943**
van   tot

zu verlassen.   hat die Genehmigung in dieser Zeit die
te verlaten.   Strassenbahn zu benutzen.

Reiseziel   **AMSTERDAM**
Plaats van bestemming

Diese Genehmigung ist nach Ablauf der bewilligten Zeit SOFORT der ausstellenden Stelle zu übergeben bezw. zu übersenden.
Deze vergunning is onmiddellijk na afloop van de toegestane tijd aan de instantie, welke deze uitvaardigde, te overhandigen of
te zenden.

DER BEFELHSHABER

LAGER WESTERBORK, den   **16. Januar 1943**   der Sicherheitspolizei und des SD
für die besetzten Niederländischen Gebiete

LAGER WESTERBORK

Siegel

-Obersturmführer

K 540

Permission for OD man Jechiël Roselaar to travel from Westerbork to Amsterdam.

The *Kommando* was immediately used in Amsterdam to pick up sick and elderly Jews. The first assignment consisted of the emptying of Jewish nursing homes. Under the supervision of the *Ordnungspolizei*, the OD members loaded the elderly, who could barely or not at all walk because of illness or old age, onto stretchers and brought them to the trucks. In general, the Borneokade was the intermediate station. There, the OD men had to transfer the men and women they had picked up into wagons. The train then drove to Westerbork.[68]

The first transport, with about 250 sick Jews, left on the night of 18 to 19 January and arrived at the camp at midday. Until 16 February, the OD was sent almost daily to Amsterdam. The total of 12 transports usually arrived at night in Westerbork and consisted of several hundred Jews each time. The night transport of 10 February had a different composition. With this train, about 150 Jewish orphans were brought to Westerbork from Amsterdam orphanages.[69]

During their stay in Amsterdam, the OD members enjoyed certain privileges, which most Amsterdam Jews had lost some time ago. Despite the curfew, the group was allowed to walk on the street until 22:00. In addition, they were allowed to travel by tram.[70] This latter led to confusion, because the yellow Star of David on the overalls was clearly visible to everyone. After showing a consent form signed by Aus der Fünten, as well as showing they were part of the *Jüdenpolizei*, the journey could usually be continued without further delay. Those who could visit family, friends or acquaintances during their stay in Amsterdam were given permission to spend the night there.[71] If this was not possible, *Die Jüdische Unterkunft*, located at the Jan van Eijckstraat 19, was the alternative. Certain privileges eventually expired, so that the building on the Jan van Eijckstraat became the only permitted residence for all Jews who had to be in Amsterdam or the surrounding areas from Westerbork in connection with a mission. Among the staff of the Jewish residence, which consisted of residents of Camp Westerbork, were three OD members. This small Security Unit was monitoring the place day and night, arranged the roll call and checked the phone calls of the temporary residents. In addition, they kept the card catalogue up to date and filled in the journal.[72]

GEMEENTETRAM-AMSTERDAM.

Amsterdam,   4 Februari 1943.

Houder dezes: Jechiël Roselaar,
Houdster
geboren: 14-8-1920 te Amsterdam,
wonende: Lager Westerbork,
mag, in afwijking van het bepaalde bij kennisgeving A.D. No.92,
op vertoon van het schrijven van den Befehlshaber der Sicherheitspolizei und des SD für die besetzten niederländischen Gebiete d.d.   16 Januari 1943 , in de wagens der Gemeentetram
vervoerd worden tot 16 Februari 1943.

De Directeur,

Permission to travel by tram.

Jechiël Roselaar[73], born in Amsterdam, joined the OD on 18 January as a stretcher bearer. Before the occupation began, he worked as an accountant at an accounting firm in Amsterdam. Because of anti-Jewish measures, he lost this job and, like all unemployed Jewish men, had to go to a labour camp in the second half of 1942. Jechiël ended up in a camp near the village of Geesbrug in Drenthe.[74] There he had to work on the land and help with the construction of a concrete shoring along the canal Coevorden-Zwinderen, together with a few hundred colleagues.[75] Jechiël may have come into contact with a bridge guard from Geesbrug while he was there, because he received food packages through him that his wife sent to the address of the bridge guard. Jechiël married Eva Roselaar on 5 August 1942. It is likely that Jechiël was already in Geesbrug at that time, because Eva remembered that he was given leave and returned to Amsterdam one day before the wedding. In Amsterdam the raids had started and only those who had an exemption were safe. Eva received such an exemption because she sewed black mourning gowns for Germany as a seamstress in a workshop.

At the beginning of October 1942, the Jewish men in the labour camps had to leave for Westerbork. On Saturday 3 October it was the turn of those in Camp Geesbrug. The men walked in a long line to Hoogeveen, more than 10 kilometres away. A packed train then took them to Hooghalen. Once again, a considerable distance had to be travelled on foot before the group finally reached the camp. Jechiël saw the opportunity to join the OD as a 'new' camp resident. Because he was married and Eva had an exemption, he was able to stay with her during his work in Amsterdam.[76]

On 16 February 1943, 31 of the 40 groups of the '*Kommando* Amsterdam' returned in Westerbork at the same time as a night transport. According to the OD report, two members of the commando unit were missing.[77] The missing ones, who turned out to have fled, were Ernest Frank[78] and Jechiël. Shortly before the group left for Westerbork, he told Eva that she had to come to Westerbork too as her exemption was about to expire. Eva replied that he could go if he wanted, but that she would not go with him; she chose to go into hiding. After a brief consideration, Jechiël decided to go with her. After they quickly packed some stuff, they left Amsterdam, with Bussum as their destination. An uncle and aunt of Eva lived there, to whom they could turn for the time being. However, this stay was short lived, because they had to flee and look for another safe house because of a raid by the *Ordnungspolizei*. Together they left by train to Assen and then to Geesbrug. There they knocked on the door of the bridge guard Jechiël had met, asking if he could help them get to a safe house. A son of the bridge guard worked for a farmer in Nieuw Zwinderen and after they had discussed it, the couple could turn to this farmer.

In the countryside, the Roselaars got to rest for a while. They were even able to spend their day usefully. Jechiël helped the farmer on the land and Eva sewed, among other things, a wedding gown for the maid. Three weeks later, this relatively quiet and normal life came to an end. After the Mayor of Gramsbergen informed the farmer one evening of an impending invasion, presumably as a result of treason, Jechiël and Eva had to leave the farm that same evening. Both returned to the bridge guard. There someone from the resistance was ready to take Eva to a new safe house; there was no place for Jechiël at this address. Eva advised Jechiël to go to friends of her parents in Zwolle. However, he was only allowed to stay there for two days, because these people were too afraid to hide Jews in their homes.

Jechiël wandered around for a while after this. He finally decided to return to the farm in Nieuw Zwinderen. The farmer's wife had become cautious after the raid. She immediately called the Police saying she was being harassed by a Jewish man. Two Dutch Policemen came to the farm and arrested Jechiël, who was then taken back to Westerbork as an S-Case. On 18 May 1943 he went on transport to Sobibor, where he died three days later. Eva did experience the liberation.[79] Ernest Frank went into hiding in Utrecht after his escape from Amsterdam and made it to the liberation as well.[80] To prevent escapes during a permitted stay outside the camp, Gemmeker issued a bail. This measure also applied to the OD, because when an OD man left the camp, five family members would be chosen to be put on transport if he did not return. If there were not enough family members present in the camp, the missing number was supplemented by fellow OD members. Fate determined who qualified for this.[81]

Meanwhile, not all Jewish institutions had been evacuated in Amsterdam yet. That is why the strength of the OD command was increased. On

1 March the OD's stretcher bearers had to assist the occupier in the emptying of the building 'De Joodse Invalide' (the Jewish invalid) on the Weesperplein. Since this institution had been left alone until that date, it was seen as a safe place, so many Jews had volunteered there. The Jewish Council warned them in time for the imminent evacuation, which allowed a large part of this group and the other staff to flee. However, the disabled residents did not stand a chance. They were removed from the building with the help of the command.[82] According to a witness, this was not always done in a gentle way. For example, he saw that elderly residents were thrown down the stairs. The story does not tell whoever was responsible for this.[83]

That there was indeed some degree of violence is proved by Ernest Frank's report. He described how things went during the first action in which he participated:

[...] Our car stopped for the first time in the Zuider Amstellaan. With a snarl, the accompanying SS man ordered us to get out and he told two of us, Ab Velleman and me, to follow him. After consulting a list, he rang the bell persistently at a certain address, and when the door was finally opened, he stormed up the stairs, three steps at a time. He shouted at us to follow him and soon we were in a neat salon, where a little lady of over 60 years was shivering in bed with fear. The German, who later became known to us as Grünberg, pulled out her call from a pile of papers, barked at her to show her ID and roared (without reason) that she had to be down in the car within two minutes. The poor woman, completely helpless, burst into tears, sobbing and asking him to let her wait for her husband, who had just gone out to run an errand. Then came a burst of anger from the German; he screamed, frothing at the mouth, and repeated his threat, that if she was not downstairs within two minutes, he would personally throw her out of the window.

We were pale and trembled with fear and anger at such a display of sadism and roaring. As we understood that we had to help, we tried to calm the woman with a few words and lift her out of the bed. But we encountered strong resistance. It was perfectly logical that she saw in us two enemies and we did not succeed in calming her down. Grünberg had now walked through the house, broken open cabinets and drawers and had thrown everything through the room. Indeed, he came back after a few minutes and when he saw that we had not progressed much, he drew his revolver and began to threaten with the weapon and with violent curses and roars. I must confess I was terrified and my colleague also looked grim. What was left for us to do, other than to grab the lady by her arms and legs and carry her to the stairs like that? But the little woman kicked, bit and scratched, though the only result was that we were unable to carefully carry out the transport, like we had wanted.

Hounded by a madman, we could not pay attention to our patient and this descent appeared a lot like leading a pig to slaughter. Without luggage, without blankets, only in her nightwear, we had to drag the poor lady into the car, where she drew the attention of the surrounding inhabitants with her miserable screams. When we closed the door, it became too much for Velleman and he started crying. Immediately I gave him a strong slap in the face, after which he quickly got over his hysterical mood. We decided to make

An OD man during a raid in Amsterdam.

the best of it. I must confess that I was deeply ashamed of lending myself for such inhumane work, but we did not know it in advance either. [...][84]

On the night of 2 to 3 March the train brought 285 Jewish invalids and nursing staff to Westerbork. Of this group, 116 people went directly to the Camp Hospital. After the Dutch Israeli Hospital on the Nieuwe Keizersgracht and the adjacent home for the elderly had been emptied on March 3, the *Kommando* Amsterdam was temporarily disbanded. With the last transport of 6 March, in addition to the 40 men, Hans Eisinger and Heinz Wolf returned to the camp.[85]

On 25 May 1943, 50 OD members left in the afternoon to Amsterdam, including Hans Margules, again led by Hans Eisinger. According to the OD report, the purpose and duration of this trip was unknown. Upon arrival, it became clear quickly why the men of the OD had been sent to Amsterdam. A big raid took place in the centre and in the eastern part of the city the next day. During this raid, the OD had to assist the German and Dutch Police. After the entire neighbourhood was blocked off, every house was investigated. The Jews found were taken away. According to Hans Margules, he had to collect the luggage with the other OD men and load it into trucks, because the trains were not designed to hold that much stuff. The OD would have had nothing to do with the arrest of Jews.[86] Hans was probably wrong, because the task of the OD also consisted of getting Jews out of the house who, due to illness or old age, found it difficult to move or were no longer able to walk. The task of the OD was also to guide the arrested Jews to the trams. These trams brought the Jews to an area of the Muiderpoort station, which served as a gathering place.[87]

Often after many hours of waiting, the packed trains left for Westerbork. These transports caused a busy period in the camp. Until the night of 27 May, five trains entered the camp, which delivered a total of 4,353

OD men on the sports fields of the Amsterdam Olympiaplein, where they helped the Police in the raid, 20 June 1943.

Amsterdam Jews. Four days later, the work was finished for 37 OD members in Amsterdam. They returned to Westerbork. Hans and Heinz remained with 14 OD members in Amsterdam.[88]

On the night of Sunday 20 June, around 2:00 AM, 20 members of the *Fliegende Kolonne* and 100 OD members received a call without prior notice to get ready. Shortly thereafter, the entire group left for Amsterdam. They probably arrived just in time to assist German troops and members of the auxiliary Police, which mainly consisted of National Socialists, in the last major raid. In the early morning, the south of the city and part of the east were blocked off. There were still relatively many Jews in these districts, who had been left alone during previous raids. On that Sunday they were instructed to report to nearby gathering points. These included the Daniël Willinkplein, Olympiaplein, Sarphatipark and Polderweg. From these places, trucks and trams departed to the Muiderpoort station. Some groups were escorted to the station on foot. The task of the OD was the same as during the raid on 25 May: carrying sick people and invalids and guiding this group and other Jews to various gathering places and to the station. On the day of the raid, the first transport arrived in Westerbork; there were two more the next day. The total number of people taken in the raid amounted to 5,550 Jews. On the third train, which arrived in the camp around 8:40 AM and which had 1,605 people on it, there were also the OD members. Part of this group was immediately deployed in the handling of the transport after arrival. This work lasted until 20:00.[89] On 29 September 1943 the last raid took place in Amsterdam. Although most of the work had been done, a command of 15 OD members still left for the capital city the next day as stretcher bearers.[90]

The removal of the last Jews meant that Amsterdam had become *Judenrein*. This also brought an end to the work of the Jewish Council.[91] The command, which had left for Amsterdam after the last raid and was once again led by Hans Eisinger, was ordered to guard the buildings abandoned by the Jewish Council. Around 12 October, Hans suddenly received a telephone message that he had to return to Westerbork. The reason for this order was not disclosed. After arriving at the camp, Hans first wanted to visit his girlfriend, Hannelore Cahn, but she turned out not to be present in her barracks. Partly because of her job as a dancer at the camp shows, Hannelore and Hans had a more or less protected status. Hans's hope that she was staying elsewhere in the camp quickly disappeared. He heard from the other members of the barracks that she was missing. When Hans reported to the OD in the OD barracks, this information turned out to be correct. The day he had left for Amsterdam, Hannelore went missing. An investigation inside and outside the camp produced nothing. Hannelore seemed to have fled.

This assumption was correct, because she had escaped from the camp with help from outside. The Jewish actor Rob de Vries, to whom she had been engaged in Amsterdam and who had joined the resistance, helped Hannelore escape. After considerable preparation, Rob was able to drive into the camp as a temporary employee of the railways alongside the driver of the mail train. After a failed attempt, Rob managed to get Hannelore to hide in the train, and thus the escape was successful. After a nerve wracking train journey, which ended in Amsterdam, Rob took Hannelore to a friend, where she could go into hiding.

Hans had to show up in front of Pisk, Schlesinger and Gemmeker. The fact that Hannelore went missing the day he left for Amsterdam raised questions and did not work in his favour. Gemmeker held him responsible for the disappearance of his girlfriend. If she did not return to the camp, Hans would have to go on the next transport. During one of the conversations, he indicated that he might be able to figure out where Hannelore was staying. First, he started an investigation within the camp. From a fellow barracks member of Hannelore, he heard that she had once spoken about a friend in Amsterdam. She also knew part of the address. Hans was allowed to return to Amsterdam and continued his search there. With the clues he got, he found her at the safe house. After some effort, he managed to convince Hannelore to return to the camp with him. On 5 November she was on the train again, with as final destination the place from which she had fled in such a spectacular way less than a month ago.[92]

According to the OD report, number 22 returned to the camp that day around 22:00 with his bride.[93] Before Hans had left for Amsterdam, Gemmeker had promised not to punish Hannelore, a promise the Camp Commander kept. Hannelore and Hans married and stayed in the camp until after the liberation.[94] After his return, Hans was no longer sent to Amsterdam. This did happen with many other OD members, because despite the fact that most Jews had been transported from Amsterdam, a group of the OD remained seconded to that city. From the end of March 1944 onwards, the OD men of the *Kommando* Amsterdam were relieved every other month. Since the OD report was kept only until 20 May 1944, it is not clear when the *Kommando* was disbanded and what its task was.

Other Activities Outside The Camp

On 10 June 1943 Pisk compiled a list with the names of 24 OD members, including Albert Moses and some other long time colleagues, such as Werner Bloch and Peter Margules. Under the leadership of Pisk, this group had to go to Camp Amersfoort to assist in picking up 572 residents.[95]

This group consisted of men, women and children, most of which had dual nationality. Because the investigations on this subject had not yet been completed, the group had been brought to Amersfoort a month earlier from Westerbork for a short period of time. As a result, there was space in Westerbork for the accommodation of the Jews collected in Amsterdam. There was no shortage of space in Amersfoort yet, because after a temporary closure, the camp had been reused as *Erweitertes Polizeigefängnis*.[96] The task of the OD likely consisted mainly of guiding the group during the return trip. There would hardly have been any fear of escapes, since this group did not yet qualify for transportation to the camps in Eastern Europe because of their special status.

On 29 September 1943 the alarm signal for the OD was sounded around 4:15 AM. The men immediately came into action. Since the reason for the alarm was unknown, they speculated about it among themselves. It was suspected that another transport from Amsterdam was approaching. This proved to be partly correct, because in the afternoon and evening, a number of transports arrived from Amsterdam. However, never before had the alarm signal been sounded so early in the morning. The real reason had to do with a special assignment outside the camp, for which 50 OD members were selected.[97] Before this command left the camp at about 6:30 AM under Pisk's leadership, together with 170 members of the *Notbereitschaft* (NB), Pisk addressed his men. During this speech, he warned his subordinates. Any person who violated the rules or was not disciplined enough would be sent to Poland.[98]

The trip ended in Barneveld. There, the command will initially have been deployed to accompany a special group of Jewish men, women and children. This so-called Barneveld group, which occupied a privileged position within the Jewish community and which consisted of more than 650 people, had been housed at two different locations in Barneveld since December 1942. The largest group, of more than 460 people, had been staying in a castle called De Schaffelaar, while the rest had been housed in the De Biezen house. Although there was an internment and limitation of privacy, and there were guards in the buildings, the Barneveld group seemed to have more privileges than the Jews in Westerbork. For example, they were allowed to bring their own musical instruments, books, beds and other furniture. However, they could not have access to it, because these things were locked up in egg sheds in Barneveld. Both groups owed this special treatment mainly to two Dutch officials. One of them was the Secretary General of the Ministry of the Interior, Frederiks.[99]

At the time when anti-Jewish measures succeeded one another rapidly in the Netherlands, Frederiks contacted the German authorities in the interest of the Jewish community. Since Rauter was mainly responsible for 'the Jewish question', Frederiks first knocked on his door. This had no results, but Frederiks did not let it go and contacted a rival of Rauter: *Generalkommissar zur besonderen Verwendung* Fritz Schmidt. This tactic, whether deliberately chosen or not, was successful, because Schmidt granted Frederiks permission to exempt some Jews from deportation. After Seyss-Inquart had also given permission, the plan could be implemented.[100] Initially, the 'List-Frederiks' consisted of five Jewish friends, but the number soon grew, giving more Jews the coveted exemption stamp in their identity certificate. The selection criteria for a place on the list were at first rather arbitrary and not strict. Acquaintances and those with a special position, such as artists and scientists, had a good chance of getting on the list.[101]

A colleague of Frederiks, Prof. Dr. Jan van Dam, Secretary General of the Ministry of Education, Culture and Science, copied the plan and compiled a list himself. Both lists were merged over time. Because the Jewish community soon knew that these lists existed, more and more requests began coming in rapidly. As a result, the selection criteria had to be made a little stricter. Jews who had a special note on their card in the card catalogue of the *Zentralstelle für Jüdische Auswanderung* were placed on the lists, even when they did not ask for it.

Despite the promise that the persons who were on the lists would not be deported and could stay in the Netherlands, Frederiks came up with a plan B, just to be sure. According to him, the likelihood of the group of Jews being safe was increased if they were to be housed in a Municipality in the east of the country. There were certain conditions attached to the plan. A large building had to be available and the Mayor was expected to be of the old school. Barneveld met these conditions.[102] As Schmidt agreed as representative of the occupier, the plan could be implemented. Most of the chosen Jews responded to the call and departed from December 1942 onwards to Castle De Schaffelaar in Barneveld. When this location was full, the De Biezen house was used as an annex.[103]

On 29 September Frederiks learned via Rauter that the Barneveld group would still be brought to Westerbork and that this had already been started. Frederiks could no longer go to Schmidt for help or complaints, because he had died in France under suspicious circumstances. Complaining to Rauter did not help, because according to him, the action met the agreements, because they remained in the Netherlands.[104] The group had little time to get ready for the trip. They were not allowed to take suitcases with them; these would be sent to Westerbork later on. The *Ordnungspolizei* was in charge of carrying out the action. There were likely not enough men to cordon off the areas entirely, because 22 people managed to escape through a fence that had been left unguarded.[105]

The other 637 Barnevelders arrived in Westerbork at about 21:40 hours, together with 42 OD men. The registration and completion of this transport lasted until 5:00 AM of the next morning. Eight OD members and all 170 members of the NB remained in Barneveld. They were ordered to check the suitcases. The valuable goods had to be removed from them. This work may have taken several days.

On the night of 2 October, three OD men and 61 members of the NB returned to the camp.[106] The remaining group had to help with the emptying of the buildings and the sheds that had been filled with furniture. During the work, the OD members, and possibly the members of the NB, could not resist the temptation to get their hands on the stuff of their peers who had been taken away, despite Pisk's warning. In any event, the men would have had no difficulty with devouring the various types of alcoholic beverages and delicacies, which were virtually not available in the Netherlands anymore, unless one was willing to pay large sums. In addition, clothing items, including almost new costumes, proved to be in demand among the men. The clothing they wore under the overalls, clothing that was mostly in poor condition, was exchanged for these costumes. As the Supervisors participated themselves, the OD members and members of the NB were free to do as they pleased. On 7 October they returned to the camp.[107]

Notbereitschaft

The NB, which participated in the work in Barneveld, will mainly have been there to support the OD, because this Reserve Service was set up on 1 May 1943. This date was not chosen by chance; it had to do with events outside the camp. Although the Dutch population remained relatively calm during the initial stage of the occupation, the activities of the resistance took on greater forms over time. The occupiers thought that with warnings and harsh measures they could suppress the resistance, but that did not turn out to be the case. Because the occupying forces mainly accused former Dutch Soldiers of participating in the resistance, it was announced on 29 April 1943 in the newspapers that all former Dutch demobilised Soldiers would be taken away again as prisoners of war. This announcement caused a lot of unrest among the population.

The first reaction came from Hengelo. That is where the staff of most large companies went on strike. The strike spread to other places in Twente. The German authorities were concerned that the strike actions, known as the April to May strike, would spread over the rest of the Netherlands and spread to other European countries. That is why the disturbances had to be combated by all possible means. By taking measures, such as curfew, the occupying forces hoped to limit the strikes to the province of Twente. The reports of the next morning indicated that this had not been successful, as the strike had spread to large parts of the country. In the afternoon, the so-called 'politiestandrecht', also known as a summary execution, was proclaimed for the provinces of Overijssel, Limburg, Noord-Holland and Gelderland, which meant that 'suspects' could be shot without trial. One day later, the measure was enforced in the whole country. Due to the massive number of arrests and the carrying out of death sentences, the strike ended after a few days.[108]

On 1 May, Gemmeker announced through a *Lager-Sonderbefehl* that the summary execution also applied to the camp. In addition to this measure, he stipulated that curfew would be set between 20:00 and 6:00 from that moment onwards. No one was allowed to leave the barracks unless they had been given special permission to do so. Furthermore, the order stated that the NB had been appointed to support the OD. The NB's instructions, as well as those of the OD, had to be followed. The alarm signal for fire and air threats would also be used when the NB came into action. The men of this emergency service were given blue overalls as uniform and a white armband with the letters NB.[109] It was pointed out several times that an NB man was only allowed to appear in this uniform when there was an emergency. At any other time, he was not allowed to wear the overalls and armbands.[110]

For the formation of three NB companies, a large number of Jewish men was appointed, because each Company consisted of 112 men. The leadership came into the hands of the German Dr. S.A.J. Wachtel, who had also acted in Westerbork as a representative of the Committee for Jewish Refugees and of the Jewish Council. To promote discipline and camaraderie, the men had to exercise regularly under the directions of the OD and participate in practical exercises. A few days after its creation, such an exercise already took place, in which all three companies participated. During the exercise, the men were instructed to shield barracks 55 to 73 from the remaining barracks due to unrest among some of the residents.[111]

Armband Notbereitschaft.

It was not all just practice. For example, the Second Company of the NB had to move out in the early days, because several farms in the vicinity of the camp were on fire. If there were not enough OD members in the camp to supervise the incoming and departing transports, the NB or part of it was also-called on.[112] Because the emergency personnel were only called on when needed, they generally had another job to do during daytime, in contrast to the OD members. Most men probably were not queueing for a position at the NB. This is evidenced by a call received by Salomon Boas from Wachtel in mid-December 1943. According to the call, Salomon had to report to the NB service at the roll call place in front of the OD barracks the day after he received the message. If he could not appear for health reasons, he had to be able to provide a certificate from a Doctor. Staying away for no reason meant that an investigation would be started. This was therefore clearly not something for which people volunteered.[113]

Exemption

Serving in the NB would have been more attractive if the residents had been granted the coveted exemption, also known as *Sperre or Zurückstellung*, from deportation. The exemption system was introduced when the persecution of the Jews in the Netherlands began, with the Jewish Council being given permission from the occupier to grant these exemptions. Especially the Jews belonging to a certain category, such as those in a mixed marriage, Jews working for the German (war) industry, and the employees of the Jewish Council, were eligible for this. As the Jewish Council was allowed to select its own staff, it drew up a list of 35,000 Jews who were eligible for an exemption. The occupiers found this number too high and gave permission for only half. The selection and the exemption procedure would not have been entirely flawless. There would have been corruption and nepotism, causing chaotic circumstances at the Jewish Council offices.[114]

Those who were lucky received the exemption stamp in their identity documents. In return, some categories of exempted persons had to work for the Jewish Council or the occupying forces, thereby contributing to a greater or lesser extent to keeping the deportation or war machine running. The number of the stamp showed to which category someone belonged. The numbers 60,000 to 80,000 were reserved for the so-called *Rüstungsjuden*. This stamp was given to the Jewish men and women who worked in the clothing, fur, or diamond industry.[115] The numbers 80,000 to 100,000 were reserved for members of the Jewish Council, while those in a mixed marriage received the following series of numbers: 100,000 to 110,000[116].

The exemptions did not serve as a definitive safeguard. According to the text in the stamp, its owner was exempted *bis auf weiteres* (until further notice). This had been the intention of the occupier since the introduction of the exemption system. It never intended to keep the Jewish community alive, not even part of it. The Netherlands also had to become *Judenrein*. That is why the trains continued to go to Westerbork. The number of Jews living in villages and towns was decreasing, with as result that the Jewish Council had to reduce its workforce and that exemptions were lost. Those who exercised one of the specific professions turned out not to be so indispensable, since their exemption was withdrawn over time. The loss of the exemption had another disadvantage: in Westerbork, the persons from different ranks, who had formerly been given an exemption, were generally admitted as ordinary residents in the camp community. A position in one of the service groups could ensure that someone was again granted an exemption and a privileged position. Often immediately after arrival, the struggle for a stamp on the camp card began.

These so-called Z stamps (for *Zurückstellung*) were initially blue or green; the red colour came later. Each colour had a certain meaning. The blue 'Z' had a more general character than the two others, because this stamp was meant for several groups. Members of the Jewish Council, the Barneveld Group, the baptised Jews and the foreign Jews were eligible for this

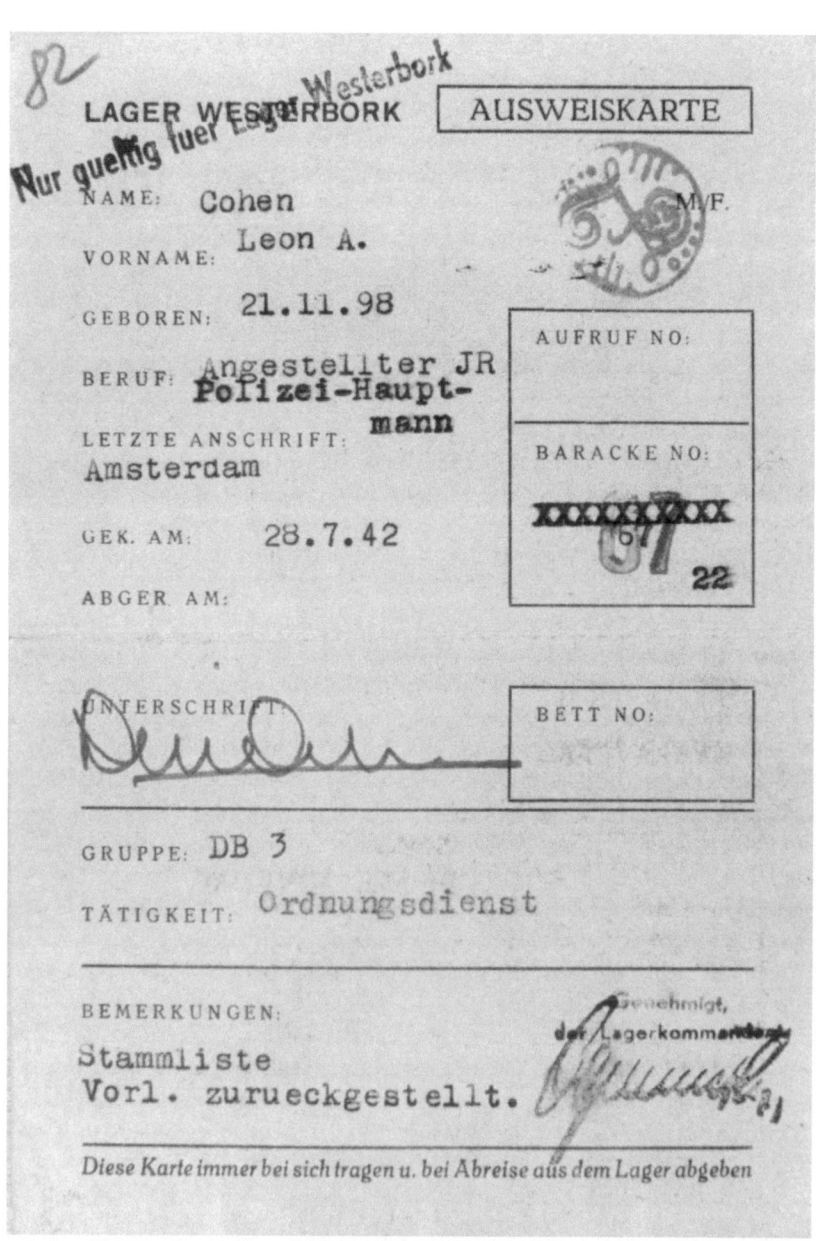

LAGER WESTERBORK   AUSWEISKARTE

Nur queltig fuer Lager Westerbork

82

NAME: Cohen   M/F.

VORNAME: Leon A.

GEBOREN: 21.11.98

BERUF: Angestellter JR   AUFRUF NO:
Polizei-Haupt-
mann

LETZTE ANSCHRIFT: BARACKE NO:
Amsterdam

                                           XXXXXXXXXX
GEK. AM: 28.7.42   67
                                                    22
ABGER. AM:

UNTERSCHRIFT   BETT NO:

GRUPPE: DB 3

TÄTIGKEIT: Ordnungsdienst

BEMERKUNGEN: Genehmigt,
                                           der Lagerkommandant,
Stammliste
Vorl. zurueckgestellt.

Diese Karte immer bei sich tragen u. bei Abreise aus dem Lager abgeben

Camp card of Léon Cohen with the stamp of exemption.

exemption. The stamp with the green colour, also known as 'the work stamp', was given to residents when they were included in the labour process and performed an important function in it, such as the nursing staff of the Camp Hospital. A red stamp initially offered the best protection. This exemption was granted to the old residents (*Alte Kampinsassen*). This group consisted of persons who had been living in the camp since before 15 July 1942. They were later placed on the so-called *Stammliste*. These residents had helped build up the camp and therefore enjoyed more prestige and protection.[117]

In addition to an exemption, the stamps provided even more advantages. On 24 March 1943 Gemmeker announced in camp order 19 that smoking in the camp was allowed only for the 'carriers' of the red and blue 'Z stamps'. Three days later, another privilege was added: the owners of the same stamps were allowed to have 250 guilders. This amount of money could be sent to them from outside the camp. In addition, they were given the opportunity to send 10 guilders once a month. Larger sums had to be authorised first. All other newcomers had to hand in all their money at the support centre of the bank Lippmann, Rosenthal & Co. They were not allowed to possess and/or receive money. In mid May 1943 it was also announced that curfew for the exempted persons did not start until 22:00, while the other residents had to be inside at 21:00. Because of these favours, the exempted ones became a special and even elitist group within the camp. Because the OD members, depending on their background, received one of the three stamps on their camp card, they also belonged to this group. As a result, it was attractive for the women in the camp population to start a relationship with one of them and get married as soon as possible, because the wife of an exempted person was generally also given a stamp.

As far as is known, more than 10 OD men had a marriage certificate drawn up at the Assistant Secretary of the civil registry in the camp. In some cases, a marriage could not be arranged on time. This was true for Ernst Rosendorff and his future wife Henny Nol. Both signed the prenuptials in the camp. The final wedding ceremony could not take place, because Henny had already been put on transport. She died in Auschwitz on 31 July 1944[118].

For those who did have enough time to get married, things changed immediately. Netty Kater, the wife of OD man Maurits Beetz, later said that there was not always an exuberant love affair or love at first sight. However, obtaining an exemption could have a positive effect on a relationship and was an incentive to quickly arrange a marriage. When Netty arrived at the camp, she was still married to another Jewish man. He was no good, according to her, nor was he staying in the camp, so she divorced him. This could, like marriage, also be arranged in the camp. Whether she knew Maurits at that point, she did not know. She initially thought Maurits was a nice man who knew a lot and helped her with certain things. The contact between the two slowly grew into a relationship. In order to stay together, Maurits and Netty decided to marry in 1944.

In addition to some certainty, the couple was offered a residence in the camp. Two couples could be accommodated in this house, as it consisted of two separate rooms. Each room had a kitchenette, a sleeping area and a living area. Although the cottages were small, it was a world of difference from the barracks, where Netty had stayed before. She enjoyed much more privacy and did not have to stand in line for a visit to the toilet. Netty could also enjoy her night's sleep because she was not kept awake by screaming and pacing barracks members anymore.[119] Like Hannelore Cahn and Hans Eisinger, the couple Beetz-Kater remained in the camp until after the liberation. This was only reserved for a small group, because most of the exempted persons eventually had to go on transport anyway.

In the camp order of 7 July 1943, which concerned the reorganisation of the camp, Gemmeker also had a message for the exempted persons. First of all, he announced that the stamps of all residents, with the exception of those with a blue 'Z', were no longer valid. The holders of a green 'Z' were therefore no longer safe. In addition to the blue 'Z', a new group was formed, consisting of a maximum of 1,623 men and women between 14 and 65 year old. They had to be able to be fully deployed in the labour process.

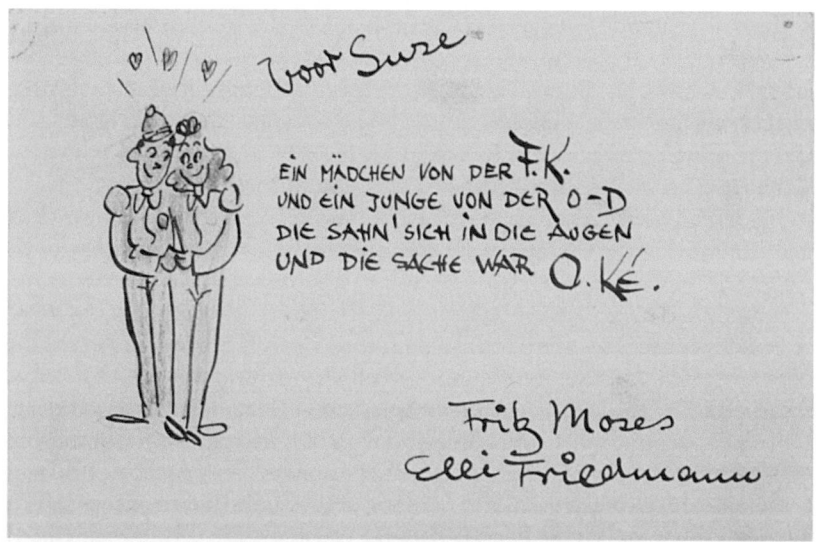

Various relationships arose between OD men and female camp residents.

The residents of the new group received a red 'Z' on the camp card. The distribution took place among the various service groups. The OD was granted 80 exemptions. Because 117 OD men were still employed in the camp in August, some of them entered the 'danger zone'. The remaining stamps could be withdrawn at any time, so that the owner had to go on transport, even though he was part of the OD.[120]

OD Members On Transport

Among the transports that departed from Westerbork, there were 27 transports with which one or more OD members were deported. Of these, 11 trains drove to Auschwitz. The German Ernst Adam[121] and Otto Max Mayer[122], who resided in Westerbork from the beginning of October 1942, were the first OD members to be put on transport. They had to go on the 38th transport, which left to Auschwitz on Tuesday 24 November 1942 with more than 700 Jews aboard. Both went in a different direction during the selection. Otto, 51 year old, was murdered in the gas chambers three days later. Ernst, 6 years younger than Otto, was considered sufficiently capable of carrying out work. He came through the selection and probably had to go to a labour camp. There he lasted 16 months, but eventually he died somewhere in the middle of Europe at the end of March 1944.

For many, work meant hope for a better future. This was not always true, because some of the OD members employed died after two months due to malnutrition, illness, exhaustion or abuse. The rest, who seemed stronger, eventually had to give up the battle as well. Of the 29 OD members deported to Auschwitz, eight suffered the same fate as Otto. They were selected for the gas chambers immediately after arrival. From Auschwitz, no OD man returned alive. The same was true for at least 44 OD men who arrived at the Polish Extermination Camp Sobibor with 8 different transports from Westerbork.[123]

In addition to Auschwitz and Sobibor, trains with OD members left to Theresienstadt and to the Bergen-Belsen Concentration Camp in northern Germany. If one of these two camps was the (temporary) final destination, there was a greater chance of survival. Of the seven OD men who were brought to Bergen-Belsen with three different transports, three were able to endure a difficult period and lived to see the liberation. One of these three survivors was David Chajes. Together with his wife, two daughters and more than 200 other residents, he was brought to Bergen-Belsen on 15 March 1944. According to daughter Peppie, despite the fact that it was against the rules, her father had spoken with Gemmeker in Westerbork about the fact that he and his family preferred to go to Theresienstadt. Gemmeker advised him to go to Bergen-Belsen anyway. Instead of on a freight train, the Chajes family left Camp Westerbork in a normal passenger car. The journey was not without danger, as trains were a willing prey for allied aircraft.

Eventually, the transport reached its final destination after three days. SS men with shepherd dogs were waiting for the newcomers in Bergen-Belsen. Because some children had signs of polio, the entire group had to be quarantined for the first six weeks; then they were transferred to the main camp. This is where the Chajes family met a cousin of the Mother. She looked like a walking skeleton and described the camp as a living hell. It was not long before the newcomers themselves felt how hard life in the camp was. The food turned out to be bad and very limited. Because of overcapacity, two residents had to sleep in one bed, on a mattress minimally filled with straw and under a thin blanket. The roll call continued regardless of the weather and sometimes lasted five hours. Everyone had to show up for this, even if he/she was old and/or ill. If someone was unable to go himself, he was taken out of the barracks by the guards and put in line. After the roll call, a hard and long working day followed for most residents.

Because of the heavy work, David got lumbago, so he could not get out of bed. However, this was not a valid reason not to go to work, and guards therefore dragged David out of bed. They then took him to a pit that had to be filled by night time. If he failed to do this, they threatened to bury David alive in this pit. There was likely insufficient supervision, so David could return to his barracks after much effort. However, this was not the end of the suffering. Guards often loved to mistreat residents without cause. David also got his turn: an SS Officer grabbed a chair and hit David several times, causing him to get some heavily bleeding wounds.

Because of the approaching front, the situation changed in the first week of April 1945. Those who were still able to walk had to leave the camp and were taken to a train with three wagons. Daughter Peppie was too sick and too weak to walk that distance. Luckily she could ride along on a cart, so that David's whole family was in one of the wagons. The destination was Theresienstadt, but because this camp could not be reached, the train, with a total of 2,500 Jews, drove aimlessly between the front lines for two weeks under the guidance of German Soldiers. That is why this transport is also-called 'the lost transport'. David was not the only OD member who was on this train. His colleague Arnold Alfons Spitzer[124] was also required to join him. On 23 April the guards left the train in the town of Tröbitz, located between Leipzig and Dresden. There, the prisoners were soon liberated by Soldiers of the Russian Army. The constant going back and forth took its toll, because about 550 people did not survive the journey. In Tröbitz prisoners also died later on from the effects of the infectious disease typhus, including Arnold Spitzer.[125]

After several transports had already left Westerbork, it was reported for the first time on 17 April 1943 in the OD report that OD men would be put on transport. According to the registration, 18 OD members had to go to the town of Terezin, 60 kilometres north of the Czech capital Prague. Terezin had been renamed by the Germans as Theresienstadt.[126] During the Wannsee conference, the decision was made to make Theresienstadt a special Concentration Camp. Of the two forts that made up the town, the largest was put into use as a ghetto. The small fortress served as a Police Prison for the Gestapo of Prague.[127]

The intention was to house in the ghetto the elderly German Jews and Jews who had been severely injured or who had received a high distinction during the First World War as a German Soldier at the front. Soon this group was expanded with Jews who had made themselves useful for Germany.[128] Because of its special character, Theresienstadt could be used perfectly for the propaganda apparatus of the Third Reich. By acting like this Jewish city was a paradise for Jews or a spa for the older German Jews, the German Government wanted to show that, contrary to the many negative reports, it did treat the Jews well. Theresienstadt would be Hitler's gift to the Jews.[129] That is why it had to be seen as a special camp for special Jews. The fact that 80 OD members were brought there seemed a logical step in view of their function in Westerbork.

On the evening of 20 April 1943, around 22:00, 196 residents were selected in Westerbork and temporarily housed in barracks 93. Most of them belonged to the special category of Jews. Among this group, there were at least 15 OD members. Two of them had the Dutch nationality, while the others were former refugees. Because they had all been staying in Westerbork only since May 1942, no one fell under the category 'old residents'. OD man Albert Sachs and his wife were also selected that evening. Their daughter Friedl stayed behind in Westerbork, because she was over 15 year old, but she followed later.[130]

On Tuesday 4 May, two weeks after Albert's train had left Westerbork, a number of OD members had to go on transport. This time, eight OD men and their families were among the 1,200 people. With the exception of a German couple, this OD group consisted of Dutch Jews. Because they were not part of any of the special groups, the train took them to Sobibor. There, probably immediately upon arrival, they were killed together with all their family members in the gas chambers on 7 May.[131]

As all the exemptions had been withdrawn, the OD members with a green stamp on their camp card were given the opportunity to go along with the transport of 18 January 1944 to Theresienstadt. If they did not, they also lost their exemption, and then they could be sent to any camp. A group of 32 OD members responded to this call and left 'voluntarily' on 18 January to Theresienstadt. According to the OD report, from 25 February onwards, there was no OD man left in Westerbork with an exemption, because in the long run, all exemptions lost their value. Even those who had been there since the beginning and who were on the *Stammliste* could end up on a transport list.[132] Because the decrease in the number of OD members was equal to the decrease in the number of residents, enough staff remained in the camp to preserve the internal order. The Gendarmerie Detachment was still responsible for outdoor surveillance.

6. OUTDOOR SUPERVISION AND SURVEILLANCE

The separation between indoor and outdoor surveillance took place in January 1943, after the *SS Wachbataillon Nordwest* had left. Since the train was able to enter the camp directly via the railway line from the beginning of November 1942, the Gendarmerie Detachment's assistance during the transport from and to Hooghalen station was discontinued. Supervision from the outside remained.

The Gendarmerie Detachment

The organisation of the Police Force was dealt with on a national scale, because with the entry into force of the *'Verordening Organisatie Politie'* (VOP; Ordinance Organisation Police) on 1 March 1943, the objective of the occupier to set up the Dutch Police according to the German model was achieved. From that moment on, state authorities began to exercise Police authority. The Police work became a state matter and the Directorate General of the Police (DGvP) was once again entrusted with the effective management of the Dutch 'State Police'. The chief commissioners of the Municipalities of Amsterdam, Rotterdam, The Hague, Utrecht, Haarlem, Groningen, Arnhem and Eindhoven were given the new title of Police President. They would now act as leaders of the State Police Organisations. The Police Presidents of Amsterdam, Rotterdam, Eindhoven, Arnhem and Groningen also assumed the role of Regional Police President and each received authority over the Police in a number of provinces. They took over the task of the Attorney General. The former Commander of the 8th Division, Major Ynto de Boer, became responsible for the provinces of Groningen, Friesland and Drenthe as acting Regional Police President. Because he was therefore responsible for all Police Departments in the region, De Boer also gained control over the Gendarmerie.[1]

From a letter written by De Boer on 15 March 1943 to all Department Commanders in the region and the Detachment Commander of Camp Westerbork, it is clear what position he took on the matter of the Jews. The contents of the letter had to be discussed with the staff. First of all, De Boer mentioned the core of the problem:

[...] These days, by order of the Occupying Power, all Jews in the Region had to be transferred to the Lager Westerbork. [...] This measure is the result of the decision of the Führer to put an end in Europe to the danger posed by those of the Jewish Religion, who, by means of capital, by means of Bolshevism and other underground political powers, tries to achieve world domination. After all, when world domination is achieved, the Messiah of the Jews will appear on earth. For Christianity, this pursuit represents a serious threat. Christ is regarded by the Jews as a threat, and His followers may be freely lied to and deceived by the chosen people. In order to break the power of the Jews, all Jews are removed from European society and, as long as they are not ill, transferred to Poland, where a large region is reserved for them. [...] It is the duty of each, in the interest of his own culture, to contribute to the fight against this danger. As for the Police: these Military formed corps have the orders given in this regard by the Occupying Force to execute orders of service without delay. [...]

Furthermore, De Boer argued that some thought that the Führer, by destroying Judaism, actually meant that the Jews themselves should be destroyed. According to him, this was, of course, the greatest possible nonsense.

[...] In reality, no Jew who does not resist is hurt at all. Any unnecessary harshness is even avoided by leaving the families intact during transport. [...]

De Boer wrote the letter because Police Officers from his region, including 11 Gendarmes from the Grootegast group, had refused to pick up Jews a few days earlier. Dirk Boonstra, who was at the post Grijpskerk, belonged to the Grootegast group and was the first to receive the order to pick up an elderly Jewish couple and bring them to Camp Westerbork. Boonstra resolutely refused this. When ten of his colleagues were given a similar task shortly thereafter, they also adopted a passive attitude. The entire group was then given the opportunity to carry out the assignment after all. Because everyone stuck to their former decision, they were arrested and transport to Camp Vught followed.

According to De Boer, the refusal of the Gendarmes from Grootegast caused the Dutch Police to be found unreliable in the eyes of the occupier. The transfer of Police work to the German Police and the removal of Dutch Police Officers to Germany could be possible measures against this. De Boer therefore urged his Gendarmerie staff to act reliable and loyal.[2]

Boonstra's choice had to do with his reformed faith.[3] He probably knew the contents of the letter that had been read out loud on 21 February 1943 in the churches. The letter was considered a strong protest from the church against the orders and measures of the occupiers. The core of the letter was clear. Among other things, it said: 'For the sake of the right of God, no one should cooperate in acts of injustice, because it makes one guilty of injustice.' The injustice was also clearly described: 'The obligation of labour service as a National Socialist Institute, the forced employment of Dutch workers in Germany and the persecution of Jewish fellow citizens.' These were tasks that were considered unjust and that Christians were not allowed to participate in.[4] This letter resulted in a moral dilemma for several Police Officers because of their faith.

Gendarme Folkert van der Werf had to go to Camp Westerbork in mid-April 1943. Through stories from colleagues who had been there before, he knew what the work there entailed. Because he, as a Catholic, had heard of the letter in church, the Detachment caused confusion and doubt. That is why he contacted Father Van Oostrum from Oosterwierum first before leaving. After careful deliberation, he would have advised him to go, although he had to be as passive as possible. The Pastor added as an argument that if he did not go, another Gendarme would be sent to Westerbork instead. However, according to the Pastor, responding to the call meant that he might still be able to do something for the Jews, if there was an opportunity to do so. Folkert also realised that refusing and leaving the service could cause problems for him. He knew what had happened to his colleagues from Grootegast. He also knew that a colleague from Dokkum, who had run away with his service weapon, was risking his life. Folkert therefore left for Westerbork.[5]

As evidenced by a publication in the *Nederlandsch Algemeen Politieblad* of 11 February 1943, not everyone fulfilled the Detachment assignment:

> The Comm. of the Gendarmerie in Groningen requests the investigation, arrest and arraignment of the Gendarme Abraham Gerard VAN DER LINDE, Brigade Gorredijk, post Bakkeveen, d.o.b. 16 Nov 1918 in Zeist. Van der Linde disappeared without a trace in the night of 4 to 5 February 1943, dressed in uniform and armed with an F.N. gun, n°. 702, cal. 9mm, with matching ammunition. His escape is due to the fact that he was to be seconded on 5 Febr. 1943 to Camp Westerbork, where he had to provide security services. Description: approx. 1.76 m tall, dark appearance, thick black hair, sideburns, pale face colour, sturdy figure, speaks quickly and briefly. He left with his bicycle and a suitcase with his civilian clothes. Van der Linde's closest family relationship lives in Zeist, Gerolaan 93.[6]

Van der Linde (a.k.a. Bram Hoekstra) went into hiding with his brother Willem, who was also in the Gendarmerie, and joined the illegal scene in Friesland. They formed the core of an assault group there.[7]

Some Gendarmes who fulfilled their secondment assignment for Westerbork observed the place carefully. Folkert van der Werf was one of them. He shared some details with his family in letters. For example, he wrote that things in Westerbork were just as he had imagined they would be. In addition, there were Gendarmes who informed their loved ones about their daily activities. They would have night shifts one week and day shifts the next. According to a schedule, the Gendarmes would do their rounds throughout the camp for two hours in the night under any weather conditions. Then they were relieved and allowed to spend the next two hours in the waiting room, until it was their turn again to watch the camp from outside the barbed wire fence. During the day shift, instead of doing rounds, the men had to occupy the seven watchtowers for two hours on and off. Especially when the wind was blowing and sand was being blown around, it was difficult to serve in the towers. For this reason, the Gendarmes wore large goggles to protect the eyes.[8]

The Gendarmerie Detachment had to perform other tasks in addition to manning the watchtowers and doing patrol rounds, such as guiding Jewish workers to their jobs outside the camp. Gendarmes also joined as Supervisors when sick residents had to be operated in the University Hospital of Groningen. At the beginning of June 1943, this came to an end, because an independent Surgical Department was opened in the camp. The intention was to use Westerbork as a Military Hospital for wounded German Soldiers after the departure of the last Jews. In the end, it never came to that.[9]

Gendarmes were forbidden to be in contact with residents unless they had a valid reason for doing so. Especially during guidance tasks, it was difficult to stick to this rule. This rule was therefore regularly violated. This was the case for the Gendarme Jenne Boering, born and raised in Assen. During his secondment, he met several Jewish boys with whom he had attended school in Assen. He was in contact with some of them in the camp. They regularly asked him for a favour, such as taking a letter with him or arranging tobacco, and in many cases Jenne complied with these requests. In addition to tobacco, he got meat from a butcher's shop in Assen. He smuggled these scarce and therefore precious goods into the camp in his panniers and divided them among his acquaintances.[10]

Gendarmes oversee labour groups outside the camp.

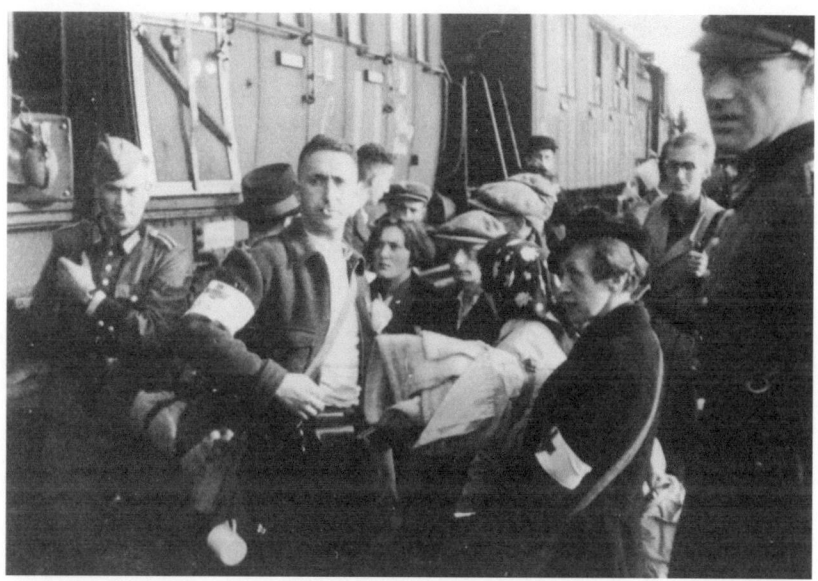

German Police Forces during the preparation of a transport.

As a young Gendarme, Jenne was part of a surveillance system that had to help keep the deportation machine running. The Gendarmerie Detachment had little to do with the handling and supervision of incoming and departing transports, an important and especially difficult part of this machine, after they took over outdoor surveillance, because the OD was mainly used for this purpose. The *Westerborkfilm* by Breslauer shows Dutch Police Officers armed with carbines during an incoming transport. They were not part of the Detachment, but had joined the group on the train as Supervisors.[11]

The footage of a departing transport shows mainly people dressed in German uniforms. They belonged to the Camp SS or to the German Police who guided the train to the final destination. These escorts were troops of the Police Battalion 105, which originally came from Bremen and was composed of troops from the *Schutzpolizei* and the Reserve Police. At least 120 Policemen from the Battalion admitted after the liberation that they had accompanied a transport from Westerbork as Supervisors. Over 30 Policemen stated that they had joined a transport four times. Many had volunteered because of the extra food and the few days of special leave they received for this. The days of leave were to be spent in Bremen on the return trip. Before a transport departed from their Dutch station, the men were brought to Westerbork by train or truck. There they took over the transport and travelled in a passenger car to the final destination.[12]

That no Gendarmes can be seen on the transport[13] filmed by Breslauer was confirmed by Jenne. According to him, he and his colleagues no longer played any role in these transports after some time. When the train left, they were still ordered to walk along the railway track. There they had to pick up and return all the letters, money and other items thrown out of the wagons.

Most of the latter did not happen. Jenne hid the letters and small items, such as a fountain pen with a gold pen, under his uniform coat and later took them with him. The letters, which usually had no stamp, he would add a stamp to and send. Jenne kept the small number of objects to return them to the rightful owner later. These actions could be dangerous, because not every colleague was reliable, so when such a colleague came along, Jenne returned the found items according to the regulations. Sometimes unannounced checks also took place. Jenne was once warned by his colleague Meye Haagsma about such a check, which was carried out by the then Detachment Commander, Derk Klavers. Jenne was able to destroy the letters hidden under his clothes in the toilet just in time. Fortunately, nothing was found in his locker either. Had this happened, it would in all likelihood have resulted in arrest and imprisonment in a camp.

A colleague of Jenne, Gendarme Johnnie Trompert, did receive this sentence. He was arrested after being betrayed because he had written anti German texts with a pencil on the walls of watchtower number 3, which stood east of the camp. Derk Klavers made a Police report of this fact on 26 March 1943. This shows that Johnnie had written the following under the text '*SS-Wachtbataljon N.V. Amersfoort*', which had been carved in the wood: 'Murder that bunch of traitors; they must hang the scum. Despicable lackeys of the Krauts'. He then wrote under a different text 'Das Internationale Judentum sprecht nun in Amerika', which was drawn with ink on one of the window frames: 'An international band of thieves is now plundering our Netherlands'. After consultation with Gemmeker, Klavers informed the Sicherheitspolizei in Assen.[14] Johnnie had to be brought to the Detention Centre in Assen on the evening of 26 March. Later he ended up in Neuengamme via Camp Amersfoort. He did not return alive.[15]

Johnnie had grown up in Alkmaar. Before being placed as Military man in the depot of the 21st Infantry Regiment because of the mobilisation in 1939, he worked for some time as a machine operator. Whether he participated in the battles in the May days of 1940 is unknown. In any case, he was demobilised in the rank of Corporal. In October 1940 he joined the Gendarmerie. Before Johnnie came to Westerbork, he was seconded to the city of Groningen and to Winschoten, Veenhuizen and Echten.[16]

During the period that Jenne worked in Westerbork, some of his colleagues were arrested. According to Mechanicus, some Gendarmes had been captured in the vicinity of Assen in the second half of October 1943, because they had been too friendly to the Jews in the camp. After their arrest followed imprisonment in Ommen.[17] Although other sources do not support this fact, it is likely that this measure has been implemented and served as a warning. Because of the chance to be arrested, the Gendarmes, most of them fairly young, tried to abide by the rules as best as possible. This was not an easy task. Especially the night shifts were monotonous, which made it difficult to stay awake. For such a small violation as sleeping during the shift, the coveted weekend off had to be handed in as a rule. Apart from being young, many members of the Detachment belonged to the so-called 'war Gendarmes'. This group, which consisted of demobilised Military personnel, would probably never have chosen to join the Gendarmerie under normal

These overview photos were taken secretly from a watchtower. The creator knew he was risking his life by making these photos.

Op het namen van deze foto's stond de deodstraf.

Kamp Westerbork.

het Jodenkamp.

'Taking these pictures was punishable by death. Camp Westerbork, the Jewishcamp.'

circumstances. This was true for Jenne Boering and Folkert van der Werf, for example.

The fact that Camp Westerbork was not a popular workplace is evidenced by the fact that men also had to go there as a disciplinary punishment. Gendarme Roelof Hemkes was a victim of such a forced transfer in August 1943. He received this penalty because he had adopted an attitude that was considered too passive several months before, during the April May strike in the Municipality of Leek. After his two-month secondment ended, an involuntary transfer to the town of Oldehove in Groningen followed.[18]

Gendarme Joop Floor did not go to the camp at his own request either. In 1942 he was placed with the Brigade Grootegast. When this Brigade was supposed to deliver personnel for the Security Detachment, no one was eager to volunteer. Because Joop was the last person to come in, he was chosen. He did not like what he observed in Westerbork. For example, he would have witnessed how a train filled with children was emptied in a very rough manner. Partly because of this, Joop did not feel at home in his new workplace and decided to go into hiding. Not long after arriving, he surreptitiously grabbed his bike and rode to Beilen. Eventually he found a safe house at a farmer's place in the Zaanstreek.[19]

Especially when the Gendarmes were still in charge of escorting the transports, they could, like Joop, be confronted with harrowing situations. Even after outdoor surveillance became their main task, those who were open to it saw enough to get a good idea of the situation in the camp. This was evident, among other things, from the letters to their families and loved ones. On 27 February 1943 H.J. Droppers wrote to his sister the following:

> Here are continuously always about ten thousand Jews. Things always continue to go on here with these people. Almost not a day goes by or something comes up again. But every week, probably 1,200 of them go to Poland. Which, of course, is always a terrible thing for those people. But fortunately, we do not have to help, because (now you should not start laughing) the Jews themselves take care of that. They do everything themselves here in the camp. You often have to feel sorry for them, because no one can approve of what is being done to the Jews at the moment. But the mentality of the Jews is often expressed here. For they stand here, as it were, with one foot already in the grave, but if they are able to sacrifice each other, they will.[20]

Folkert van der Werf made a similar remark about the fate of the residents in a letter dated 20 May 1943.

> There are so many Jews passing through lately. Things are happening to those people that I cannot write, but that simply affect God in his power. Fortunately, that doesn't happen here in this camp. But I do not think that we will ever see again that the Zaailand (Leeuwarden FvR) is a Jews Market.[21]

Both quotations show that the censorship of letters probably only applied to residents and not to the Gendarmes of the Detachment, which meant that information about the conditions in the camp and about the supposed fate of the Jews also reached those outside the camp. Whether the Dutch knew during the occupation what happened to the Jews after they had been deported from Westerbork was a question that has been asked for decades and has led to many discussions. Bart van der Boom came to the conclusion in his 2012 book *Wij weten niets van hun lot. Gewone Nederlanders en de Holocaust (We know nothing of their fate. Ordinary Dutch people and the Holocaust)* that the ordinary Dutch did not know about the Holocaust. According to him, they suspected and assumed that the Jews would suffer greatly, that they would have to do hard work under poor conditions and that many would die in the long run. But they did not know that a large majority of the deportees were killed immediately upon arrival; most of them could not even imagine that, according to Van der Boom.[22]

It is difficult to see the Gendarmes of the Surveillance Detachment as ordinary Dutch people in this context, because they were in or near the intermediate station of the murder factories, as Camp Westerbork was later called. During their short period of secondment, they undoubtedly saw and heard more than the ordinary Dutchman and, as both letters showed, came to the most farfetched conclusions. Because both Droppers and Van der Werf shared this with their loved ones independently of each other, the possibility that the atrocities were much more widely known than has always been assumed cannot be ruled out. It is also plausible that after the liberation the men have forgotten it, deliberately repressed it, or have chosen not to talk about it anymore. Folkert, who wrote down his memories of the German occupation in 1999, became aware that his memory about the fate of the Jews was not exactly in line with what he had described in a letter to his family from 1943. He wrote in 1999 that during his stay in Westerbork, he had experienced at least one 'transport'. He could not remember any emotional farewells. As far as he could remember, he and his colleagues did not know that the Jews were sent to gas chambers. He thought they assumed they were going to Poland and would end up in a labour camp again there. Folkert then explained that from the last sentence in his letter of 20 May 1943 about the market at the Zaailand, one could conclude that he did think the Jews would be murdered. However, he did not remember this in 1999.[23]

While the main characters wanted to leave the past behind as soon as possible after the liberation, criticism of their performance in Camp Westerbork continued to increase. That criticism was not in line with the opinion of a number of residents. According to Mechanicus, the Gendarmes stood watch from the towers with 'the rough helmets on their boorish heads and the frightening carbine within reach', or they patrolled the barbed wire fence. Although they looked brutal and strict, according to Mechanicus they were fair in their performance, which they did with much reluctance.[24] Mirjam Bolle, a camp resident who also kept a diary, shared the opinion of Mechanicus. She wrote: 'The Gendarme is generally good, and hates that they have to work for the Germans.'[25]

The comments of Mechanicus and Bolle, which once again show that a large part of the Gendarmes was reluctantly serving, are supported by a quote from a letter from Frans Spoor. On 1 February 1943 he came from The Hague to the Jewish cemetery in Assen to attend the funeral of Izaäk Herman Meijer, who died on 28 January 1943 in Camp Westerbork at the age of 66. His son Herman and his wife were staying in the camp at that time. They were brought to the cemetery under the guidance of a Gendarme. Spoor wrote about this event as follows:

> [...] Then we went back to the cottage where we could wash our hands and eat our bread. The idea that the time was approaching to say goodbye was not pleasant. The moment also came to give our gifts, which were received very gratefully, as I mentioned earlier. All this was done under the supervision of a Gendarme, who, armed with his revolver, kept to himself very modestly. In answer to a question from me if he wanted bread, he told me that he needed nothing. He only accepted a cup of tea, but he refused bread, drinks and cigarettes, of which he had enough already. So he was a pleasant person, who had to act that way and toughened up because of the situation. [...][26]

Despite the difficult task, the reputation of which got worse and worse after the liberation, it can be said with certainty that most of the Gendarmes of the Detachment were actually good people. For example, Folkert van der Werf wrote on 21 April 1943 in a letter that the evening before, a feast was served in the cafeteria because of the Führer's birthday.[27] Of the entire Detachment, only four Gendarmes attended this meal. Most of the men wanted nothing to do with the New Order or National Socialism. However, this did not apply to those responsible for the management of the Detachment.

The Detachment Commander And His Dubious Role

The Gendarmes were led by a Detachment Commander in Westerbork. The first (Acting) Commander, who also spent the longest period in the camp, was Albert de Jong.[28] He knew the camp from the period when it was still in use as a refugee camp, because in 1941 he had been seconded to the camp for one month. On 15 July 1942, he was sent to Westerbork again on the basis of a secondment from Emmen. In November of the same year, this turned into a temporary transfer. It is likely that from this moment on, as acting Detachment Commander, he was in charge of the command. According to him, the request for transfer was submitted by Schol and by some prominent Jews, because they did not want the SS to take over all the surveillance tasks of the Gendarmerie.[29]

Gemmeker was initially positive about De Jong's view of the new situation in the Netherlands. From their conversations Gemmeker got the impression that De Jong believed that Germany would win the war, although he remained neutral when it came to the National Socialist view of the world. According to Gemmeker, De Jong had a great sense of honour. First Service Leader Kurt Schlesinger even described his attitude as 'terribly ambitious'.[30] Two reports made and signed by De Jong on or around 2 September 1942 show that he tried to perform his service in the camp very seriously:

> I have the honour of suggesting to send Julius Bick, d.o.b. 16 Febr. 1880, on the next transport, since he was caught here one of these days buying sausages in a clandestine way and, as it seems to me, has never done anything but trade illegally. He is in my view unfit to carry out labour here in the Lager. Wmr. A. de Jong.[31]

This report did not miss its purpose, because Julius Bick was sent along with the next transport on 4 September and was immediately killed after arriving in Auschwitz; the date of death was set on 7 September 1942.[32] The second report of De Jong, dated 2 September 1942, relates to an attempt by residents to illegally smuggle postcards from the camp:

Commander! When I was checking the work teams, I found three Jews, each of whom was writing a postcard. These cards, which were written during a rest period and from which it can be deduced that they had to be sent to the post in a clandestine manner, I have added as proof. Because writer POONS has already given us his false declaration concerning the disappearance of his daughter, may I advise you politely to send this person and, if possible, the two others on the next transport.

On the postcards De Jong not only noted the names of the captured writers, but also that they came from barracks B4a. They were Lyon (Lion) Poons, Mozes Logger and D. Bos. It is known that Poons was transported to Theresienstadt on 4 September 1944. It is not known, however, whether the other two were sent on the next transport.[33]

In the file drawn up against De Jong in the context of the post war Special Court, no data has been found to show that both reports have been taken into account during the trial. It turns out, however, that by using violence, he wanted to get into the good graces of the German camp leaders. According to the file, 25 people were interviewed, including some colleagues from De Jong and some former residents. A large part of the latter group stated that De Jong also used violence during incoming and departing transports. They had seen him beat and kick people. Some even talked about assaulting. He would have done this especially if there were SS people nearby. OD member Hans Margules was one of the witnesses. Among other things, he saw that De Jong beat and punched Jews at the train and in the main hall. During a transport, Hans saw an old woman in barracks 11 lean with her backpack against the windowsill. De Jong attempted to get this woman to hurry and turned her arm around, with which he was trying to get the woman to move. Hermann Wingens[34], also a member of the OD, confirmed Hans's statement. He had only seen De Jong hit people, but made the remark that he did not hit softly. Some witnesses stated that De Jong did not distinguish between men, women, children or elderly people during the beatings. The victims were mainly Jews who, loaded with luggage, did not move quickly enough in the eyes of De Jong.

During his interrogation De Jong denied that he had been brutal to the Jews who had to go on transport. He did confess to using violence during an incident in a barracks in early October 1942. He also admitted to boxing someone's ears or giving them a push sometimes, but he had never done this without cause. At times he gave Jews who had to go on transport and who were dilly dallying or did not want to go a shove or a kick against the butt. Someone with luggage that was too heavy had once fallen down because of this, but he had helped him on his feet directly. According to him, the ones he used physical force on were always men; he had never touched women. Camp resident Ernst David claimed the opposite. He saw De Jong assault a woman on one of the first transports. When Ernst asked De Jong the next day how he could do such a thing, the answer was: 'Yes, but it's so hard for me. The Jews don't want to go, and the Germans are above me, and then I have to. The nerves will get the better of me.' In the long run, De Jong could not control his nerves anymore and became burnt out. As a result, he was no longer able to serve from 12 December 1942 until about 15 February 1943. He spent all or part of his sick leave in the camp, but was nevertheless involved in one or more cases.

On 12 January 1943, around 17:00, when he was walking outside with the permission of the Doctor, Gemmeker summoned him to his office. Gemmeker informed him that he had to remove Officer Winters from the camp immediately, or else Winters would be sent to a Concentration Camp after arrest. The reason for this penalty was a conversation between Winters and a driver of the SD, which had made Gemmeker feel offended. Winters would have told this driver that he did not think it was normal for the Commander to leave a Jew standing at the barbed wire fence from 8:00 to 18:00 as punishment. De Jong started an investigation, which indeed showed that Winters had said such a thing to the driver. After this conclusion, he contacted the acting district Commander in Assen, who gave him permission to return Winters to Hoogeveen. Winters was still punished with a few days of light arrest for insulting Gemmeker.

Clearly De Jong continued to interfere in service matters, although in the meantime, the command had been taken over by another Officer. Nevertheless, after his recovery, he was not again put in charge of the Detachment, because by order of Rauter, a Dutch Police Officer was entrusted with the command. The reason for this appointment would have to do with the fact that this Officer had to be a member of the SS. Because De Jong had not joined any National Socialist Organisation, he was not allowed to get the position of Commander again. He had to settle for the position of Chief of Office, which meant that his work would consist of conducting service correspondence. Because of this, he had less contact with residents than before. This contact had already lessened since the departure of the *Wachbataillon*, because the Gendarmerie was mainly in charge of the outdoor security.[35]

De Jong was succeeded by Derk Klavers[36]. Little is known about his work in the camp. He could not be interrogated after the liberation, because he was shot down by two members of the Groningen resistance group on 22 September 1943 in Zuidhorn. He died that same day in a Hospital from his injuries. At that time, Klavers had already not been working in the camp for several months. As a Group Commander in the province of Groningen, he became a fanatical accomplice of the Germans. The appointment of Klavers in Westerbork fulfilled the wish of the occupying forces, because they wanted National Socialists to take over all important posts. The command of the Surveillance Detachment Westerbork certainly belonged to these posts. It is very likely that he was not a member of the SS, as De Jong claimed[37], although he had joined the National Socialist Rechtsfront, an organisation from the NSB, and had been with the Police for a long time.

When Klavers was eight year old, it did not look like he was going to build this career in the Netherlands. Possibly due to economic circumstances, his parents, along with their eight children, left for Germany. There the family settled in Eschendorf, now a part of the town of Rheine, not far from the Dutch border. While Germany was still in the middle of the First World War in 1916, Derk Klavers decided to return to his hometown Deventer. Although the Netherlands remained neutral, many men had to be prepared to fight. Klavers also exchanged his civilian clothes for a Military uniform: he ended up in the infantry, where he was promoted to Sergeant in 1918.

While this commitment will not have been voluntary, the next step in his career was: on 27 September 1919, Klavers joined the Royal Gendarmerie. After completing his training in Apeldoorn and serving as a Sergeant for a short period of time in the Municipalities of Wijhe and Emmer-Compascuum, Brigade Dwingeloo became his new place in 1924, the year in which he married. In 1935 the transfer to the Brigade Assen followed. In the same year, Klavers was also appointed a traffic expert within the Gendarmerie, a title he acquired partially by writing some legal manuals for bicycle traffic. After being in Assen for three years, Klavers left for the Brigade Veenhuizen.38 Shortly before that, he had also been temporarily seconded to the *Gemeentelijke Dactyloscopische Inrichting* (Municipal Dactyloscopic Institute) in Amsterdam, where he was promoted to Sergeant Major First Class.[39]

Early October 1940, the Netherlands had been occupied for almost five months, Klavers returned to Dwingeloo as the new Sergeant Major. He was put in charge as Commander of this Brigade, where he served for the longest time.[40] Despite being somewhat advanced in age, he participated in the Officers training given at Police Officers School (POS) in Apeldoorn in mid-1942. That this was exceptional is evidenced by the speech made during his funeral by the Regional Police President Y. de Boer. De Boer indicated that, given his age, a lot was asked of Klavers during this training at the POS. Nevertheless, he was an example for a number of younger trainees because of his cheerful mood.[41] After completing the Officers training in early January 1943, Klavers was assigned as Chief Lieutenant to the region of Groningen. He probably left Apeldoorn shortly after his return to go to Westerbork, because he was considered a suitable candidate for commanding the Detachment.

De Jong was not happy with the appointment of Klavers. He would have felt offended and hurt, because he had to play second fiddle from now on. According to Gemmeker, De Jong therefore sought more rapprochement with him. During conversations, De Jong argued several times that, in terms of qualities, he was no less than Klavers, who had owed his appointment and promotion mainly to his membership of a National Socialist Organisation. In the long run, Gemmeker got the impression that De Jong had slightly changed his view on national socialism and that instead of his previous neutral attitude, he was now very sympathetic towards it. This attitude, changed in the eyes of Gemmeker, did not get De Jong the desired position, not even when Klavers, due to one or more incidents, was relieved of his position a few months after his appointment. De Jong was present during one of these incidents, where Klavers fired four shots inside the barracks of the Gendarmerie. The withholding of important information by Gendarme Johnnie Trompert would have triggered this shooting. Trompert knew that a few farmers from the area around the camp had offered help to American pilots. Contrary to what had been stipulated in the guidelines, he had not reported this information to his superior. Klavers blamed De Jong for not having done enough against this unauthorised behaviour. The quarrel that arose as a result of this escalated to such an extent that Klavers pulled his service weapon and fired.

Gendarme Hendrik de Kruijff made a statement about a similar incident. During the period in which Klavers was in charge, De Kruijff transported a Polish pilot. The intention was to put him on the train to Amsterdam. Klavers likely observed some things he did not like. Without knowing who he was dealing with, he fired four shots, all of which missed their target. Klavers informed De Jong about the event, and although De Jong knew that De Kruijff was involved, he did not mention his name. It is not clear whether this refers to the same incident. In any case, Gemmeker was very dissatisfied with Klavers' actions, because of which the much-needed peace and order within the Detachment and possibly also in the camp could be disturbed. The decision was made to find Klavers a different workplace immediately.[42]

He returned as District Commander to the province of Groningen in early May and moved into a home in Zuidhorn, where he was liquidated almost five months later by the resistance. What was so special about this act of resistance is that the two perpetrators, Willem Homoet and Hielke van der Heide, were former Gendarmes and therefore colleagues of Klavers. Both had refused to arrest a Jewish couple from Bedum and to transfer them to Westerbork. Because of this refusal, they were no longer able to continue their service at the Gendarmerie. To escape captivity, going into hiding was the only alternative. Via their safe house in Adorp, the farm of a provincial leader of the resistance, Willem and Hielke came into contact with the world of crime, in which they both began to play an active role. It is possible that Klavers got too close to the resistance groups in the north, so liquidation was the only solution for them to stop him. Willem and Hielke did not make it to the liberation either: both were arrested and died in Bergen-Belsen and Vught.43

The successor of Klavers, Jan Rebel[44], was a young Police Officer with little experience. Among other things, he was a member of the NSB and the Rechtsfront. In April 1941 he had also voluntarily registered as a member of the *Nederlandsche SS*. Four months later, he applied for a job at the Police. He probably took this step to prevent transfer to the Eastern Front. Because Police training in the Netherlands was centralised, Rebel had to go to Schalkhaar to be trained at the Police Training Battalion (POB) to become a kind of Police Soldier.[45]

After the training, which lasted six months, Rebel was placed with the 1st Company of the Police Battalion Amsterdam as a Police Officer on a bicycle.[46] Besides the right political colour, he probably met the demands of the New Order there, because almost a year and a half later Rebel was allowed to participate in the Officers training in Apeldoorn. Six months later he was transferred to Leeuwarden in the rank of Ensign and in August 1943 he was promoted to Lieutenant and was seconded to Assen. In connection with his promotion, Rebel came into contact with Major Waschke, Liaison Officer of the *Befehlshaber der Ordnungspolizei* in Groningen. The topic of the conversation was the application for the Waffen SS. Although they could not force him, Rebel felt the pressure and he realised that he could get into trouble if he refused. Still, he did not respond to this call. According to him, he was sent to Camp Westerbork as a Detachment Commander as punishment, where he stayed for five months. De Jong saw the SS runes on Rebel's uniform and felt that he was fully integrated into the teachings of the New Order. Rebel would have tried to convey this doctrine to his men, for example by exercise. Yet he was not a very difficult person in the eyes of De Jong, but since he was an Officer of the New Order, De Jong felt they had to watch out for him anyway.[47]

Even though De Jong had not been given the positions he had desired several times, according to Gemmeker, he continued to perform his duties in the camp in an excellent way. Gemmeker's conviction about the compliant attitude of De Jong was confirmed in September 1943, when he arrested Johan Ernst Polak[48] in Groningen, a Jewish Lawyer who had escaped from Westerbork. Polak had been arrested at the end of March 1943 for concealing weapons. He was first brought to the Scheveningen Prison and was then taken to Westerbork as a criminal case. Polak saw the opportunity to flee from the camp's Criminal Barracks in early June; an intensive search by the OD did not yield any results.

Johan Ernst Polak

On Monday 13 September 1943 De Jong travelled to Groningen to celebrate the birthday of a sister-in-law. When he was walking in civilian clothes on the Oude Kijk in't Jatstraat near the Academieplein, a man passed him, going in the opposite direction. De Jong immediately recognised him as the one who had escaped from the Criminal Barracks and immediately grabbed Polak – as he later claimed, instinctively – by one of his shoulders. The man began to scream loudly: 'You are robbing me of my freedom!' He then denied being the wanted person. Because there were many pedestrians on the street and De Jong wanted to avoid a commotion, he transferred Polak to the Police Station at the Ossenmarkt as soon as possible. Along the way, he would have doubted the justness of his action. According to him, there was no way back, because there were too many dangers. For example, there was a possibility that Polak had started working as a traitor for the occupiers after his escape, while he also had to take into account any 'false' witnesses. At the station, an investigation revealed that De Jong had indeed brought in the wanted Polak. The transport from Polak to Camp Westerbork took place the same evening or night, because he was sent directly on a transport to Auschwitz the next day. Polak was probably selected for the gas chambers immediately after arrival, as he died on 17 September 1943.

After the liberation, De Jong declared that he regretted his action. If he had known everything in advance, he would have let Polak go. It had never been his intention to deliberately bring the Jewish man into the hands of the occupying forces. The occupier, represented by Gemmeker, was satisfied with De Jong's performance. Before that, he had already discussed a possible promotion with the direct supervisor of De Jong, Department Commander Abraham Bouma. Because De Jong was already sympathetic towards national socialism, they would try to convince him to join the SS. After all, this had a positive impact on the request for promotion. After Polak was arrested, Gemmeker contacted Major Oosterhoff (Commander of the Gendarmerie in Groningen) and pointed this action out to him, because in order to be eligible for an extraordinary promotion, a reason had to be provided[49].

On 17 February 1944 De Jong was promoted in the camp, together with his colleague Paridaen. As mentioned earlier, Paridaen became Sergeant Major and De Jong was given the position of Sub Lieutenant. According to the report on the event, Oosterhoff described De Jong as an exemplary Officer, who had always performed his often difficult task as Commander of the Detachment in an excellent manner. Partly in view of Gemmeker's favourable reports, the promotion to the next rank was very appropriate, according to Oosterhoff. He also announced that De Jong was again entrusted with the command over the Detachment with effect from 1 March. At the end of the ceremony, De Jong thanked the authorities on behalf of Paridaen for the nomination for promotion, which had come very unexpectedly for both. He assured them that they would continue to fulfil their task with no less ambition than before[50].

On 29 February 1944, a few days before De Jong took over Rebel's command, Oosterhoff visited the camp again, now for a comradeship evening in the cafeteria of the camp. In addition to the 70 Gendarmes and Gemmeker, the Department Commander from Assen, Chief Lieutenant

Bouma, Rebel and De Jong were present. Gemmeker took the opportunity to thank Rebel for the way in which he had conducted the command and stated that he was very satisfied with the services of the entire Detachment. After this, Oosterhoff took the floor. He argued that he was pleased to hear that the Camp Commander was very satisfied with the service of the Gendarmes in the camp and that he was convinced that they would continue their good work.[51]

The 70 Gendarmes present probably did not all belong to the Detachment of the camp, because a few months later, at the end of April 1944, Oosterhoff submitted a proposal to increase the number of Gendarmes to 76 in connection with an incident that had occurred on the night of 18 to 19 April. Around 1:00 AM, two OD members were ordered to transfer a tipsy Gendarme to the Camp Hospital. In the reports, this incident, which may have occurred at the eastern guard post, was described as an invasion of the camp. The posts on the eastern and western sides had been occupied by the Gendarmerie since September 1943. In addition, the men occupying the posts were ordered to patrol the camp from 23:00 to 7:00 AM.[52]

After the incident, ten pairs of the OD patrolled the camp from 3:30 to 6:00 AM. The next day, five OD members had to look for shell casings on the outside, but nothing was found. For the Gendarmerie and the OD, a signal for help was established so that they could assist each other during an emergency situation.[53] Oosterhoff proposed to replace the single posts with double posts during the darkness. For this reason, 16 more Gendarmes were needed per day. Because there was not enough staff available in the region of Oosterhoff to add to the Detachment, he asked the DGvP if the extra staff could be obtained from other Gendarmerie regions. If this was not possible, he suggested that perhaps additional staff could be removed from other parts of the Dutch Police.[54] In the meantime, the Gendarmerie's watch post on the east side was left by the Gendarmes and completely taken over by the OD.[55]

Initially, the measures taken were intended to be temporary. This setup did not succeed, because the camp was not given the desired reinforcement of the Detachment. The reply of the DGvP showed that it was not possible to post staff from other regions in Groningen for the extension of the secondment.[56] De Jong therefore had to make do with the staff he had at his disposal. He would have done his utmost to accomplish his task; after all, this was his promise after being promoted. After the liberation, De Jong stated that he had not been aware of his promotion and that he did not appreciate this gesture at that time either. However, witnesses, including Gemmeker, claimed the opposite. According to Gemmeker, De Jong had tried his best to obtain a higher rank. The arrest of Polak and the statements about using violence show that he sometimes acted quite fanatically. De Jong also played a role during an incident in which one of his subordinates was caught doing something he should not have.[57]

The Case Smallenbroek

Contacts between Gendarmes and residents were only allowed if it was necessary. However, this rule was frequently ignored. There were even (love) relationships between young Gendarmes and camp residents. Johan Hendrik

Smallenbroek was seconded to the camp at the end of 1943. On 23 December, his birthday, Johan had agreed to meet with the 19-year-old Jewish girl Charlotte Weisz[58] around 18:10 at the barbed wire fence near the Camp Hospital. The intention was to make further arrangements with her regarding the receipt of letters, which he would send for her. Johan was on duty from 16:00 to 18:00 and again from 18:30 to 19:30, so he only had half an hour. After his break had started and he had clocked out according to the regulations in the barracks of the Gendarmerie, he headed towards the agreed location. He did not go directly to the barbed wire fence, but first walked up and down a few times. When he could not find anything suspicious, he went in the direction of the fence.

Although it was already dark, he saw Charlotte standing behind the fence at a distance of about 8 meters. Near her walked a yellowish dog, which Johan recognised as Gemmeker's dog. Because it was not the first time the dog was roaming around the camp, he paid no attention to it and walked on. At the moment he was about one and a half meters away from the fence, a bright light suddenly shone in his direction. At first Johan still assumed that it was just one of his colleagues doing his rounds, but when his eyes were accustomed to the light, he saw Gemmeker and De Jong standing in front of him. Both were dressed in civilian clothes and wore raincoats with a cap. Johan heard Gemmeker say, 'Also wachtmeister, Sie sind verhaftet.' He was transferred directly to Gemmeker's office. De Jong would have entered the camp to pick up Charlotte, while Gemmeker declared that he had ordered her to report to his desk through the gate. The interrogation that followed, done by Gemmeker himself, lasted about an hour. According to De Jong, Gemmeker continuously spoke about *Rassenschande* during this interrogation and asked questions several times about physical contact between the two arrestees. Charlotte and Johan kept denying that anything of the sort had happened. After the interrogation, the Jewish girl was transferred to the Camp Prison, while De Jong took Johan to the office of Detachment Commander Rebel. There the Gendarme was questioned again and a report was made of what he said.[59]

Johan Hendrik Smallenbroek

When Rebel left the room briefly during the interrogation, Johan would have asked De Jong what he had to say. De Jong advised him to say that 'that the Jewish girl' looked a lot like a Christian girl and that he was therefore attracted to her. Furthermore, Johan should never admit that he had had physical contact with her. Johan did as he was told, but according to De Jong, the report showed that Johan and Charlotte were dating. That same evening SS men brought Johan to the Military Police Station in Assen. After spending some time in a Detention Centre and then in the Scheveningen Prison, he ended up in Camp Amersfoort. As a Police Officer, Johan had to appear before the *SS und Polizeigericht*. This Court condemned him to six months imprisonment for 'Military Disobedience'[60]. Via Camp Amersfoort, he ended up in a camp in Egestorf, Germany, where he was liberated by the Americans on 8 April 1945[61].

A few days after her arrest, Charlotte was interrogated in the waiting room of the Camp Prison by Chief Lieutenant Bouma and De Jong. According to De Jong, Charlotte stated that there was a relationship between her and Johan and that they had made love several times behind the warehouse. De Jong deliberately did not include the latter in the report.[62]

Charlotte was born in Vienna and had come to the Netherlands together with her family as a refugee before the occupation. She had been staying in Camp Westerbork since 1940.[63] Gemmeker stated after the liberation that he had managed to ensure that only she and not her whole family had to go on transport. Charlotte died on 31 March 1945 in Bergen-Belsen.

As far as Gemmeker could remember, De Jong himself had seen from his home that Johan was seeing Charlotte or had heard this from another Gendarme. At least he knew for sure that De Jong had communicated this to him by telephone the night before the arrest. He would also have had contact with Rebel by telephone. The next day Gemmeker discussed the situation with De Jong. The outcome of this conversation was that they would be arrested that same day. Around the time Johan and Charlotte were going to meet, both men put on their civilian clothes and waited at the location of the appointment in a potato pit for what was going to happen. De Jong denied calling Gemmeker the night before the two were arrested. He would not have spoken to him the morning after that. Only on the evening itself, when he was on his way from the Detachment Office to his home, did he meet Gemmeker, who ordered him to dress up in civilian clothes and go with him. On the way, De Jong would have heard for the first time what was going on and what was about to happen that night. On the other hand, according to him, Rebel would indeed have been informed before the event. Rebel denied this and also that he had informed Gemmeker of the relationship between Johan and Charlotte.[64]

As Manager of the Camp Prison, Paridaen would have received many complaints about colleagues who, while they were married, maintained 'shameful' relations with girls from the camp. These girls had a bad reputation.[65] Because this remark of Paridaen is not supported by any other source, it is difficult to imagine that most of the complaints were related to relationships between married Gendarmes and Jewish women with poor moral habits. Since Paridaen lived in the camp and many of the offenders, including Charlotte, stayed as 'guests' in the cells with him, he did know what was going on in the camp. One of the places where unauthorised contacts between residents and Gendarmes could also emerge was Camp Heidelager, a few kilometres from the camp. This is where the Gendarmes slept and stayed when they were not working.

Camp Heidelager

From July 1942 onwards, the troops of the *SS-Wachbataillon* were staying in Camp Heidelager. After the *Wachbataillon* had left in early January 1943, the Gendarmerie Detachment moved from the barracks in the camp to the labour camp. Because the work of the Gendarmes shifted from the inside to the outside, they only occasionally entered the camp itself. Gemmeker announced this move at the beginning of March via *Lagerbefehl* nr. 12. Part of the Dutch administrative staff also moved with the group. The order also showed that the small camp officially got the name 'Heidelager'.[66]

Drawing of Camp Heidelager.

Gendarme Jenne Boering stayed in this Lager during his secondment. As far as he could remember, the barracks consisted of two parts. One of them was furnished as a sleeping area and in the other part, there were tables and chairs, as this was where the Gendarmes would spend their free hours.[67] Because there was little to do for the men in the middle of the moor, much free time was spent on card games, such as blackjack. A high stake of 1 guilder per round happened fairly often. This shows that the men had enough money. This is confirmed by Folkert van de Werf. He wrote in a letter that they paid less fees than other Detachments and that they were also given a temporary allowance. He too participated in card games to get through the boring hours and won a sum of 7 guilders one night. He did remark that almost all money was gone quickly. Both Droppers and Folkert indicated that the food was pretty good. There was at least enough bread, jam, broth and butter.[68] The food was cooked in Camp Heidelager, because besides living barracks, it had a kitchen and a cafeteria.

```
Heidelager, den _____ 31/1 ____ 194 4 .

            R E C H N U N G
            _____

für Herrn Wmr.Zwuup _____
Verpflegung für die Zeit
vom ____ 1/1 ____ bis ___ 31/1 ____ 1944 _____

        ___ 2 ___ Tage abwesend

__ 29 _ Tage à f 1,40 = f ___ 40.60 ____
                       ================

Betrag erhalten:
Heidelager, den _____ 31/1 194 __ 4 __
                                    i.A.

Distributiestammkarte)
   "      "    bescheiden)   erhalten:



Heidelager, den ___ 31/1 _____ 194 4 .

            R E C H N U N G
            _____

für Herrn _ Wmr.Zwuup _____
Miete für die Zeit
vom _____ 1/1 __ bis _ 31/1 ___ 194 4 _____

_____ Tage à f _____ = f _ 1.50 ____
                            ============

Betrag erhalten:
Heidelager, den _____ 31/1 __ 194 4 __
                           i.A.
```

Gendarme Willem Pieter Zwuup, like his colleagues, had to pay for his stay in Camp Heidelager.

Cleaning and other chores like that, which a corps such as the Gendarmerie often had to do, were no longer part of the day-to-day tasks of the seconded personnel. For this and other domestic work, about 20 to 30 male and female residents came to Camp Heidelager. The famous Dutch Jewish sports reporter Han Hollander, known from the radio, also belonged to this group. He won during the 1936 Olympics in Berlin. As a memento, he received a certificate signed by Hitler personally. Initially, he believed that this document and his fame offered him protection and that he could thus escape persecution. This turned out to be a misconception, because he ended up in Westerbork with his wife and daughter. Here, however, Hollander did benefit from his special background.[69]

According to Mechanicus, as administrator of Camp Heidelager, Hollander had the most envied job of the entire camp, because he could use various facilities there and had a lot of freedom.[70] He lost this privileged position abruptly after his wife got into a fight with a German Jewish woman. The words she pronounced during the quarrel, 'There will be another time. We will get you, you Krauts!', were reported by a camp resident. The struggle between privileged Jews and the rest once again reached a low point, fuelled by envy and distinction. Via the Camp Prison, Han Hollander and his wife were transported to Sobibor in early July 1943 as punishment. There they both died a few days later.[71]

Less than half a year later, the Jewish staff of Camp Heidelager were re-employed in the transit camp. The good relationship between them and the Gendarmes was the reason for this transfer. In addition to the development of relationships, smuggling parcels and sending letters were among the prohibited activities. It had become an art to perform these actions as inconspicuously as possible, because traitors were always lurking. Shortly before the transfer, a package was found that had been meant for a Jewish girl. A Gendarme had taken it into Camp Heidelager for her from outside. It was initially not known who this Gendarme was, but after the girl had been put under pressure, she still mentioned his name. Whether the Gendarme was punished for this is unknown. The work in Camp Heidelager was transferred to old residents who had been in Westerbork for a long time and were older than their predecessors. For most of them, this certainly did not mean an improvement in position, because they had often been living in separate houses within the camp for years. In addition, partially because they had the right contacts, they had built up a special status which allowed them to escape from compulsory employment. Performing household duties in Camp Heidelager meant that this status and the acquired rights were significantly diminished. As a result, the differences between residents were further smoothed out. A few days after beginning to work in Camp Heidelager, some women were clearly confronted with their new situation. When making the beds of some SS workers also housed in the camp, they used gloves. For some reason, women were not allowed to wear these protective garments. As punishment, they had to clean the toilets. This measure was mainly seen as a way to humiliate them.[72]

In certain cases, such as in the event of a fire hazard or in order to prevent other emergencies, the OD had to serve in Camp Heidelager. During the

April to May strike of 1943, several NSB farmers were the targets of dissatisfied citizens. In Elp, not far from the camp, activists set fire to two NSB farms, and as a result of sparks flying around, three other farms also fell prey to the flames.[73] To prevent the sparks from reaching Camp Westerbork or Heidelager, precautions were taken. In addition to placing OD posts on the corner towers and outside the barbed wire fence, six OD members had to keep watch during the night for almost two weeks in Camp Heidelager.[74]

The Gendarmes were allowed to spend their days off outside Heidelager, provided that they did not have to work extra as disciplinary punishment. However, all leave was cancelled when, due to the outbreak of some epidemic, everyone had to remain in quarantine. In the autumn of 1943 there were several infectious diseases in the camp, and because of this, it was decided to declare an overall quarantine state. Any contact between the camp and the outside world was limited as much as possible, so travelling for business as well as taking leave was no longer possible. In order to compensate for the withdrawn leave, a party evening was organised in Heidelager in mid-November for the SS and the Gendarmes. Whether this evening helped improve the morale is not known. Because of the quarantine state, more work had to be done within the camp and at the gate. Especially the guard posted at the barrier got extra work to do. Incoming transports had to be surrendered to the guard and escorted further into the camp. Suppliers of goods were obligated to unload them at the barrier. All these measures were meant to ensure stricter control.[75] When there was no quarantine state, these kinds of checks were generally much less intense.

Police Force In The Camp

Under normal circumstances, the detection of criminal offences was one of the regular tasks for a corps like the Gendarmerie. In Camp Westerbork, however, things were different. Outdoor surveillance was the main task for the Surveillance Detachment. The detection of criminal offences did take place, but that was often done on Gemmeker's order. One of the tasks that was carried out continuously was checking incoming and outgoing letters and parcels in case they contained prohibited texts and content. Among other things, they were looking for clues regarding hidden possessions, persons who had gone into hiding and Military news.[76] One of the offences that had to be taken care of according to Gemmeker was the smuggling of letters and parcels and evading censorship of post. Because some Gendarmes were also secretly guilty of this, it was difficult to deal with this offence. Nevertheless, the Gendarmerie had to carry out stricter checks, because Gemmeker and the SD in Assen received complaints about the smuggling of letters and parcels. During these checks, several persons who were in possession of prohibited postal items were arrested. Among the arrests were mainly civil servants and workers from outside the camp, such as a Conductor and a Train Driver of the Dutch Railways, as well as masons and carpenters. Gemmeker warned them during an overall roll call, after which they were released again.

For freight forwarder Jetse Sikkema from Beilen, it did not end so well. When Sikkema was in the camp on 8 September 1942 around noon, he was arrested by De Jong and his colleague Hendrik de Kruijff. This arrest took place on behalf of the SD. The Gendarmes took Sikkema to the Detachment Office in the camp. That is where his clothes were searched for forbidden objects. This resulted in at least a notebook, which showed that Sikkema smuggled letters for Jews and received money for it: sums that ranged from 1 to 4 guilders. In combination with the discovery of a bundle of letters in the cabin of the truck, the evidence was provided and the case was completed. Sikkema was transferred to the SD in Assen. They calculated that Sikkema would have earned about 10,000 guilders from his business. Whether he had actually earned this much money is not entirely clear. It can be assumed that Sikkema was locked up for some time because he had helped the Jews.[77] Willem Willing confirms that a fee had to be paid for the smuggling of letters. In a letter of 10 October 1943 he wrote: 'Every secret letter costs f3.'[78]

Gendarmes were not the only Supervisors who acted against unauthorised activities. Sometimes fanatical SS members who worked in the camp as well dealt with it too. In early January 1944, a patient from the infirmary was pressured to give the names of persons who had sent letters illegally. The patient succumbed to this pressure and told them the names. The confiscated letters were thoroughly studied. With the evidence found, Hendrik van Dam immediately initiated a follow up investigation: he ordered all women from the punishment barracks and from the sewing workshop to show up at the roll call. Women with the first name Beppie from the punishment barracks had to step forward and the women from the sewing workshop with the first name Clär were given the same order. After this selection, Van Dam ordered the women who wrote the letters to report to him. This did not happen, but Van Dam did not give up. Later that day, the selected women were expected to pass a writing test in the barracks of the OD. They had to write down a number of lines and their handwriting was then compared to that in the letters. Whether this resulted in the exposure of the perpetrators is unknown. However, some men whose names were included in the letters did get arrested. They had to go to the punishment barracks. The others in the camp felt sorry for the victims, but according to Mechanicus, they did laugh at the foolish way Van Dam had handled the whole situation.[79] The OD report briefly mentions this incident. Several persons were transferred to the punishment barracks and Camp Prison on the day in question because of the smuggling of letters.[80]

Aside from the smuggling of letters and parcels, there was also a lively black market. Persons from outside who had to be in the camp because of work brought the often scarce goods with them and then sold them to residents for a considerable sum of money. On the orders of the commander, the Gendarmerie had to warn these persons several times. If they were caught again, confinement in Camp Amersfoort would follow for the duration of six months. When De Jong returned to the camp one afternoon after visiting family in Emmen, it turned out that the SD had caught about 30 people trading goods illegally with residents. Because of the earlier warning, the camp's management, after consultation with the authorities in The Hague, intended to send the whole group to Camp Amersfoort. At the request of some of the traders, De Jong would have asked the camp's management not to carry out this sentence. Eventually, Gemmeker agreed, provided that they worked in the camp for three weeks without pay. During these three weeks, the group was not allowed to leave the camp. The Gendarmerie was ordered to guard them day and night. De Jong did comment on the supposedly good intentions of the group of workers. In reality, they did not sell their goods to help the Jews, but because they made a lot of money from it. If Gendarmes discovered black trade, they took action in a number of cases. A Police report was made against the trader. De Jong himself also fined several people. A Police report was filed against a driver from Nieuw-Weerdinge, because he sold two pounds of bread for 15 guilders to a camp resident.[81]

Despite the Police reports and the threats to punish them, the black market continued to exist as it was a lucrative affair. In mid-January 1944 an article was published in several regional newspapers with the headline 'Outrageous smuggling trade in Westerbork' or 'Extensive trade in food'. According to one of the articles, it was a public secret that the Jews in Camp Westerbork were not doing so badly. On payment of a lot of money, they could still get the best stuff, such as slaughtered chickens, butter, eggs, tobacco, sugar and grain. Outside the camp, and especially in the big cities, these scarce goods were increasingly difficult to obtain. The distribution system had to ensure a fair distribution. The smuggling trade came to light when the Gendarmerie from Assen checked some Jews who came to collect milk at the dairy of Hooghalen. Although these Jews were almost certainly escorted from the camp by Gendarmes or OD members, they were in possession of three and a half kilos of butter, two slaughtered chickens and a few boxes of cigarettes. The investigation that was initiated after this discovery resulted in even more evidence and a suspect. Baker's boy E.W. from Assen stated that he had been smuggling food into the camp for some time. His merchandise now consisted of 100 pounds of butter, 65 packs of tobacco and cigarettes, bread and numerous slaughtered chickens. What punishment E.W. received is not known.[82]

The discovery of the smuggling trade and the media coverage of it undoubtedly once again embarrassed the occupying authorities. Although it is not clear what role the Gendarmerie's Surveillance Detachment played in this, it would have been yet another indication for the occupier that the Detachment was unreliable. In addition to not adequately supervising the smuggling of food, letters and parcels, Gendarmes also helped people escape and entered into illegitimate relationships with camp residents. As a result, the work of the Gendarmes was considered increasingly questionable. On 1 June 1944 the Surveillance Detachment of the Gendarmerie was replaced by a Company of the Police Battalion Amsterdam.[83] Unreliability of the Gendarmes was without any doubt the main reason. According to Lindwer, the men from Amsterdam consisted for the most part of very feared policemen who had followed an SS based training.[84]

Police Company Amsterdam

On 2 May 1941, it was announced that vacancies in the Dutch Police Force could only be filled by persons trained at the Police Training Battalion

(POB) in Schalkhaar. Those who wished to join the Police Force had to be loyal from that moment on. They could only go to the village of Schalkhaar near Deventer for Police training, where just outside the built-up area was the Westenberg barracks. In this barracks, Dutch men were trained to become Police Soldiers with a National Socialist spirit and according to German models. According to Rauter, the intention was to place all the candidates in Closed Units after their education. They would stay with these units until their 27th year of life, after which they were given the opportunity to move to a Police Force. The goal was to have the corps be gradually nazified.

The first group of Officers trained in Schalkhaar were destined for the Amsterdam Police Force. This group arrived on 4 March 1942 and joined the Police Battalion Amsterdam (PBA). The personnel cards show that this Battalion consisted of men who were loyal to the occupier. Almost every card indicated that the person in question was a member of the Rechtsfront, the NSB and/or the SS. It soon became clear that these Police Soldiers met the wishes of the occupying authorities, because the members of the PBA were referred to as good servants of the Germans and henchmen of the German Police because of the brutal actions at the raids.[85] The first Police Soldiers trained in Schalkhaar could without a doubt be generally regarded as collaborators and minions of the German Police. For the majority of the groups that later went to Schalkhaar, this did not apply in the long run; among them, there were fewer and fewer National Socialists. Instead of being sent to Germany for labour, young men deliberately chose a job in the Police Force. That they had to follow a training course based on German models in Schalkhaar, they simply considered necessary.[86]

Within the Amsterdam Battalion, the various political preferences had led to friction. Due to the low reliability in the eyes of the occupier, the work of the Battalion was limited to the guarding of objects. After the first important buildings in Amsterdam had been dealt with, almost the entire Battalion was seconded to various places in the Netherlands to guard the employment agency in September 1943.

On 1 June 1944 most of the First Company came to Camp Westerbork to take over the outdoor surveillance of the 'unreliable' Gendarmerie Detachment.[87] According to Lieutenant Andries van Santen, one of the managers, the transfer had to be seen as a penalty measure, because 80 percent of his personnel were anti German and anti NSB. This negative attitude of his subordinates towards the New Order was very obvious.[88] The Company consisted of 108 men of various ranks. This group, whose average age was between 20 and 25 years, was housed in Camp Heidelager. Entering the camp site was only allowed once a week. Then the men were allowed to visit the bathhouse of the camp in groups.[89]

Of the entire Gendarmerie Detachment, De Jong was the only one left behind. According to his statement, his task consisted of giving theoretical lessons to the Company's men. However, it is more likely that De Jong was left behind to ensure the transfer went well, because he had been serving in Westerbork for a long period of time and as commander, he was fully aware of the circumstances in and around the camp. On 5 August 1944 De Jong's contract ended. According to his own words, he was arrested by the SD on that day for espionage. Together with a certain Major Van Beek, he would have planned to attack the camp when the allies approached, after which Van Beek would take over command. De Jong would then take care of the Police Service. It did not come to that, because De Jong was dismissed at the Gendarmerie and locked up until the liberation.[90]

The group De Jong had to teach quickly thinned out, because a few days after arrival, the number of men in the Company decreased again. Ten of them had to go to the Erica labour camp in Ommen, where they were assigned to the Labour Control Service. The task of this special service was to track down and arrest those who had broken their contract or refused to work. Two of the people only found out what they were deployed for in Ommen, and because they had not volunteered, they were able to return to Westerbork that same day.[91]

Of the men remaining in Ommen, at least one had voluntarily applied. There was a suspicion that he was a member of the SS because a colleague later saw him walking in Amsterdam with the SS runes on his uniform. However, he denied being a member of the SS. He had stolen the uniform and then went into hiding. No information was found in his file to determine whether or not he had joined the SS. In the files of other men, this information is present. This supports Andries van Santen's statement that 20% of the Company was pro German. At least ten men were demonstrably members of the NSB, SS or both.

22-year-old Pieter Drent belonged to this group of National Socialists. Before joining the Dutch Labour Service (in Dutch called the *Nederlandse Arbeidsdienst*, or *NAD*) voluntarily at the end of 1941, he worked as a butcher's servant. Because of the invasion of the German Army in Russia, men were needed for the building and repairing of roads behind the front. For this purpose, volunteers were searched for within the NAD. About 400 workers, including Drent, responded to this invitation. After a month and a half of training, the group left in early June 1942 as *Gruppe Niederlande im Reichsarbeitsdienst* in the direction of Russia. Meanwhile, Drent had become a member of the NSB. Around November 1942 he returned to the Netherlands. After that, he signed up for a job with the Police, because he might otherwise have been redeployed. Together with many other members of the Company, he started Police training in Schalkhaar on 1 July 1943.[92]

Teunis Jan Versteeg, a colleague of Drent, followed a similar path. The Company Versteeg worked for at the time had many young people leave, because they had to go to Germany for labour. When his name appeared on the list, he decided to join the NAD, because he did not want to be sent to Germany. Serving at the NAD was not a difficult task for him; he felt that this service was very much like being part of the Boy Scouts. After half a year, the opportunity arose to join the Police Force. Because Versteeg had always wanted to join the Police, he traded the NAD for the Police training in Schalkhaar. He had never been particularly interested in National Socialism.[93]

The majority of the Company was not interested in this either. Officer Jacobus Johannes Bombergen also belonged to this majority. Bombergen worked at the Municipal Telephone Service in The Hague from March 1939 onwards. During the occupation, this Company also had to give up young workers for labour. At the end of May 1943, the management of the Company was told to give up part of their staff for compulsory employment in Germany. Via a friend, whose brother worked as a Secretary for the Directors of the Telephone Service, Bombergen learned that his name was on the list. Bombergen also disliked the idea of being sent to Germany and applying to the Police was almost the only way to be able to stay in the Netherlands legally. The procedure was successful, so that Bombergen was able to go to the Training Battalion in Schalkhaar on 1 July 1943. The training, which he described as quite tough, lasted until 9 February 1944. Like most students of his class, Bombergen was placed with the Police Battalion Amsterdam (PBA).

After a little over one week, the first deployment followed. On 21 and 22 February 1944, allied bombers accidentally dropped their bombs above Nijmegen and Enschede respectively. Bombergen, together with some colleagues, had to go to Enschede first to help the local Police. A few days later, the transfer to Nijmegen followed. There he was given the task of cordoning off and monitoring the affected area, so that rescue workers could do their job without hindrance. After this depressing time, in which Bombergen saw many mutilated bodies, he returned to Amsterdam around 14 March. After that, he had to go to Velsen-Noord and Beverwijk with part of the Battalion for a period of four weeks, to check whether the population was adhering to the early curfew period. The occupying forces had chosen to punish these people because an NSB member of the State Police, Chief Lieutenant Willem Ritman, had been liquidated by the resistance. Bombergen was not given a lot of time to prepare for the next secondment, because two weeks after he had returned to Amsterdam, he left with the rest of his Company to Camp Westerbork. According to Bombergen, he had not known beforehand what 'Westerbork' was.[94]

Captain Willem Hendrik Tasseron, described as fierce NSB man, was entrusted with the Command of the Company.[95] He immediately issued some orders, probably on Gemmeker's orders. In one of them, he banned any contact with the residents. It is logical that Gemmeker wanted this order to be issued. One of the reasons why the Gendarmes were relieved of their duties was these unauthorised contacts, after all. This restraining order had little effect, since good relationships between residents and various Police Officers soon arose anyway. If an Officer was caught, sanctions followed. For example, a supervisor who had been talking to punished Jews for about eight minutes was punished by six days of light arrest.[96]

The personnel files show that a large part of the Company failed to comply with the regulations one time or even multiple times. Even those who were known as pro German, such as Pieter Drent, were caught. Drent was punished three times: twice four days and once five days. The first penalty he was given for having broken a hatch during the watch with a comrade on a watchtower. The second offence was that, contrary to the regulations, Drent put his carbine down while he was at his post. The last penalty he received for the fact that he, 'while being on patrol, was found crouching in the thickets outside the patrol route, along with another Patrolman'. The probability of being caught violating the regulations depended on a number of factors. Among other things, it was important to know which guard was serving as a Watch Commander at the time, because some of them were more fanatical than others. One of the chief guards himself was punished, because he was found asleep while serving as Commander of the Camp Guard. Since he had been ordered to be particularly vigilant before the arrival of the guard, this was considered an aggravating circumstance which was taken into account in the imposition of the sentence. The chief guard was therefore given a fine of 15 guilders and had to give up three days off.[97]

According to guard Jacobus Sijstermans, his colleague, Jan Bouwens, was one of those who took their duties very seriously. If certain parts of the camp were unguarded at night, he reported the responsible guards. He also recorded other offences in a report. Most of these reports did not reach their destination because the other guards tore them apart. Bouwens had no specific purpose in mind with his performance, except that he wanted to get in his superiors' good books. As far as is known, Bouwens was not anti-Jewish, nor did he register as a member of some National Socialist Organisation. In any case, Sijstermans did not find any posting as tough as the one in Westerbork. Therefore, the non NSB men helped each other as much as possible to make the insanely tough services as light as possible.[98] Sijstermans probably meant the length of the services, because, just like the Gendarmerie, the Company did not interfere with the internal affairs or with the transports. In addition to patrolling around the camp and occupying the watchtowers, the task consisted of guiding working groups outside the camp and supervising the work.

After the liberation, Bombergen remembered that he had been ordered to supervise a group of Jewish men and women, including people from the Criminal Barracks, who had to go outside the fence to cut stones near the crematorium. With these stones, the road next to the camp was paved. Despite the ban, according to Bombergen, the Jews were spoken to. It was important to pay close attention, because there could always be a 'bad' person nearby. Bombergen was addressed once in Camp Heidelager by a Jewish man who asked him if he could take a letter for him. Bombergen hesitated, because it could have been a trap. When the man indicated that he had heard that Bombergen could be trusted, he accepted to the request.[99]

It was less risky to have conversations with the Jewish people and provide services for them, such as sending letters, when their work took place farther away from the camp. In the summer of 1944, Bombergen had to supervise a group that was working on installing a telephone wire a few kilometers outside the camp. In collaboration with the Jewish Canteen Manager of the Heidelager, a large mess tin with extra hot meals was smuggled from the men's quarters and driven to the workplace on a wheelbarrow. The Supervisors pretended there was drinking water in the tins, because this was allowed. The workers were allowed to take turns hiding in a grove to quickly eat their portion. Because of the smuggled letters and the excellent organisation, the residents were also able to receive visits from family

Three members of the Police team, including J. Sijstermans, at their barracks in Camp Heidelager.

members and friends at their workplace. This was only possible because there was mutual trust and because there was always someone on the lookout. If there was any danger, a whistle was blown and everyone would go straight to work.[100]

In mid-August 1944, Tasseron left for Amsterdam, because he was in charge of the command of the entire Amsterdam Police Battalion. Lieutenant Jacobus Willem Munnikhuizen then took over the leadership of the Company in Westerbork. Munnikhuizen only began his Police career during the occupation. After completing his training in Schalkhaar, he was assigned the position of Superintendent at the Police Battalion in Amsterdam in early March 1942. Because Munnikhuizen had been a member of the NSB since 1941, the SS and the Rechtsfront, he had the right political colour to be sent to the Police Officers School in Apeldoorn in early September 1942. After graduating, he returned to Amsterdam as Ensign of the Gendarmerie. Shortly thereafter, promotion followed to Lieutenant of the State Police. From 5 October 1943 to 15 November 1943, Munnikhuizen would have been employed in a Division of the SS in Prague in order to follow a gymnastics course. Whether he was stricter than his predecessor cannot be concluded from his file.[101]

Early September 1944 the people of the Company became restless. After a disagreement between several men and Munnikhuizen, two of them decided to go into hiding for fear of arrest. This fear was not unfounded, because about a week later, seven men were lifted from their beds by the Germans at night and transported to Camp Amersfoort. According to Bombergen, he did not know why his colleagues had been arrested. In any case, it was not conducive to the overall mood and uncertainty among the men grew. In those days, Bombergen was also on the verge of going into hiding. His doubts got worse after one of the last transports had left Westerbork in early September. One day before the departure, Bombergen heard about the transport. Although he had not noticed any of the transports before and had never cared about them, this time he felt it necessary to warn the Jews who worked in the Heidelager that, after they had finished their work, they should not return to the camp. Whether they heeded his warning is unknown.

Staying behind in the Heidelager was not an option, because then retaliatory measures would certainly be taken against family members or other residents. Bombergen probably knew that the departing transport could have consequences for those he warned, because he wrote: 'When I heard the truth, this was such a bitter disappointment for me that I made plans to disappear.' Bombergen did not get further than making plans. In addition to danger, going into hiding also posed a number of practical problems. Each member of the Company had to hand in his civilian clothing, identity certificate, registration card and tickets in advance. Wearing the uniform and not having any means of livelihood made it more difficult to hide. Bombergen did take precautions, in case the situation became untenable for him. He knew that the Veenstra family lived in Beilen. These were acquaintances of his mother. During a visit to them, he explained the situation, after which he was told by the family that he could count on them day and night.

In the meantime, things had happened in the Netherlands. On 5 September 1944, which later came to be known as 'Dolle Dinsdag' (Mad Tuesday), there had been broadcasts about the alleged liberation of Breda, which prompted celebrations in the Netherlands. In connection with these broadcasts, a large group of NSB members came to Camp Westerbork with their families in that first week of September, where they found temporary safe accommodation in a section that had been closed off for them. The Company had nothing to do with this group. A few weeks later, it turned out that something was indeed about to happen: on Saturday 16 September, Bombergen, like some other men from the Company, would go on leave for the weekend. This time the men did not receive the necessary travel order, which was normally provided in advance. The reason for this was unknown to them. As time passed, Bombergen decided to walk to the Station of Hooghalen with some colleagues. There they were told by a Railway Officer that the Company's Commander had ordered him by telephone to send the men back. Because the men did not trust it, they got into the train ready without a travel order. They instructed the Railway Officer to inform the Commander the next time he spoke to him that he had not been able to pass on the message.

Everything seemed to be going well, until the train approached Hoogeveen Station. On the platform stood, as was often the case, a group of the *Ordnungspolizei*. This time, however, there seemed to be more going on, because the German Policemen had blocked off the platform on both sides. When the train came to a standstill, they walked past all the compartments and ordered the Dutch Policemen to exit the train immediately.[102] A small number of them, including Versteeg, still saw a chance to reach the luggage section of the train, allowing them to escape. Versteeg managed to travel safely to Rotterdam. After a short period of hiding, he was recruited as a Police Officer by the Rotterdam Corps without any problems. This transition was neatly announced in mid-October 1944 via a service announcement from the Amsterdam Police Corps.[103]

The group that had been removed from the train in Hoogeveen and of which Bombergen was part was brought back to Camp Heidelager under the guidance of the German Policemen. A day later Bombergen met a camp resident on the road outside the Heidelager, who had returned from work outside the camp shortly before. During this work, which consisted of cleaning an SS building near Arnhem, the resident would have seen secret documents stating that the entire Police Station of Westerbork would be arrested the next day. Because of this message, Bombergen and a roommate decided to flee that same night from the Heidelager. Their plan succeeded and via the family in Beilen and other safe houses, Bombergen managed to stay out of the hands of the occupiers until the liberation.[104]

Bombergen had fled at the right time. The information about an upcoming action by the occupying forces concerning the Police Team of Westerbork turned out to be correct. On the morning of Tuesday 19 September 1944, men from the SD and *Ordnungspolizei* from Assen, armed with machine guns and hand grenades, surrounded Camp Heidelager. A little later, Gemmeker arrived. The SS men from the camp would also have been present. Commander Munnikhuizen was ordered by Gemmeker to gather his Company, which at that time consisted of 69 men. Once they had arrived, Gemmeker spoke to the men. He said that he had received a request from the Commander of the *Schutzpolizei* from Groningen, Major Waschke, to inform the Policemen present in Camp Heidelager that they could choose one of two options. As a first choice, Gemmeker called the possibility to switch to the *Ordnungspolizei*. Those who did not choose to do so would be dismissed and transported to Germany for labour. The group was given ten minutes to decide. In the meantime, Gemmeker's SS staff collected the weapons of the Company.

After ten minutes had passed, the men who had decided to join the German Police were ordered to step away from the others. Of the total group, including Munnikhuizen, 14 Policemen complied with this order and stepped forward. The other 55 remained in the same spot. They had to take off their tunic and in return, they were given a coat. The diversity of these garments was great. It was clear that the coats had been owned by the Jews, because although the Star of David was no longer on it, it could still be seen on some coats where the star had been.[105]

After everyone had been provided with a 'new' coat, the group was brought to buses from the *Wehrmacht* with blinded windows. Under the guidance of the German Police, the buses left for an unknown destination. The journey ended that day, not in Germany, but in the camp of the German *Organisation Todt* (OT) in Delfzijl. Many of the people who were forced to work for the OT worked on the line of defence along the coast, which was part of the *Atlantikwall*. The next day, the entire group was transferred under very strict surveillance to the labour camp of the OT in the nearby town of Termunten.[106]

Upon arrival, the men were ordered to stand in line, after which the men who were professionals at certain crafts had to come forward. Because James Romeijn had held a hammer once, he considered himself able to be qualified as a carpenter. In hindsight, he was glad he had stepped forward, because most colleagues had to push heavy carts with cement for the bunkers that were being built all day long. A few months later the group returned to Delfzijl. From there, they were sent to different places to build roadblocks. About half of the Company fled during the stay in the north with the help of the resistance from Winschoten. The rest, including Romeijn, was released around April 1945. Romeijn later realised that the group had been taken care of better during captivity than all the people in the west of the Netherlands. Indeed, they had not suffered hunger and there had been no victims.[107]

The deportation of the men and the dissolving of the remaining Dutch Battalions and companies partially had to do with the diminishing trust. The Acting Company Commander of the Police Company Eindhoven wrote in a report at the end of June 1944 that the Company under his command had lost its right to exist because about 30 percent of the men were completely unfit for the task. While some of them went into hiding during the invasion of the allies, others refused to search for Jews and other people in hiding.[108] The 14 Policemen who had stepped forward in Westerbork had deliberately chosen to join the *Ordnungspolizei*. There was no immediate transfer, since they remained in Westerbork until the second half of November 1944. To maintain the Heidelager only for them was probably too costly and not necessary because all facilities were present in the camp. Therefore, the Dutch Policemen who had chosen to serve the Germans were housed in barracks 42 of the camp.[109]

7. THE LAST CHAOTIC MONTHS

Before the net slowly closed in on the Police Battalion and the last trains left Westerbork, a large part of the Dutch population was under the assumption at the beginning of September 1944 that the liberation was coming. On 6 June 1944 allied troops landed on the beaches of Normandy and thus formed a western front. Despite the fierce battle, the advance to the north was initially successful. After the liberation of Paris on 25 August, it was the turn of the remaining villages and cities in the north of France. Initially, it seemed that the allies had stopped at the northern French border, but on Monday evening, 4 September, the message was spread that Brussels had been liberated that afternoon and that allied troops were on their way to Antwerp.

After this, the coverage of the allies' movements became chaotic. In the evening Prime Minister Gerbrandy announced via Radio Oranje that the troops had crossed the Dutch Border. The Dutch Section of the BBC interpreted the information differently and revealed that Breda was now one of the liberated cities. The next day, 5 September, which would go down into history as 'Dolle Dinsdag' (Mad Tuesday), the British Newspapers took over this news and made it even more optimistic by writing that armoured columns were already on their way to Rotterdam. The Dutch population got into a very cheerful mood after hearing this news. Dutch flags appeared everywhere and in an unknown number of places, the people spontaneously celebrated. The panic that broke out among the occupying forces and their National Socialist accomplices as a result of the reports also had an impact on Camp Westerbork.[1]

The Last Transport

Since the Third Reich was shaken to its foundations and was even about to collapse, the BdS, Dr. Karl Eberhard Schöngarth, ordered and (partially) carried out some precautionary measures at the beginning of September. To prevent the advancing allies from getting their hands on some documents containing sensitive and incriminating information, Gemmeker had to destroy the entire camp's administration.[2] This was only a small part of the ultimate goal, because in order to remove as many traces as possible, he was also instructed to evacuate and demolish the camp completely. Another destination had already been found for the barracks; these would be transferred to the Ravensbrück Concentration Camp. Gemmeker objected to a complete evacuation. In order to break down the barracks, he needed several hundred workers. He eventually got permission to keep 600 of the 4,000 Jews still present in the camp. The rest had to go on transport.[3]

On 2 September 1944 the residents were informed by Gemmeker that the camp would be relocated and that the number of residents had to decrease. The transport that left the next day brought 1,019 Jews to Auschwitz. 2,087 Jews left to Theresienstadt with the transport of 4 September. In addition to some groups that had initially received an

On 27 July 1942 Siegfried Frank married Margot Cohen in the camp. The OD man on the right is Erich Gottschalk and second from the left is Fritz Hartog. Siegfried died on 23 April 1945 (place of death unknown).

exemption, such as the Barneveld Group and the baptised Jews, 30 OD members were on that transport.[4] At least eight of them, including Werner Bloch, Hans Dieter Blume, Siegfried Frank and Ernst Rosendorff, were old residents.

Werner, who was not able to 'celebrate' his five years stay in Westerbork, had to sit in a freight wagon, together with his seven-month pregnant wife Helga Bloch-Lipinski, whom he had married more than a year before. The young couple had to share this wagon with about 60 other people. The journey, which Werner described as a lurid honeymoon, was far from pleasant. For urinating and defecating, there was a wooden barrel in the wagon. Because there was no partition of any sort, there was no privacy. Due to the fact that this barrel was only emptied once during the days long journey and only a few ventilation slots had been installed in the wagon, the stench of vomit, urine and faeces was often unbearable. According to Werner, the train journey caused another change: as an old camp resident, he had acquired a certain status in Westerbork, but on the train this status seemed to have disappeared almost immediately. Upon arrival in Theresienstadt, the people in the wagon were considered a group of newcomers from a Dutch Transit Camp.[5]

A better fate initially seemed to await those sent to Theresienstadt than those who had been sent to other camps. After all, they had ended up in the 'better' camp because of their special services or other extraordinary circumstances, but it soon became clear that it was not some health resort where the 'chosen ones' would enjoy better treatment. Due to over-population, little food and poor sanitation, infectious diseases began spreading quickly and many people died. In order to fight overpopulation in another way, a large number of residents were transferred to other camps.

In many cases Auschwitz/Birkenau was the next and last destination. Of the 15 colleagues with whom Albert Sachs had arrived in Theresienstadt at the end of April 1943, nine were transferred after a few months to Auschwitz, where most of them were murdered immediately upon arrival. The group of OD members who left for Theresienstadt on 18 January 1944 seemed to have better chances of survival. Although the majority also soon moved to Auschwitz and the usual selection took place there, this time they were not brought to the gas chambers but were chosen for labour. Among the 1,000 men who were considered suitable, there were about 15 OD members.

The group had to go on transport again. The train arrived on 3 July in the German town of Schwarzheide, where a Sub Camp of the Sachsenhausen Concentration Camp was located. Close to this new and small camp was the *Braunkohle-Benzin-AG* factory, where important products for German warfare came from, such as synthetic gasoline and paraffin. It was crucial for the allies to stop this production. That is why the factory was bombed regularly. After such a bombing, those chosen for labour had to repair the damage as quickly as possible. The circumstances in this camp, which was located about 40 kilometres north of Dresden, were particularly poor. Hundreds of these men, including former OD members Abraham Hoogstraal[6] and Jacob Magnus[7], starved or died because of an illness. In mid-April 1945, the camp was suddenly abolished. The remaining men, together with several tens of thousands of prisoners from the Sachsenhausen Concentration Camp and some Sub Camps, started the so-called death march through Germany.[8]

Werner Bloch experienced some perilous adventures first before he had to walk in this death march. After three weeks of staying in Theresienstadt, he was transferred to a labour camp near Dresden, together with a group of men. Along the way, the train stopped, not because they had arrived at the destination, but for another reason. The men were ordered by some members of the SS to write a card with a mandatory text to their partner. One man who refused to do this was instantly shot right in the head. The men had to mention on the card that life in the new camp was pleasant and that each family had its own room. They had to give their wives the advice to request a transfer to this camp as soon as possible. After the cards were handed in, the train continued. Given the time that had passed since they had begun their journey, the train should have been near Dresden by far, but that was never the intention. Before the departure from Theresienstadt, it had already been established that Auschwitz would be the final destination.

Although several women did not trust the situation, many still chose to go after their husbands. Werner's wife also went with this group to Auschwitz. Part of the promise had become true because the men and women ended up in the same camp. However, they were never reunited as they had hoped or given the better housing they had been told about. The women were brought to the gas chambers immediately upon arrival. Werner never saw his wife again, who at that point had been eight months pregnant.[9]

During the selection in Auschwitz, Werner's physical condition was found to be good, making him suitable for labour. Ludwig Trier, Albert Moses, Mozes Benjamin Zimmern and Hans Dieter Blume, who had been

Stolpersteine for the former homes of Albert and Emma Sachs at Lantmanstraat 34 in Borne.

transported to Theresienstadt by the same train as Werner and also ended up in Auschwitz, were less fortunate in the selection: they were killed in Auschwitz on 30 September and on 1, 17 and 26 October 1944 respectively.[10]

Werner had to remain alert and responded immediately when there was a call for carpenters. His experience of several months in Westerbork's carpentry workshop came in handy now. In the meantime, he had lost his identity in addition to his status, because he had to trade it for a number. Werner left to a small Sub Camp in the south of Poland as number B-12379, which was tattooed clearly on his arm. This camp was located near a refinery. There was no carpentry work at all. Together with the other prisoners, he had to clean up debris after bombings that took place during the night. This work was heavy, the treatment rough and the food very meagre. The chances of survival decreased at a rapid pace. After four months, it was January 1945, the roars of cannons of the approaching front became more and more audible. As a result, the hope of an early liberation by the Russian Army grew. It never came to that, because the Camp Guard was ordered to evacuate the prisoners. Men who were too sick and weak to travel could stay behind. Many belonged to this category, but because they found staying too risky, they gathered all the strength and courage together for the journey. They had assessed the situation well, because the 50 people who had chosen to stay behind were shot to death a few hours after the departure.

Werner belonged to the group that was still somewhat mobile. Together with about 200 other men, he embarked on a difficult journey on foot, which lasted four days. The men who were unable to continue along the way suffered the same fate as those left behind in the camp. The journey ended on a rail yard, which was also used for men from other camps as an intermediate station. The group had to sit in open freight wagons that were covered in snow. Because it was freezing and there was nothing to shelter them from it, this transport went down into history as 'the frozen meat transport'. Werner described the atrocities he witnessed along the way. Sleep had to be kept to a minimum, otherwise the body's temperature could drop too much. Despite the will to survive, many fellow passengers died along the way. The survivors turned this to their advantage, because the bodies of the victim were put into use as benches. Although this will appear cruel and disrespectful, it was simply one of the survival strategies. Sitting or lying on the snowy floor could lead to freezing to the floor. By sitting on the bodies of the deceased, this danger was somewhat reduced. Upon arrival at the Concentration Camp Sachsenhausen, it appeared that there were more 'benches' than men in a number of wagons. Werner had a frozen toe after the five-day train journey, and amputation had to prevent him from losing the rest of his foot as well.

The net closed in on the once powerful German Army quickly; troops from various countries were coming in from all sides. This was the reason for evacuating the camp population of Sachsenhausen and some Sub Camps. On 21 April 1945 a procession of more than 30,000 people set themselves in motion in the direction of Schwerin, located in northern Germany. They started the death march, which eventually lasted ten days.

Because of the wound on his foot, Werner could barely walk. He even collapsed a few times. Staying behind was not one of the options this time, as this would have resulted in certain death. Werner gathered his last remnant of courage and strength and continued the journey as well as he could. During the day, a distance of several tens of kilometres was covered. At night, they could often rest in the open field. Due to malnutrition and exhaustion, many fellow sufferers once again succumbed along the way. A large part of the guards saw the end was near and left. This did not change the situation for those left behind, because where could they go?

Werner was running on his last bit of strength when white trucks from the International Red Cross passed the remaining people participating in the death march. The first vehicles were already full and did not stop. Fortunately, the other vehicles were not yet full. A truck that had almost no one in it came to a standstill near Werner. Along with some other exhausted men, he was lifted into the vehicle. When the vehicles with the survivors in them had been on the road for some time, they ran into a Russian tank blocking the road. Continuing to drive was too dangerous, because further down the road, there were still fierce battles going on. Russian Soldiers helped them get out. After spending a night in a nearby village, vehicles of the Red Cross appeared again. After an exhausting journey, they delivered the former prisoners to an Emergency Hospital in Lübeck. A number of Werner's colleagues did not survive the death march.[11]

Accommodation National Socialists

Because of the reports on the advancing allied troops on 4 and 5 September 1944, which were spread quickly, the National Socialists fled, fearing retaliatory measures. Additional trains brought women and children from the south and west to the east. That Camp Westerbork and other places were used as a shelter for this group of refugees is not surprising: it was close to the border; all facilities were present and there was enough space after the recent transports. According to the Jewish camp resident Hans Bial, who wrote extensively about the September days of 1944 in his diary, the reports about the arrival of the refugees had already reached the camp at an earlier stage. On the evening of 4 September Bial heard that 40 women and 50 children of the SD would arrive at the camp from Zeist the next morning. All other residents had to move to the old part of the camp to make room for them. After that, the empty barracks were cleaned thoroughly.

According to reports that reached the camp the next day, large groups of National Socialist refugees were on their way to Drenthe. Presumably, 10,000 NSB people had to be cooked for. The reports on the arrival of the refugees proved to be correct. On Wednesday 6 September 1944 the first NSB men drove into the camp with their packed cars. Not much later, the stream of refugees really started. In and on everything that still had some wheels left and could drive, but also on foot or by train, the fleeing NSB people tried to reach the camp.[12] The Dutch civil servant Aad van As saw the group nearing the camp. He compared the entry of the National Socialists with that of the Jews and saw many similarities. Exhausted, insecure and with only those possessions they were able to carry with them, the newcomers entered the camp.[13] This caused a tense situation. In order to avoid conflicts between the two groups, a barbed wire barrier was laid around the old part of the camp. An NSB man armed with a rifle was placed at the only passage to that part of the camp. Armed NSB members were also placed at other strategic points in the camp. Residents were allowed to leave their part of the camp, but this did not apply to the NSB people: they were stopped at the old part. Once it was past curfew, the guard posts could only be passed if one knew the password. Initially, only the Service Leaders knew the password, but according to Bial, soon the rest of the people knew it too.[14]

It will not have been difficult to select NSB members who had held a weapon before for manning the posts. Among the group was an unknown number of men from the 'Landwacht Nederland'. The National Socialist newspapers described these guards as the new Police Soldier, who was ready day and night to keep the people safe. The leader of the NSB, Anton Mussert, wanted to use the Landwacht as a self-protection corps of the NSB. However, Rauter had other ideas about this: he wanted the Landwacht to take over Police tasks, because the Dutch police did not cooperate sufficiently and was considered unreliable. As a compromise, the Landwacht received tasks related both to the security of the camp and the Police Service.[15]

The reports on the rapid advance of the allied troops proved to be incorrect. The cheerful mood disappeared instantly and the occupiers no longer felt that there was much cause to panic. Although the allies still liberated the south of the Netherlands, the area above the major rivers remained in the hands of the occupying forces. The NSB men present in the camp probably felt that the situation in the occupied part of the Netherlands was not safe enough, because mainly the women and children left for Germany by train after a few days. This had little or no influence on the state of mind of the residents, because they would have much preferred seeing the men leave.[16] That only happened on 18 September, after they had been inspected first. Those who were considered suitable were included in The Emergency Company of the Landwacht.[17]

The relief felt by the Jews who were left behind was short lived. According to a message, a new group was to come to the camp on the evening of 18 September, consisting of all the men of the SD present in the Netherlands and their Dutch accomplices. Although the group did indeed consist of SD men and their accomplices, it was not directly a large group that arrived. That night, about 40 SD members arrived. The next morning there was also something going on outside the camp: in the Heidelager the men of the Amsterdam Police Battalion were asked to choose between the aforementioned options. The minority of them who opted to join the German Police Force was housed in the camp, so there was still sufficient supervision. According to a camp order, the SD patrolled the camp. The SD was authorised to ask for access to the camp cards. One of the camp residents recognised among the SD men someone who had arrested him and interrogated him in Rotterdam. This observation is consistent with the facts. Among the newcomers were 15 members of the SD *Fahndungskommando*, the Political Service of the Rotterdam Police.

In mid-1942, the Police Forces of the larger cities, where no Political Service was yet active, were instructed by the occupying forces to set up one. However, several large cities already had such a 'dreaded' service before the order. In The Hague this was the *'Documentatiedienst'* (Documentation Service), in Amsterdam the *'Bureau Inlichtingendienst'* (Bureau Intelligence Service) and in Rotterdam the service was initially called Group 10. These services, which consisted mainly of National Socialist Police Officers, were tasked with carrying out orders for and by the occupying forces. When the persecution of the Jews began, special groups were formed within the political services for the search for Jews who had gone into hiding, among other things. Partly as a result of this work, the political services became an extension of the occupying forces. In Rotterdam, Group 10 was even under the command of the *SD* as *SD Fahndungskommando* from March 1944 onwards. On 20 September 1944 the *Fahndungskommando* would have left for an unknown destination. Because the leaders of the Police Force thought that the members of the command had gone into hiding, they immediately sent a telex message to the DGvP in Zwolle and blocked the accounts. A few days later, they received the reply that the *Fahndungskommando* had not gone into hiding, but had been evacuated to Camp Westerbork by order of the *Aussenstellenleiter*.[18]

Probably during the same period, or perhaps a little later, several employees of the political services from Amsterdam and The Hague were sent to Westerbork as well. After the liberation, Chief Detective Hendrik Johannes Buunk, who had belonged to the Rotterdam service, made a statement about his short stay at Camp Westerbork. Together with his colleagues in Rotterdam, he spent about ten days in the camp. His work there consisted of security tasks inside and outside the barbed wire fence. On Monday 25 September Buunk's group and the remaining SD members were replaced by an unknown number of Police Officers from The Hague, according to Bial. The Amsterdam men followed a few days later. Buunk and his colleagues did not return to Rotterdam. They were given new stations in the east of the country, where they had to carry out orders for the SD. Buunk ended up in Apeldoorn.[19]

After the last train with almost 280 Jews in it had left for Bergen-Belsen on 13 September 1944, the remaining part of the camp population was still in danger of having to leave Westerbork too. When the railway strike began four days later, no transport could leave, as the train traffic had almost entirely stopped.

As previously mentioned, the coming and going of large and small groups of National Socialists with different backgrounds was not conducive to the peace within the camp. Some of the Jewish camp people abused this troubling situation, for example by calling in sick. That is why Schlesinger and Pisk visited the barracks in the Jewish part at the end of September. They took the camp cards of those who were found there while they were not sick. This action was successful, because these people went straight back to work. Residents who thought that supervision had become less stringent because of the circumstances were proven wrong.[20] The SS became increasingly involved in internal affairs. In the period from May to August 1944, six men were added to this group.

War Crimes In And Around The Camp

Hartog Walvis[21] was brought to Westerbork shortly before the chaos around Mad Tuesday broke out, together with an unknown number of Jews from Camp Amersfoort. The Landwacht had arrested him three months before during a raid in Amsterdam. Because one person was ill, the entire group was housed in a separate barracks. After more than a week, Hartog heard that he and the others in this barracks would go on transport to a camp in Germany. Soon thereafter, a plan to escape arose, but because of the great risk, more and more people refrained from participating after all. In the end, only Hartog and four other young men were left.

On 5 September 1944 John Ancona, Johan Engers, Samuel Goldstein, Ernst Katan[22] and Hartog left the barracks shortly before the evening roll call. Using the darkness as protection and taking a pair of pliers with them, they snuck to the ditch surrounding the camp. When they got there, Hartog heard whistling from another part of the camp. Because he thought that their absence had been discovered and the guards would therefore be searching for them, he suggested that they stopped the attempt to escape. The other four were not keen on this idea and decided to continue. Hartog left them by the ditch and returned to the barracks. In order to have dry clothes after crossing the ditch, the four men undressed and tried to enter the water as quietly as possible. This failed. Due to the silence in and around the camp, some of the Police Battalion, who were in charge of surveillance on the outside of the barbed wire fence, heard something. The Dutch Policemen walked in the direction of the sound and saw the four refugees. They immediately fired a number of times with their rifle; whether the rifles had been aimed at the men is unknown.

The four men could not go anywhere, because three of Gemmeker's men,

Edmund Xaver Breil   *Fritz Lübbecke*

the German SS members Edmund Xaver Breil, Fritz Lübbecke and Heinz Martin Max Lemke, came running to the place where they had heard the sound of the shots. They arrested the men and immediately brought them to the barracks in which the *Kommandantur* was located. There they reported to Gemmeker that the guards had caught the four arrestees in the act trying to escape the camp. During the subsequent interrogation, denying was of little use, since they had been caught in the act. Gemmeker would have told Lemke that he himself was not authorised to impose penalties. To do this, he had to get permission from the BdS.

Gemmeker sent a telex message describing the incident. The answer already came after half an hour. Deppner ordered Gemmeker via an order signed by him to shoot the four men that same night. Gemmeker fulfilled the assignment and assembled a firing squad. He chose Breil, Lemke and Lübbecke, who had arrested the men, for the job and added the Dutch SS man Johannes Otto von Henning to the squad as well.

The SS members brought the men condemned to death to the crematorium located a few dozen metres outside the camp. There they were arranged in a row, with their faces in the direction of a side wall. The SS men pulled their guns and stood about half a meter from the men. After that, they aimed the weapon at the neck of the man standing in front of them and pulled the triggers. A neck shot was chosen because it gave the assurance that the men would immediately be struck fatally. It seemed that they had achieved this goal, because after the shots, all four victims collapsed. After about twenty minutes, the SS men returned to the camp. Because the key to the crematorium was missing, they left the victims at the execution site.

Lemke, Lübbecke and Von Henning were among the six SS men who had been added to Gemmeker's group between May and August 1944. Von Henning, who was the only Dutch person of this group, came from an NSB family and had become a member of the movement himself in 1938. In March 1941 he volunteered for the *Waffen SS* in Rotterdam, knowing that he was entering into German Military Service. After training, he served six months at the Eastern Front with the anti-aircraft artillery and then became driver of the staff. On 16 May 1944 Von Henning came to Camp Westerbork as *Polizeiangestellter*. On his SS uniform he wore the rank of an *Unterscharführer*. Von Henning was initially a telephone operator and worked in the kitchen for some time. Like the other SS members in the camp, he also had to carry out other tasks, which would later be included in the category of war crimes. Participation in the firing squad certainly belonged to this category.[23]

Dentist Heinz Wolf was late at work in the Dental Office of the camp on the night of the execution. At one point he heard a scratching sound at the door and from that same direction came whimpering. When Wolf opened the door, he saw a person who was visibly injured. Blood came from the victim's neck and mouth. Together with someone who came to his aid, Wolf put the wounded man on a stretcher and they took him to the Hospital. Then surgeon Salomon Kuttner was woken up and asked to come to the Hospital. He examined the wounded man, who was fully conscious. Kuttner saw that the bullet had entered the man's neck next to the spine and had exited through his lower jaw. Having provided him with emergency aid, the man could talk. He introduced himself as Goldstein and told them what had happened that night. Before Kuttner continued treatment, such as taking X rays, he first informed his chief, Fritz Spanier, about the incident. Spanier then contacted Gemmeker directly by telephone, who decided that Goldstein should not be treated further. He was therefore taken from the treatment table and put on a bed. As evidenced by various statements, further treatment would certainly have helped, because the injuries were relatively minor.

An OD man was ordered to guard the wounded man all night. After the liberation, Breil stated that he was sent to the Hospital by Gemmeker in the early morning with another German SS man, Emil Walter Frentzel-Beijme. There they had to instruct Spanier to put Goldstein under anaesthesia using a syringe. It was Gemmeker's intention to make Goldstein believe that the anaesthesia was necessary for surgery, so he would not notice what they were actually planning to do with him. After the liberation, Spanier stated that this story was not correct. He was told by Frentzel-Beijme to give Goldstein a lethal injection. As a Doctor, Spanier considered it only natural for him to refuse to fulfil this order. According to Frentzel-Beijme, there was nothing more to do in this case than to kill Goldstein by shooting him. Because Spanier thought the alternative was terrible, he consulted with his colleague Nico Speyer to try and decided what they should do. They came to the conclusion that the administration of a sedative was still within the limits of their medical profession. Goldstein would not notice the second attempt on his life this way.

After Frentzel-Beijme approved this proposal, Goldstein was given a syringe with a firm sedative and he immediately fell into a deep sleep. To transport Goldstein to the crematorium, Frentzel-Beijme contacted the main guardhouse of the OD. He ordered for two OD members and a stretcher to be brought to the Hospital. Peter Margules, who was present in the main guardhouse at that time, went to the Hospital with his brother Hans. Both OD members were under the assumption that the man they were supposed to put on the stretcher had died, since they had to take him to the crematorium. After the brothers had placed Goldstein in the hallway of the crematorium, they were ordered to go with Frentzel-Beijme. He took them to a clearing near the crematorium. There they found, quite unexpectedly and to their great dismay, three more bodies, which they also had to take to the hallway of the crematorium. When Peter and Hans were finished with their task, they returned to the camp.

When leaving the crematorium, they came across Isidoor Fontijn. This Jewish man, who had only been working in the crematorium for a short time, had been told by his boss to burn the four corpses in the cremator. Breil and Lübbecke helped Fontijn burn the first corpse. Then they left the crematorium and left Fontijn with the three remaining corpses. Afterwards, Fontijn understood that the first body must have been Goldstein's. He explained a number of special circumstances. The differences between Goldstein's body and the other corpses, in combination with his later experiences, made him realise that Goldstein was probably still alive when he was put into the cremator. According to Breil, however, Goldstein had not entered the cremator alive. He had been ordered by Gemmeker to shoot Goldstein in the hallway of the crematorium. By shooting him in the temple, he had complied with this order. After burning all four corpses, Fontijn buried the ashes near the crematorium.

According to Gemmeker, the execution was justified, because everyone in the camp knew what the consequences were of trying to escape. In addition, due to the circumstances in the Netherlands, a state of emergency had been declared in the camp, which could be seen as an additional warning. Other witnesses considered this justification questionable because the group to which the four men belonged had only briefly been in the camp and was housed in the punishment barracks. There was therefore a possibility that they were not aware of the special circumstances.

A few weeks later, the SS members were involved in an incident that

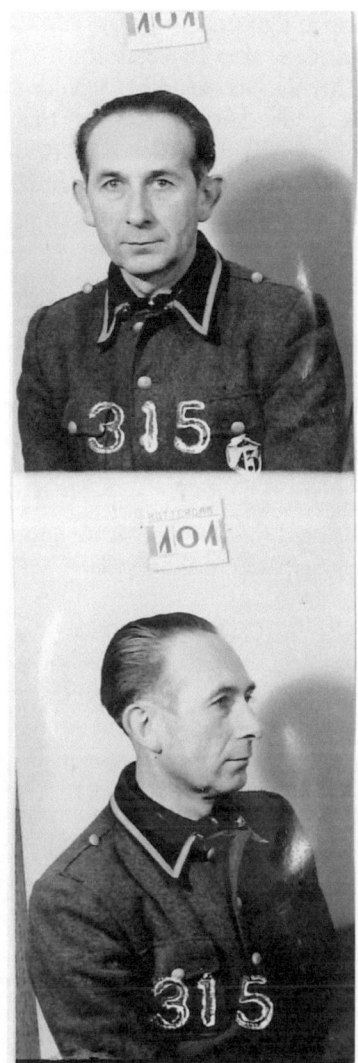

Emil Walter Frentzel-Beijme   Walter Hanitsch

occurred outside the camp, but in which they played a significant role. On 17 September 1944 the staff of the Dutch Railways went on strike after a special code message was sent via Radio Oranje on behalf of the Dutch Government in London. As a result of this railway strike, the train traffic in the Netherlands stopped almost entirely. The aim was to stagnate the transport of German troops and war equipment as much as possible. Because this also endangered the supply of food, the strike negatively affected mainly the citizens in the west of the country in the long run, with the so-called *Hongerwinter* (Dutch famine of 1944/45) as result. The occupiers tried to change their minds by means of retaliatory measures.

A number of those who were still hiding fell prey to the vengeful Germans and their accomplices after all. On 30 September 1944 Gemmeker received a note from Deppner, who was in the camp at that time, with five addresses in Hooghalen. Railway workers lived at three of these addresses, while the other two were those of the head of the Christian school in Hooghalen and one of the teachers working there. Both were also hiding. It is likely that an order to empty these homes and set them on fire had also been written on this note. Any residents present had to be arrested. Gemmeker ordered a number of his subordinates to execute this order. In addition to these SS members, the Dutch members of the Police Battalion who were still in the camp were also sent to these addresses. They were already wearing the German uniform at that time.

The entire operation was led by Lieutenant Munnikhuizen. The group drove to the specified addresses in two trucks, one of which was driven by the Jewish camp resident Siegfried Sommerfeld. First, the men took all the useful objects out of the homes. They also took the animals, such as chickens. When the trucks were full, they drove it back to camp and unloaded the cargo. In the meantime, the ones left behind destroyed the homes and then set fire to them.[24] Several SS members declared that Soldiers from another German unit had also joined them and participated in the action.

The Centre Of Power

These Soldiers possibly belonged to the *Zollgrenzschutz*. In the last week of September 1944 Bial had to clean some barracks together with other residents, because between 800 and 1,000 *Grenzschutzleute* would be coming to the camp. Whether that many actually came in the end is doubtful. In any case, from the beginning of October, care and shelter were arranged for 14 persons from the *Zollgrenzschutz Fortbildungs Kompanie*. During that month, this Company grew to just over 200 men.[25]

At the beginning of November 1945 Derk Jan Stoel, as head of the Political Investigation Service, drew up a report on the 'Zollschutzpolizei Westerbork' for the Mayor of Westerbork. In this report, Stoel stated that he was personally aware of the fact that the Officers of this Department were stationed in the camp. They would be trained there in the SD school, which was also located in the camp, to become an SD member. Whether there was in fact such a school in the camp cannot be said with certainty.[26] However, it is plausible because the BdS, Schöngarth, and his staff had set up part of the camp as headquarters from October to the beginning of December 1944. As a result, Westerbork became partly the centre of the occupying power.[27]

The barracks had to be cleaned and decorated. In one of them, the office of the *Brigadeführer*, even linoleum was laid. Furniture and household items needed for the decoration had to be taken from the residents' homes. F. David-Heller had been staying in the camp with her husband, chef Ernst David, since 1939. As a Government Official, she was allowed to take all of her furniture with her. The couple initially lived in a villa next to the later casino. When the camp was put into use as a transit camp, they had to move to barracks 10, behind the central kitchen. SS member Walter Hanitsch was ordered by Gemmeker to help claim furniture. In the context of this assignment, he visited the couple.

According to Mrs David-Heller, the way Hanitsch worked was extremely humane. Hanitsch did not 'claim' anything, but for every piece of household items he had to bring, he asked whether it could be missed. Hanitsch refused to take anything from the nursery, where the couple's daughter was sleeping during his visit. Mrs David-Heller was convinced that he was carrying out the assignment against his will. She further described Hanitsch as a very humane person, who was always friendly and polite to the residents and who was always the first to greet the other when passing by.

The Jewish camp resident M. Montezinos was also positive about Hanitsch's actions. He got to know him as a 'correct' man, who, in his opinion, had a very exceptional position compared to the other SS men. This was not true for his background, by the way. In June 1942 Hanitsch left for the Eastern Front as a Soldier from an *SS-Polizei Division*. There, he was severely injured during a reconnaissance, which caused him to lose his left arm. After a recovery period of several months, he was employed at the telephone service of the Sipo in The Hague. As he needed a lot of fresh air on his Doctor's advice, he was transferred to Camp Westerbork in early August 1944, where he was given a position in the *Bauleitung*. This service was occupied with building and repairing barracks[28].

For residents it was important, even after the departure of the Dutch National Socialists, to keep an eye on who they were dealing with. With the arrival of the SD members, their accomplices and other representatives of the occupying forces, it was still difficult to estimate who they could trust. Sometimes, in the part of the camp where these newcomers were staying, things happened that no one from the Jewish part was allowed to see. In the first days of October, OD members were placed in front of the entrance to the Jewish part. They were meant to prevent residents from attending speeches by dignitaries. The Jews were usually allowed to enter the other part if it was for work. As such, they witnessed what was happening in the camp. Bial saw how the Border Guards were being prepared for their new position. Although he did not feel sorry for them at all, Bial found it depressing to see that these generally older men, often between 50 and 60-year-old, could not do anything right and had to fulfil all orders on command. Bial thought what he saw was inhumane. If a dog were treated in this way, he would either run away or bite after a few minutes. From mid-October onwards, residents were able to come into contact with the Border Guards, as they took over the surveillance from the heavily reduced Police Battalion.

This remaining group was officially assigned to the *Polizei Freiwilligen Bataillon Niederlanden* in mid-November 1944. Shortly after they had put on the uniform of the *Ordnungspolizei* and had taken the oath on the Führer, they were transferred to the barracks of the *Ordnungspolizei* at the Grote Markt in Groningen. In addition to guarding the Detention Centre, troops of the former Battalion were involved in incidents that were described as war crimes after the liberation. For example, Pieter Drent was part of a firing squad consisting of members of the *Ordnungspolizei* and of the SD at the beginning of April 1945. This squad executed a number of persons on the Military grounds of what used to be Peest airport. Drent also participated several times in raids on illegal workers in the city of Groningen, Grijpskerk and Roodeschool. His superior in Westerbork, Jacob Munnikhuizen, became known as a war criminal because of his actions during a raid in Tijnje, where he severely abused those arrested and where two innocent men died.[29]

The departure of the Dutch Police did not pose any problems for the leaders of the camp, because the deployment of the Border Guards meant that there was some continuity in surveillance. The rapid change of these men was not a problem either, because when the first group left after about a month, their place was taken by a new group. The men of the *Zollgrenzschutz* would have treated the residents correctly almost without exception. Occasionally, one or more Border Guards had to be warned that talking with Jews was forbidden. This could only be done if this was in the interest of the service.[30]

The work of the Border Guards was not limited to occupying the guard posts outside the camp. They also patrolled the area and carried out road checks in the Municipality of Westerbork. In order to track down people in hiding, they mainly checked the identity documents of young men. In addition, Border Guards were placed with SD commands in surrounding villages, such as Zweeloo and Beilen. In this latter Municipality, an incident involving Border Guards from the camp occurred around 21 October 1944. SS man Frentzel-Beijme was ordered by Gemmeker to empty the farm of Lammert Zwanenburg, located at the Beilervaart in Beilen, together with Border Guards and some residents. The furniture and the cattle had to be transferred to the camp. Frentzel-Beijme himself shot a bull, which was then slaughtered on the spot by a Jewish butcher. The meat also went to camp.

When the action was in full swing, Zwanenburg's wife was brought home by the Landwacht. They had arrested her a day before. Before Frentzel-Beijme sent her off the premises, she was able to observe a few things. Her husband and daughter were picked up in Diever on the night of 18 to 19 October. Frentzel-Beijme could remember that this action was related to the hiding of American pilots. Zwanenburg's wife admitted that they had helped pilots, but according to her, the Germans were not yet aware of this, because she had only been questioned about hiding a forbidden radio.[31] Normally, Gemmeker would not have received the order to carry out this action, but since the leaders of the Sipo and SD were operating from the camp, he did get this order. In addition, sufficient personnel from various units were present to carry out certain assignments.

The whole Zwanenburg family was involved in all kinds of illegal activities, such as sheltering (Jewish) people in hiding. When the Landwacht of Diever arrested and questioned a person in hiding, he mentioned the name Zwanenburg. Soon afterwards, the arrest of father, mother and daughter followed. The son was staying elsewhere and thus managed to stay out of the hands of the Officers. Those in hiding were not found on the farm because they had been able to escape in time. Initially, nothing was found during the search, but inspection of the cesspool yielded a box with ration stamps, identity certificates and photographs of allied pilots. Some contacts of Zwanenburg, including Lambertus Bruulsema and Hendrik Wiegers, were also arrested. Meanwhile, a unit of the SD from Assen and some men of the *Ordnungspolizei* had come to Diever for an interrogation. Zwanenburg in particular was allegedly abused.[32]

In the case of Bruulsema, Wiegers and Zwanenburg, evidence was found that they had been guilty of illegal activities. On 19 October, the day of their arrest and the subsequent interrogation, the verdict had to be reached as soon as possible, according to the so-called *Niedermachungsbefehl*[33]. Under the guidance of the SD men from Assen, the trio was taken by car to Camp Westerbork. Gemmeker would not have been informed in advance of the arrival of the three people who had been sentenced to death. He first asked for permission from his superior to execute them and then appointed a place near the crematorium for the execution. Three former Dutch Policemen who had switched to the SD in Assen were instructed by their Commander to form the firing squad. After they had pulled the trigger, an Officer probably gave them a final shot to the head. The two residents who were in charge of operating the cremator were commissioned shortly afterwards to burn the three bodies. Gemmeker was not present at the execution. However, he ordered his own SS men to close the roads in the camp. This statement matches those of his subordinates.[34]

Edmund Breil stated that he had been ordered to block off the entire area and all roads with the other SS men from the camp on the evening of 19 October. They were ordered by Gemmeker not to admit anyone, and if the convicts tried to flee, they were obligated to shoot at them. To do so, the SS men were armed beforehand with American machine guns. Even Reiser, who had only one arm, was given such a weapon. During the remaining four executions that took place near the crematorium in October 1944, the SS members of the camp were given the same task.[35]

It is likely that OD members supervised the cremating of the executed, because both Hans Eisinger and Sandor Salmagne made a statement about this after the liberation. During one of the execution days, Sandor went to the crematorium. In front of this building stood a number of civilians, as well as Gemmeker, Deppner and a number of troops from the *Ordnungspolizei*. Sandor saw the civilians disappear behind the crematorium and heard gunfire immediately afterwards. A little later, men of the Ordnungspolizei appeared, dragging a number of bodies by their legs into the hallway of the crematorium. When he arrived there, the cremator had been lit. Hans Eisinger later took over Sandor's shift and also saw a number of corpses lying in the hall.[36] In the camp itself, the OD will also have had a task, because on the days when an execution took place, no one was allowed to leave his or her barracks.

During the turbulent September days of 1944 and the tense period thereafter, order and discipline remained important. The person who violated the rules did not go on transport anymore, but could still be punished. For example, there was a camp resident who asked an Amsterdam SD man if he could send a letter for him, although others had advised him not to ask. Instead of responding to the request, the man immediately arrested the resident and brought him to the appropriate authority. The man would have been chased through the camp for an hour and a half by a Police Officer, while in the meantime, he was ordered to lie down and get up again. After this public display followed confinement in the Camp Prison.[37]

Internal Supervision Maintained

In a relatively short and chaotic period, much changed when it came to surveillance. The OD remained one of the fixed factors. Although this service had declined in strength due to the last transports, at least 32 OD members were still supervising the Jewish part of the camp. Some of the SS members in the camp had to fill the empty spots in the security. They were assigned vacant spaces, such as the penal barracks and the Camp Prison.

Since residents continued to violate the rules and the Detachment of Gendarme Paridaen came to an end, a new Prison Guard had to be found. SS man Heinz Lemke was seen as the most suitable person for this task. Lemke had to join the Military in 1941 and was assigned to the *SS Polizei Division*. With this Infantry Division, he fought on the Eastern Front near Leningrad. In 1942 he suffered such severe injuries that he lost his right eye. After being nursed in the Military Hospital of Darmstadt and in another Hospital in Vught, he was assigned to the *Referat IV B 4*, the so-called *Judenreferat*, in The Hague.[38] There and in Scheveningen he participated in raids, in which he allegedly abused several Jews.[39]

Around May 1944 Lemke came to the camp, where Gemmeker gave him the task of supervising the Prison at the end of that year. A number of sources, such as statements, show that the cells were not often occupied. It is therefore plausible that the surveillance was carried out from the *Kommandantur*. Lemke had to visit the prisoners three times a day, so he was there much less frequently than his predecessor. Gemmeker knew the conditions in the cells were not great. The central heating did not provide enough heat, because wood was used instead of coal. He did not know if there were blankets. He did not think so, because when the NSB refugees came to the camp in early September 1944, all available blankets were given to them.

Gemmeker was aware of the fact that there were no sanitary facilities in the cells. Urinating and defecating had to be done during Lemke's visits. Because Gemmeker assumed that the prisoners were in good hands with Lemke, he did not check this. He would have heard only after the liberation that the treatment had been very bad. Several people who came into contact with Lemke made an incriminating statement about this.

The Jewish resident Mozes Kisch belonged to this select group. Kisch worked as a stoker in the boiler house and as a driver on the camp's train. With this train he drove to Groningen every ten days to store food. During the trip, Kisch smuggled letters out of the camp. On the way back, the train crew themselves secretly took food, which they traded on the black market in the camp. These illegal activities came to light because a resident of the punishment barracks was willing to commit treason in return for better circumstances. The investigation initiated by Gemmeker resulted in eight suspects. Because of previously imposed retaliatory measures, four of them were already in the Criminal Barracks, because two other prisoners had fled from their original barracks. The remaining four, including Kisch, lived in the so-called 'free part'. Initially, all eight suspects were imprisoned in the Camp Prison. Gemmeker decided to make the sentence of the four men in the Criminal Barracks even tougher. In addition to three weeks of imprisonment, they had to live on bread and water during this sentence. The four suspects from the free section were transferred to the Criminal Barracks after a few days.

Evidence shows that Lemke did indeed treat 'his' prisoners badly. They did not get enough bread and water. It even happened a few times that Lemke only came to deliver the meagre meal after two or three days. There were generally no straw mattresses on the wooden benches they were supposed to sleep on, so the night had to be spent on slatted bases. Because there were no blankets, the capacity of the heating was insufficient and no extra clothing could be worn over or under the overalls, the prisoners were constantly cold. There was no tin for urinating and defecating in any cell. The men used a clog as a urinal and threw the contents out between the bars.

Max de Jong was imprisoned on 10 February 1945. According to him, the treatment in the cell was terrible. In addition to all the other inconveniences, such as the bad bed and the unbearable cold, he had no other choice but to defecate in the corner of his cell. He had to clean up the faeces himself, and in the absence of resources, this was an unhygienic job. De Jong had ended up in Prison because he had told someone that food intended for the residents was sent to the SS. As Gemmeker said this was a lie, De Jong had to go to him and explain his actions. He was sentenced to 20 days in Prison for incitement. Before he went to jail, Lemke searched him first. This investigation resulted in a piece of paper on which De Jong had written messages from the English channel. The broadcasts were listened to illegally at the casino. De Jong came there regularly, because he was in charge of keeping a fire going. Spreading messages could still be dangerous to discipline, and that is why the matter was taken so seriously. During one of the interrogations, Lemke would have punched De Jong in the face, but he continued to deny he was guilty of incitement. Gemmeker sent De Jong's statements to the BdS, who subsequently sentenced De Jong to death. When the BdS came to the camp a day later, Gemmeker discussed this case with him and indicated that there was too little evidence. Following these consultations, De Jong's sentence was converted into five years of imprisonment in the Criminal Barracks.

After the liberation, Lemke denied that he had mistreated the prisoners. According to him, there were straw mattresses and blankets. He did admit that there was no proper heating. Without skipping a day, he would have brought water, bread and occasionally even coffee. He could not remember whether the prisoners were given the same amount of bread as the other residents.[40]

From mid-September 1944 onwards, the original Criminal Barracks were no longer used as such. The closure was a logical consequence of the circumstances. Most of the punished people will have been sent along with the last transports, while the arrival of Jews stopped for some time. When the advance of the allied troops came to a halt at the beginning of September, the search for Jews who were hiding was resumed above the big rivers. Those who were found came back to the camp as S-cases. In addition, residents could also be eligible for imprisonment. At the end of 1944, barracks 21 and 22 were used to house these newly arrived Jews.[41]

Jewish drivers Siegfried Sommerfeld and Fred Goldstein were the first prisoners in mid-December 1944. Goldstein brought some suitcases with

Sommerfeld's properties to Assen because the man had asked him to do so. This sounded like an attempt to escape from the camp, leading to Sommerfeld receiving a sentence of one year of imprisonment and Goldstein half a year. After Max de Jong had served his Prison sentence, he was also transferred to the Criminal Barracks.

The four suspects who had been sent to Prison for the smuggling of letters were also transferred to the punishment barracks. Although they got a little more freedom here, they also complained about the care. SS man Wilhelmus van Eck was in charge of the barracks. A few months before, on 15 August 1944, Van Eck had left for Officers training to Bad Tölz, located in southern Germany. Although he had lost his right eye at the front, he was still approved for the Officers training, which lasted six weeks. Then he would be redeployed to the front. Van Eck stated that fighting the allies seemed to him an 'unforgivable' act, so he tried to get out of Bad Tölz as soon as possible. After about a month he succeeded in this and he was given the opportunity to return to Camp Westerbork.

Van Eck was initially appointed head of the garage, but when he was no longer needed there, Gemmeker appointed him Commander of the Criminal Barracks. Van Eck chose some of the people who had been imprisoned there to supervise according to the 'divide and rule strategy'. In Van Eck's eyes, those who were in the barracks had to do the most difficult work during a long working day. Gemmeker would have given him the authority to make them exercise for 30 minutes or longer after their work if the work had not been carried out properly. According to Van Eck, he had only done so sporadically. Men and women who were unable to participate because of old age or physical health issues were allowed to stay in the barracks. Gemmeker was convinced that Van Eck had indeed not abused this power. Some residents had a different opinion because of their own observations.

According to David Gudema, Van Eck made them exercise almost daily. He saw that the man kicked the prisoners several times. Especially when he was drunk, which they claimed was common, they had to stay out of his way. All residents would have been afraid of this 'half madman'. He was constantly watching them in order to catch them, including people who had not received any sentence whatsoever, in the act of failing to perform given assignments. If this was the case, he could, among other things, force the offender to participate in the notorious punishment exercise. In addition, he regularly made people wait for a long time before they were allowed to go to the bathroom. Only at times randomly chosen by him, he allowed visits to the toilet. Emanuel Blok stayed in the Criminal Barracks for some time. He also stated that Van Eck had prisoners exercising almost daily. In most cases, he was obligated to participate. If someone made a mistake, he had to run at least ten minutes on clogs. Because of his brutal performance, Van Eck was also-called 'the terror of Camp Westerbork'.[42]

The combination of fanatical SS members, the coming and going of dignitaries and their accomplices, and the constantly changing reports about the advance of the allies caused a lot of uncertainty among the residents. They regularly wondered what the occupying forces had planned to do with them, now that the end of the Third Reich was slowly but surely approaching.

Towards The End

A short visit by Aus der Fünten to the camp in the second half of October 1944 was enough to trigger a flow of rumours. It was widely speculated that half of the 600 residents would be taken away. On the one hand, it was difficult to keep the camp running with only those who had stayed behind, while on the other hand, it did not seem desirable to keep so many capable men concentrated in one place. People became even more tense when a train entered the camp on 10 November and stopped at the place from which the transports used to depart. At the end of the morning, Bial had walked along the main street, where at that time it was still very quiet. A little over an hour later, however, this had completely changed, because the train had arrived. According to Bial, it was a tram which normally operated between Assen and the Stadskanaal. It consisted of two locomotives, two open and fifteen closed freight wagons and two passenger cars. Meanwhile, groups of residents had begun discussing the purpose of this train. Was there enough room for the transport of 600 persons or was it destined for the Soldiers present in the camp?

In the late afternoon, the camp's management clarified that the train was intended for the people in the camp. What was meant by this remained unclear and the information was insufficient to defuse the tension. It made people even more nervous when the train was cleaned a few days later and the windows were blacked out. Although the fear of 'being put on transport' did not disappear altogether, it appeared in the second half of November that the train was indeed simply used for services such as bringing supplies to the camp. With a resident as a train driver, the train regularly drove to Groningen and then returned with food and/or fuel.[43]

Between the end of 1944 and early 1945, the camp's management observed several times that the discipline was somewhat problematic. Because of the many rumours about the situation in the camp and at the fronts, the tension got worse and people stopped following the rules as well as they were expected to. For example, some residents arrived late at work in the morning or returned to the barracks too late in the evening. Whoever committed this offence could be locked up in the Criminal Barracks for eight days. Censorship of outgoing mail still took place during this period. If the assessor saw certain words or phrases in a letter that he considered to be inappropriate because they could be offensive to the occupier, the writer of the letter might have been in trouble. Camp resident Emmy P. wrote at the end of January, for example, that she has been working for the cleaning service for three weeks and that her hands were suffering because of it. This lament could be received negatively by those who lived outside the camp and were starving. For this thoughtless deed, P. had to stay in the barracks for eight days.

The Criminal Barracks had no shortage of prisoners during that period. At the beginning of 1945 Jews were still brought to the camp from all parts of the Netherlands. In most cases, they were small groups. At the end of January and in early February this pattern was broken, because three larger transports arrived within a short period of time. The first transport, consisting of 25 Jews, came from Camp Amersfoort. Two men from this transport saw the chance to flee from the camp a few days after arrival. They probably crawled into the freight wagon of the camp train, which one morning drove to Groningen. As before, ten Jews were taken to the Criminal Barracks from the barracks where the men should have been staying, so the policy of sanctions had still not changed much.

A week later, the train drove to Beilen and picked up 82 Jews from the Prison in Scheveningen. At night another transport should have arrived from Amsterdam. However, it never came and no one knew why. The next day residents suddenly had to turn two halls of a barracks into a Hospital in the afternoon, because the transport from Amsterdam had been shot by allied aircraft on the way. Of the 34 Jews, only 12 reached the camp. Ten of them were wounded. The rest had either died, fled or had been taken elsewhere.[44]

Due to the arrival of new residents, the camp population had increased to 848 people at the beginning of March 1945[45]. It is not known what role OD members had in these transports and whether they had been given the same tasks in the camp as before. Little has been recorded about the tasks of the OD in the period from the September days of 1944 to the liberation. In addition to occupying a number of permanent posts and supervising residents, not many tasks will have been added. In any case, OD members had no function in the new Criminal Barracks. Only a handful of times, OD men had to show up for other tasks.

For example, SD Officers had one time decided to go on a hunting trip at the end of October 1944. Ten OD men and 20 other residents were ordered to drive the wild animals towards the hunters. According to Bial, the animals knew that the terrain around the camp was dangerous, because no animal was shot that day. OD members were given other tasks as well. For example, when the garage was looking for skilful staff, Peter Margules had to go there. Pisk was responsible for managing visits to the hairdresser, because near the end, only one hairdresser was still staying in the camp. Residents were allowed to have their hair cut every four weeks. Those whose turn it was to visit the hairdresser had to get some sort of ticket from Pisk the night before. He kept a record of who had gotten his permission, because the administration had to be complete.[46]

In the first week of March 1945, residents were ordered to prepare the former Criminal Barracks, numbered 65, 66 and 67, for the housing of female prisoners. Because of the arrival of this group, part of the camp was changed into a Concentration Camp. For residents, this was another reason to think about their future. A few days later, barracks 65 was bustling with people. These and the other two barracks had not been used and had been rather neglected after the departure of the last convicts. About 100 residents were ordered to make them habitable again. Beds and mattresses were moved. Others cleaned the place and helped in the laying or repairing of cables and water pipes. In addition, the barbed wire fence had to be installed again and a guard house, which was still at the Hospital, was moved to the entrance of the three barracks. The sewing workshop of the camp was also given assignments, such as making numbers that the female prisoners had to wear on their overalls. Because there were too few blue overalls available to dress all women, the residents were informed that they had no obligation to wear them anymore. For the female guards (*Aufseherinnen*), the seamstresses made blouses out of parachute silk. These guards were also given a place to stay in the camp, but that had not yet been furnished. The necessary furniture and other useful objects were again taken from the homes of residents. As a result of this collection, people became somewhat upset, because no one liked to give away their possessions. The taking of cutlery took place via the barracks' leaders. If not enough stuff was collected, the barracks would be searched.

Contacting the newcomers was strictly prohibited. Residents who ignored this ban had to appear before a Court. 50 Border Guards were appointed for the surveillance of the women's camp, mainly for outdoor surveillance. In addition, 60 guards of the Landwacht came to the camp. They were trained by the Border Guards. Because of all these precautions, Bial concluded that the women had to be very dangerous persons.[47] This conclusion turned out to be true in a sense. The occupying forces indeed considered the women to be dangerous individuals, because they had all participated to a greater or lesser extent in resistance activities. As a result, they were considered 'political prisoners'.

After the September days of 1944, members of the resistance arrested by the SD and their accomplices were punished more severely than before. A large number of them were in Prison as so-called *Todeskandidaten*. Initially, it was their turn to be punished whenever people who were on the side of the occupier died due to resistance activities. As a retaliatory measure, a number of *Todeskandidaten* were then shot by a firing squad. Due to the changed circumstances, the BdS ordered the SD's *Einsatzkommandos* to shoot all *Todeskandidaten* if the allied forces approached.

In several cities in the northern and eastern provinces, including Velp, Apeldoorn, Doetinchem, Deventer, Zwolle, Steenwijk, Meppel, Assen, Delfzijl, Heerenveen and Sneek, SD commands had settled. Some existing commands, such as those of Enschede, Groningen and Leeuwarden, received back up. Because of the active investigation policy, these groups arrested a large number of resistance fighters, who ended up in danger because of the order. The Chief of the *Einsatzkommando*-Groningen, Bernard Georg Haase, was not willing to fulfil the order. Refusing to fulfil the task or claiming that there were no *Todeskandidaten* were not among the options, because then Haase himself would be in trouble. However, permission was granted for the transfer of the prisoners to another Prison. At the time of the order, Haase was staying in the Achterhoek. There too he had some influence, because he ordered the Commander of the SD Prison 'De Kruisberg' in Doetinchem to release as many people who had received a sentence for small offences as possible.

Those who had committed more serious crimes had to be transferred elsewhere. A group of about 50 women ended up in the separate part of Camp Westerbork. Female resistance fighters were also transferred to the women's camp from other penal institutions. One of these women, Jacqueline Theodora Kuyck, wrote a book about her experiences, which is titled *Partisanenvrouwen* (Partisan Women). She was imprisoned for some time in the Koning Wilhelm III barracks in Apeldoorn.[48]

Partisan Women

Together with her friend Netta Verkerk, Jacqueline Kuyck provided shelter to children from broken families at the shelter 'De Lichthoeve' in Santpoort. During the occupation, they also included Jewish babies and children. This went well for a long time, until a local NSB man did not trust the situation and went to the occupying forces. The NSB man probably put forward sufficient arguments, because in 1942 the institution had to close the doors at the orders of the Germans. Jacqueline and Netta left for Garderen, where they were able to stay in a holiday home on the Zonneland estate. They housed the children in a nearby country house.

Jacqueline was a woman who liked to help people, partly because of her belief. For example, when a ranger knocked on her door, asking whether she could house people from the resistance and people who had chosen to go into hiding, he immediately received an affirmative answer. In the vicinity of the summer house, a hole was dug, into which ten young men could safely retreat. From there they performed their actions during the night, such as blowing up the railway near Assen. Due to these acts of resistance, the occupier was extra active and discovered at least one shelter nearby. Zonneland also became noticed more and more. After somebody chose to rat them out, providing the final clues, the SD knew exactly where to look with the help of a drawing.

On the evening of 26 October 1944, shortly before a raid took place, a good Policeman from Garderen went to the holiday home and warned the residents. Just in time, the men managed to leave the place and hide the weapons present. Therefore, the search did not produce the desired result, but by chance the weapons were found. This discovery and the discovery of the hole the men had been in provided sufficient evidence to arrest Jacqueline. In revenge, Zonneland was also set on fire. For Jacqueline, hiding was not an option, because her 'foster children' would be in danger. There was nothing else for her to do but accept her fate, which consisted of imprisonment in an overpopulated cell of the Koning Wilhelm III barracks in Apeldoorn.[49] This barracks originally did not function as a Prison, but because the Koepel Prison in Arnhem was unreachable due to operation *Market Garden*, alternative facilities were put into use.

Jacqueline was interrogated and threatened several times, but did not reveal her secrets. That is why she stayed behind bars. As time passed, circumstances did not improve. There was less and less food and it became worse as well, while she and the other women who were trapped often suffered from the cold. Even after they were transferred to a larger room, their circumstances barely changed. The women tried to get through the day and the night as well as they could. Although, according to Jacqueline, the guards were good for them in their own way, they had to be extremely careful. Because of the poor conditions for the Germans at the fronts and the increasing tension, the generally German female and male guards regularly drank too much, which caused their mood to change quite abruptly at times.

However, when it became clear that the Third Reich was about to collapse, even the most fanatical guards suddenly became more humane.

If it had been an earlier stage of the occupation, the women would have been transferred to the German Concentration Camp Ravensbrück, which was specially equipped for them, but there were no longer any transports to this camp. Therefore, because the allies were approaching, it was decided to place them somewhere else. On the evening of 21 March 1945, almost five months after Jacqueline was arrested, the guards suddenly appeared in the room and, using a card system, they called the names of the women who had to leave immediately. Only the oldest woman and Jacqueline were left behind. Initially, it was unclear where the women would be taken. There was a rumour that the transport would be going to Westerbork. A few hours later, Jacqueline and the other woman had to get in a truck as well. The other passengers were Jewish women and children, so the rumour about Westerbork seemed to be correct.

After a bumpy and tiring journey of many hours, the transport indeed arrived in Westerbork. The Jewish people had to go to the part reserved for them. Jacqueline was immediately enthusiastically welcomed in the women's camp by the women who had arrived there earlier. One of the female guards, dressed in a German uniform, addressed the new camp residents. As usual, this speech included various warnings and threats. Then the registration took place, after which the women had to exchange their clothes for blue overalls and clogs. The overalls had a red shoulder pad and on the back was a red number. Jacqueline got number 12. After their hair had been cut by a Jewish hairdresser, the women showed many similarities with the former Jewish criminal cases.[50]

A total of 116 female political prisoners were staying in the women's camp, all of which had a different background and age. Prisoner 89 was 23-year-old Corry Polderman. As a courier she had delivered letters for the resistance and helped her brother stencil *Het Parool*, edition Zwolle. Her parents had also offered help, because the Polderman family offered to let the Commander of the Zwolle resistance group use their house as shelter. In March 1945 the SD arrested this Commander outside Zwolle. The occupiers probably knew where he had stayed, because a search took place a few days later in Corry's parental home. The next day she was arrested and transferred to the Detention Centre in Zwolle.[51] There she was placed for 14 days with six other women in a cell that was much too small for them all.

On 2 April, the second day of Easter, German Soldiers took the women out of Prison and brought them to a bus, which then drove to Westerbork. The bus arrived at the camp in the middle of the night. Given the time, Corry's group was taken directly to a barracks, where they were instructed to get in the unoccupied beds. They were not allowed a lot of rest, because a few hours later, at 5:00 AM, they had to get up again. In the scarcely lit barracks, they could catch a glimpse of the other members of the barracks. Those women looked peculiar in the eyes of the newcomers. They wore overalls and were pitch black. After the roll call, these women left for their workshop. What kind of work they did there, Corry did not know. She herself stayed behind with her own group.

The chief guard addressed them. Among other things, she stated that Corry and her associates were no longer people, but numbers. Corry thought this was horrible. After the speech, the usual ritual followed: registration, swapping their clothes for overalls and getting their hair cut. The next day Corry and her group began following the same routine as the other female prisoners: Get up at 5:00 AM and go to work after the roll call at 6:00 AM. Corry quickly found out what her daily work would be. Together with the other women, she was transferred to a barracks, where she had to disassemble batteries. The raw materials that remained were intended for the war industry. Supervisors explained what the best way was to reach the daily quota of several dozens of kilos.[52] If they did not succeed, several sanctions could be imposed, such as the withholding of a meal.[53] At noon the women could return to the barracks. After the mandatory roll call, the afternoon shift began at 13:00. This lasted until 18:00. The work was rather unhealthy, because the lignite from the batteries was swirling through the workshop. As a result, the group of Corry quickly became as black as the rest.[54]

In the early morning of Saturday 7 April, the last 22 women and girls arrived. In the evening they were brought to the camp from the Groningen Detention Centre in a bus.[55] Jacqueline Kuyck wrote that the camp was in turmoil that Saturday, so the women barely got any work done. According to Bial, however, there was a disturbing silence in the camp. Both did see that the camp train was being loaded with all kinds of stuff. Typewriters, uniforms and even the slaughtered and still living cattle was put on the train. The transport left a day later, but the train did not return. On Monday, a guard hinted that she and her colleagues were about to leave the camp, as the allied troops were getting closer. Sounds of machine guns and artillery could be heard all the way to the camp, indicating that there was fighting nearby.

On Tuesday afternoon, 10 April, all the guards turned out to have actually left. The Border Guards, who were still present, did not bother the female prisoners. Because of all the developments, things seemed to be moving in the right direction. They were no longer obligated to work or wait for the roll calls. The whistle that announced the new working day every morning at 5:00 was no longer there the next day either. The women were able to think in peace about their release that Wednesday, because Aad van As, to whom Gemmeker had left the command of the camp on 11 April, said during a speech that they would be released on the same day. With a bath and more freedom of movement in mind, the women took their own clothes out of the warehouse and got changed.

The hours passed and it looked like the women would have to spend another night in the camp. Jewish camp residents invited the women to spend the evening with them. Around 16:00, Van As appeared at the barracks. The group was ordered to stand in line. The message of Van As was contrary to what the women had expected. Instead of information about their release, he told them that they would be transferred to another destination under the guidance of the Border Guard the same evening. The message felt as if they had been captured again and they began to panic.[56] Van As negotiated with the Commander of the Border Guards in the evening

Corry Polderman is being picked up by her fiancé. She is wearing her overalls from the camp with number 89 on them.

about surrender and disarmament of his men. The Commander refused to accept this because he had been ordered to leave the camp and take the women with him. Van As saw this as an opportunity to lay the responsibility for the safety of the women with the commander.[57]

They still had to wait another few hours for the final journey, because it was too dangerous to go out with such a large group during the day. Meanwhile, the women were given the opportunity to pack their meagre belongings, including a blanket and work overalls. When darkness fell, everyone had to stand in line to be counted. This took longer than expected, as the number turned out to be incorrect after counting them several times. It was suspected that the missing women had taken advantage of the chaotic situation and had fled. During a search, some women were found hiding in the camp. After they were added back to the group, the march to the unknown destination began on Wednesday 11 April around 22:00. In rows of five, just over 100 women left the camp under the guidance of about 150 Border Guards. The women were singing as they walked. Those who could barely walk or not walk at all were allowed to sit on one of the horse-drawn carts.[58] Bial witnessed the departure. According to him, the whole thing had looked eerie.[59] Jacqueline also started the journey on foot, but soon she could not keep up with the pace and threatened to fall behind. She was allowed to sit on the chef's cart.[60]

The destination remained unclear on the way. There were rumours that the Prison in Leeuwarden was the final destination. If that place could not be reached, the guards would leave their prisoners in Groningen. According to Loe de Jong, the women had to be taken to the Scheveningen Prison via the Afsluitdijk.[61] Some of them, including Greetje van der Molen, spoke with the Border Guards shortly before the departure. They, too, expressed their desire for a swift end of the war. Despite this, they had been ordered to bring the women to Groningen. According to the original order, they had to shoot their prisoners on the way if they could not reach Groningen, but they would not execute this order in any case. Along the way, the promise of refusing the order was repeated again and there was even a certain fraternisation between the prisoners and their guards.[62]

Once morning had come, the group made its way through Assen after a journey of 25 kilometres. The moment the few spectators present realised that they were witnessing something special so early in the morning, the group had already left the city. After a while they stopped at a farm. There the women were allowed to rest for several hours in a barn, because they had not slept much. They continued on their journey while it was still light. This was earlier than planned, probably because the allied troops were approaching. The poor conditions they had lived in before leaving the camp took their toll, because more and more women were barely able to travel long distances on foot. In order to avoid too much delay, horses and wagons were confiscated from farmers in the area. The Border Guards often had something that looked like a bicycle. After a long journey of more than 13 hours, Quartermasters of the Border Guard outside the city of Groningen once again found a place to stay at a farm. Once more, they did not get much sleep and during the roll call held the next morning, it turned out that a dozen women were too sick to continue the journey; they were allowed to stay behind. The rest was not much better off. Nevertheless, they had to go on into the dark night.

Initially, the women were afraid that they would be driven from Groningen to the east. The relief was great when it became clear that they were going west, in the direction of Leeuwarden. Meanwhile, the Commander of the Security Unit had left for the Scholtenshuis in Groningen to get new instructions. At the dawn of the new day, they became tense again. Leeuwarden as possible final destination was at more than 30 kilometres from the new resting place. The owner of the farm in Pieterzijl was not eager to take in the group, but after a number of threats, he had to allow them to stay. In a large barn the exhausted women, along with their guards, waited nervously for the commander's return. When he finally showed his face, the sun was already going down and the night was coming. They had to stand in line immediately. The women were waiting anxiously for what the Commander was going to tell them. The assignment he had received initially did not allow for many changes. The prisoners had to be delivered to Leeuwarden without any delay. Only if the journey became too dangerous for the men, the Commander was given the authority to decide on the fate of the women himself.

He probably did not need much time to make a decision, because he would have heard and/or seen enough along the way for him to conclude that he and his men would not gain anything from taking them to Leeuwarden. The women were left in the dark for a few more minutes before the Commander said they were free. The word 'free' did not get through to them immediately. It came unexpectedly and had to be processed first, before they began showing the first signs of joy. The Border Guards did not wait and left immediately. Soon the roles were reversed, because not long after, the guards came across Canadian Soldiers, who took them away as prisoners of war. Because the farmer had been forced to let these uninvited guests stay, they were not welcome for much longer, so the women left the premises as soon as possible. Most of them ran to the nearby village of Grijpskerk. There they received a warm welcome from the population. To prevent them from being mistaken for NSB women because of their short hair, they swapped their clothes for the blue overalls they had worn in the camp. Nobody cared either way, because they were finally free.[63] That did not apply to the residents who had stayed behind in Camp Westerbork.

8. WEIGHED FREEDOM

On Tuesday 10 April the events in and around Camp Westerbork happened quickly after one another. The reports of the fighting showed that the allied troops were getting closer and closer. Everything indicated that Gemmeker and his men were about to leave soon. His car was parked behind his apartment, ready for the approaching retreat. At 22:00 it was rumoured that Gemmeker had informed Spanier by phone that the camp was free. A message was read out loud in the barracks at the same time that the next morning, they had to work as usual. Nevertheless, everyone would get their identity card back, starting at 8:30 AM, while the OD would be disbanded. As soon as the occupier had left, the *Notbereitschaft* had to take over the guard posts to prevent looting.

At 23:00 Bial walked through the camp for a while and found that the situation had hardly changed. For example, German Soldiers were still at the guard posts, armed with guns. Shortly thereafter, an OD man appeared in the barracks, who had been ordered by Schlesinger to spread the message that the occupying forces would not be leaving and that everything would remain the same after all. The next morning, Wednesday 11 April, Gemmeker, some members of his staff and Border Guards were still present. The OD also turned out to still be around. In the afternoon, the residents were ordered by Schlesinger to remove the star from their clothes, because the German Soldiers still walking through the camp did not need to see what the camp's population consisted of. Around 16:00, the identity cards were actually given back to them in the barracks. At 18:30, the news that Gemmeker and his entourage had left spread through the camp like wildfire. The guard posts were no longer occupied and the barrier had been raised. That same evening the Border Guards left with their female political prisoners.[1]

Freedom Behind Barbed Wire
Before Gemmeker left, Schlesinger spoke briefly with him and received an object. Aad van As witnessed this. Right after the cars had disappeared from sight, Schlesinger went to find Van As and handed him the object in question. Van As saw that it was a leather case containing a small model revolver. By handing over Gemmeker's personal weapon, Schlesinger symbolically transferred the camp's command to Van As. First, the new Commander had the barrier brought down again. Furthermore, he decided that the curfew and the covered windows would stay, because German Soldiers were still staying outside the camp and from the sounds coming from the direction of the Oranjekanaal, it was clear that there was still a big battle going on. With regards to their own security, no one was allowed to leave the camp.[2]

With the exception of a few changes, Van As kept the service groups as they were. The OD, with Pisk as the service leader, also continued to exist. As the number of OD men was not sufficient to occupy all vacated posts and watchtowers, Van As appointed a number of residents as guards. In addition, he appointed five residents as his confidants, with whom he formed the camp's leadership. The Dutch OD man Abraham van Witsen[3], who had been in the camp since 12 August 1942, was one of these five. The new leadership had a meeting all night. The results of this meeting were announced the following morning by the first order of the free camp. In addition to the announcement of the appointments and information on the changed working hours, Van As took the opportunity to encourage everyone to fulfil their duty as well as possible and to maintain discipline in the camp. Van As warned that he was not afraid of taking action against those who would somehow try to disturb the camp's peace. What measures he was thinking of was not specified in the order.[4]

In the afternoon the new Commander sent all residents, except the sick ones, to the main hall and addressed them. Suddenly somebody in the back of the hall called out that there was a telephone call for him. When asked who was on the phone, the answer was that the Tommies had been spotted at the camp's farm. According to Van As, a gunshot would have had less of an effect, because in no time the room was empty and everyone moved in the direction of the farm as quickly as possible. The Canadian Military quickly retreated into their tanks when they saw the frenzied crowd coming at them. However, after they found out why the residents had made a run for them, they were escorted to the camp.[5] On Thursday afternoon, 12 April 1945, about 900 residents of Camp Westerbork, together with the Canadian Military, celebrated the liberation of the camp.

The green overalls of the OD soon caused some commotion. While some OD members were busy cordoning off a road, one of them introduced himself to the liberators and said he was an Austrian. A Dutch Liaison Officer, who had arrived in the camp shortly before, gave the order to take all guards with a different nationality as prisoners of war. The misunderstanding was quickly cleared up, allowing at least 18 OD members of foreign nationality, including Pisk, to remain in the camp.

After some time, all residents had to come to the main hall for the second time that day. There they were addressed by the Intelligence Officer of the Canadian Military, Captain D.F. Morris. He urged them to keep calm. He also indicated that no one was allowed to leave the camp because the war was not over. To prevent stagnation in the advance of the allied troops, everyone had to stay in the camp for a few more days. The patience of many residents was tested, as it took more than three weeks before the entire country was liberated. According to the information in the camp order of Van As, residents had to get back to work as soon as possible. Bial was critical when he wrote about the OD's continued presence in the camp. He asked the reader if they could imagine that the OD was walking around with orange armbands with 'Camp Police' on it in blue letters. Pisk also had 'Chief' on his armband. In addition, the OD members continued to wear the green overalls, although the cap was no longer mandatory. Bial, like other residents, will have felt that the members of the OD had gone too far during the occupation in aiding the Germans and that this service group should have been disbanded.

The people in the camp became noticeably more and more dissatisfied with the fact that they had to continue working. Many residents wanted to go on strike, because the Service Leaders remained at their posts and did nothing.[6] On 17 April, the first edition of *De Westerborker* appeared. In this newspaper for the camp population, Van As, who had now been given the post of Camp Intendant, devoted the foreword entirely to the impending labour dispute. He had found that not everyone kept their promise to continue working to maintain the camp. The day before that, 30 of the 80 women who should have worked in the kitchen had not showed up. In addition, Van As saw healthy men walking through the camp during working hours. He threatened that if he did not see any improvement, he would publish the names of those who refused to work, but he hoped that this measure was not necessary.

The Military Commissioner of Drenthe, Lieutenant Colonel A.H. Stok, once again explained the situation in an article. Because they were still in the middle of a war, everyone had to be patient, because the allied leadership tried to limit traffic as much as possible. Stok expected that all the instructions given in the camp would be followed closely and that escapes were a thing of the past. These words hardly had any effect, as a growing number of residents refused to go to work as long as the old Service Leaders remained at their posts. These actions were successful. In the second edition of *De Westerborker* on 18 April, Van As announced the new camp organisa-tion, which would consist of six Divisions.[7] On the recommendation of Van As, all but three Service Leaders had resigned.[8]

Division III, housed in barracks 86, consisted of the Security Service and Police, of which A. van Witsen became the leader. Although Pisk was no longer a service leader, he was still given a limited managerial position, because he became responsible for the Security Service and the Fire Brigade as Chief. Léon Cohen was going to perform the function of Chief of the Criminal Investigation Department. In addition to the renewed camp organisation, the instruction regarding passes required to enter or leave the camp was also brought to the attention. It stipulated that everyone should be in possession of a special pass when entering or leaving the camp. This pass was issued only if certain conditions were met and if the highest Military authority present in the camp had approved the request. Although the residents were given more freedom of movement and more facilities, there was still that wide ditch and barbed wire fence that separated the camp from the outside world[9].

This strict policy had a reason. According to the Military Commissioner, residents enjoyed the same freedom as the other residents of the province of Drenthe during the first week of the liberation. Soon it became apparent that some residents were unable to cope with this freedom because they were trading illegally or were embezzling camp property. Although only a few people were guilty of this, the restrictive measures applied to the whole camp. This was not the only reason why the authorities had taken the decision. They also simply did not trust the residents. Many wondered why the occupying forces had chosen to spare this group while deporting others to the Extermination Camps. Had they sometimes helped the Germans? The National Socialists outside the camp, who had deliberately taken the side of the occupying forces because of their political preference, were arrested and placed in one of the many detention camps during the preliminary investigation[10].

Detention Camp Westerbork

Around 20 April 1945 it was announced that Camp Westerbork would soon be taken over by the Dutch Military. The plan was to use part of the camp as a detention camp for NSB members, members of the *Waffen SS* and men of the Landwacht who had been arrested in Drenthe. The first group would arrive around 23 April. Bial had to have extra beds transferred to barracks 65, 66 and 67. These former Criminal Barracks were extremely suitable for this purpose, because residents had made them habitable for female political prisoners less than two months before. Furthermore, there was still a barbed wire fence around it. For the surveillance of the 'collaborators', as the group of 'bad' Dutch people was also-called, troops from the Internal Armed Forces (*Binnenlandse Strijdkrachten* or *BS*) had already been directed to the camp. The number of men of this unit, which largely consisted of former resistance fighters, was not sufficient, because according to an article in De Westerborker, former Soldiers were asked to sign up for the Camp Police. The intention was to increase the number of men from 30 to 60. Residents who opted to join the Police received a payment of 35 guilders per week in addition to bed and board. To be recognisable, the Camp Police started wearing dark brown overalls, along with an orange armband. For the OD members who decided to switch to the new Camp Police, the same dress code was applied. They had to exchange their green overalls, and their armament consisted of batons and guns.[11] Hans Margules, who made the switch, got a gun pressed into his hands, even though he had no clue how it worked.[12]

They began using the old regulations on dealing with prisoners again. For example, Jewish residents were not allowed to speak with the newcomers, unless they had to do so for work. In case of the latter, it was not allowed to have these conversations last for a long time, unless there was a good reason for it. Over time, the curfew was introduced again. After 10:00 PM, no one was allowed to be outside the camp. Guards were ordered to shoot at anyone who was there anyway.

On Tuesday 24 April the first collaborators arrived in the camp. The sick were brought in by truck in the afternoon. Some 200 people followed on foot a few hours later. In *De Westerborker* a report on the arrivals was published a day later, titled *De dag der dagen* (*The day of days*). Many Jews witnessed the arrivals. According to the article, the newcomers were very disciplined. After entering, they underwent the same ritual as their predecessors. First of all, the whole group had to stand in line in the roll call area. That is where they got the first instructions from the Camp Police. After that, the registration took place. The procedure was successful that first time. That was not always the case later on, especially when large groups arrived, because then the registration could take a lot of time. Those who were in charge of the registration would leave to have lunch in the afternoon, even though there was still a long queue waiting. Many tried to get out of imprisonment in the camp during registration by claiming that there had been a misunderstanding, a case of mistaken identity, or that they had been forced to join a German Company. This had no effect whatsoever, because after the administration, everyone went on to the next station to be searched. Large amounts of money were sometimes found. There was no need to speculate on the origin of this money: in many cases it involved spoils of war. After their things had been taken from them, they were assigned to a barracks. There everyone received a bracelet with the personal registration number on it. The whole ritual ended with the shaving of the heads.[13]

The confrontation between the former oppressors and the oppressed did not always go smoothly. Although the Camp Police in general dealt with the newcomers in a rather harsh manner, the BS took things even further. In some cases, an individual Jewish resident lost their cool and then the pent-up tension and anger came out. The collaborators were then called traitors, crooks or *Herrenvolk*. A more violent reaction followed when someone noticed the one who had arrested him among the group of newcomers. This happened to Leo Benninga. He saw the SD man from Amsterdam who had arrested him come in. He and some other residents surrounded the man, after which they taunted, spit, beat and laughed at him.[14] According to the camp's management, this kind of behaviour was unacceptable. In an article in *De Westerborker*, they acknowledged the suffering of the Jewish residents or their relatives, which made it understandable that they took out all of this frustration and pain on the new prisoners on impulse. However, they should not resort to using the same methods of which they themselves had been victims. That is why the camp's management asked them not to be vindictive towards the National Socialists.[15]

With the exception of a few skirmishes, the last German Soldiers laid down their weapons in the Netherlands on Saturday 5 May 1945. This brought an end to five years of occupation. Everywhere people celebrated this exuberantly. The news of the surrender of the German Army also reached Camp Westerbork. In the afternoon, many listened to the impressive speech on the radio of Prime Minister Pieter Sjoerds Gerbrandy in the main hall. Many tears were shed.[16] A few days later the situation looked quite different yet again. For the majority of the Jews still present, the festive mood had turned into disappointment. Commander J.G. Buijvoets tried to change this by allowing more freedom of movement. On Saturday 5 and Sunday 6 May, the Jews were allowed to walk in a radius of 2 kilometres outside the camp from 14:00 to 17:00 hours. On departure and return, the guards had to check the identity cards first. They were not allowed to take any luggage with them. People who tried to use the walk to score food were disappointed; they had to turn in all goods upon entry.[17]

On Wednesday evening 9 May, things became so tense that the situation threatened to escalate. A group of dissatisfied Jews gathered in front of barracks 33 and complained to the camp's management about the bad conditions. Despite the liberation, a group of about 700 Jews was obligated to stay in the camp. By the way they were treated, it seemed as if they were still trapped. The message was apparently clear, because two days later the camp's management organised an important meeting in the main hall where subjects such as the release of the camp population, more freedom of movement and the general attitude of the Jews were discussed. Buijvoets addressed the group. No one was forced to stay inside from that moment on and everyone was allowed to move freely in a zone of 6 kilometres around the camp. Any small amount of food obtained from farmers nearby was no longer confiscated. Buijvoets also explained how the actual release would go. Three groups were made. These groups would be released at different times.

The first group consisted of people who had been brought to the camp after 4 September 1944. They were allowed to leave after the weekend. The second group, whose date of arrival was between 10 May 1940 and 4 September 1944, was to be released soon afterwards, on one condition: Everyone had to prove beforehand that he or she had a place to stay outside the camp. Among the third and last group were those who had been living in the camp since before 10 May 1940. They received a disappointing announcement. Since they had come to the Netherlands as refugees and were labelled as' stateless', the Government still had to decide on their release.[18] About ten members of the OD, including Pisk, Salmagne and the Margules brothers, were part of the latter group.[19] They had to be patient for some time, while more and more Jewish residents left every day. In the first weeks after the liberation of the camp, the first Jews left with or without permission.

According to an official list of the camp's administration, 883 Jews were still in the camp on 12 April. In August the number had fallen to 428. Despite the faster depopulation, 120 Jews from the category of 'stateless persons' were still in the camp.[20] A large part of this group was probably allowed to leave the same month. Hans Margules found an address in Amsterdam via an acquaintance. He wrote him a letter asking him if he could rent a room. When he received an affirmative reply, his stay in the camp ended after more than five and a half years. As a passenger of an allied Army truck that was loaded with food and chocolate, he arrived safely in Amsterdam.[21]

The release of the Jews took so long because all 900 of them first had to undergo a security check. Three non Commissioned Officers would have started this on 27 April. They probably did this very carefully, because only eight to ten people got their turn each day.[22] The purpose of this investigation was to get a number of important questions answered: Why had the occupier spared this group, while others with the same background were sent to Extermination Camps? Had this been a case of (survival) collaboration or did fate simply decide it that way? These were questions that could be answered mainly by the parties involved. After the investigation, release followed in almost all cases.

Survival As A Reward For Services Rendered?

Initially, the majority of the 32 OD members still present during the liberation of the camp were not investigated as a separate group. They would often have faced the same questions as other residents during the investigation. Some of them will have struggled themselves with the question of why they were allowed to stay while 160 of their colleagues had to go on transport sooner or later. It is likely that any hypothesis raised new questions. Gemmeker himself would have ordered for this group to not be deported.[23]

The complete answer cannot be traced from the composition of this group of survivors. That Pisk, along with his wife and son, survived to the end is not strange, because of his position as the leader of the OD. It is not possible to find a valid explanation based on who the other members were, who had survived. There is nothing to be found in the available data that suggests they had one particular thing in common. The ages were pretty far apart. The youngest member still present in the camp was no older than 23 in May 1945, while the eldest at that time had reached the age of 58. How long they had been staying in the camp also seemed to have nothing to do with it. Ernst Rosendorff had been in the camp from the beginning of November 1939 and was therefore one of the 'old' residents, while Léon Cohen had arrived as a newcomer only on 22 July 1943. Léon was one of the 14 Dutch people. The other 18 men were former refugees from Germany or Austria. Therefore, place of origin was not a criteria for survival either.[24]

Since this investigation did not reveal any incriminating facts for most members of the OD, everyone except Pisk could leave the camp after a while. Pisk was arrested in mid July 1945 for allegedly committing a political crime. Léon Cohen, who joined the Amsterdam Police Force again after his release, made an exculpatory statement. As a Policeman, he expressed his admiration for the way in which the leader of the OD had carried out his duties, although he felt that Pisk was also worthy of criticism on several points. Residents such as Mechanicus, who described him among other things as 'the Chief of the Jewish Gestapo', support the negative image. Paul Siegel also described him as a rude and power hungry man, who could become horribly angry. Léon confirmed that Pisk often shouted loudly and threatened to report several incidents to Gemmeker. However, most of the time, he did not follow through with his threat. Only in a few cases, such as when somebody had stolen property from fellow residents, he would have reported them to Gemmeker. Léon did not know exactly what the leader of the OD had been accused of, but it was clear to him that Pisk certainly did not deserve the title 'the brute of Westerbork'. Whenever he could, he would actually have often sabotaged Gemmeker's punishments and rules, or at least applied them in the most humane way. Camp Intendant, M. de Jong made a statement, saying that Pisk had performed his function as Chief of the Camp Police only in the interests of the residents.[25]

The investigation did not produce enough incriminating facts to build a case against Pisk. At the end of July 1945 he moved into a house at the Johannes Vermeerstraat 31 in Heemstede with his wife and son.[26] According to an unconfirmed source, Pisk's function would have contributed significantly to the fact that his wife and son were among the survivors. However, he had not been able to have his mother removed from the transport list. She died on 13 September 1944 at the age of 78 in Theresienstadt. There is a chance that his mother had been used as a kind of collateral, so that her son would continue to perform the function of leader of the OD until the end, exactly as the occupier wanted.[27]

Pisk and the others who had stayed behind often lived in uncertainty, but they eventually reached the finish line. For those who had to go on transport from the Netherlands, this was quite different, because out of the 107,000 deportees, only 5,000 returned. As most of the exemptions were withdrawn, many members of the OD lost their protected status and as a result, at least 164 of them could not escape the misery of being deported. Of the 44 members brought to Sobibor, not one survived. With the exception of one person, everyone was sent to the gas chambers immediately upon arrival. About 30 people were deported directly to Auschwitz. Two thirds of them passed the selection and were deemed good enough to do work, but no one of this group returned alive either. The 80 members who ended up in Theresienstadt seemed to be getting a better future as a thanks for their efforts. Theresienstadt, however, was a make believe world for the propaganda apparatus of the Nazis, because in due time, the majority of the deportees were sent to other camps and died there. Of all the deported men, only 15 returned. The journey back took place in most cases under very appalling conditions.[28]

Some families, such as David Chajes's, were lucky and saw the chance to stay together after leaving Westerbork. Together with his wife and two daughters, David was liberated by men from the Russian Army near the German town of Tröbitz after a difficult period in Bergen-Belsen and after a tough train journey of several weeks at the end of April 1945. David found a residence for his family. There were already people living in it, but because an apartment was present in the basement, the original residents were allowed to stay. In return, they had to cook and keep the place clean. As a result, the roles were completely reversed in a short time. The Russians searched for an interpreter among the group of survivors. Because David was born in Poland and therefore knew a little bit of Russian, he was given this task. Together with a number of Soldiers, he went to pick up food from farmers who lived nearby every day.

The danger had not yet passed, however, and now came from the direction of the liberators, because Russian Soldiers were regularly looking for alcohol and women. When one night a drunken Soldier entered David's home, his wife hid in the basement just in time. She stayed here on the following nights. The two daughters were left alone. The reason for this might have been the fact that their short hair, in combination with the weight loss due to the hunger they had suffered, caused them to look more like boys. After a two month stay, the family was transferred from Tröbitz to an American Army base in Leipzig; three weeks later repatriation to the Netherlands followed. Slowly but surely, everything got back to normal for the Chajes family, until the Hungarian Revolution broke out in 1956. Because David and his wife were afraid of another war, they sent their children to family in New York. Although the family fell apart because of this, at least the chance of having to go through the same suffering as before was kept to a minimum for the children.[29]

It is difficult to figure out how most of the other OD members who returned managed to survive. The German born Fritz Hartog[30], who left for Theresienstadt on 4 September 1944, returned because he belonged to a special group. His name was on the list of Jews rescued by the Czech-German Oskar Schindler.[31]

The data show that, compared to the total number of Jews deported via Westerbork, more OD members returned proportionally. This difference can somewhat be explained, because as a service group, the OD consisted only of men who had a greater chance of survival than, for example, the deported children and the elderly, due to the work they were able to do. In addition, a considerable part left only with the last transports to Theresienstadt. If the number of OD members who returned is added to the 32 colleagues who were able to stay in the camp until liberation, it turns out that about 24 percent of the total group had survived. A third of this group was made up of those who had been in the camp since before the German invasion in May 1940. It is therefore certain, on the basis of these figures, that a member of the OD did indeed have a greater chance of survival than other residents, since the difference is more than 19 percent. Despite the fact that proportionally speaking, more OD men made it out alive, it cannot be said that serving in the OD was by definition rewarded with a greater chance of survival. After all, at least 150 of them still died.[32]

Survival did not mean that the suffering was over. For many, the mourning process could only begin after the liberation, because almost every Jewish survivor lost relatives, friends and/or acquaintances during the occupation. In addition, the stories of the terrible events that took place in the Extermination Camps were now given a lot of attention. The general judgment on the behaviour of the Dutch during five years of oppression was not too nuanced in the first years after the liberation. National Socialism was 'wrong' and everything else was labelled 'right'.

After the trial against Adolf Eichmann, the organiser of the deportations, had taken place in Jerusalem in the early 1960s, a trial that was followed by the press worldwide, many expected that the memories of the persecution of the Jews would fade. However, nothing was less true. A few years after the trial, especially *Ondergang* (*Extinction*), the two part publication by Presser, caused public interest in the Second World War to increase explosively. It also set in motion a short but violent generational conflict. This conflict had profound consequences for public opinion, because the generation that had grown up after the occupation with the myth of a 'national resistance' discovered because of Presser's publication that what they had been told was not correct and that there had been Dutch people who had worked for the occupying forces. These were now the culprits, the fanatical collaborators even more so.[33]

In light of this development, the OD was the most criticised one of all the service groups. The term 'Jewish SS' as a synonym for the OD, introduced by Mechanicus, was taken over by historians such as Presser and De Jong. It is understandable that the OD as a Camp Police was often judged very negatively, because this service was not made up of outsiders, but of fellow Jews. However, it is important for a well-balanced judgment to take into account a number of factors, such as the constantly changing composition of the group and the different periods during which the service operated.

The first group of OD members, which was made up of men from the Camp Fire Brigade, did not in any case consist of fanatical, brutal Officers. These were mainly Jewish men who had fled from Germany or Austria. They had seen with their own eyes what the Nazi regime was capable of and many had themselves been victims of the violence against Jews. Moving to one of the neighbouring countries, leaving behind all the possessions, was generally the only option. In the Netherlands the illegal refugees ended up in various shelters and many were transferred several times, until they were finally taken to an unfinished camp far outside the world of civilisation. Some of these men were placed with the OD during the period that Camp Westerbork served as refugee camp and had not yet been taken over by the occupying forces. Initially, the work consisted mainly of relatively innocent activities, such as guiding convicts and assisting the Gendarmerie. So far, there is really no reason for such a negative judgment, because no transports had left to the east yet.

The situation changed when the occupier took over the camp on 1 July 1942. Shortly afterwards, the OD had to help with the incoming and outgoing transports, together with the Gendarmerie. Because they had carried out this task, the service was immediately seen in a bad light. After the railway tracks were added to the camp, their work as guides was no longer needed for the most part. However, the OD became even more criticised, rather than less, because of the other things they had to do from that time onwards. Certain tasks, such as the guarding of the Penal Company and the Criminal Barracks, providing services during raids in Amsterdam and assisting in the clearing of the Apeldoornsche Bosch, have been described as highly reprehensible and extremely disgraceful acts. Because of their involvement in these events, the OD members were considered accomplices of the occupiers.[34]

In order to be able to carry out all tasks properly, it was important that enough OD members were available. Partially due to the increase in the number of residents, there was a need for new Jewish Officers at certain times. For the majority of men who wanted to join the OD, this was not because of the work, but because a position in this service group resulted in an exemption, which increased the chances of a longer stay in the camp and therefore of survival. That is why the Jewish men who voluntarily joined the Camp Police after the camp was taken over in July 1942 were more eligible for the term 'collaborative survival' than the former refugees.[35] Because collaboration has too much of a negative connotation, 'survival participation' may be a term that better suits the members of the Camp Police in this case.

Residents who had been there since the beginning, including Werner Bloch and Hans Margules, saw Camp Westerbork grow from a more or less innocent refugee camp to a well-oiled deportation machine. As members of the OD, they became part of this machine. Both men survived the war. While others remained silent after the liberation, these men did not leave the past alone. By participating in interviews and writing books, they tried to provide insight into the functioning of the OD. For example, Hans responded during an interview to the critical post war books and stories, which, according to him, led to the OD men being blamed for the residents being transported to the Extermination Camps. Because of the sophisticated system and the self-government being kept intact, it seemed as if they had carried out these tasks voluntarily. Hans disagreed with this. It was precisely the constant threat of being sent on transport if they refused to cooperate that kept the system functioning. In addition, many, including Hans, were convinced that SS men would have acted in a very harsh and inhumane manner if they had taken over the duties of the OD members. He was of the opinion that the OD should therefore not be blamed at all. He and his colleagues would not have acted cruelly, for example by kicking or beating with bats.[36]

Both Hans and Werner admitted that there were bad and fanatical figures in the OD. Keeping these 'show offs' under control was important. As a Watch Commander, Werner had the opportunity to give these persons tasks where they could do little damage. In addition to keeping the fanatics in check, there was another point of attention. Werner was of the opinion that the OD had to operate as a group that had ended up between two groups. On one side stood their fellow Jews and on the other side stood the Germans. According to him, they had to make sure that the OD was not used by one group against the other. Especially during the supervision of outgoing transports, the OD had to act tactically, in order to be one step ahead of the Germans. In such transports, people sometimes refused to climb into the wagons at the last minute, which threatened to slow everyone down. SS men or German Police Officers were immediately ready to force these people into the wagon. The accompanying OD men were instructed beforehand to yell at people if such a situation threatened to arise and to push them into the train themselves if necessary. This made it possible in many cases to prevent the Germans from intervening with violence. According to Werner, this tactic may have seemed unsympathetic and harsh, but in his opinion, it was still better to be pushed into the train by a member of the OD than to have to go on transport bleeding due to being beaten with a rifle.

Most of the Jews taken away will not have been aware of this strategy adopted by the OD.[37] Hans and Werner therefore understood very well that it seemed as if the OD was cooperating with the Germans. However, according to them, this interpretation was wrong. Like everyone in the camp, the OD members were constantly trying to keep themselves safe. Indeed, a job within one of the service groups resulted in the coveted exemption. Because such an exemption could only be obtained by becoming part of the OD, many of them put aside their principles and willingly accepted the job. Nevertheless, it appeared that almost the entire exemption system had been meant to mislead the Jews, since almost all exemptions lost their validity over time.

Since more and more became known about the atrocities in the Extermination Camps after the liberation, it is not surprising that those who had stayed behind and those who did return found it difficult to process the past. In addition, it will have been difficult to build a new future, especially for former Jewish refugees, who in general had no connection with the Netherlands. Therefore, many went abroad, far away from the past and in search of a new future and new happiness. For example, some former members of the OD tried to build a new life in the United States, Australia or elsewhere.

Pisk emigrated to Australia a few years after his release. He died there in 1963. After leaving Westerbork, Sandor Salmagne remained in the

Netherlands for some time. Here he built a prosperous career. After he had joined the Simson Company as Chief Clerk, he worked his way up to director and later even took over the Company. In 1962 Sandor left for Spain, where he worked in the real estate business. Eventually he emigrated to the United States in 1980 and lived in the state of Florida until his death on 13 January 1995.[38] Werner Bloch did see a future for himself in the Netherlands and officially became a Dutch citizen after a while. At the Red Cross, where he initially worked, he met his second wife. Later Werner built a successful career as an importer of toys. The camp number tattooed on his arm was a lasting reminder of the horrific past.[39]

Memories of the past could also provide clarity, as in the case of David Chajes. After the liberation, he made an important statement about the clearing of the Jewish Psychiatric Institution '*Het Apeldoornsche Bosch*', and about the role played in this by the OD. The confrontation with fate in most cases did not turn out positive, because the search for the perpetrators of the persecution of Jews in the Netherlands continued. This happened both collectively and individually. An individual case concerned the charges pressed against Joël Granade. As far as is known, with the exception of Pisk, he is the only OD man who had to justify himself after the liberation. He was suspected of 'bringing a camp resident back into the hands of the enemy' and was reported to the Bureau of National Security in Amsterdam at the end of December 1945. The crime committed by Joël, which according to the accuser was a war crime, should not remain unpunished in his view. The final sentence was in fact a disciplinary punishment: the case was dismissed conditionally and he was to be supervised by the Foundation of Political Delinquents in Amsterdam. The fact that he was also put on transport and that his wife and nine-month-old son were murdered in Auschwitz, which made him a victim of the persecution as well, was not considered a mitigating circumstance. After all, justice had to prevail.[40]

That people thought and acted in this way is not surprising, because immediately after the south of the Netherlands was liberated, members of the occupying forces and those who had worked with them had to justify their actions. Their reasons were then weighed on an imaginary scale and if the result was negative, the so-called political delinquent had to exchange his freedom for imprisonment in one of the internment camps, of which Camp Westerbork was one.

On The Scales Of Justice

In order to find out if someone had only made mistakes or had really been a bad person, an investigation had to be conducted first. Special investigative bodies, such as the Political Investigation Service (*Politieke Opsporingsdienst*, or *POD*), were set up for finding and questioning suspects. After the investigation was closed and the official report was drawn up, the Judge had to decide what punishment someone deserved. Since pre-war law was not deemed sufficient for the trial of members of the occupying forces and their Dutch accomplices, the London Government had already begun to develop a number of new laws and decrees during the occupation. Eventually, individuals could be tried under three separate regulations, depending on the severity of their actions. The so-called '*Zuiveringsbesluit*' was mainly intended for civil servants. If sufficient evidence was gathered of membership of a National Socialist Organisation or other forms of infidelity, measures could already be taken before the final verdict. These measures consisted of a strike, suspension and total or partial deprivation of freedom. After some time, the person concerned received the final judgment in writing. In addition to dismissal, it was possible to impose various disciplinary penalties, ranging from transfer to reprimand.

Those who had been guilty of helping or collaborating with the enemy had to appear before one of the 19 tribunals because of unpatriotic behaviour. These tribunals were able to impose certain measures, such as internment for up to 10 years, confiscation of assets and deprivation of rights, functions and professions. Those who had committed the most serious crimes, such as war criminals and traitors, were tried before Special Courts, of which there were five. The death penalty was even temporarily reintroduced for this group. According to the post war judiciary, whether and to what extent the men of the units and services guarding Camp Westerbork were guilty also had to be investigated by the Detective Department and the Investigative Service.[41]

The Gendarmerie Detachment, which was responsible for both the indoor and outdoor surveillance of Westerbork, was judged alternately. Some Gendarmes were even described as convinced Nazi sympathisers or as opportunists who tried to make a career by doing their best to aid the enemy. However, the majority would have carried out the task against his will.[42] This contradiction makes it clear that forming a collective judgment on the actions of the Gendarmerie in the camp is extremely difficult.

A Closer Look At The Gendarmerie Detachment

The generally young Gendarmes of the Surveillance Detachment, who had to go to Camp Westerbork for a period of several months, were not held accountable just for this fact. They only qualified for such measures if they had committed any other wrongdoings as well. For most Gendarmes, such as Jenne Boering, Reint Middel and Folkert van der Werf, Camp Westerbork was one of the many places where they were seconded during the occupation. The question of whether the behaviour of individual Gendarmes could be considered deplorable is not easy to answer. This depends on a number of things, such as the period during which the secondment took place and how one even defines 'deplorable'. In the first period, there was still little going on. Back then, Camp Westerbork functioned mainly as a shelter for foreign Jewish refugees. This changed when the occupier started using the camp as a transit camp. Together with the OD, the Gendarmerie was busy guiding groups of Jews to and from the trains. This second period, which lasted about half a year, can be considered the hardest period of the existence of the Detachment, because the Gendarmerie had to help keep the deportation machine running. During that period, more than 30 trains left for Auschwitz.

At the end of 1942, the guidance task became considerably easier, because the trains were able to enter the camp on a new railway line. The long and often difficult hikes to and from Hooghalen station were a thing of the past. In January 1943, when the *SS-Wachbataillon Nordwest* left and the Gendarmerie Detachment took over the outdoor surveillance, a new period began. For the Detachment, this essentially meant that the direct confrontation with fate ended. Most Gendarmes no longer witnessed the often chaotic and emotional departure of the trains to the Extermination Camps. Although the cooperation of the Detachment in these transports was highly reprehensible, it was not enough to punish individual Gendarmes only after the liberation. After all, they had not been seconded to Westerbork at their own request. Gendarmes who had not joined a National Socialist Organisation and had therefore not been problematic in political terms, but who had done bad things were in many cases suspended immediately while the investigation was still ongoing. If the investigation showed that the deeds had been serious enough, definitive punitive measures followed after a trial.

Paridaen was one of the few people of the Detachment who was investigated. After having been initially suspended, it turned out after a few months that there was enough evidence to arrest him. He was arrested on 12 June 1945 and kept in custody until 13 December 1945. The investigation resulted in him being charged with four offences. Three of them related to his role in the arrest of Jews who had tried to flee. The fourth offence, the beating and kicking of prisoners, was supported by several incriminating statements that were included in the official report. It is striking that these statements were mainly made by fellow Gendarmes. Some of them indicated that they had witnessed the abuse themselves, but most of them had heard people talk about it.

Paridaen denied having abused prisoners. He may have shouted louder than anyone else, sometimes kicking or hitting someone, but according to his Lawyer, this fit in with his deliberately chosen tactics. By acting Militaristic, rough and sometimes even cruel, he tried to deceive the occupying forces and any colleagues who may have been on the side of the occupier, so that he could play his double role without being suspected of anything. This other and almost invisible role Paridaen played in the Camp Prison. There he gave the prisoners a lot of freedom, extra food and cigarettes. He also smuggled letters and packages into and out of the camp for them. Although he could operate fairly safely within the Prison walls, there were risks, because traitors were always on the lookout. Much riskier was helping people escape. Paridaen managed to get Sylvia de Levier and the Schoenland couple out of the camp. After the liberation, they were able to make a statement that portrayed Paridaen in a favourable light. Contrary to a remark from a fellow Gendarme that all Jews abused by Paridaen had not returned from the Extermination Camps, the Lawyer tracked down dozens of residents who all judged him positively. Because Paridaen was not discovered, he was able to maintain his double role for a year and a half until he left the camp.

When asked why he had stayed in such a difficult position for so long, he gave several reasons. For example, he claimed that several (prominent) residents had asked him to stay, that he did not want to return to his previous Detachment because of the possibility of an unwanted promotion there, and that he was able to help Jews in this position. Which reason is the real one remains vague. In any case, research has shown that Paridaen was not a National Socialist, was not pro German, and did not help Jews for the sake of monetary gain. He was promoted in rank, but he denied that he had tried his best for this especially. He would not even have been pleased with this higher rank, because the promotion caused envy among his colleagues. At the end of May 1947, the Special Court in Assen dealt with Paridaen's case for the first time. The Court thought it had sufficient evidence to sue him for abuse, 'whereby the guilty party took advantage of the opportunity offered to him by the enemy's occupation, deliberately providing aid to the enemy in time of war, and intentionally exposing persons to detection, persecution, and limitation or complete deprivation of freedom'.

Paridaen's Lawyer wrote a 20 page pleading. First of all, he emphasised how extremely difficult the task was that the Police Force had to fulfil during the years of occupation. The service in Camp Westerbork, essentially the gateway to the gas chambers, would have been tougher than anywhere else, but according to the Lawyer, the worst part was guarding the Prison. Nevertheless, no one from the Jewish side had made an incriminating statement. After this, the Lawyer explained the strategy deliberately chosen by Paridaen and quoted about 40 witnesses. The Lawyer also tried to refute the three accusations relating to the arrest of Jews. The arrest of a Jewish man on the platform of Assen had taken place under pressure. The man had been noticed because of his appearance, after which Paridaen was ordered by an NSB member to arrest him. Since Paridaen was constantly supervised, he did not dare to let the man flee. According to the Lawyer, it could therefore not be said that Paridaen had intentionally tracked down the man and exposed him to persecution and restriction or deprivation of freedom, because the Jewish man had already been tracked down by Paridaen's higher ups.

The Court agreed with the Lawyer that the difficulties faced by the Police during the occupation should be taken into account. After all, in certain situations, a Police Officer could not always make his choice quietly. Nevertheless, the Court still considered Paridaen's actions at the station of Assen highly objectionable. They were convinced that he could have acted differently without too many risks, but he had instead sacrificed the man for his own safety. The Court and the Lawyer also disagreed about the incident in which Paridaen shot at a Jewish man who had fled the train during a transport. According to the Lawyer, there would have been no malicious intent. He had first shot in the air and then he had jumped off the train to pretend to chase the man. After all, it had been required to report what efforts had been made to find the escapee. Paridaen stated that he had been attacked by the man as he walked along the tracks. He had then fired in self-defence, causing the man to get injured and stop the attack. When Paridaen arrived at the camp with his arrestee, he could not tell the true story, because then it would have become clear that he had not actively been searching for the man. Bragging about his 'good performance' was in line with his deliberately chosen tactics. However, the Court took the view that in this case, a so-called 'camouflage act' should certainly be ruled out. They said that by pursuing the Jewish man with the aim of sending him back into the hands of the Germans, which would lead him to his death without any doubt, Paridaen had proved himself to be inhumane.

Another incident occurred after the Detachment had left the camp in the second half of 1944. In all likelihood, Paridaen was transferred to the Municipality of Vledder, because together with the NSB Mayor of the Municipality and a detection dog handler, he participated in an investigation into the theft of a number of motor vehicles. During the investigation, a suspicious man was stopped. Since it was suspected that he was a Jew, he was asked if he was, but the man denied it. Paridaen would have said something like: 'Are you not a Jew? Pull down your pants, then I'll tell you if you're a Jew, yes or no.' According to the charge, due to this method of questioning, the man became subject to prosecution, among other things. Paridaen confessed to regrettably having used such words. According to him, this behaviour was probably due to the bad influence of the occupation and, in particular, to the stay of a year and a half in Camp Westerbork. Despite this, the Lawyer denied that Paridaen had exposed the Jewish man to something bad by his actions.

Once again, the Court begged to differ. Among other things, they described the action as repulsive. Demanding of someone to show his genitals already pointed to a highly questionable mentality. Moreover, because it was made by a Christian to a Jew, the demand had an extra despicable character. In addition to a chance that the Jewish man would be mocked because he was circumcised, thereby affecting him in his religious value, the demand could have terrible consequences. The Court stressed that it did not see this as merely a crude joke, as the Lawyer wanted it to appear. It was more akin to devilish mental abuse. The Court also assumed that Paridaen must have felt most satisfied when the suspect was exposed, and he saw his power hungry, cruel and lewd act crowned with such success. However, there was not the slightest need or reason for Paridaen to act this way during the Mayor's interrogation. The Court would have taken into account Paridaen as a person when deciding on a sentence. He was described as someone with a morally low character, insolent, cynical, impulsive, adventurous and willing to do terrible things.

The findings of the Court did not correspond to those of the Lawyer in many ways. The Lawyer's final conclusion and the Court's demand show the difference of opinion on Paridaen's actions most clearly. The Lawyer ended his written pleadings stating that he did not wish to speak at all about a possible punishment; in his opinion, only acquittal could follow. The Court reiterated its disbelief that the brutal actions against the Jews in the camp had been merely camouflage acts. They thought it much more likely that the performance had arisen from Paridaen's peculiar mentality. The Court stated that, if all favourable statements had not been taken into account, an extremely severe penalty would indeed have been imposed.

Because a number of witnesses did not show up, the case was adjourned until early July. Despite the harsh words in the direction of Paridaen, the Court did take into account what he had done for the prisoners in the final assessment. As this weighed heavily, a lighter sentence was imposed. They had come to the conclusion that, in addition to doing many good things,

Paridaen had made mistakes. The Special Prosecutor took the positive opinion into account in his demand. He even finally believed that Paridaen had been deliberately good in his attitude and concluded he was not a two faced figure. Only the shooting of the prisoner who had tried to escape the train was proved and he therefore demanded imprisonment for a period of six months, minus the time Paridaen had already spent in custody. Since this sentence was equal to the time already spent in custody, Paridaen did not have to go back to Prison. However, because of his conviction, he was not allowed to return to the Gendarmerie, but he was able to make a living by working in the flax industry.[43]

There was not much difference between good and evil for Paridaen. On the one hand, he helped prisoners escape, so the Jewish saying 'Who saves a life saves the whole world' did apply to him, while on the other hand, he played a dubious role in the arrest of several Jewish men. How Paridaen himself dealt with this contradiction and the sentence imposed by the Judge is unknown. A passage from his obituary might be an indication that it was not easy for him to find his way in the liberated Netherlands. According to the obituary, he emigrated to Canada in 1950, after surviving World War II as a prisoner in a German camp and later as a Police Officer. He did not say anything about being imprisoned in a camp. It is possible that he was detained as a prisoner of war for a short time after the capitulation of the Dutch Army in May 1940, because at the beginning of September 1940 he joined the Gendarmerie. Paridaen built a new life in the vicinity of the Canadian city of Edmonton. In 1952 he married and he had seven children with his wife. After attempts to achieve success in agriculture and in some other enterprises, Paridaen worked at the *Edmonton Parks and Recreation Department* of the city of Edmonton until his retirement in 1984. He died on 13 February 2008.[44]

The question of how someone could lose control of his own actions entirely or partially and start to serve the occupying forces, even up to collaboration or war crimes, knows many answers. Determining exactly where the boundary was located was not easy. Someone could have already crossed that line without even noticing it. This shows that there is a very fine line between good and evil. The Special Courts and Committees also had to deal with this fact. They were unable to make collective judgments, so each case had to be looked at separately. If it was discovered that someone had been a member of a National Socialist Organisation during the war, this was deemed enough of a reason to fire someone. However, it was still necessary to investigate to what extent this person had helped the occupying forces. For those who had deliberately collaborated, the question of whether they were guilty could be answered quickly. The assessment of all the facts and the consideration of what punishment fit the crime was left to the Judge.

One offence could already be sufficient for a substantial sentence, as in the case of Detachment Commander Albert de Jong. He was sentenced to seven years in Prison in 1947. However, the Leeuwarder Special Court in Assen sentenced him to twelve years imprisonment for his part in the death of Johan Ernst Polak. His right to vote and to be elected was also withdrawn for the duration of his life, as well as his right to hold office. On the basis of the evidence, the Court considered that De Jong had deliberately provided aid to the enemy in time of war by exposing another person to investigation, persecution and deprivation or restriction of liberty, which had resulted in death. Showing regret and the statement that it had never been his intention to deliberately bring Polak into the hands of the occupying forces did not affect the Judge's ruling. De Jong appealed to the Court, because according to his Lawyer, it was still not established that Polak had actually died at that time. In his pleadings, this Lawyer supported De Jong's remark that it could not be considered a deliberate act. He had not been a ruthless Jew hunter in search of hiding Jews, as the encounter between him and Polak had been a result of coincidences. For a good and diligent Policeman of the old school who had managed to become a Petty Officer, arresting a resident who had fled was a natural reaction. The Lawyer was convinced that De Jong would never have been prosecuted if he had not arrested Polak.

In addition, the complaints that had been received, which would supposedly have been carefully examined, should not be taken too seriously. They had been filed by old residents who had themselves participated in sexual acts with female Jews and been guilty of corruption, extortion or betrayal. Most of the complaints could be traced back to De Jong's cooperation during the transports. Although witnesses stated otherwise, there would hardly have been any beating and kicking. If he ever harshly dragged Jewish men out of a wagon to make room for women, children and elderly people, then according to his Lawyer, he could not be blamed for this. The chaotic conditions, especially when it came to the larger transports, called for such action. It also had to be taken into account that, in addition to the complaints, many positive statements about De Jong's actions had been made as well. That is why the Lawyer asked the question whether it was not tragic that this man, who himself had been arrested in August 1944 and put in a cell with a sign on the doorstep with *Jüdenbegünstiger* on it, should stand trial for a single offence. That he would have participated in resistance activities to cover the arrest of Polak was not based on any fact, according to the Lawyer. That is why he asked the Supreme Court to annul the verdict of the Special Court. If the Supreme Court did not have sufficient grounds to do so, the Councilman suggested that the imposition of a lower penalty should be considered.

At the beginning of April 1948, the Supreme Court dealt with De Jong's case. They did not see in him the deliberate collaborator who had chosen to serve the enemy on the basis of treacherous motives or solely for the sake of his own gain and the desire for promotion. In addition, De Jong had never joined the NSB or any other party or organisation that was approved of by the occupiers. This would have made sense if he had deliberately chosen the enemy's side or if he had simply wanted promotion. Although De Jong could not have predicted the consequences of a possible arrest himself when he came across Polak, the Court believed that he would have been able to make up for 'his misplaced, in the circumstances downright criminal diligence' if he had let Polak go on his way to the Police Station. The Court decided that a Prison sentence of eight years was sufficient. In view of the fact that the arrest of Polak had resulted in his death, a serious correction was still necessary. The sentence of twelve years in Prison imposed by the Special Court of Justice was reduced 'only' by four years, because the rest of De Jong's actions in relation to the persons residing in the camp had been quite deplorable and he had certainly been too harsh.

When the final sentence was being decided on, the reports written and signed by De Jong in September 1942 were not taken into account. They were also not found in the file in the archives of the Special Court. De Jong had written them because some Jewish men had violated one of the camp rules. He also advised each time to send the offenders along with the next transport. Of at least one Jewish man, Julius Bick, it can be said with some certainty that he was indeed sent on the next transport and was murdered immediately upon arrival in Auschwitz. Why the reports have not been taken into account in the trial remains unclear. It is possible they were still in an undisclosed or unknown file, so De Jong was not questioned about the drafting of both documents. In any case, it is certain that he wrote them during his second detachment as a Sergeant. The reason may certainly have to do with De Jong's work ethic. He was described by Gemmeker and other witnesses as a man with a great sense of honour. A social worker from the Political Delinquents Foundation concluded the same thing. He described him as a person who was a Policeman through and through, but one who would have exercised the profession under any Government.[45]

Of the Gendarmes who had already been serving in the Royal Gendarmerie before the war began and who formed a minority within the greatly expanded corps during the occupation, only a small part would have collaborated with the occupier.[46] The Detachment Commanders De Jong and Klavers belonged to this group. They had already entered service before the war. Most of the lower ranking Gendarmes, who had to go to the camp for a few months, were often placed with the corps as demobilised Military, without Police training. Some residents, such as Mirjam Bolle and Philip Mechanicus, who experienced the performance of these so-called 'war Gendarmes' up close, judged almost unanimously. Among other things, they wrote that these men were generally fair in their actions and that they were good people. The occupier, on the other hand, was less and less satisfied with the performance of the Detachment. Because they had illicit affairs with camp residents, helped people escape and smuggled letters and parcels, the occupier no longer trusted the Gendarmes and instead replaced them with a Company of the Amsterdam Police Battalion in June 1944.

The replacement of the Detachment that was unreliable in the eyes of the occupier and some positive comments about their behaviour could not change the generally negative picture of the Gendarmes in Camp Westerbork. The fact that they had helped the occupiers with the transports, as well as the fanatical actions of some of the leaders, had an enormous impact on public opinion. It is therefore understandable that most Gendarmes wanted to forget this period as soon as possible and never spoke about it again, despite the fact that most of them were not persecuted after the liberation because of their actions in Camp Westerbork. There was no room for any nuance when it came to the negative view on the Gendarmes. By judging them based on knowledge only gained after the war, the exact opposite of creating a more nuanced view happened. Whether it was on purpose or not, little attention was paid to the way the Detachment functioned in Camp Westerbork. The task of monitoring the residents was considered one of the most reprehensible acts of the Gendarmerie during the occupation. It was not easily forgotten either and continued to be seen that way for a long time. That is probably why it took until 28 April 2010, almost 65 years after the liberation, before the then Commander of the Royal Gendarmerie, Lieutenant General Mr. Dick van Putten, said anything about the whole ordeal. During the official commemoration at the memorial near the camp, he stated that he was aware the Gendarmes of the Detachment had carried out awful tasks under a bad regime, in the wrong place at the wrong time. According to him, they should never have helped the enemy. After his statement, Van Putten laid a wreath at the monument, together with a Jewish survivor of Camp Westerbork and Auschwitz, as a gesture of reconciliation.[47]

However, this gesture did not mean that the Royal Gendarmerie was allowed to participate in the annual Remembrance of the Dead on Dam Square in Amsterdam the same way the other Military components did. This is mainly due to the fear that this could cause negative feelings to arise among Jewish relatives and survivors. However, Van Putten wrote in an article that he did not believe they would react that badly. He saw the wreath at the monument in Westerbork as evidence. According to Van Putten, Chief Rabbi Binyomin Jacobs, the representative of the Jewish community in the Netherlands, did not react negatively either to the full participation of the Gendarmerie in this memorial.[48] Despite this, the occupation and especially the role of the corps in the surveillance of Camp Westerbork remains a dark chapter in the history of the Gendarmerie.

Not only the Gendarmes struggled with the part they had played during the war. The Amsterdam Police Team struggled with their role as well. After all, was this Police Force not largely composed of highly feared Policemen who had been trained according to the methods of the SS, as Lindwer claimed?[49]

Police Company Purged

The majority of the Company consisted of Policemen trained in Schalkhaar under the supervision of the German Police. The Centralised Training Institute had a clear Military basis, because according to the objective of the occupying forces, it had to deliver Police Soldiers. However, keeping in mind all known facts, the training cannot rightly be linked to the SS. Many young men did not go to Schalkhaar because of a National Socialist conviction or a pro German attitude. They voluntarily opted for Police training in the Netherlands because the alternatives, working in Germany or hiding, were not options for them. The fact that the 'Schalkhaarders' as individuals and the Police Battalions as a group were seen in such a bad light was mainly due to the first group, which consisted of fanatical National Socialists who helped pickup the Jews in Amsterdam.

It was only clear what the Company truly consisted of on 19 September 1944, when they had to make an important choice. A minority of 14 members chose to continue serving the occupying forces until the end.

The rest, 55 Policemen, did not step forward. They were taken as prisoners to a labour camp. After the liberation, several committees focused on the role of the Schalkhaarders. Some committees considered a collective punishment, but this was not possible. A number of members of the Westerbork Group did not have to worry about any punishments, nor would they have to worry about that in the future. They often tried to build a normal life in their original or new place of employment.

Bombergen was able to flee shortly before the Heidelager was surrounded by German Soldiers. He joined a resistance group in the Municipality of Donkerbroek and later became a member of the Dutch Internal Armed Forces (*Binnenlandse Strijdkrachten*, or *BS*). His very recent past as Schalk-haarder proved to be no obstacle for this. Once the liberation was a fact, it took about one month before he was allowed to return to Amsterdam. That is where he applied to the Police Force. Upon delivery of a statement signed by the Commander of the BS, he was given permission to resume service immediately. Because Bombergen did not have a place to live yet, his employment was postponed for two weeks, so he could look for a place to stay. He also used those days off for other activities, such as visiting Camp Westerbork. Because of his involvement, Bombergen wanted to know what had happened to the camp and the residents in the end. The meeting with those who had remained there was emotional and he kept in touch with some of them later. According to Bombergen, this meant that the Jews did not see all the Schalkhaarders as bad people.[50]

The members of the Company who had remained in the original line and had therefore chosen to be sent to the labour camp were released in April 1945 or had already fled by then. One of these members, Johannes Frederikus Buring, fled from the labour camp on 12 October 1944 and went into hiding. He seems to have done illegal work until the liberation. Because Buring assumed that he had been dismissed from the Amsterdam Police Force due to his arrest in Westerbork by the occupying forces, he applied to the Police Force of Enschede after the liberation. At first it seemed that he could join this corps without any problems. However, when he was informed that he had not been fired in Amsterdam and thus still belonged to this corps, he had to resign officially. This resignation was granted to him on the day he joined the corps in Enschede. By giving him an honourable discharge immediately, it does not seem that Buring was held accountable for training in Schalkhaar and for his service in Camp Westerbork. Jacobus Romeijn and Klaas Koster were among the men who worked on lines of defence under supervision until their release. Like Bombergen, they had to wait some time before they could return to Amsterdam after the liberation. The reacquisition of a place within the Metropolitan Police Force was no problem for them. Koster only said he was held accountable for his actions by one of the committees dealing with those who had served in Westerbork. Bombergen and Romeijn did not speak about this at all.[51]

Initially, no measures were taken against those Amsterdam Policemen who had followed Police training in Schalkhaar but had not joined some National Socialist Organisation. The Military Commissioner of Amsterdam, Lieutenant Colonel Th. J. van Lohuizen, was instructed not to remove the

Schalkhaarders from the corps when he was appointed. However, he had to have them assessed individually by one of the committees. Koster's statement shows that the committee had probably already begun with his trial, but that they had soon stopped convicting the Schalkhaarders altogether due to a draft law. Returning them to the same rank as the Officers who joined the Amsterdam Corps after the liberation was accepted as an appropriate collective measure.[52]

The assessment of the Schalkhaarders was very diverse. Before German Soldiers surrounded the Heidelager, Teunis Versteeg was able to leave for Rotterdam by train just in time. There he was hired without any problems. A month and a half after the liberation, Versteeg found himself in a difficult situation, because he and the other Schalkhaarders from the corps were suspended in mid-June. They were instructed to write a report, in which they had to explain why they had followed the German Police training. After the report was assessed and the suspension was lifted, Versteeg was allowed to resume his service at the Rotterdam corps.[53]

No one of the Battalion was therefore punished for being part of the Surveillance Detachment of Camp Westerbork. If all the facts had been thoroughly studied and weighed, there would certainly have been a chance that some of them would have been punished. For example, on 5 September 1944 four Jewish men tried to flee from the camp. They were caught by men of the Battalion. These Policemen fired a few shots, allowing some SS members to arrest the men. As a retaliatory measure, the Jews were sentenced to death the same night. It is likely that the Policemen did not know what consequences their actions had. They may have never even known that an execution had taken place since the Battalion did not come into the camp. Chances are small that the identities of these men were actively searched for after the liberation.

Those in charge, such as Tasseron and Munnikhuizen, and the members of the Company who opted to join the *Ordnungspolizei* were interned and interrogated after the liberation. Although the files contain statements that include information about the camp's surveillance, they were generally not incriminating.[54] Most people in this group were punished for offences and crimes committed before and after their stay in the camp. Munnikhuizen was sentenced to imprisonment for life by the Court in Groningen on 20 March 1950, partly because of his part in the massacre in Tijnje. He did not serve this sentence in a Dutch Prison, because he fled to Germany, where the Public Prosecutor's Office could not find him. When a trail led back to him in 2002, Munnikhuizen turned out to have already died five years earlier.[55]

Of the Dutch Police Units, virtually no one was convicted for playing a role in the surveillance of Camp Westerbork. Those who had been part of the camp's SS often were held accountable for the role they had played in the camp during the war.

SS Members In Court

Gemmeker's employees were divided into two categories during the prosecutions after the liberation. At least four Dutch people were subject to different criteria in the trial than their German and Austrian counterparts. Before the investigations and interrogations could take place, the men had to be tracked down first. At the end of April 1945, while the Netherlands had not yet been completely liberated, OD member Hans Eisinger travelled through the country for five days and visited several internment camps, with the aim of identifying camp SS members.[56]

The investigations into the conduct of the 'political offenders', as the Germans and their accomplices were called after arrest, took a lot of time. Calls appeared regularly in the newspapers asking witnesses to come forward. On 31 January 1947, in an article in the *Nieuw Israëlietisch Weekblad* (*New Israelite Weekly*) the head of the Political Investigation Department in The Hague asked those who could provide information about the Dutch SS man Hendrik van Dam to contact his service. This request was followed by a brief summary of Van Dam's work during the occupation. According to the article, after being placed at the SD in The Hague, he had worked as an *Unterscharführer* for quite some time in Camp Westerbork, where he had allegedly abused residents.[57]

Van Dam had already been arrested by the BS in Zwammerdam on 5 May 1945. After a short stay in the Scheveningen Prison, he was imprisoned in Rotterdam in early June until his trial began. During the interrogations, he tried to twist his personal war history. He probably did not want to be known as a reckless drunk who beat residents during the occupation and treated them badly. He stated that he had volunteered for the Waffen SS in December 1940. After a training of several months, he fought with the Volunteer Legion Netherlands (*Vrijwilligers Legioen 'Nederland'*) on the Eastern Front from July 1941 onwards. Van Dam then stated that he had to be admitted to Hospital because of a gunshot to the head. After he had healed, he was again forced to go to the Eastern Front in November 1943. Because he refused to do so, he was locked up in the Prison of Apeldoorn. This version of the story did not last long.

Partly as a result of the call for witnesses in the newspapers, enough witnesses showed up to invalidate his story. For example, Van Dam had lied about his participation in the fights in Russia, because he had never even been there. He did not suffer the injuries to his head when fighting at the front, but when he had driven into a tree in a drunken state. The statements also show that during the occupation he boasted about his violent behaviour in Westerbork. He often spent his leave in The Hague. There he regularly visited café restaurant Monopole. There he met up with colleagues from the SD. Among the wait staff, Van Dam was known as the 'Jew Torturer', because they had heard him say that he threw Jewish children against the wall in the camp. Although this never actually happened, he was known to the residents as the fiercest and most dangerous employee of Gemmeker.

During the interrogation, Van Dam denied almost all accusations made against him. Only the excessive consumption of alcohol he admitted. Because he felt locked away from the outside world in the camp, he was often tempted to drink alcohol, of which there was no shortage. In spite of the various testimonies, Van Dam denied he had abused Jews. He could at least recall no such incident. Such a form of (temporary) amnesia occurred in

In other newspapers, calls for witnesses appeared as well.

several individuals. It is possible that they had deliberately suppressed their memories or simply refused to admit their shortcomings. The investigation then had to show to what extent someone had been guilty of misconduct during the occupation.

During the trial against Van Dam, which only took place before the Special Court of Justice in The Hague on 19 March 1948, the Judge probably had sufficient evidence against him. According to the indictment, the former subordinate of Gemmeker was suspected of having mistreated and abused one or more camp residents, while he had also unlawfully taken things for himself that belonged to one or more Jewish persons. The Court believed there was enough evidence to say with certainty that Van Dam had intentionally helped the enemy several times during the war and that he had also deliberately taken advantage of the opportunity to get something out of it for himself. For these crimes, the Court sentenced him to eight years in Prison. The period during which he was in custody, from 17 January 1946 until the verdict, was deducted from the sentence. Van Dam did not agree with this last addition, because he had been in Prison since 5 May 1945. He submitted three petitions for pardon. At the end of February 1949, the sentence was reduced by one year.[58]

Another Dutch SS member, Wilhelmus van Eck, who would have been considered one of the most hated SS men and was even called 'The Terror of Camp Westerbork', had to go to jail for one year more than Van Dam. The Special Court of Justice of Arnhem postponed the case in February 1948, because the investigation was not yet complete. The Court considered it necessary to have his mental capacity evaluated first. According to Gemmeker, Van Eck could indeed be weird sometimes. He assumed that his mind had suffered somewhat because of the injuries he had suffered on the Eastern Front, in which he had also lost his right eye. However, after examination, a neurologist came to the conclusion that Van Eck's injuries had not resulted in any severe neurological or psychological abnormalities. In the opinion of the Doctor, he was a weak, egocentric figure who had no interest in the world around him, unless it was in his own interest. The study also did not prove he suffered from any disorder or a reduction in mental abilities. Van Eck could therefore be held accountable for his actions.

Contrary to the statements of witnesses about his brutal actions, Van Eck stated that he had never been guilty of drunkenness, abuse, unacceptable comments or other misbehaviour. His attitude towards the Jews in the camp would instead have been very mild, because he did not agree with the isolation of these Jews from Dutch society. He could not have exhibited this view openly during the occupation, so that, according to him, there would have been nothing for him to do but adopt a strict and correct Military attitude. His choice to join the enemy's Military Service weighed heavier in the final verdict than his brutal actions in the camp as Commander of the Penal Barracks. Overall, the Court sentenced Van Eck to nine years of imprisonment.[59]

Entry into foreign Military Service as a Dutchman was also one of the two facts for which the Dutch SS man Johannes Otto von Henning stood trial on 5 December 1946 in Assen. Because he had also formed a firing squad in the camp with Breil, Lübbecke and Lemke in early September 1944 and was therefore complicit in the death of three residents, a life sentence was demanded. Two weeks later the Court sentenced Von Henning to 20 years in Prison. Von Henning took advantage of the opportunity to file an appeal in cassation. The case served before the Supreme Court in October 1947. Before the Court took a decision a few weeks later, a Chaplain who had worked in internment camps for two years and in one of them had met Von Henning's wife tried to get the Court to lower the sentence. In a letter, the Chaplain urgently asked for leniency, because Von Henning would have acted under pressure during the occupation. After being egged on by his parents and fellow students, he joined the SS, which resulted in being sent to the Eastern Front. He did not dare to desert, because he was afraid of what might happen to his parents if he did.

With regard to the second alleged crime, the Chaplain believed that Von Henning was not to blame for the death of the residents. It would have been an unfortunate coincidence. He claimed Von Henning was under the assumption that he had to bring the Jewish men to the Criminal Barracks because of an attempted escape. Only at the last moment would he have been ordered to be part of the execution squad. Because he feared that retaliatory measures would follow against him or his parents, refusing the order was not an option for him. Therefore, he would have decided to hit Samuel

Goldstein in such a way that he could still flee. He succeeded in this setup, because Goldstein was only slightly injured by the gunshot. If Von Henning had truly been someone with cruel intentions, he would certainly have participated in the execution with more conviction, according to the Chaplain. In this case, the situation had been beyond his control. As such, the Chaplain was of the opinion that Von Henning should not be treated as a war criminal who had murdered a man in cold blood and that he did not deserve a long and severe punishment. Rather than that, he was a boy with a very soft character and a good heart. The Court was not swayed by the Chaplain's arguments. These arguments were dismissed on the ground that the offences committed by Von Henning were classified as particularly serious.[60]

Herman van Laer had to appear before the Special Court of Justice in The Hague on 19 August 1948 for treating residents in the camp cruelly, for the unlawful appropriation of food and cigarettes intended for residents, and for the withholding of an amount of 5,000 Dutch guilders. During the trial, two witnesses were heard. According to a newspaper article, these witnesses made such favourable statements that only the withholding of the money was left. The Public Prosecutor demanded a sentence of seven years in Prison, minus the time already served, and deprivation of the right to vote for life.[61] The Court ruled otherwise and imposed a sentence of five years and six months imprisonment in connection with the support he lent to the enemy. In mid-December 1948, the remainder of the sentence was suspended. At that time, Van Laer was detained in the Passart State Labour Institution in Treebeek and probably worked in the Emma Mine.[62]

The trial of the representatives of the Nazi regime who were based in the Netherlands seemed at first to have been well organised and properly prepared. At the beginning of 1942, the allies signed a treaty in London, in which they promised to assist in the detection and trial of German war criminals after the occupation. In the following period, the treaty became more detailed. In August 1945 it was decided that German leaders would be prosecuted by an International Court that still had to be founded. In the Netherlands, only Seyss-Inquart was eligible for such a trial. The other German offenders could be prosecuted by the Special Courts of the occupied countries themselves. As such, the Dutch Government in London started to create rules that would enable the trial of both Dutch people and members of the German occupying forces.

After the liberation, the Dutch Government thought it had sufficient regulation to ensure that the former members of the occupying powers were successfully tried by the special judicial bodies. However, the Supreme Court ruled differently on 17 February 1947. According to this Court, the Dutch Court had no jurisdiction to judge war crimes committed by the occupying forces in the light of the rules in force at that time. It was necessary to amend the *Besluit Buitengewoon Strafrecht* (a special decree regarding criminal justice) in order to grant the Court that jurisdiction. Since this change took place only on 10 July 1947, the trial of the occupier was delayed quite considerably. Most members of the occupying force were therefore tried after 1947, which did not cause any adverse consequences for themselves. In fact, the penalties were milder for various reasons. The growing lack of interest in the Special Courts of Justice and the better opportunities for cassation were part of the reason.[63]

The German and Austrian SS members too learned only after a few years of internment of what they were suspected and what was supposed to happen to them. Breil, Frentzel-Beijme, Lübbecke and Reiser were still detained in Groningen at the end of December 1948. The Investigating Officers of the Assen Municipal Police, who had been seconded to the *Bureau Opsporing Oorlogsmisdrijven* (the Department tasked with tracking down war criminals), did their best to complete the cases against these men. On 21 April 1948 the investigation concerning 'the conduct of persons who worked in Camp Westerbork' was closed. Although suspects like Gemmeker, Lemke, Reiser, Van Dam and Van Eck were interrogated, this investigation focused mainly on Lemke's work in the Camp Prison. It is clear from the reports that during the investigations, attempts were made to reveal the misconduct of as many individuals as possible. Nevertheless, there was barely any difference between the charges of non-Dutch SS members. Those of Reiser, Frentzel-Beijme, Breil and Lübbecke, dated 28 December 1948, stated that they had committed the following war crimes: deliberately assisting in illegally depriving a large number of persons of their freedom and participating in the plundering, destruction and burning down of residences as retaliatory measures. Nevertheless, in view of the time spent in custody, the four SS members were unconditionally excluded from prosecution. On 30 December they were transferred to the Crailo camp in Laren, after which they were allowed to return to Germany quickly. Lemke's indictment was equal to that of the others. His case was dismissed on 14 March 1949.[64]

Almost all SS members who had worked in the camp declared that they had acted on the orders of the commander. The non-Dutch SS men could as such rely on the '*befehl ist befehl-principle*', because they had not joined a foreign Military Service. In most cases, the Judge therefore considered the detention for this group a sufficient punishment and did not impose any longer custodial sentences. Camp Commander Gemmeker was often mentioned as the person who had given the orders.

'Ich Habe Es Nicht Gewusst' – 'I Didn't Know'
After the liberation, Policeman Jan Schoenmaker, Sergeant Major of the State Police, seconded to the *Bureau Opsporing Oorlogsmisdrijven* of the Assen Police, investigated Gemmeker's performance as Commander of Camp Westerbork. Schoenmaker recorded his findings in an extensive report.

The search for information on Gemmeker's predecessors yielded less data in some cases. This is not surprising, because these Camp Commanders had stayed in Westerbork for a shorter time or had had a less prominent role. Jacob Schol built up a well-functioning camp organisation as Commander of the refugee camp in the period before the occupation, which lasted two years. The occupier happily made use of this and after they had taken over, they largely kept the organisation the way it was. After the takeover, a German official was put in charge of the camp and Schol's role became more limited. In March 1943 Gemmeker forced him to leave the camp, after which Schol moved in with his in laws in Hengelo. When the Department of Justice terminated his employment contract on 1 November 1943, he no longer had an income. He remained unemployed until the liberation. Immediately after the liberation of Hengelo, in early April 1945, Schol reported to the head of the local Police, with the aim of being employed as an Officer in the further liberation of the Netherlands.

After a test by the registration office for war volunteers and a conversation with the chairman of the committee of the National Criminal Investigation Department, Schol received the rank of captain at the 21st Army Group. As Commander of the Central Volunteer Camp I, he ended up in the Ernst Casimir barracks in Roermond. His previous position at Camp Westerbork did not seem to stand in the way of a new Military Career at first. However, a phone call from a member of the local Advisory Committee led to the POD of the Police in Hengelo starting an investigation on 15 June 1945. This member said that Schol had been employed as Commander of the Lager Westerbork, with the Sipo in The Hague as employer. Schol's response to these charges was very convincing. After the surrender of the Dutch Army, he was appointed Commander of Westerbork, back then still a refugee camp, by the Department of Justice. When the Dutch Jews started being brought in, Schol wanted to resign from his position, but he chose to stay at the request of the Jewish Council. Soon after, he was dismissed because he was considered politically unreliable and he had to go into hiding until the liberation. He ended his statement by saying that he had never been appointed by the Sipo and had not started working for this German authority.

At the end of November 1945, the case was opened once again because some former residents, including OD member Max Levy, filed complaints against Schol. These complaints concerned the abuse of some residents with a whip at the roll call area in November 1942. After the witness statements had been recorded, the report was forwarded to the Political Investigation Department (*Politieke Rechercheafdeling*, or *PRA*) in Limburg at the end of February 1946, because Schol was still in Roermond at the time. Schol was questioned in the barracks by the Regional Director of the PRA. The result was that Schol was classified as a suspect, but he was not arrested. He had strongly protested against the claim that he had used his whip for just about any reason. As far as he could remember, he had never even whipped anyone at all. He admitted that sometimes he had to use a strong and powerful voice, but according to him, he had never lost his temper, even when some residents did almost get under his skin.

Schol stated several times that he could not remember certain facts, while his memory seemed to work fine at other times. Particularly when it came to incriminating facts, he would suddenly suffer from amnesia. All the incriminating statements were made by witnesses, some of whom had not actually experienced Schol's brutal actions themselves, but had heard about them from others. The victims themselves could not be traced, probably because they had died in an extermination camp. One year after the start of the Limburg investigation, the case was dismissed, because Schol's abuse and work at the time he fulfilled his position as Camp Commander were considered not severe enough to impose a sentence. After the results were announced, the file did not disappear definitively in the archive, because at the end of 1948 the journalist Werner Stertzenbach also made an incriminating statement. Werner saw Schol beat a woman with his whip at the roll call area. He did not know the reason for this, nor did he know what had been the consequence of this action. Since the statement did not produce any new facts, there will have been no reason to reopen the case.

A question that was asked to everyone who had been involved in any way in the persecution of the Jews and which led to much discussion over time was whether people had known what was happening to the Jews in the East. Schol expressly stated that he had never known what horrors had awaited the Jews who had been sent on transport.[65] This statement is questionable, because even those who had played a less prominent role in the camp and had stayed there for a shorter period of time, like some Gendarmes, had suggested they had been aware of this. It is very likely that at least the German commanders had indeed known what would happen to the deported Jews.

Erich Deppner was the first German to take command after the camp was taken over in July 1942. He only stayed there for two months. During that period, the transports to Auschwitz began. His choice to add a group of orphaned children to the first transport immediately caused a lot of commotion. Still, this would not have been the reason he was replaced so quickly. At the very beginning, Deppner had already stated that he was only temporarily fulfilling the position. The moniker 'murderer' with Officers attitude was not given to him because of his actions in Westerbork, but because he had previously been involved in the execution of 77 Russian prisoners of war in the vicinity of camp Amersfoort. Deppner's superiors were probably satisfied with his performance, because after his departure from Westerbork he returned to The Hague. There he was appointed head of the *Referat IV* of the *Sipo*. This Department, also known as the Gestapo, tracked down and detained opponents of the Nazi regime.[66]

As head of that Department, Deppner played a very unfavourable role in a situation taking place in Westerbork in early September 1944, involving four residents who died. The four victims, John Ancona, Johan Engers, Samuel Goldstein and Ernst Katan, were discovered during an attempt to escape the camp. They were arrested at the barbed wire fence. According to Gemmeker, he was no longer authorised to impose penalties at that time. For this he had to contact the BdS in The Hague. Deppner responded fast. He ordered Gemmeker to shoot the four men the same night. This assignment was part of the so-called *Niedermachungsbefehl*, in which Deppner was closely involved. For example, at least 450 people, mainly resistance fighters, were shot to death in Camp Vught at his command during the same period.[67]

After the liberation, Deppner could not be interrogated in the Netherlands about these and the other facts because he had returned to Berlin at the beginning of 1945. After the Russian Army had won the violent battle for that city, he was taken away as a prisoner of war to one of the camps in the East. Deppner returned to Germany in 1950. His past did not stand in the way of a new career, because he joined the Organisation Gehlen as agent V-616. This secret service, founded in 1946 under the supervision of the American Occupation Authorities, was led by the former Major General of the Wehrmacht, Reinhard Gehlen. Together with a large number of other representatives of the defeated Nazi regime, he built up a spy network to keep an eye on mainly the Soviet Union as a new enemy. Deppner, who used the aliases 'Egon Dietrich' and 'Ernst Borchert', was in charge of Section 12, also known as GV-G. This Department spied from Berlin in the GDR. In 1956 the Bundesnachrichtendienst was established. All employees of the *Organisation Gehlen*, including Deppner, were placed with this Intelligence Service.[68]

In the meantime, those in charge of post war justice in the Netherlands made many attempts to take Deppner to Court because of his war crimes. He was finally arrested in July 1960 for complicity in the massacre of Russian and Dutch prisoners in Germany. During the investigation, he was in custody for nine months, after which he was released. Although a request for a trial had been rejected several times, Deppner still faced the jury in Court in München at the end of January 1964. The indictment focused on his complicity in the murder of the 77 Russian prisoners of war. Camp Westerbork was not mentioned at all. The trial began on 20 January and lasted for several days.

On the second day of the trial, Deppner's Lawyer handed a White Paper to the President of the Court. This document, which caused quite a stir, according to a newspaper article, was drawn up by Hitler's Ministry of Foreign Affairs during the occupation. It showed that the execution in Amersfoort was a retaliatory measure for the atrocities committed by the Russian Army against German Soldiers on the Eastern Front. Therefore, as opposed to what many people believed, the execution had not been merely a matter of killing sick and weak Russian Soldiers for no reason. Deppner wanted to prove during the trial that it had never been his intention to cover up what had happened. When he had returned to Germany in 1950, he had wanted to go to the Netherlands immediately so he could explain his actions, but his legal advisers had dissuaded him.[69]

The Prosecutor hinted at acquittal on this second day of the trial. This happened a day later. The Court assumed that the shooting of the Russian prisoners of war had indeed been a justified retaliatory measure. The Bavarian Minister of Justice, Hans Ehard, was dissatisfied with the judgment of the Court. Two weeks after the verdict, he ordered the Public Prosecutor of Baden-Württemberg to review the judgment of the Court of München. Deppner was expected to appear before the Federal Court in Karlsruhe after about six months.[70]

Whether this trial actually took place is not clear. Deppner was later acquitted on appeal. A trial in the Netherlands was not possible because Germany did not extradite its citizens. Representatives of the Dutch Public Prosecutor's Office did not give up. They wanted justice. In 1980 district attorney Mr. L. de Beaufort, who was responsible for tracking down war criminals in the Netherlands, once again submitted a request to Germany for a trial against Deppner. This request was rejected. De Beaufort's successor, Mr. P. Brilman, saw a small opportunity three years later to ask West Germany to investigate whether the prosecution of Deppner was possible. This attempt did not produce the desired result either.[71] Deppner was able to enjoy his retirement for a long time. He died on 13 December 2005 in the southern German town of Anzing.

What happened to Josef Hugo Dischner, Deppner's successor after he was forced to resign as Camp Commander because of his behaviour and his alcohol abuse is not clear. After the liberation, no criminal investigation followed, nor did anyone insist later on bringing him to Court. Dischner's involuntary departure was mainly due to the way he had acted during the transport of 5 October 1942. As a result, he had put the order and peace inside the camp at risk. Because there were more and more transports at the time, he had to ensure that the deportation machine was running at full speed and without delay.

Gemmeker was seen as an extremely suitable person for this task. During the period when the 'uncrowned king of the Jewish capital city' was in command, the trains drove to the (destruction) camps perfectly on time and with the right number of Jewish victims. If Gemmeker came across an irregularity in the camp, he did not hesitate but dealt with it immediately. The threat of putting the offender on the next transport usually yielded the desired result. Without major incidents and with only a small number of men at his disposal, Gemmeker managed to make it almost to the end. When it became clear that the allied troops were approaching, he left the camp with his entourage. Via the Afsluitdijk the Company reached Amsterdam, where he could work as a *Verwaltungsführer* at the *Aussendienststelle*. This new career quickly ended, because after the German Army capitulated and the Dutch population celebrated the liberation, he was taken as a prisoner of war.

The interrogations would have started right away. For some facts, such as the shooting of four residents in which Gemmeker was directly involved, he was questioned separately. After several months in Prison in Amsterdam, a transfer to the Prison in Assen followed. Sergeant Major Jan Schoenmaker made a detailed report after the interview. Particular attention is paid to the deportation of the Jews. Schoenmaker added some critical comments about several passages. A point of discussion may be whether this fit within his field of responsibility, because he should have been neutral and impartial in his position. In any case, it shows that Schoenmaker felt closely involved in the case of the former Camp Commander. When Gemmeker claimed that he had tried with great difficulty and risks and without the knowledge of his superiors to turn the transit camp into a labour camp, which could have saved part of the Jewish population, Schoenmaker commented that Gemmeker did this only to secure his own position.

During the interrogation, Gemmeker was also questioned about issuing one of the most controversial camp orders. In this order, number 5, he stipulated that ten residents would be put on transport as retaliation for each person who escaped. According to his statement, he had managed to prevent this measure from being implemented in almost the entirety of 1943, even though residents had fled. Only once did he have no choice but to pass on the names of the relatives. The initiative was not taken by him, but by the

BdS. In the conclusion of the report, Schoenmaker wrote that all good choices had supposedly been made by Gemmeker entirely and the bad actions had happened purely on the orders of his superiors. Schoenmaker found this illogical and confronted Gemmeker several times with it, but he stuck to his story. Schoenmaker rightly doubted Gemmeker's sincerity, because the facts show a different picture. The retaliatory measure which followed an attempt to escape has been demonstrably applied more than once by him or on his order.

Ensuring that peace and order reigned within the camp was most likely the chief task of the commander, as chaotic conditions could be devastating for the well running deportation machine. With few men under his command, Gemmeker managed to keep the residents under control. He made various statements as to how he succeeded in this. In some cases, his memory had abandoned him somewhat, and sometimes he claimed not to have known that his men had acted brutally.

After Schoenmaker had collected enough facts, he finished the report on 5 June 1948. The indictment was no surprise and mainly focused on Gemmeker's involvement in the deportation of 80,000 Jews. As a result, he had been guilty of kidnapping. He had brought persons across the borders of the *Reich* in Europe, with the aim of unlawfully bringing them under the control of another person or placing them in a position in which they were helpless. For this crime, he could be sentenced to a maximum of twelve years.[72]

During the entire preliminary investigation, Gemmeker stayed in the Prison of Assen. Shortly before the trial took place, he was imprisoned in Camp Westerbork for some time. The reason for this temporary transfer is not clear. It is possible that he was transferred there with the aim to intimidate him before the trial. The imprisonment of the former Camp Commander in the camp over which he had ruled in the past will undoubtedly have unleashed something in him.

On 9 December 1948 the trial against Gemmeker began before the Special Court of Justice in Assen. It lasted a total of three days. Articles discussing the first day appeared in the newspapers. In one of them he was described as a typical German: strictly submissive to the orders given to him and someone who honoured the *befehl ist befehl-principle*. This was mainly related to the questions asked by the members of the Court. To the question of President Mr. A. Maassen whether Gemmeker had protested against his appointment as Commander of Camp Westerbork and whether he had later tried to escape from it, he replied in the negative. He had accepted the appointment because he had taken it as an order. Maassen also asked whether Gemmeker did not believe interning elderly people and children was going too far. According to Gemmeker, he could not criticise or oppose the regulations of the Reich Government. He took the view that there were important reasons for the adoption of these regulations, which meant that he had no choice but to implement them. Maassen noted that this involved a kind of blind obedience to orders. On the one hand, Gemmeker agreed with this remark and on the other hand, he did not, because he realised only after some time what was happening to the Jews. Counsellor Mr. Berghuys asked whether Gemmeker did not consider the treatment of the Jews inhumane. Gemmeker replied as follows:

> I could not oversee everything. I had grown up in a world that was against the Jews, so it was no problem for me. However, I did have conflicts of conscience, but there was only one thing left for me: to do everything that was possible. I was told that internment was the harshest punishment the Jews were given. The fact that so many died was only made known to me after the end of the war. They spoke of employment in Germany, for example the demolition of aircraft. I thought it was just forced labour, and I took those stories as facts.

Gemmeker had no objection to interning and deporting the Jews, because he believed it was necessary for Military and political reasons. He added that, in his opinion, this was not against the laws and customs of war and humanity.

On the first day of the hearing, attention was also paid to the retaliatory measures which followed attempted escapes. This included, for example, the incident in which Gemmeker sent 20 sick Jews on transport at the beginning of April 1943 after two residents had escaped. The barracks leader described Gemmeker's actions as extremely cruel, while Gemmeker himself judged this retaliatory measure as a lawful action. In any case, he felt that these retaliatory measures had reached their goal, because during the period in which he acted as Camp Commander, no more than 100 people would have escaped.[73] Some historians, including Presser and De Jong, concluded on the basis of a list made immediately after the liberation that 210 Jews had fled the camp. According to a more recent study, which includes a list of names, some 300 Jews illegally left camp during the occupation.[74] Although it is therefore not possible to determine exactly how many escapes took place, Gemmeker's remark on the effectiveness of the retaliatory measures has a high level of truth to it. Indeed, the number of escapes was in stark contrast to the large number of deportees. The warning that other members of the barracks, family members or acquaintances would be sent along with the next transport was in many cases enough to prevent someone from attempting to escape.

After this particular subject had been dealt with and after one of the witnesses explained how the selection process worked in Auschwitz, the hearing was adjourned until Tuesday 28 December. During this second day, the Public Prosecutor, Mr. J.E. de Ranitz, held his prosecution speech. In this he argued that he would certainly have demanded the death penalty if Gemmeker had been a Dutchman. Since he aided in the extermination process as a Camp Commander and De Ranitz took his mentality into account, he demanded 12 years imprisonment minus the time already served.[75]

During the last day of the trial, which was held on 6 January 1949, Gemmeker's Defence Lawyer, Mr. J.W. Boonk, was given the opportunity to make his plea. He tried to prove that Gemmeker was not guilty of committing a war crime or a crime against humanity. After all, he had carried out the orders of his superiors. In addition, the Defence Lawyer was of the opinion that Gemmeker had not deliberately acted unlawfully during the transport operations. He did not know what was happening in Auschwitz. From what he heard of it; he assumed it was a labour camp. When four Jewish men tried to escape and were shot, according to Boonk, Gemmeker did not act on his own authority, because the order for this came from the higher ups. Boonk finished his plea with the remark that Gemmeker had tried to make the best of it and that any other German who could have been placed in his position would probably have done less well. Therefore, he considered the punishment demanded to be far too high. Finally, Gemmeker got his chance to speak. After emphasising once again that he had wanted to turn Westerbork into a labour camp, he thanked the Court for the way in which his case had so far been handled. Gemmeker remained a gentleman.[76]

According to the media, the process shed a bright light on the awful things that had taken place within the barbed wire fence for several years. The Court had to judge how great Gemmeker's role had been in this. The final verdict was announced on 20 January 1949. The former Camp Commander was sentenced to 10 years imprisonment minus the time he had already served. The Court could not prove that he knew what had happened to the vast majority of the deported Jews in the Extermination Camps. The sentence was also lower because the Court took into account the correct treatment of residents.

Gemmeker filed an appeal in cassation a few days later. Whether the Supreme Court dealt with the matter is not clear and will not have been important, because on 20 April 1951 Gemmeker was allowed to leave the Netherlands as a free man. His sentence had been reduced because of his good behaviour, as well as his choice to work in the mines in Limburg. This was probably better than confinement in a cell or in an internment camp.[77]

Gemmeker returned to Düsseldorf and in 1953 married a woman 21 years younger than he was. Instead of in a large villa overlooking the heath, the couple lived in a grey and modest apartment. Working for The Government again was not an option for him, because he wanted to be independent as much as possible. As a result, he lost his pension, so he had to continue working until his death, according to his own words. The fact that he worked long hours as a salesman in a tobacco shop did not bother him. He mainly tried to lead a withdrawn existence, but he did not always succeed, because the past continued to haunt him.[78]

In 1959 the *Norddeutsche Rundfunk* managed to get Gemmeker in front of the camera. The decor looked boring. Dressed in a slightly oversized costume, he answered the questions. He admitted that he did know where the transports were going and named Auschwitz as the destination. The question of whether he knew what was happening there did not come as a surprise, because it had already been asked many times. His answer was also predictable. He kept repeating: '*Ich habe es nicht gewusst*'.[79]

It was not long before Gemmeker received media attention again, because in early March 1960 the Public Prosecutor in Dortmund announced that a preliminary investigation had been opened.[80] A lawsuit against some communists had been the cause. During the interrogation, one of the accused demanded that they prosecute the fascists, not the antifascists. According to an article in *De Waarheid*, he used Gemmeker as example and revealed that the former Commander of Camp Westerbork was walking around freely and lived in Düsseldorf. Because of this statement, the Court was forced to initiate a preliminary investigation. Gemmeker's name was not mentioned by chance. The accused communist wrote in a letter that he had come to the Netherlands with his parents as immigrants before the outbreak of the war. His parents were later deported to Bergen-Belsen via Westerbork, where they starved to death.[81] The preliminary investigation probably did not produce enough new evidence, because Gemmeker did not have to go to Court again.

However, employees of the *Zentralstelle für NS-Verbrechen* in Ludwigsburg and the National Institute for War Documentation in Amsterdam continued to collect evidence against the former Camp Commander. At the end of January 1967, the so-called 'Westerbork trial' started in München. There, the former BdS in the Netherlands, Wilhelm Harster, his Secretary Gertrud Slottke and the head of the IVb4 Division, Wilhelm Zöpf, stood trial for their complicity in the murder of thousands of Jews who had been taken away from the Netherlands. Although there was not enough evidence for a new trial against Gemmeker, it was established that he must have known what happened to the Jews after they were taken away from Westerbork. That was a good reason to continue the investigation. New witnesses were interviewed in the Netherlands, but also in the United States and South Africa. The statements were both incriminating and exculpating, which did not help the employees create any new accusations.[82]

The media regularly speculated about a possible new lawsuit against Gemmeker. However, despite all efforts, it was not possible to prove with certainty that he had known what would happen to most of the Jews once they arrived in the Extermination Camps. He himself continued to deny this until his death in 1982. The discussion did not stop after this. Many, including survivors and historians, were convinced that he was aware of the *Endlösung der Judenfrage* and thus knew what terrible fate awaited the vast majority of Jews after their departure from Westerbork. A higher punishment or a new trial would certainly have been appropriate to satisfy the survivors and their families.

If Gendarmes, who were only in charge of surveillance for a few months, were already aware that a terrible fate awaited the Jews who were deported, then Gemmeker must certainly have known what was happening in Auschwitz and the other (destruction) camps. The question can be asked whether he could have done anything against this as a Camp Commander. According to his statement, he would have tried to turn the transit camp into a labour camp, which could possibly have saved part of the camp population. For many Jewish men, women and children, this change would have been too late anyway, because they had already been deported and murdered at an earlier stage. Gemmeker could also have decided to resign. This would not have jeopardised the survival of the camp, because then a new Camp Commander would have replaced him, one who might have introduced a stricter and tougher regime. Although the Commander held an influential position in the camp, he was only part of the deportation machine. He had to make sure that Westerbork continued to function as a transit camp and in the end, he successfully carried out this assignment.

The Success Of A Refined System

Gemmeker and his predecessors were not the reason the system became so successful. They were able to use a system that had been developed in the Drenthe countryside since 1939 on behalf of the Dutch Government and at the expense of the Jewish community. After the takeover on 1 July 1942, it was easy to build on the already existing and well-functioning organisation. With a minimal number of physical security measures, the refugee camp was easily transformed into a transit camp.

After the liberation, the roles people had played during the war were reviewed. Those who could clearly be regarded as perpetrators had to be held accountable, because there was evidence they had acted in a wrong way. They had to show up in Court and sentences were demanded against them. The assessment and subdivision of the rest proved to be a more difficult task. Did the Gendarmes, the Policemen and the OD members belong to the perpetrators, bystanders, followers, accomplices or, as in the case of the OD men, possibly also to the victims? The answer to these questions was not always unanimous and changed over time, as more and more became known about the terrible fate of the Jews deported via Westerbork. As a result, the benevolent Gendarme changed from a friendly bystander, confirmed by a couple of residents, into an accomplice who had shown great negligence towards the Jewish community.[83]

The transition from 'relatively good' to 'very bad' was mainly due to their cooperation in the transports. In the period of almost half a year in which the Gendarmerie had been in charge of escorting transports, one third of the total number of transports left to the destruction camps. Taking over the outdoor surveillance was considered a less incriminating task, but this could not restore the violated image. After all, the damage had already been done. Even if more attention had been paid to the fact that this Detachment consisted to a large extent of ordinary young men who carried out their difficult task at an unusual time, without political ideology and often reluctantly, this will have had very little impact on the negative image.

The question to what extent the Gendarmerie Detachment was guilty and whether the men had indeed neglected the Jewish community is difficult to answer without sufficient knowledge of the facts. Factors such as period of secondment, position and personal circumstances are important elements to keep in mind for the final judgment. For this purpose, particular attention should be paid to individual performance and/or shortcomings. Negligence as a collective reproach towards the Detachment is certainly understandable with the knowledge the public gained afterwards, but it is not entirely justified, because if the whole persecution of the Jews is considered, one can only say that the Detachment was merely a small cog in the large and well-functioning deportation machine.

Forming an opinion on the OD, which consisted of Jewish men, is even more complex, because they did do dirty jobs for the occupiers, both inside and outside the camp. However, this group did not necessarily consist of brutal men who had deliberately and with conviction chosen to bother the other residents. They chose to take one of the scarce opportunities to get an exemption, in the hope that they would survive. However, the majority was deceived because the entire exemption system ceased to exist before the end of the war. Although the chances of survival were slightly higher for OD members than for the other residents, a large part was nevertheless victim of the ongoing deception. There was no distinction between German and Dutch Jews. Transfer to Theresienstadt seemed a reward for the services rendered, but that too was a big misconception. It also belonged to the sophisticated system of deception, with the result that the majority was put on transport again and eventually died in one of the (destruction) camps. Many of the OD members were thus themselves victims of the system.

That those who had to go on transport thought differently about this is completely understandable. The OD members were the ones to load the Jews into trains and to help the enemy during the pickup operations in Amsterdam and Apeldoorn, in some cases screaming at the victims and pushing them around. This would supposedly have been part of the deliberately chosen tactics, because the OD members were convinced that the Germans present would have acted much worse. Because of the difficult position the OD men were in, it is hardly possible to make an informed and fully accurate judgment about their actions. Given the circumstances, 'Jewish SS' is certainly not the right name for them. 'Collaborative survival' is less heavy a term, but also does not quite fit. If a specific term has to be used to describe the actions of the OD, 'participation for survival' would probably be the best term.

Except for the tactics of screaming and pushing used by the Supervisors, physical violence in the camp was scarce. This was not necessary either, because the imposition of penalties and the constant threat of being put on the next transport promoted discipline within the camp. Because of this type of psychological pressure, combined with the hierarchical self-government, the model of indoor and outdoor surveillance functioned well within the refined system, so that it was not necessary for the occupier to deploy a large number of own personnel. After all, the trains drove from Camp Westerbork to the (destruction) camps according to a tight schedule, with the right number of Jews.

9. CAMP SURVEILLANCE IN EUROPEAN PERSPECTIVE

In almost all countries occupied by Germany, one or more transit camps were set up for the controlled transport of Jews and smaller groups of Sinti and Roma. These way stations differed greatly from each other in terms of size and original destination. In Luxembourg, most Jews were housed in the Monastery Fünfbrunnen, while the former prisoner of war camp in northern Italy, near the village of Fossoli, served as a transit camp. Apart from a diversity of way stations, the surveillance of temporary residents was virtually nowhere organised in the same way.

In Belgium, the Dossin Army barracks in Mechelen was found to be suitable as a central *SS-sammellager für Juden*. Mechelen was the ideal location for setting up such a camp, because it is located between Antwerp and Brussels, the Belgian cities where most Jews lived, and there was also a good railway connection. The maximum capacity of the barracks was about 2,000 people.[1] Between 4 August 1942 and 31 July 1944, about 25,483 Jews were deported from Mechelen. This required a total of 27 deportation trains, which were guarded up to the German border by Flemish SS members and by the *Ordnungspolizei*.[2]

The Dossin Barracks in Mechelen (1942).

As in many other (transit) camps, a German Officer was entrusted with the management of this camp. Initially SS-Sturmbannführer Philipp Johann Adolf Schmitt, who was also Commander of Camp Breendonk, was given this function. Schmitt was described as brutal, as he would hit Jews. He would have exercised a harsh regime. In addition, the conditions in terms of hygiene and food were poor. All this was not the reason why he was replaced by Hans Frank in April 1943. Corruption and embezzlement would have led to his forced departure. The opinion on Frank, who remained until the end of the camp in September 1944, was somewhat more positive. If he was present at the camp, the other SS members would be less abusive. In addition, he tried to improve food supply and hygiene.[3] This had little to do with a consciously more humane policy. Due to the delay in transport operations, the residents had to remain in Dossin for longer periods of time, with the result that the camp was in danger of becoming overpopulated. The improved conditions were meant to have a positive effect on the order within the barracks. After all, dissatisfied residents could revolt.[4]

The temporary residents of the barracks were assigned various tasks, such as administrative and maintenance work. In addition, a Jewish leader was appointed and in each room came a person who was responsible for everything that went on in there. Although these residents supervised the order and discipline in the camp, there was no equivalent to the Ordedienst they had in Westerbork.[5] For the outside surveillance, *Wehrmacht* Soldiers were initially appointed. They did not interfere in internal affairs. In November 1942 more than 90 Flemish SS members of the *SD Wachgruppe* took over this task. Contrary to their colleagues in Westerbork, these were not the SS men returning from the Eastern Front, who had suffered a wide variety of injuries and therefore could no longer participate in the battle. The regular (Military) Police of Belgium, if this already existed in such a form during the occupation, did not play any role in the surveillance of the barracks.[6]

As in Westerbork, this did happen in the largest French transit camp Drancy. In this suburb to the north east of Paris, the building complex called *Cité de la Muette* was put into use around July 1942, even if the building had not been finished yet. The complex consisted of a large U shaped apartment building, which was originally built as part of a social housing project. In June 1940 the Germans took over the complex. After the installation of a double barbed wire barrier around the camp and the installation of four watchtowers, it initially served as an internment camp, with a total capacity of about 6,000 people. In France, several smaller camps were also located in the occupied zone, such as *Beaune-la-Rolande, Compiègne* and *Pithiviers*, and *Gurs* in the unoccupied zone. Although from the first three camps, also under the supervision of the French Police, some trains with Jews left for the Extermination Camps, Drancy was the camp with the greatest capacity. The Jews from the unoccupied zone often went via Drancy to Auschwitz.[7]

As a result of the German invasion of Russia in June 1941, the communist resistance in France grew. In addition to arresting communists, the French Police were ordered to arrest some 6,000 Jews during a large-scale action that took place in the 11th district of Paris on 20 August 1941. Since the target number was not reached, the action had to be extended to other districts the following days. Eventually, a total of 4,232 Jewish men were arrested. They were between the ages of 18 and 50 and of different nationalities. They were taken to the nearby camp in Drancy, making it a hostage camp that was now destined only for Jews.[8] *SS Hauptsturmführer* Theo Dannecker was in command of the camp. He will have done this from the Paris based *Dienststelle* of the *Sipo und SD*, because he was appointed there as a so-called *Judenreferent* and was therefore responsible for the persecution of Jews in France.[9]

French Gendarmerie men and Officers of the regular Police were in charge of both indoor and outdoor surveillance of the complex. The conditions, as in food supply and medical care, were particularly bad from the very beginning, because the camp was not prepared for the housing of so many people.[10] Initially, there was a strict Military regime. Residents were not allowed to communicate with the outside world or to receive goods from outside the camp. A number of men already died of hunger and illness after a few weeks. The person who gained the trust of a French Policeman was able to arrange something through him after paying a hefty fee. However, this was exceptional, because according to a witness, most Police Officers were sadistic profiteers. This witness based his or her verdict on facts. Over time, the residents were given permission to send a card twice a month and receive one parcel.[11] However, on entry, the French Law Enforcement Officers first searched the parcels for food and cigarettes and confiscated them for their own use or for the black market, which was thriving in the camp. The conditions remained bad for a long time and partly because of this, nearly 900 sick and starving men started a riot in October 1941 that could only be stopped after the use of violence. They were released in November 1941[12].

As in other occupied countries, the deportation of the Jewish population in France began in June 1942. The camp in Drancy was given the function of transit camp. In the early morning of 16 July 1942, about 4,500 French

The accommodation block at Drancy with French policeman on guard (1941).

Police Officers in Paris took part in a major pickup operation. Almost 13,000 Jews were arrested. Singles and married couples without underage children were brought to Drancy. The rest was housed in the *Vélodrome d'Hiver*, which temporarily served as a gathering place.13 The first train with 1,000 Jews departed from Drancy to Auschwitz on 22 June. A month later the frequency of departing transports was increased. Until August 1944, more than 64,000 Jews were deported from Drancy.[14]

The trains were escorted to the German border by French Police Officers and not by members of the *Ordnungspolizei*, as in Westerbork. The French Police also remained in charge of supervision in and around the camp, but because of the growing dissatisfaction, they left part of the internal organisation to the Jewish residents. In addition to creating a hierarchical structure, more than 30 service groups were created, including main and subgroups. One of these groups, which was formed in August 1942, was the M.S. (*Membres de la Surveillance*). This Internal Surveillance Service was mainly composed of former Jewish Reserve Officers. It would have consisted of three Brigades of seven men. Each group was led by a Sergeant. The M.S. supervised the camp and checked whether members of the Office of Jewish Affairs (*Bureau Joodsche Zaken*) and French Officers did not take valuable goods for themselves when the newcomers arrived. As a distinctive sign, these Jewish regulators wore a red armband. The employees of the other service groups were recognisable by the white armbands.[15]

After the last train had left from Drancy on 25 March 1943, the transports stopped temporarily because there were not enough Jews to fill the trains. The fact that the French Police was less and less cooperative was one of the reasons. The denaturalisation law was intended to get the influx of Jews back on track. As the existing organisation did not suffice, Alois Brunner, who had a small SS unit at his disposal, was entrusted with Drancy's command from 10 June 1943 onwards. This confidant of Adolf Eichmann was known as the deportation specialist, as he was responsible for transporting Jews from Vienna, Berlin and Thessaloniki.[16]

Brunner took drastic measures immediately. He made the camp regime considerably stricter than before. The French Police Officers were banished from the camp and were only allowed to deal with outdoor security. For internal surveillance, a Security Service was compiled, consisting of members of the M.S. and of other Jewish residents. This service was supervised by SS members.17 The men of this renewed service received a yellow armband with the text *Service d'ordre juif – Jüdischer Ordnungsdienst* on it.[18]

After the reorganisation, Drancy's outdoor surveillance was organised in almost the same way as in Westerbork. This was not exactly the case for the Jewish service group known in Westerbork as the OD, or *Ordedienst*. It seems that this service group played a less prominent role in Drancy than in the Dutch transit camp. Locations where Jewish service groups similar to the OD were also used, and where at least they had a prominent role, were the more than 1,100 ghettos in Eastern Europe. The Jews there were centralised and housed in districts, closed or not, with their family. In this way they could be kept under control better, which was supposed to make the deportations easier and without too many problems. A difference with the (transit) camps was that the Jews in the ghettos mostly remained in an environment familiar to them. As a result, there was no forced and much more radical move to a location far away from civilisation, as was the case with the Jews in the Netherlands. Nevertheless, the residents of the ghettos often had to deal with the same bad circumstances.[19] The size of the ghettos was often decisive for the number of men in the 'Jewish Ghetto Police', as the service groups were also-called. In the Lodz ghetto, for example, 1,200 Jewish Police Officers were present and in Lvov, there were 500 of them, while in Warsaw in 1943 there were 2,300 men.

The tasks of the Ghetto Police could vary depending on the ghetto. This had to do with several things, such as location, size of the ghetto and the person in charge of the management, for example. Initially, the tasks consisted of 'normal' Police activities, such as supervising, regulating traffic, confiscating valuables, preventing smuggling and escorting residents to the jobs. In addition, they could even punish people here and there, for example, for leaving the ghetto without a pass or not wearing the Star of David. Later, the Jewish agents also actively participated in the deportations. This cooperation therefore went further than removing people from their homes and attending to those in need, as their colleagues from Camp Westerbork had to do in Amsterdam and Apeldoorn.

In the ghettos, it was also important to have the right contacts to obtain a function within the Jewish Police Force. Family members of Jewish Councils and strong young men had an advantage over the rest. Protecting ghetto residents from violence could have been one of the reasons someone enlisted. Over time, little was left of this helpful and selfless attitude, as the men began to copy the questionable behaviour of the occupying forces. For example, they allowed children outside the closed ghettos to get food. When they returned, they took the often scarce goods and then sold them on the black market themselves. The occupying forces did not stop this unseemly behaviour, but even encouraged it, so that they could count on willing accomplices if necessary.

The cooperation of the Jewish Officers became crucial when the deportation of the ghetto residents began. Initially, the German Authorities left the execution of the actions to the Jews themselves. To encourage their cooperation, the Officers of the Ghetto Police were promised that they and their family members would be exempted from deportation. As the actions progressed, however, the willingness to cooperate faded, partially due to doubts about this promise. In the Warsaw ghetto, the occupier responded to this by introducing a quota. Every Officer had to deliver five ghetto residents every day. The enemy threatened that if he failed to do so, he and his family members would be added to the transports. This threat led to the active search for Jews. Some became specialists in locating ghetto residents who had gone into hiding. Because over time the German Police, SS and non-Jewish accomplices got involved in the pickup operations and the number of ghetto residents decreased, the number of men in the Ghetto Police could be reduced.

There was no exemption as reward for services rendered. Some Police Officers were even shot or hanged in the ghetto. The vast majority ended up going with the transports to the Extermination Camps and died there. Those who survived this often tried to trivialise their part in this war. The Commander of the Jewish Police Force in the Vilnius ghetto, Jacob Gens, stated that during some actions, he had sent mostly old and chronically ill Jews along, so that he could save others. Furthermore, Gens justified the actions of the Ghetto Police with the most frequently heard remark that if they had not done this, the Germans would have taken over, and he believed they would undoubtedly have been much more violent. Saving Jews from the clutches of the Germans was also an extremely idealistic goal which could not be reached, because the ghettos had to be cleared entirely.

The similarities between the transit camps were broadly related to outdoor surveillance, but did not apply to the organisation of indoor surveillance. Outside Westerbork, almost no camp had a service like the OD that consisted of Jewish men. Only the ghettos could have a Jewish Police Organisation. Just like the men in Westerbork, the Officers of the Ghetto Police cooperated mainly in the hope that they would have a greater chance of survival. However, in many cases, their actions went beyond what their colleagues in Westerbork did. Therefore, this was much more a matter of survival collaboration than survival participation, as was the case in Westerbork.[20]

Notes

Introduction

1. J. Presser, *Ondergang* en L. de Jong, *Het Koninkrijk der Nederlanden in de Tweede Wereldoorlog.*
2. Willy Lindwer, *Kamp van hoop en wanhoop*, 38.
3. J.J. Bombergen, *Terugblik 1943-1945.*
4. De Jong, *Het Koninkrijk*, deel 8, tweede helft, blz. 737-739.
5. Philip Mechanicus, *In Depot*, 22.
6. Jacob Boas, *Boulevard des Misères*, 65.

Chapter 1

1. Irmgard Loosen, *Erinnerungen an die Jüdische Gemeinde in Linnich.*
2. Albert Moses, born Sept. 22, 1890 in Linnich. Arrived at Westerbork November 11, 1942. Transported from Westerbork to Theresienstadt on September 4, 1944. Died in Auschwitz on Oct. 1. 1944. Source: hckw archive and http://www.joodsmonument.nl/page/546361/nl
3. Kurt Moses, *Home at Last. Auschwitz Survivor*, 37.
4. Susan Stanelle e.a.: *Die nationalsozialistische Judenverfolgung – Die Verfolgung in der Zeit von 1933 – 1938.*
   – Dirk van Laak: *"Arisierung" und Judenpolitik im "Dritten Reich". Zur wirtschaftlichen Ausschaltung der jüdischen Bevölkerung in der rheinisch-westfälischen Industrieregion.*
   – *Der Spiegel*, 1 april 2008: *75 Jahre "Machtergreifung" 1933: Kampfansage vor dem Kaufhaus.*
   – http://www.holocaust-chronologie.de (*Deutsche Allgemeine Zeitung*), 4 april 1933.
   – http://www.judentum-projekt.de
5. Irmgard Loosen, *Erinnerungen an die Jüdische Gemeinde in Linnich.*
6. Moses, *'Home at Last', Auschwitz Survivor*, 37.
7. De Jong, *Het Koninkrijk*, deel 1, 412.
8. Corrie K. Berghuis, *Joodse Vluchtelingen in Nederland 1938-1940*, 10.
9. Albert Sachs, born May 19, 1896 in Werther. Arrival at Westerbork October 6, 1942. Transported from Westerbork to Theresienstadt on April 21, 1943. Died February 28, 1945 in central Europe. Source: hckw archive and http://www.joodsmonument.nl/person/473782/nl
10. Hennie Noordhuis e.a., *In verdrukking, verzet en vrijheid. Borne, Bornerbroek, Hertme, Zenderen, 1940-1945* and http://www.steinheim-institut.de/cgibin/epidat?function=Ins&sel=e11&inv=9000 .
11. Berghuis, *Joodse Vluchtelingen in Nederland 1938-1940*, 11.
12. Siegfried Frank, born May 7, 1913 in Velen. Arrived at Westerbork November 9, 1939. Transported from Westerbork to Theresienstadt on September 4, 1944. Died April 23, 1945 (place of death unknown). Source: hckw archive, http://www.humberghaus.de and http://www.joodsmonument.nl/person/543918/nl
13. Norbert Fasse, *Das Amt Velen-Ramsdorf 1918-1945. Katholiken und NS-Herrschaft im Münsterland.*
14. na, 2.04.58, Ministerie van Binnenlandse Zaken, Zorg voor vluchtelingen uit Duitsland, inv.nr. 133.

15. Hermann Anspacher, born Oct. 22, 1887 at Achim. Arrived Westerbork Dec. 31, 1942. Remained in Westerbork until liberation. Source: hckw archive

16. NIOD, 250i, inv.nr. 494 and http://www.stolpersteine-bremen.de.

17. Wet van den 13den augustus 1849, tot regeling der toelating en uitzetting van Vreemdelingen, via www.vijfeeuwenmigratie.nl.

18. Berghuis, *Joodse Vluchtelingen in Nederland 1938-1940*, 223.

19. Hans Margules, born May 5, 1918 in Berlin. Arrived Westerbork January 10, 1940. Remained in Westerbork until liberation. Source: hckw archive.

20. Peter Margules, born May 26, 1920 in Berlin. Arrived Westerbork January 10, 1940. Remained in Westerbork until liberation. Source: hckw archive.

21. Lindwer, *Kamp van hoop en wanhoop*, 134.

22. Werner Bloch, born Sept. 15, 1920 in Calvörde. Arrived at Westerbork November 23, 1939. On September 4, 1944 from Westerbork on transport to Theresienstadt. Returned. Source: hckw archive.

23. Werner Bloch, *Confrontatie met het noodlot*. (manuscript, hckw).

24. Lindwer, *Kamp van hoop en wanhoop*, 134.

25. Bloch, *Confrontatie met het noodlot*.

26. Siegmund Keller, born Sept. 19, 1920 in Höngen. Arrived Westerbork April 22, 1942. Remained in Westerbork until liberation. Source: hckw archive.

27. na, 2.04.58, Ministerie van Binnenlandse Zaken, Zorg voor vluchtelingen uit Duitsland, inv.nr. 133.

28. Berghuis, *Joodse Vluchtelingen in Nederland 1938-1940*, 45.

29. Ibidem, 47.

30. Jean-Philippe van der Zwaluw en Joop van der Hor, *Heijplaat in verzet*, 69.

31. *Rotterdamsch Nieuwsblad*, 20 januari 1939.

32. Lindwer, *Kamp van hoop en wanhoop*, 134.

33. Sjra Vintcent, *75 verhalen uit Reuver*, 93.

34. *Het Vaderland*, 25 december 1938.

35. Sjra Vintcent, *75 verhalen uit Reuver*, 91.

36. On 25 December 1938, 87 refugees were housed in the Reuver shelter. na, 2.04.58, Ministerie van Binnenlandse Zaken, Zorg voor vluchtelingen uit Duitsland, inv.nr. 66.

37. Bloch, *Confrontatie met het noodlot*.

38. na, 2.04.58, Ministerie van Binnenlandse Zaken, Zorg voor vluchtelingen uit Duitsland, inv.nr. 66.

39. na, 2.04.58, Ministerie van Binnenlandse Zaken, Zorg voor vluchtelingen uit Duitsland, inv.nr. 66.

40. Sjra Vintcent, *75 verhalen uit Reuver*, 98

41. Bloch, *Confrontatie met het noodlot*.

42. Ernst Rosendorff, born 18 April 1921 in Schlochau. Arrived at Westerbork 8 November 1939. Transported from Westerbork to Theresienstadt on 4 September 1944. Died on 6 June 1945. Source: hckw archive and http://www.joodsmonument.nl/person/545948/nl

43. A.L. Jonker, *Joodse vluchtelingen in Hellevoetsluis 1938-1940*, 109, 332

44. Fred Schwarz, *Treinen op dood spoor*, 27.

45. *Het Vaderland*, 4 januari 1939. Ernst stayed in Hellevoetsluis for

just under two months.
On 28 February 1939, he was deregistered from the residence register of Hellevoetsluis municipality. With nine other youngsters, he had been transferred to Eindhoven. From: C.L. van den Heuvel, Joodse vluchtelingen in het kamp in Hellevoetsluis, 413.

46. Berghuis, *Joodse Vluchtelingen in Nederland 1938-1940*, 71, 75.
47. Ibidem, 193.
48. Ibidem, 62 and *De Tijd*, 29 december 1938.
49. *Stichting 'Ford aan den Hoek van Holland', De vluchtelingen-opvang te Hoek van Holland, 1999* en *Het Volksdagblad*, 2 maart 1939.
50. Berghuis, *Joodse Vluchtelingen in Nederland 1938-1940*, 95.
51. Dick Houwaart, *Westerbork. Het begon in 1933*, 62.
52. Berghuis, *Joodse Vluchtelingen in Nederland 1938-1940*, 97.
53. *Het Vaderland*, 19 maart 1939.
54. Ibidem, 24 maart 1939.
55. Ibidem, 13 juni 1939.

Chapter 2

1. Dirk Arie Syswerda, born 5 juni 1899 te Gorinchem, died 8 oktober 1986 Arnhem.
2. na, 2.04.58, Ministerie van Binnenlandse Zaken, Zorg voor vluchtelingen uit Duitsland, 91.
3. Houwaart, *Westerbork. Het begon in 1933*, 145.
4. Verslag over de maand oktober, op 3 november 1939 opgemaakt door Syswerda, Hckw archive.
5. Ibidem.
6. Berghuis, *Joodse Vluchtelingen in Nederland 1938-1940*, 199.
7. Hans Dieter Blume, born 23 November 1921 in Opladen. Arrived at Westerbork on 23 November 1939.
   On 4 September 1944 from Westerbork on transport to Theresienstadt. Died in Auschwitz, October 1944. Source: hckw archive and http://www.joodsmonument.nl/person/562978/nl.
8. Dirk Mulder en Ben Prinsen (red.), *Vluchtelingenkamp Westerbork, Westerbork Cahiers 7*, 55.
9. na, 2.09.53, Ministerie van Justitie, DGvP, inv.nr. 262.
10. na, 2.04.58, Ministerie van Binnenlandse Zaken, Zorg voor vluchtelingen uit Duitsland, 93, 333
11. na, 2.09.45, Ministerie van Justitie, Rijksvreemdelingendienst, 1839.
12. Frank van Riet, *'t Uwen dienst*, 46-56.
13. Drents Archief, archief Commissaris der Koningin, toegangsnr. 0040 en archief gemeente Midden-Drenthe, personeelsdossier Barteld Lukas Knol en info via Libbe T. Henstra.
14. na, 2.04.58, Ministerie van Binnenlandse Zaken, Zorg voor vluchtelingen uit Duitsland, 92.
15. Berghuis, *Joodse Vluchtelingen in Nederland 1938-1940*, 202.
16. na, 2.04.58, Ministerie van Binnenlandse Zaken, Zorg voor vluchtelingen uit Duitsland, 91.
17. *Leeuwarder Courant*, 10 mei 1940.
18. Brief van de secretaris-generaal, waarnemend hoofd van Binnenlandse Zaken Frederiks aan de waarnemend Opperbevelhebber van land en Zeemacht van Alphen, 18 mei 1940 (zie Berghuis, *Joodse Vluchtelingen in Nederland 1938-1940*, 165).
19. Berghuis, *Joodse Vluchtelingen in Nederland 1938-1940*, 210.

20. na 2.09.45, Rijksvreemdelingendienst, 1888.
21. Ibidem, 1847, He was not out of work, as between December 1942 and the end of January 1944, Syswerda worked at the Department of Trade, Industry and Shipping as chief of the Internal Organisation and Branch Offices Department.
22. na, CABR, dossier Jacob Schol, pf Assen 2340 en pra Enschede 3642, Born 9 September 1890 in Amsterdam, died 27 May 1966 in Delden. 23. after 2.09.45 Rijksvreemdelingendienst, 1901.
24. na, CABR, J. Schol, 88.972 (pra Enschede), 108.897 (pf Assen).
25. Drents Archief, 0126, *Centraal Vluchtelingenkamp Westerbork*, nr. 18.
26. Born on 8 March 1886 in Beckum. Windmüller died in Auschwitz on 10 September 1943 (source: www.joodsmonument.nl).
27. na 2.09.45 Rijksvreemdelingendienst, 1901.
28. Ibidem, 1847.
29. Ibidem, 1901.
30. Drents Archief, 0126, *Centraal Vluchtelingenkamp Westerbork*, nr. 18.
31. Sandor Salmagne, born 30 April 1922 in Recklinghausen. Remained in Westerbork until the liberation.
32. na, 2.09.45, Rijksvreemdelingendienst, 1901.
33. Lindwer, *Kamp van hoop en wanhoop*, 72.
34. na 2.09.45, Rijksvreemdelingendienst, 1901.
35. Frank van Riet, *Handhaven onder de Nieuwe Orde*, 145.
36. Ibidem, 27.
37. na, 2.09.53, Ministerie van Justitie, DGvP, inv.nr. 262.
38. Ibidem.
39. Ibidem.
40. na, 2.09.45, Rijksvreemdelingendienst, 1839.
41. na, 2.09.53, Ministerie van Justitie, DGvP, inv.nr. 262.
42. na, 2.09.45, Rijksvreemdelingendienst, 1839.
43. Harm van der Veen, *Westerbork 1939-1945*, 25.
44. Hckw archive.
45. Reint Middel, born 13 December 1919 at 2e Exloërmond.
46. Interview Reint Middel op 27 maart 2007, hckw archive.
47. na, CABR, J. Schol, 88.972 (pra Enschede), 108.897 (PF Assen).
48. na, 2.04.58, Ministerie van Binnenlandse Zaken, Zorg voor vluchtelingen uit Duitsland, 82.
49. OD-rapport, hckw archive.
50. Maarten Ternede, *De Ordedienst van kamp Westerbork*, 24.
51. NIOD, 250i, inv.nr. 721, 006.
52. De Jong, *Het Koninkrijk*, deel 8, tweede helft, 707.
53. Mechanicus, *In Depot*, 146.
54. na, CABR, dossier A. Pisk, inv.nr. 86558.
55. G.L. Durlacher, *Verzameld werk*, 361.
56. Lindwer, *Kamp van hoop en wanhoop*, 133.
57. na, CABR, dossier A. Pisk, inv.nr. 86558.
58. Correspondence Aad van As, december 2009.
59. OD-rapport, hckw archive.
60. Van Riet, *Handhaven onder de Nieuwe Orde*, 131.
61. Van der Veen, *Westerbork 1939-1945*, 25.
62. Van Riet, *Handhaven onder de Nieuwe Orde*, 183-185.
63. Van der Veen, *Westerbork 1939-1945*.
64. na, 2.09.45, Ministerie van Justitie Rijksvreemdelingendienst, 1901.
65. Ibidem, 1839.

Chapter 3

1. Lindwer, *Kamp van hoop en wanhoop*, 26.
2. na, 2.09.45, Ministerie van Justitie, Rijksvreemdelingendienst, 1839.
3. na, CABR, J. Schol, 88.972 (pra Enschede), 108.897 (pf Assen).
4. Verzameling kamporders en kampbevelen, collectie hckw.
5. N.K.C.A. in 't Veld, *De SS in Nederland*, 114 en C.B. Cornelissen, *Sipo en SD in Twente*, 145.
6. De Jong, *Het Koninkrijk*, deel 4, eerste helft, 79.
7. Geraldien von Frijtag Drabbe Künzel, *Kamp Amersfoort*, 106.
8. Presser, *Ondergang*, deel ii, 326.
9. Proces-verbaal Gemmeker, nr. 414, dd 4 juli 1948 (privately owned).
10. Via www.kranten.kb.nl.
11. In 't Veld, *De SS en Nederland*, 373-375.
12. Ibidem, 374.
13. na, Ministerie van Jusitie, DGvP, inv.nr. 262.
14. Lagerbefehl no 225 of 17 December 1942, Verzameling kamporders en kampbevelen, collectie hckw.
15. In 't Veld, *De SS en Nederland*, 374.
16. na, Ministerie van Jusitie, DGvP, inv.nr. 262.
17. OD-rapport, hckw archive.
18. Drents Archief, inv.nr. 0126, 17.
19. OD-rapport, hckw archive.
20. Presser, *Ondergang*, 247.
21. Van Riet, *Handhaven onder de Nieuwe Orde*, 415.
22. NIOD, 250i, inv.nr. 204. Willem van der Veen, born 1 november 1921 in Apeldoorn.
23. OD-rapport, hckw archive.
24. De Jong, *Het Koninkrijk*, deel 8, tweede helft, 693-695.
25. Schwarz, *Treinen op dood spoor*, 113.
26. De Jong, *Het Koninkrijk*, deel 8, tweede helft, 693-695.
27. OD-rapport, hckw archive.
28. Schwarz, *Treinen op dood spoor*, 113.
29. Presser, *Ondergang*, deel ii, 296.
30. De Jong, *Het Koninkrijk*, deel 8, tweede helft, 693-695.
31. Presser, *Ondergang*, deel ii, 296.
32. OD-rapport, hckw archive.
33. Van Riet, *Handhaven onder de Nieuwe Orde*, 242.
34. Proces-verbaal Gemmeker, nr. 414, dd 4 juli 1948 (privately owned).
35. Presser, *Ondergang*, 326.
36. Proces-verbaal Gemmeker, nr. 414, dd 4 juli 1948 (privately owned).
37. De Jong, *Het Koninkrijk*, deel 8, tweede helft, 691 and hckw archive, inv. nr. 9209, do 1047.
38. Nanda van der Zee, *De Trein*, 111.
39. Thursday, September 17, was one such day. Trains carrying Jewish people travelled from various towns to Hooghalen at that time. First in the morning, a transport from Amsterdam arrived with about three hundred people. At 12.45 pm, one followed from The Hague (about two hundred), at 6 pm from Nijmegen (about twenty) and between 10 pm and 11 pm one from Enschede and one from Rotterdam. The handling of this last transport, which brought in a total of one hundred and twenty people, lasted until 4.30am. OD-rapport, hckw.
40. Ibidem.
41. Niek van der Noord, *Jodenkampen*, 9, and www.joodsewerkkampen.nl.
42. Guido Abuys, *De Joodse werkkampen in Oost-Nederland*, Cogiscope 2/10, http://www.cogis.nl/uploads/documents/345.pdf, and mr. D. Giltay

Veth en A.J. van der Leeuw, *Het Weinrebrapport*, 9-21.

43. Waldemar Ochs, born 23 August 1894 in Gmünden. Arrived at Westerbork on 3 May 1942. On 14 September 1943 from Westerbork on transport to Auschwitz. Date and place of death unknown. Hckw archive and http://www.joodsmonument.nl/person/474549/nl

44. Karl Hecht, born 6 January 1896 in Rengsdorf. Arrived at Westerbork between 3 and 5 October 1942. On 18 January 1944 from Westerbork on transport to Theresienstadt. Died on 28 February 1945 (place of death unknown). Source: hckw archive and http://www.joodsmonument.nl/person/474553/nl

45. www.joodsmonument.nl.

46. www.joodsewerkkampen.nl.

47. Noordhuis e.a., *In verdrukking, verzet en vrijheid. Borne, Bornerbroek, Hertme, Zenderen, 1940-1945*.

48. www.joodsewerkkampen.nl.

49. Onderdrukking en verzet, aflevering 24, *Kroniek der Jodenvervolging*, 108.

50. Presser, *Ondergang*, deel I, 301.

51. Onderdrukking en verzet, aflevering 24, *Kroniek der Jodenvervolging*, 108.

52. David Chajes, born 24 October 1903 in Przemislany. Arrived at Westerbork between 3 and 5 October 1942. On 15 March 1944 from Westerbork on transport to Bergen-Belsen. Returned after liberation. Source: hckw archive.

53. Peppie Chajes, Peppie Dekker's *Holocaust Experience as seen through the eyes of a child.*

54. OD-rapport, hckw archive.

55. na, dossier Albert de Jong, inv.nr. 75961.

56. Collection Jewish Historical Museum, inv.nr. 00012408.

57. na, CABR, J. Schol, 88.972 (pra Enschede), 108.897 (PF Assen).

58. Collection Jewish Historical Museum, inv.nr. 00012408.

59. Lindwer, *Kamp van hoop en wanhoop*, 27 and Nanda van der Zee, *De trein*, 32.

60. Presser, *Ondergang*, deel ii, 326-328.

61. NIOD, Doc I 520, I-5.

62. Minutes Gemmeker, no. 414, dated 4 June 1948 (privately owned).

63. De Jong, *Het Koninkrijk*, deel 8, tweede helft, 698.

64. Minutes Gemmeker, no. 414, dated 4 June 1948 (privately owned).

65. NIOD, 250i, inv.nr. 1011.

66. Minutes Gemmeker, no. 414, dated 4 June 1948 (privately owned).

67. Frank van Riet, *'n Papieren Monument*, 32-37.

68. Presser, *Ondergang*, 331.

69. Steffie van den Oord, *Westerbork Girl*, 78.

70. Van der Veen, *Westerbork 1939-1945*, 59.

71. Presser, *Ondergang*, 332.

72. Proces-verbaal Gemmeker, nr. 414, dd 4 juli 1948 (privately owned).

73. Presser, *Ondergang*, 331.

74. Max Levy, born 31 March 1896 in Carolinensel. Arrived at Westerbork 3 October 1942. Would have returned to Amsterdam on 20 April 1943. Survived the occupation. Source: hckw archive.

75. na, CABR, J. Schol, 88.972 (pra Enschede), 108.897 (pf Assen).

76. Proces-verbaal Gemmeker, nr. 414, dd 4 juli 1948 (privately owned).

77. As it is not always clear who belonged to the SS, we chose to use 'SS man' as the title in general.

78. The Report regarding ss- and sd-people who worked in camp Westerbork, drawn up on 14 April 1945, lists about 35 names of ss- and sd-people who worked in camp Westerbork. Besides those of commanders Deppner, Dischner and Gemmeker, the list also includes the names of Germans who were temporarily in the camp, such as two employees of the Zentralstelle für jüdische Auswanderung from Amsterdam. Behind almost every name a function is listed. Many of them are administrative positions. This corresponds to the data from the archives, as virtually no SS or SSD staff were sent to Westerbork as guards. Source: NIOD, 250i, inv.nr. 50.

79. na, CABR, various personal files.

80. H.G.J. Reiser, born 22 November 1921 in Mainstockheim.

81. na, CABR, Hans Georg Johann Reiser, inv.nr. 87503.

82. na, CABR, Heinz Lemke, inv.nr. 2029.

83. Wilhelmus Severinus Antonie van Eck, born 21 August 1919 in Voorburg.

84. na, CABR, W.S.A. van Eck, inv.nr. 66642.

85. Edmund Xaver Breil, born 10 November 1919 at Gelsenkirchen, na, CABR, dossier Breil, inv.nr. 87494.

86. Herman Benjamin van Laer, born 5 October 1914 in The Hague.

87. na, CABR, inv.nr. 87540 (Bureau Opsporing Oorlogsmisdadigers Assen 0-66).

88. Hendrik van Dam, born 30 December 1916 at Schoonhoven.

89. na, CABR, dossier Hendrik van Dam, inv.nr. 70145.

90. na, CABR, Heinz Lemke, inv.nr. 2029.

91. na, CABR, dossier Hendrik van Dam, inv.nr. 70145.

Chapter 4

1. Minutes Gemmeker, no. 414, dated 4 June 1948 (privately owned).

2. Mededeling aan de barakleiders, 9 februari 1943, hckw archive.

3. OD-rapport, hckw archive.

4. Lagerbefehl no 2, 14 January 1943, collection Jewish Historical Museum, inv.nr. 00000561.

5. Lagerbefehl no 6, 14 February 1943, collection Jewish Historical Museum, inv.nr. 00000563.

6. www.joodsmonument.nl.

7. Minutes Gemmeker, no. 414, dated 4 June 1948 (privately owned).

8. Presser, *Ondergang*, deel ii, 339.

9. Mechanicus, *In Depot*, 96.

10. NIOD, 250i, inv.nr. 110.

11. Mechanicus, *In Depot*, 96.

12. Lagerbefehl no 42, 27 July 1943, collection Jewish Historical Museum, inv.nr. 00000606.

13. Mechanicus, *In Depot*, 239.

14. Ibidem, 94.

15. NIOD, 250i, inv.nr. 123.

16. Lagerbefehl no. 41, 14 July 1943, collection Jewish Historical Museum, inv nr. 00000589.

17. NIOD, 250i, inv.nr. 118.

18. Schwarz, *Treinen op dood spoor*, 170-172.

19. Presser, *Ondergang*, deel ii, 361.

20. Schwarz, *Treinen op dood spoor*, 170-172, and Bloch, *Confrontatie met het noodlot* (manuscript, hckw).

21. In August 1943, Gemmeker said it was necessary to 'apply a stricter summary of all available forces and a unification of the camp

organisation'. In connection with this 'camp necessity', the post of first service leader was created with immediate effect. For this position, the service leader of service group two (Verwaltung), Kurt Schlesinger, was appointed. Schlesinger had to give orders necessary for the joint organisation of the camp according to Gemmeker's directives, and he was also chief of all service leaders. As a result, Schlesinger can be seen as the mayor of Camp Westerbork, who headed the self-government and was only accountable to Gemmeker (Lagersonderbefehl, 12 August 1943, Jewish Historical Museum collection, inv.nr. 00000626).

22. NIOD, 250i, inv.nr. 721.
23. Mechanicus, *In Depot*, 145.
24. Statement Werner Bloch in: minutes Gemmeker, no. 414, dated 4 June 1948 (privately owned).
25. Leo van Messel, born 3 October 1920 in Koekelberg.
26. NIOD, 250i, inv.nr. 113.
27. Abraham Gudema, born 23 March 1913 at Wedde Blijham.
28. Minutes Gemmeker, no. 414, dated 4 June 1948 (privately owned).
29 Ibidem.
30. Eva Moraal, *Als ik morgen niet op transport ga, ga ik 's avonds naar de revue*, 271.
31. Presser, *Ondergang*, deel ii, 315.
32. Drents Archief, archive Commissaris der Koningin, access no. 0040, and archive municipality of Midden-Drenthe, personnel file Barteld Lukas Knol and info via Libbe T. Henstra.
33. Berthrandus Herman Paridaen, born 30 August 1919 in Sint Kruis. Emigrated to Canada on 15 June 1950. Died there on 13 February 2008. Source: http://www.obitsforlife.com/obit uary/38622/Paridaen-Bertrand-Herman.php.
34. na, CABR, dossier Paridaen, 76897.
35. *De Nederlandsche Politie*, jrg. 2 (15 maart 1944), nr. 6.
36. na, CABR, dossier Paridaen, 76897.
37. na 2.09.45 Rijksvreemdelingendienst, 1901.
38. OD-rapport, hckw archive.
39. Minutes Gemmeker, no. 414, dated 4 June 1948 (privately owned).
40. http://www.niod.knaw.nl/nl/ vraag-en-antwoord/ gedeporteerde-joden
41. Hans Marsalek, *Die Geschichte des Konzentrationslager Mauthausen*, 288, and J. Presser, *Ondergang* deel I, 90-96.
42. *Het Joodsche Weekblad* (Heruitgave, deel 1 en 2).
43. D. Giltay Veth en A.J. van der Leeuw, *Het Weinrebrapport*, 118.
44. na, CABR, dossier Hendrik van Dam, inv.nr. 70145.
45. Presser, *Ondergang*, deel ii, 315.
46. Minutes Gemmeker, no. 414, dated 4 June 1948 (privately owned).
47. Mechanicus, *In Depot*, 242 en 248.
48. OD-rapport, hckw archive.
49. Carol Ann Lee, *Anne Frank 1929-1945*, 220.
50. http://www.annefrank.org.
51. Salomon Sluijter, born 26 January 1895 in Amsterdam. Arrived at Westerbork 3 May 1942. Remained in Westerbork until liberation. Source: hckw archive.
52. Hermann Kirschen, born 29 March 1894 in Nizniow. Arrived at Westerbork between 3 and 5 October 1942. Remained

in Westerbork until liberation. Source: hckw archive.

53. Ludwig Trier, born 24 April 1894 in Aschaffenburg. Arrived at Westerbork 8 August 1942. Transported from Westerbork to Theresienstadt on 4 September 1944. Died on 30 September 1944 in Auschwitz. Source: hckw archive.54. NIOD, 250i, inv.nr. 130.

55. Lindwer, *Kamp van hoop en wanhoop*, 140.

56. Willem Willing, *Afdrukken van indrukken*, 20.

57. OD-rapport, hckw archive.

58. Willing, *Afdrukken van indrukken*, 59.

59. OD-rapport, hckw archive and R. de Winter-Levy, *Aan de gaskamer ontsnapt*, 10.

60. NIOD, 250i, inv.nr. 109 en 120.

61. Mozes Benjamin Zimmern, born 13 October 1885 in Bruchsal. Arrived at Westerbork between 3 and 5 October 1942. On 4 September 1944 from Westerbork on transport to Theresienstadt. Died on 17 October 1944 in Auschwitz. Source: hckw archive and http://www.joodsmonument.nl/person/526537/nl

62. Mechanicus, *In Depot*, 242.

63. Hckw archive.

64. Lindwer, *Kamp van hoop en wanhoop*, 40.

65. Lee, *Anne Frank 1929-1945*, 225.

66. Minutes Gemmeker, no. 414, dated 4 June 1948 (privately owned).

67. Mechanicus, *In Depot*, 198.

68. OD-rapport, hckw archive.

69. Mechanicus, *In Depot*, 118.

70. Ibidem, 167.

71. Ibidem, 172.

71. Presser, *Ondergang*, deel ii, 315.

73. Minutes Gemmeker, no. 414, dated 4 June 1948 (privately owned).

74. OD-rapport, hckw archive.

75. Mechanicus, *In Depot*, 33-36.

76. Guido Abuys and Dirk Mulder, *Een gat in het prikkeldraad*, 31.

77. Nanda van der Zee, *de Trein*, 113.

78. Mechanicus, *In Depot*, 35.

79. Abuys and Mulder, *Een gat in het prikkeldraad*, 31.

80. Jacob Barzilay, 7 januari 1920 at Amsterdam.

81. NIOD, doc I, 520, map B, stuk 10 verhoren Gemmeker 9 december 1948

82. Joël Granade, born 28 August 1919 in Amsterdam. Arrived at Westerbork 18 July 1942. On 4 September 1944 from Westerbork on transport to Theresienstadt. Returned. Source: hckw archive.

83. na, CABR 105340 (Procureurfiscaal Amsterdam T-11669).

84. Mechanicus, *In Depot*, 135.

85. OD-rapport, hckw archive.

86. Wils 't Hart, *Ik zou in mijn tranen willen wegzwemmen*, 40.

87. Avi Magid, *Ontsnapping uit Westerbork*, 35-37.

88. jhm, inv.nr. 00000020.

89. Minutes Gemmeker, no. 414, dated 4 June 1948 (privately owned).

90. OD-rapport, hckw archive.

91. Minutes Gemmeker, no. 414, dated 4 June 1948 (privately owned).

92. Ibidem.

Chapter 5

1. NIOD, 250i, inv.nr. 724.

2. Ibidem, 527.

3. OD-rapport, hckw archive.

4. Leo Janowitz, born 12 October 1892 at Olchowetz. Arrived at Westerbork on 30 September 1942. On 1 January 1944 from Westerbork on a transport to

Bergen-Belsen. He returned.
Source: hckw archive.

5. Lea Andriesse-Janowitz, interview
4949, Visual History Archive. Usc
Shoah Foundation Institute, 1995.
Viewed at Jewish Historical
Museum

6. Chajes, Peppie Dekker's *Holocaust
Experience as seen through the
eyes of a child.*

7. Betty Loonstein, interview 4613,
Visual History Archive. usc Shoah
Foundation Institute, 1995.
Viewed at Jewish Historical
Museum.

8. Maurits Beetz, born 13 November
1916 in Amsterdam. Arrived at
Westerbork between 3 and
5 October 1942. Remained in
Westerbork until the liberation.
Source: hckw archive.

9. Interview J. Beetz-Kater,
transcription archive
Remembrance Centre Camp
Westerbork, RA1914.

10. Bloch, *Confrontatie met het noodlot.*

11. Ernest Elie Frank, *'Dagboek 2'*,
120 (manuscript, hckw).

12. Lindwer, *Kamp van hoop en
wanhoop*, 157-160.

13. Barend Scheffer, born 19 August
1922 in Amsterdam. Arrived at
Westerbork on 21 November
1942. Transported from
Westerbork to Theresienstadt on
18 January 1944. Died on 31 May
1945 in Bergen-Belsen. Source:
hckw archive and
https://www.joodsmonument.nl/
nl/page/37625/

14. Jewish Historical Museum,
Document Collection, inv.nr.
10289, ordner ii.

15. R.E. Taselaar, *'Avegoor en het
kamp "Palästina" in Ellecom'*,
Terugblik '40-'45, maandblad van
de Documentatiegroep '40-'45
(oktober 2008) nr. 9.

16. Heiman Natan Scheffer, born
27 September 1915 in Amsterdam. Arrived at Westerbork
18 July 1942. On 18 January 1944
from Westerbork on transport to
Theresienstadt. Died on 18 March
1945 in the Senftenberg outer
commandment. Source: hckw
archive and
http://www.joodsmonument.nl/
person/ 501630/en.

17. na, Ministerie van Justitie, DGvP,
inv.nr. 262.

18. The group that originally came as
refugees from abroad grew from
18 to 76, while the strength of the
Dutch group increased from 42 to
85.

19. OD-rapport, hckw archive.

20. NIOD, 250i, inv.nr. 105.

21. OD-rapport, hckw archive. The
number of Dutch nationals among
these 182 od men was 106 men.
In August 1943, of the 117 od
men, 66 were of Dutch origin.

22. NIOD, 250i, inv.nr. 0721.

23. Léon Albertus Alexander Cohen,
born 21 November 1898 in
Amsterdam. Arrived at
Westerbork 22 July 1943.
Remained in Westerbork until the
liberation. Source: hckw archive.

24. *'Een eeuw van Léon Cohen'*, *Het
Parool*, hckw archive, RA1580.

25. na, CABR, A. de Jong, 75961.

26. Kampbevel nr. 27, dd 23 april
1943, hckw archive.

27. Ternede, *De Ordedienst van kamp
Westerbork 1939-1943*, 38.

28. OD-rapport, hckw archive.

29. Lindwer, *Kamp van hoop en
wanhoop*, 41.

30. Mechanicus, *In Depot*, 11.

31. OD-rapport, hckw archive.

32. Nanda van der Zee, *De Trein*, 113.

33. Mechanicus, *In Depot*, 148.

34. Boas, Boulevard des Misères, 65.

35. http://www.youtube.com/user/

Herinneringscentrum.

36. Lindwer, *Kamp van hoop en wanhoop*, 151.

37. Paul Siegel, *Locomotieven trekken wagons*, 112.

38. OD-rapport, hckw archive.

39. Mechanicus, *In Depot*, 167, 250 en 281.

40. NIOD, Doc. I, dossier 500, map A, nr. 8.

41. Ternede, *De Ordedienst van kamp Westerbork 1939-1943*, 59.

42. na, CABR, dossier Gemmeker, BRvC 135/49, pra Amsterdam 60326.

43. NIOD, Doc. I, dossier 500, map A, nr. 8.

44. Van Riet, *Handhaven onder de Nieuwe Orde*, 392.

45. Presser, *Ondergang*, deel I, 326.

46. na, CABR, dossier Gemmeker, BRvC 135/49, pra Asterdam 60326.

47. Boas, *Boulevard des Misères*, 65.

48. NIOD, Doc. I, dossier 500, map A, nr. 8.

49. Presser, *Ondergang*, deel I, 328.

50. NIOD, Doc. I, dossier 500, map A, nr. 8.

51. na, CABR, dossier Gemmeker, BRvC 135/49, pra Asterdam 60326.

52. NIOD, Doc. I, dossier 500, map A, nr. 8.

53. na, CABR, dossier Gemmeker, BRvC 135/49, pra Asterdam 60326.

54. *Oranjekrant*, 22 januari 1943, via: www.kranten.kb.nl, uit: NIOD, coll. 556, doos 57.

55. De Jong, *Het Koninkrijk*, deel 6, eerste helft, 311.

56. OD-rapport, hckw archive.

57. NIOD, Doc. I, dossier 500, map A, nr. 8.

58. Presser, *Ondergang*, deel I, 331.

59. Bloch, *Confrontatie met het noodlot*.

60. OD-rapport, hckw archive.

61. Collection Jewish Historical Museum, inv.nr. 00012409.

62. OD-rapport, hckw archive.

63. Van Riet, *Handhaven onder de Nieuwe Orde*, 301.

64. Ernest Elie Frank, *'Dagboek 2'*, 163 (manuscript, hckw).

65. Hans Eisinger, born 12 July 1919 in Drösing (Austria). Arrived at Westerbork 10 May 1940. Remained in Westerbork until the liberation. Source: hckw archive.

66. Heinz Wolf, born 28 April 1914 in Dortmund. Arrived at Westerbork 22 April 1940. Remained in Westerbork until liberation. Source: hckw archive.

67. OD-rapport, hckw archive.

68. Presser, *Ondergang*, deel I, 320.

69. OD-rapport, hckw archive.

70. Interview Eva Pellinkhof-Roselaar, transcript hckw archive.

71. Van den Oord, *Westerbork Girl*, 146.

72. NIOD, 250i, inv.nr. 0129.

73. Jechiël Roselaar, born 12 June 1917 Amsterdam. Arrived at Westerbork between 3 and 5 October 1942. Transported from Westerbork to Sobibor on 18 May 1943. There, he died on 21 May 1943. Source: hckw archive and http://www.joodsmonument.nl/person/501765/nl

74. Interview Eva Pellinkhof-Roselaar, transcript hckw archive.

75. www.joodsewerkkampen.nl and www.herdenking.nl.

76. Interview Eva Pellinkhof-Roselaar, transcript hckw archive.

77. OD-rapport, hckw archive.

78. Ernest Elie Frank, born 2 April 1915 in Rotterdam.

79. Interview Eva Pellinkhof-Roselaar, transcript hckw archive.

80. Ernest Elie Frank, *'Dagboek 2'*, B10 (manuscript, hckw).

81. NIOD, 250i, inv.nr. 0131.

82. Presser, *Ondergang*, deel I, 341.
83. De Jong, *Het Koninkrijk*, deel 6, eerste helft, 313.
84. Ernest Elie Frank, *'Dagboek 2'*, 166 (manuscript, hckw).
85. OD-rapport, hckw archive.
86. Lindwer, *Kamp van hoop en wanhoop*, 142.
87. Guus Meershoek, *Dienaren van het gezag*, 290.
88. OD-rapport, hckw archive.
89. Ibidem.
90. Ibidem en NIOD, 250i, inv.nr. 721.
91. Mechanicus, *Ik woon, zoals je weet, drie hoog*, 37.
92. Van den Oord, *Westerbork Girl*.
93. OD-rapport, hckw archive.
94. Van den Oord, *Westerbork Girl*.
95. NIOD, 250i.
96. Geraldien von Frijtag Drabbe Künzel, *Kamp Amersfoort*, 167.
97. Mechanicus, *In depot*, 173.
98. T.M. Sjenitzer-van Leening, *Dagboekfragmenten 1940-1945*, 337.
99. Abel J. Herzberg, *Kroniek der Jodenvervolging, 1940-1945*, 172-175.
100. K.J. Frederiks, *Op de Bres*, 74.
101. De Jong, *Het Koninkrijk*, deel 6, eerste helft, 276.
102. Frederiks, *Op de Bres*, 74.
103. De Jong, *Het Koninkrijk*, deel 6, eerste helft, 276.
104. Frederiks, *Op de Bres*, 75.
105. R.E. Taselaar, *'Het kamp Barneveld en zijn bewoners'*, *Terugblik '40-'45* (september 2003), nr. 9
106. OD-rapport, hckw archive.
107. T.M. Sjenitzer-van Leening, *Dagboekfragmenten 1940-1945*, 337.
108. Van Riet, *Handhaven onder de Nieuwe Orde*, 502.
109. OD-rapport, hckw archive.
110. Collection Jewish Historical Museum, Lagerbefehl 34, 20 May 1943, inv nr. 00000584.
111. Bloch, *Confrontatie met het noodlot*.
112. OD-rapport, hckw archive.
113. NIOD, 250i, inv.nr. 725.
114. www.joodsmonument.nl.
115. Presser, *Ondergang*, deel I, 290. Eva Roselaar fell into this category because she was a seamstress in a workshop sewing black mourning gowns destined for Germany. Her identity card was stamped with the number 62,691. (Pellinkhof family archive).
116. Presser, *Ondergang*, deel I, 290.
117. NIOD, 250i inv.nr. 510.
118. www.joodsmonument.nl.
119. Interview J. Beetz-Kater, transcript hckw archive, RA1914.
120. NIOD, 250i inv.nr.110 en 721.
121. Ernst Adam, born 11 February 1897 in Berlin. Arrived at Westerbork 2 October 1942. On 24 November 1942 from Westerbork on transport to Auschwitz. Died in middle Europe on 31 March 1944. Source: hckw archive and http://www.joodsmonument.nl/person/546448/nl
122. Otto Max Mayer, born 11 July 1891 in Mannheim. Arrived Westerbork 3 October 1942. On 24 November 1942 from Westerbork on transport to Auschwitz. There he died on 27 November 1942. Source: hckw archive and http://www.joodsmonument.nl/person/453721/nl
123. Hckw archive.
124. Arnold Alfons Spitzer, born 28 November 1889 in Janowitz. Arrived at Westerbork 10 August 1942. On 1 February 1944 from Westerbork on transport to Bergen-Belsen. He died on 7 June 1945 in Tröblitz. Source: hckw archive and

http://www.joodsmonument.nl/person/495857/nl

125. Chajes, Peppie Dekker's *Holocaust Experience as seen through the eyes of a child.*

126. OD-rapport, hckw archive.

127. Wolfgang Benz, *Theresienstadt*, 9.

128. De Jong, *Het Koninkrijk*, deel 6, eerste helft, 282-290.

129. www.ushmm.org and www.kampwesterbork.nl.

130. OD-rapport, hckw archive.

131. Ibidem and www.joodsmonument.nl.

132. OD-rapport, hckw archive.

Chapter 6

1. Van Riet, *Handhaven onder de Nieuwe Orde*, 463.

2. De Jong, *Het Koninkrijk*, deel 6, tweede helft, 635.

3. http://www.niod.nl/sites/niod.nl/files/Augustus%20Dirk%20Boonstra.pdf.

4. H.A.J. van Rens, *De vervolging van joden en Sinti tijdens de Tweede Wereldoorlog in de Nederlandse provincie Limburg*, 111.

5. Folkert van der Werf, '*Mijn oorlogsverhaal, politieman op het platteland tijdens de Duitse bezetting*' (manuscript, Den Oever, 1999), 15-18, Letter from F. van der Werf to his mother, brothers and sisters, 16 March 1943. Not exactly documented, but according to oral tradition of the family, there is another argument why Folkert decided to go to Westerbork. If he did not go and had to go into hiding, a search of his mother's house would possibly follow. This would put her and her hiders in danger. The resistance activities of 'the little widow Van der Werf ', of her daughter Wally and her sons Jacob and Catharinus are mentioned in P. Wijbenga, Bezettingstijd in Friesland, deel iii, Het laatste bedrijf (Leeuwarden 1978), 88-89.

6. *Nederlandsch Algemeen Politieblad*, jrg. 92 (11 februari 1943), nr. 6, issued on behalf of it Departement van Justitie.

7. P. Wijbenga, *Bezettingstijd in Friesland*, 46, and info via Henk Westland. By early July 1944, Van der Werf was also out of stretch. At that point, he belonged to the Ferwerderadeel group, based in Blija. From there, his duties included serving in Ferwerd, where he was in charge of guarding the Distribution Office. On Tuesday 4 July, he was ordered to transfer a person in hiding, who had been arrested the previous day by two members of the Labour Control Service, to the police station in Leeuwarden. At around 1.15pm, he and the person in hiding, Wik Jalink, a 21-year-old student from The Hague, left Ferwerd by bus. The next day, it turned out that Van der Werf had not appeared at his guard post at the Distribution Office. Information was received from Leeuwarden that neither he nor his detainee had arrived there. Research in the boarding house yielded the same result: he had not returned there either after leaving for Leeuwarden. However, his service weapon and its ammunition were found in a cupboard. The head sentry, who conducted the investigation, concluded from the facts that Van der Werf had gone into hiding, and this proved to be the case. Folkert had to move to another hiding address several times for his own safety. At the risk of his own

life, he helped the illegals. Report drawn up on 6 July 1944 by chief watchman W. Kuipers, in the collection of the Van der Werf family. and Van der Werf, *Mijn oorlogsverhaal*, 1999, 26-42, familiearchief Van der Werf.

8. Van der Werf, *Mijn oorlogsverhaal*, 15-18, letter from Folkert van der Werf to his mother and brother, 21 April 1943, and letters H.J. Droppers, archief hckw.

9. Mechanicus, *In Depot*, 23 en 30.

10. Interview Jenne Boering, born 23 October 1919, hckw archive.

11. www.kampwesterbork.nl (aankomst en registratie).

12. Karl Schneider, *Auswärts eingesetzt*, 10.

13. www.kampwesterbork.nl (uitgaand transport).

14. na, CABR, A. de Jong, 75961.

15. Jacobus Cornelis Trompert, born 28 March 1920 in Alkmaar, died on 26 March 1945, probably during a transport from Neuengamme. (Judith Schuyf, *Nederlanders in Neuengamme*,

16. Info via Henk Westland.

17. Mechanicus, *In Depot*, 187.

18. Roelof Hemkes, born 28 February 1919 (source: Leeuwarder Courant, 3 February 1979).

19. Joop Floor was betrayed by a colleague at his hiding place in the Zaan region and arrested. During interrogation in Groningen, he was mistreated. It is likely that his choice to go into hiding was not badly judged against him, because although he was rejected for active police service in the Marechaussee, he was later assigned to the Police Motor Service (source: http://www.oktober44.nl/html/detoekomst.html).

20. Letters H.J. Droppers, hckw archive.

21. Letter from Folkert van der Werf to his mother, brothers and sisters, 20 May 1943.

22. Bart van der Boom, *Wij weten niets van hun lot. Gewone Nederlanders en de Holocaust* (418).

23. Folkert van der Werf, *Mijn oorlogsverhaal,* 19-21, and letter from Folkert to his mother, brothers and sisters, 20 mei 1943.

24. Mechanicus, *In Depot*, 50.

25. Mirjam Bolle, *Ik zal je beschrijven hoe een dag er hier uitziet*, 149.

26. Letter from Frans Spoor from archive of Meijer family.

27. Letters from Van der Werf family collection.

28. Albert de Jong, born 2 January 1909 in Groningen.

29. na, CABR, A. de Jong, 75961.

30. Ibidem.

31. NIOD, 250i, inv.nr. 910.

32. www.joodsmonument.nl.

33. NIOD, 250i, inv.nr. 908.

34. Hermann Wingens, born 2 January 1919 in Cologne. Arrived at Westerbork 22 February 1940. Remained in Westerbork until liberation. Source: hckw archive.

35. na, CABR, A. de Jong, 75961.

36. Derk Klavers, born 8 May 1891 at Deventer.

37. na, CABR, A. de Jong, 75961.

38. Herman en Willem Brinkman, *Derk Klavers 1890-1943. Wolf in Schaapskleren.*

39. *Nieuwsblad van het Noorden*, 2 april 1937.

40. *Provinciale Drentsche en Asser Courant*, 25 september 1940.

41. *De Nederlandse Politie*, jrg. 1 (oktober 1943), nr. 22, 15.

42. na, CABR, A. de Jong, 75961.

43. Herman en Willem Brinkman, *Derk Klavers 1890-1943.*

Wolf in Schaapskleren. 349

44. Jan Rebel, born 25 februari 1922 Huizen (nh), personeelskaart politie Amsterdam.
45. na, CABR, J. Rebel, inv.nr.: 39410.
46. Personeelskaart archief politie Amsterdam.
47. na, CABR, J. Rebel, inv.nr.: 39410.
48. Johan Ernst Polak, geb. 3 juli 1911 in Amsterdam. Polak's name is mentioned on the Roll of Honor of Fallen 1940-1945
49. na, CABR, A. de Jong, 75961.
50. *De Nederlandsche Politie*, jrg. 2 (maart 1944), nr. 6, 15.
51. Ibidem, jrg. 2 (1 april 1944), nr. 7.
52. na, Ministerie van Justitie, DGvP, inv.nr. 474.
53. OD-rapport, hckw archive.
54. na, Ministerie van Justitie, DGvP, inv.nr. 474.
55. OD-rapport, hckw archive.
56. na, Ministerie van Justitie, DGvP, inv.nr. 474.
57. na, CABR, A. de Jong, 75961.
58. Charlotte Weisz, geb. 9 februari 1924 in Wenen. https://www.joodsmonument.nl/ nl/page/25260/charlotte-weisz.
59. After the liberation, Rebel stated that he had drawn up a report in response to Smallenbroek's statement and that the official report was written by Gemmeker. No evidence was found in the files to support this allegation.
60. na, CABR, A. de Jong, 75961.
61. http://www.archieven.nl/nl/ zoeken?mivast=0&mizig=210&m iadt=5&miaet=1&micode=2183 &minr=1183312&miview= inv2&milang=nl.
62. na, CABR, A. de Jong, 75961.
63. www.joodsmonument.nl.
64. na, CABR, A. de Jong, 75961.
65. na, CABR, dossier Paridaen, 76897.
66. Lagersonderbefehl, 5 maart 1943, collection Jewish Historical

Museum, inv.nr. 00000980.
67. Interview Jenne Boering, 23 oktober 1919, hckw archive.
68. Letter from Folkert van der Werf to his mother and brother, April 21, 1943; to his mother, brothers and sisters, May 20, 1943; to his mother, brothers and sister, June 4, 1943, and from HJ Droppers, hckw archive.
69. Trouw, 18 januari 1999.
70. Mechanicus, *In Depot*, 74.
71. Presser, *Ondergang*, deel 2, 350-355
72. Mechanicus, *In Depot*, 234.
73. http://www.encyclopedie drenthe.nl/April-mei%20staking.
74. OD-rapport, hckw archive.
75. Lagersonderbefehl, 19 oktober 1943, collection Jewish Historical Museum, inv.nr. 00000625.
76. Mechanicus, *Ik woon, zoals je weet, drie hoog*, 29.
77. na, CABR, A. de Jong, 75961.
78. Willem Willing, *Afdrukken van indrukken*, 57.
79. Mechanicus, *In Depot*, 134.
80. OD-rapport, hckw archive.
81. na, CABR, A. de Jong, 75961.
82. *Arnhemse Courant*, 15 januari 1944, en *Dordrechtsche Courant*, 14 januari 1944 via kranten.kb.nl.
83. De Jong, *Het Koninkrijk*, deel 8, tweede helft, 738.
84. Lindwer, *Kamp van hoop en wanhoop*, 38.
85. Van Riet, *Handhaven onder de Nieuwe Orde*, 294-296.
86. Ibidem, 331.
87. NIOD, Doc. ii, Politie Amsterdam, doos 384.
88. Personeelsdossier Theunis Postema, archief politie Amsterdam.
89. Personeelsdossiers, archief politie Amsterdam.
90. na, CABR, A. de Jong, 75961.
91. Personeelsdossier Reinder ten

Hoope, archief politie Amsterdam.

92. Pieter Drent, born 21 september 1921 in Vries. Personeelsdossier archief politie Amsterdam.

93. Interview Teunis Jan Versteeg, born 28 juni 1923 te Rotterdam, dd 21 juni 1999.

94. Bombergen, *Terugblik 1943-1945*.

95. Willem Hendrik Tasseron, born 28 augustus 1910 te Düsseldorf.

96. NIOD, Doc. ii, Politie Amsterdam, doos 384.

97. Personeelsdossier Dirk Veerdig, archief politie Amsterdam.

98. Personeelsdossier Jan Bouwens, archief politie Amsterdam.

99. Interview J.J. Bombergen, born 5 juli 1924 te Winterswijk, dd 6 december 1997.

100. Bombergen, *Terugblik 1943-1945*.

101. na, CABR, Jacobus Willem Munnikhuizen, born. 7 september 1918 te Velsen, inv. nr. 4386.

102. Bombergen, *Terugblik 1943-1945*.

103. Interview Teunis Jan Versteeg, born 28 juni 1923 te Rotterdam, dd 21 juni 1999. 351

104. Bombergen, *Terugblik 1943-1945*.

105. Interview K. Koster, born 17 februari 1921, dd 20 september 2000.

106. NIOD, 250i, inv.nr. 1011 en Doc. ii, Politie Amsterdam, doos 384.

107. Interview Jacobus Romeijn, born 13 september 1921 te Haarlem, dd 6 oktober 1998.

108. Van Riet, *Handhaven onder de Nieuwe Orde*, 515-517.

109. Hans Bial, *Briefe an Hetty, Tagebuch aus dem Lager Westerbork*.

Chapter 7

1. Van Riet, *Handhaven onder de Nieuwe Orde*, 569.

2. na, CABR, dossier Gemmeker, BRvC 135/49, pra Asterdam

60326.

3. De Jong, *Het Koninkrijk*, deel 10, eerste helft, 182.

4. Informatie via Guido Abuys, hckw.

5. Bloch, *Confrontatie met het noodlot*.

6. Abraham Hoogstraal, born 18 mei 1917 in Assen. Arrival Westerbork 3 May 1942. On 18 January 1944 from Westerbork on transport to Theresienstadt. Died on August 24, 1944 in Schwarzheide. Source: hckw archive and http://www.joodsmonument.nl/person/512696/nl

7. Jacob Magnus, b. March 6, 1919 in Assen. Arrival Westerbork 19 August 1942. On 18 January 1944 from Westerbork on transport to Theresienstadt. Died on November 30, 1944 in Schwarzheide. Source: hckw archive and http://www.joodsmonument.nl/person/474241/nl

8. www.ghetto-theresienstadt.info.

9. Bloch, *Confrontatie met het noodlot*.

10. Hckw archive.

11. Bloch, *Confrontatie met het noodlot*.

12. Bial, Briefe an Hetty, *Tagebuch aus dem Lager Westerbork*.

13. Aad van As, *In het hol van de leeuw.*

14. Bial, *Briefe an Hetty.*

15. Van Riet, *Handhaven onder de Nieuwe Orde*, 551.

16. Bial, *Briefe an Hetty.*

17. na, CABR, dossier Pieter Boot.

18. Van Riet, *Handhaven onder de Nieuwe Orde*, 707.

19. na, CABR, dossier Hendrik Johannes Buunk, born 25 January 1899 in Renkum, pra Hilversum 94547, brc 75219.

20. Bial, *Briefe an Hetty.* 352

21. Hartog Walvis, born 29 January 1922 in Amsterdam.

22. John Ancona, born 8 december 1919 in Hilversum, Johan Frederik

Theodoor Engers born 7 june 1919 te Batavia, Ernst Katan, born 30 april 1923 te Hilversum, Samuel Goldstein, born 1 december 1917 te Amsterdam.

23. na, CABR, Johannes Otto von Henning, born 28 August 1919 in Zwolle, inv.nr. 75299, BRC 310/47.

24. na, CABR, dossier H.M.M. Lemke, inv.nr. 2029 en NIOD, 250i, nr. 0969.

25. A meal was provided to 3,990 members of the border police in Westerbork throughout the month of October. Source: NIOD, 250i, 0058.

26. Archief Gemeente Midden-Drenthe, inv.nr. 41a.

27. na, CABR, dossier Gemmeker, BRvC 135/49, pra Amsterdam 60326.

28. na, CABR, Walter Hanitsch, born 9 January 1911 te Fürstenhagen, inv.nr. 87503.

29. Personeelsdossier Pieter Drent, archief politie Amsterdam.

30. Bial, *Briefe an Hetty*.

31. NIOD, 250i, nr. 0969.

32. Ibidem, nr. 0971.

33. At the end of July 1944, the German authorities announced stricter measures to combat terrorists and saboteurs in the territories they occupied. According to the so-called Führererlass, those who were arrested as such usually received the death penalty after a detailed investigation. Due to the circumstances, the Befehlshaber found it necessary in September 1944 to announce even stricter measures. The Niedermachungs-befehl stipulated that all Dutch persons guilty of certain offenses were to be shot immediately during or shortly after their arrest. From: Van Riet, *Handhaven onder*

de Nieuwe Orde, 255.

34. NIOD, 250i, nr. 0971.

35. Ibidem, nr. 0969.

36. Ibidem, nr. 0967.

37. Bial, *Briefe an Hetty*.

38. na, CABR, dossier Heinz Martin Max Lemke, born 13 november 1920 in Lauenburg, inv.nr. 2029.

39. D. Giltay Veth en A.J. van der Leeuw, *Het Weinrebrapport*, 118.

40. na, CABR, dossier Heinz Martin Max Lemke, inv.nr. 2029.

41. Bial, *Briefe an Hetty* and RA 2071 hckw; Bevrijdingscartotheek Rode Kruis, 353

42. na, CABR, Wilhelmus Severinus Antonie van Eck, inv.nr. 66642.

43. Bial, *Briefe an Hetty*.

44. Ibidem.

45. Presser, *Ondergang*, deel ii, 363.

46. Bial, *Briefe an Hetty*.

47. Ibidem.

48. De Jong, *Het Koninkrijk*, deel 10b, 1143-1145.

49. *Terdege*, 27 april 2011, en www.refdag.nl.

50. J.Th. Kuyck, *Partisanenvrouwen*.

51. www.rotterdamsdagblad.nl, 19 maart 2005.

52. Interview C. van der Stel-Polderman, hckw.

53. Kuyck, *Partisanenvrouwen*, 150.

54. Interview C. van der Stel-Polderman, hckw.

55. Interview Greetje van der Molen, dd 7 februari 1996, hckw.

56. Kuyck, *Partisanenvrouwen*, 158, en Bial, *Briefe an Hetty*.

57. Aad van As, *In het hol van de leeuw*.

58. Kuyck, *Partisanenvrouwen*, 158, en Bial, *Briefe an Hetty*.

59. Bial, *Briefe an Hetty*.

60. Kuyck, *Partisanenvrouwen*, 162.

61. De Jong, *Het Koninkrijk*, deel 10, tweede helft, 1145.

62. Interview Greetje van der Molen, dd 7 februari 1996, hckw.

63.   Interview Greetje van der Molen en C. van der Stel-Polderman, Kuyck, Partisanenvrouwen and W. Kamminga, *Grijpskerk van crisis tot bevrijding*, 128-130.

Chapter 8

1.   Bial, *Briefe an Hetty. Tagebuch aus dem Lager Westerbork.*
2.   Aad van As, *In het hol van de leeuw.*
3.   Abraham van Witsen, born 15 augustus 1891 in Amsterdam.
4.   NIOD, 250i, nr. 0983.
5.   Aad van As, *In het hol van de leeuw.*
6.   Bial, *Briefe an Hetty.*
7.   Collection Jewish Historical Museum, De Westerborker, inv.nr. 00000318 en NIOD, 250i, nr. 0983.
8.   Bial, *Briefe an Hetty.*
9.   Collection Jewish Historical Museum, *De Westerborker*, inv.nr. 00000318 en NIOD, 250i, nr. 0983.
10.   Presser, *Ondergang*, deel ii, 354, 363
11.   Bial, *Briefe an Hetty* and *De Westerborker*, Collection Jewish Historical Museum inv.nr. 0000 0318, en NIOD, 250i, nr. 0983.
12.   Interview Hans Margules, december 2010, hckw.
13.   Joods Historisch Museum, *De Westerborker*, inv.nr. 00000318, en NIOD, 250i, nr. 0983.
14.   Bial, *Briefe an Hetty.*
15.   Joods Historisch Museum, *De Westerborker*, inv.nr. 00000318, en NIOD, 250i, nr. 0983.
16.   Bial, *Briefe an Hetty.*
17.   Joods Historisch Museum, *De Westerborker*, inv.nr. 00000318, en NIOD, 250i, nr. 0983.
18.   Bial, *Briefe an Hetty.*
19.   Archief od, hckw.
20.   Presser, *Ondergang*, deel ii, 366-369, and NIOD, 250i, nr. 0984.
21.   Interview Hans Margules,

december 2010, hckw.
22.   Drents Archief, inv.nr. 027.
23.   Mechanicus, *In Depot*, 153.
24.   Archief od, hckw.
25.   na, CABR, Dossier Arthur Pisk.
26.   Drents Archief, inv.nr. 027.
27.   http://www.joodsmonument.nl/person/540875/nl
28.   *De Telegraaf*, 3 november 2012.
29.   Chajes, Peppie Dekker's *Holocaust Experience as seen through the eyes of a child.*
30.   Fritz Hartog, b. on May 23, 1913 in Haren (Germany). Fritz came to Westerbork on May 10, 1940. On 4 September 1944 from Westerbork on transport to Theresienstadt. Returned after liberation. Source: hckw archive.
31.   http://auschwitz.dk/schindlerslist.htm.
32.   Hckw archive.
33.   Van Riet, *Handhaven onder de Nieuwe Orde,* 14.
34.   Collection Jewish Historical Museum, inv.nr. 00006259.
35.   N.K.C.A. in 't Veld, *De Joodse Ereraad*, 10.
36   Lindwer, *Kamp van hoop en wanhoop*, 139.
37.   Bloch, *Confrontatie met het noodlot.*
38.   www.simson.nl and http://www.death-record.com/d/n/Sandor-Salmagne.
39.   *De Telegraaf*, 3 november 2012.
40.   na, CABR 105340 (Procureurfiscaal Amsterdam T-11669), en NIOD, 355 250i, inv.nr. 962.
41.   Van Riet, *Handhaven onder de Nieuwe Orde*, 665.
42.   Abuys en Mulder, *Een gat in het Prikkeldraad*, 70.
43.   na, CABR, dossier Paridaen, 76897.
44.   http://www.obitsforlife.com/obituary/38622/Paridaen-Bertrand-Herman.php.
45.   na, CABR, dossier A. de Jong, 75961.

46. J. Jansen, *De Marechaussee in de bezettingstijd*, 35.
47. www.marechausseecontact.nl.
48. *Kmar Magazine* (mei 2011), nr. 5. At the 2016 commemoration, Marechaussees were allowed to take their place in the guard of honor on Dam Square for the first time (information via Nationaal Comité 4 en 5 mei).
59. Lindwer, *Kamp van hoop en wanhoop*, 38.
50. Bombergen, *Terugblik 1943-1945*.
51. Interview K. Koster, dd 20 september 2000 en J. Romeijn, dd 6 oktober 1998.
52. Guus Meershoek, *Dienaren van het gezag*, 357.
53. Van Riet, *Handhaven onder de Nieuwe Orde*, 662.
54. na, CABR, dossier Willem Hendrik Tasseron, 5881, en dossier Jacobus Willem Munnikhuizen, 4386.
55. na, CABR, dossier Jacobus Willem Munnikhuizen, 4386.
56. Bial, *Briefe an Hetty*.
57. *Nieuw Israëlitisch weekblad*, 31-01-1947.
58. na, CABR, Hendrik van Dam, inv.nr. 70145.
59. na, CABR, Wilhelmus Severinus Antonie van Eck, inv.nr. 66642.
60. na, CABR, Johannes Otto von Henning, born 28 augustus 1919 in Zwolle, inv.nr. 75299.
61. *Nieuwsblad van het Noorden*, 19 augustus 1948.
62. na, CABR, inv.nr. 87540 (Bureau Opsporing Oorlogsmisdadigers Assen 0-66).
63. Van Riet, *Handhaven onder de Nieuwe Orde*, 687.
64. na, CABR, dossier Heinz Lemke, inv.nr. 2029, na, CABR, dossier Edmund Xaver Breil, inv.nr. 87494 en na, CABR, dossier Hans Georg Johann Reiser, inv.nr. 87503.
65. na, CABR, J. Schol, 88.972 (pra Enschede), 108.897 (pf Assen).
66. Van Riet, *Handhaven onder de Nieuwe Orde*, 247.
67. De Jong, *Het Koninkrijk*, deel 10a, eerste helft, 74.
68. *Der Spiegel*, nr. 13, 2006.
69. *Limburgsch Dagblad*, 22 januari 1964. 356
70. *Nieuwsblad van het Noorden*, 6 februari 1964.
71. *Limburgsch dagblad*, 18 februari 1983.
72. Proces-verbaal Gemmeker, nr. 414, dd 4 juli 1948 (privately owned).
73. *Nieuwsblad van het Noorden* en *De Tijd*, 10 december 1948.
74. 't Hart, *Ik zou in mijn tranen willen wegzwemmen*, 104.
75. Nanda van der Zee, *De trein*, 86.
76. Collection Jewish Historical Museum, inv.nr. 00001327 (newspaper article) and *De Tijd*, 7 January 1949.
77. *Nieuwsblad van het Noorden*, 20 January 1949, 22 January 1949 en 16 November 1968.
78. *De Tijd*, 16 November 1968.
79. www.geschiedenis24.nl.
80. *Friese Koerier*, 2 maart 1960.
81. *De Waarheid*, 3 maart 1960.
82. *Nieuw Israëlitisch Weekblad*, 30 maart 1973.
83. Moraal, *Als ik morgen niet op transport ga, ga ik 's avonds naar de revue*, 309.

Chapter 9
1. Pim Griffioen and Ron Zeller, *Jodenvervolging in Nederland, Frankrijk en België 1940-1945*, 424.
2. Ward Adriaens e.a., The Belgian exhibition in Auschwitz. The book, 19, www.kazernedossin.eu and Griffioen en Zeller, *Jodenvervolging in Nederland, Frankrijk en België 1940-1945*, 532.

3. Rudi van Doorslaer e.a., *Gewillig België. Overheid en Joden-vervolging tijdens de Tweede Wereldoorlog*, 940-947.

4. Informatie van Laurence Schram.

5. https://training.ehri-project.eu/deportation-jews-nazi-transitcamps-drancy-france-and-malines-belgium.

6. Jos Hakker, *De geheimzinnige kazerne Dossin. Deportatiekamp der Joden*, 19 and http://www.ehri-project.eu/

7. Wolfgang Benz and Barbara Distel, *Der Ort des Terrors. Geschichte der nationalsocialistische Konzentrationslager.*

8. Griffioen and Zeller, *Jodenvervolging in Nederland, Frankrijk en België*, 271.

9. http://www.massviolence.org/The-Drancy-Camp?cs=print.

10. Benz and Distel, *Der Ort des Terrors.*

11. http://www.go2war2.nl/artikel/3694/Sammel-en-Durchgangsla357ger-Drancy.htm?page=1.

12. http://www.deportati.it/e_lager/drancy.html.

13. Griffioen and Zeller, *Jodenvervolging in Nederland, Frankrijk en België*, 401.

14. Benz and Distel, *Der Ort des Terrors.*

15. http://www.massviolence.org/The-Drancy-Camp?cs=print.

16. Benz and Distel, *Der Ort des Terrors.*

17. Griffioen and Zeller, *Jodenvervolging in Nederland, Frankrijk en België*, 407.

18. http://www.massviolence.org/The-Drancy-Camp?cs=print.

19. *Die Yad Vashem enzyklopädie des Ghettos während des Holocaust*, deel xx-xxii.

20. http://www.deathcamps.org, http://www.holocaustresearchproject.org en Isaiah Trunk, Judenrat. 358

Literature

Abuys, Guido en Mulder, Dirk,
Een gat in het Prikkeldraad.
(Hooghalen/Assen 2003)
Adriaens, Ward, e.a.,
*De Belgische tentoonstelling in
Auschwitz. Het Boek*, uitgegeven door
het Joods Museum van deportatie en
Verzet in 2006
As, Aad van, *In het hol van de leeuw.*
(Westerbork 2004)
Benz, Wolfgang, Theresienstadt.
*Eine Geschichte von Täuschung und
Vernichtung.* (München 2013)
Benz, Wolfgang en Distel, Barbara,
*Des Ort des Terrors. Geschichteder
nationalsocialistische Konzentration-
slager*, band 9. (Munchen 2009)
Berghuis, Corrie K.,
*Joodse Vluchtelingen in Nederland
1938-1940, Documenten betreffende
toelating, uitleiding en kampopname.*
(Kampen 1990)
Bial, Hans, *Briefe an Hetty,
Tagebuch aus dem Lager Westerbork,
17 sept. 1944 -12 Mai 1945.*
(manuscript, Herinneringscentr. Kamp
Westerbork)
Bloch, Werner, *Confrontatie met
het noodlot.* (manuscript,
Herinneringscentrum
Kamp Westerbork)
Boas, Jacob, *Boulevard des Misères.*
(Amsterdam 1985)
Bolle, Mirjam, *Ik zal je beschrijven
hoe een dag er hier uitziet.*
(Amsterdam/Antwerpen 2003)
Boom, Bart van der,
*Wij weten niets van hun lot. Gewone
Nederlanders en de Holocaust.* (2012)
Brinkman, Herman en Willem,
*Derk Klavers 1890-1943. Wolf in
Schaapskleren.* (Groningen 2012)
Chagoll, Lydia,
*'Zigeuners'. Sinti en Roma onder
het hakenkruis.* (Berchem 2008)
Chajes, Peppie, Peppie Dekker's

*Holocaust Experience as seen through
the eyes of a child*
Cornelissen, C.B.,
SIPO en SD in Twente. (Meppel 2010)
Cottaar, Annemarie,
*Kooplui, kermisklanten en
andere woonwagenbewoners.
Groepsvorming en Beleid 1870-1945.*
(Amsterdam 1996)
Dominicus Henny E.,
Mauthausen een gedenkboek.
(Amsterdam 1999)
Doorslaer, Rudi van, e.a.,
*Gewillig België. Overheid en
Jodenvervolging tijdens de Tweede
Wereldoorlog.* (Brussel 2007)
Durlacher, G.L., *Verzameld werk.*
(Amsterdam 1997)
Fasse, Norbert,
*Das Amt Velen-Ramsdorf 1918-1945.
Katholiken und NS-Herrschaft
im Münsterland.* (Bielefeld 1997)
Frank, Ernest Elie, *Dagboek 2*
(z.j., manuscript, hckw)
Frederiks, mr.dr. K.J., *Op de bres*
(Den Haag 1945)
Frijtag Drabbe, Künzel Geraldien von,
Kamp Amersfoort (Amsterdam 2003)
Giltay Veth, D. and Leeuw, A.J. van der,
Het Weinrebrapport (Den Haag 1976)
Griffioen, Pim and Zeller, Ron,
*Jodenvervolging in Nederland,
Frankrijk en België 1940-1945.*
(Amsterdam 2011)
Hakker, Jos, *De geheimzinnige kazerne
Dossin. Deportatiekamp der Joden.*
(Antwerpen 1944)
Happe, Katja, e.a.,
*Die Verfolgung und Ermordung der
europäischen Juden durch das
Nationalsozialistische Deutschland
1933-1945.* (Berlijn 2015)
Hart, 't Wils,
*Ik zou in mijn tranen willen
wegzwemmen.*
(Doctoraalscriptie OU 2003)

Herzberg, Abel J.,
Kroniek der Jodenvervolging, 1940-1945. (Amsterdam 1985)
Het Joodsche Weekblad (Heruitgave. Deel 1en 2 Den Haag 1979)
Heuvel, C.L. van den,
Joodse vluchtelingen in het kamp in Hellevoetsluis. (Hellevoetsluis, 1995)
Houwaart, Dick,
Westerbork. Het begon in 1933. (Kampen 2000)
In 't Veld, N.K.C.A.,
De ss en Nederland. (Den Haag 1976)
In 't Veld, N.K.C.A.,
De Joodse Ereraad. (Amsterdam 1989)
Jansen, J.,
De Marechaussee in de bezettingstijd (1940-1945). (Maastricht 2000)
Jong, L. de,
Het Koninkrijk der Nederlanden in de Tweede Wereldoorlog. (Amsterdam 1995)
Jonker, A.L.,
Joodse vluchtelingen in Hellevoetsluis 1938-1940. (Hellevoetsluis 1995)
Kamminga, W.,
Grijpskerk van crisis tot bevrijding. (Zuidhorn 1986)
Kuyck, J.Th.,
Partisanenvrouwen. (Den Haag 1945)
Lee, Carol Ann,
Anne Frank 1929-1945. Het leven van een jong meisje. (Amsterdam 2009)
Lindwer, Willy,
Kamp van hoop en wanhoop. (Amstelveen 1990)
Loosen, Irmgard,
Erinnerungen an die Jüdische Gemeinde in Linnich. (Linnich 1994)
Magid, Avi,
Ontsnapping uit Westerbork. (Putten 1998)
Marsalek, Hans,
Die Geschichte des Konzentrationslager Mauthausen. (Wenen 1995)
Mechanicus, Philip,

Ik woon, zoals je weet, drie hoog. Brieven uit Westerbork. (A'dam 1987)
Mechanicus, Philip, *In Depot. Dagboek uit Westerbork.* (Amsterdam 1988)
Meershoek, Guus,
Dienaren van het gezag. De Amsterdamse politie tijdens de bezetting. (Amsterdan 1999)
Moraal, Eva,
Als ik morgen niet op transport ga, ga ik 's avonds naar de revue. (Proefschrift UvA 2013)
Moses, Kurt,
Home at Last. Auschwitz Survivor. (Harrisburg 2007)
Mulder, Ad A.J.,
Verzetsman in uniform. (Westerbork 2001)
Mulder, Dirk and Prinsen, Ben (red.),
Vluchtelingenkamp Westerbork. Westerbork Cahiers 7, (Westerbork 1999)
Noordhuis, Hennie e.a.,
In verdrukking, verzet en vrijheid. Borne, Bornerbroek, Hertme, Zenderen, 1940-1945. (Hengelo 1990)
Oord, Steffie van den,
Westerbork Girl. (Amsterdam 2008)
Oord, Niek van der,
Jodenkampen. (Kampen 2003)
Presser, J, *Ondergang. De vervolging en verdelging van het Nederlandse Jodendom 1940-1945.* (Den Haag 1965)
Rens, H.A.J. van,
De vervolging van joden en Sinti tijdens de Tweede Wereldoorlog in de Nederlandse provincie Limburg. (2013) via: http://dare.uva. nl/document/2/119638
Riet, Frank van, *'t Uwen dienst.* (Schiedam z.j.)
Riet, Frank van,
'n Papieren monument. (Rotterdam 2000)
Riet, Frank van,
Handhaven onder de Nieuwe Orde.

(Zaltbommel 2008)
Schneider, Karl,
*Auswärts eingesetzt. Bremer
Polizeibataillon und der Holocaust.*
(Essen 2011)
Schuyf, Judith (red,),
Nederlanders in Neuengamme.
(Zaltbommel 2005) 361
Schwarz, Fred,
Treinen op dood spoor.
(Badhoevedorp 2005)
Sijes, B.A.,
*Vervolging van zigeuners in Nederland
1940-1945.*
(Den Haag 1979)
Siegel, Paul,
Locomotieven trekken wagons.
(Westervoort 2000)
Sjenitzer-van Leening, T.M.,
Dagboekfragmenten 1940-1945.
(Den Haag 1954)
Stanelle Susan, e.a.,
*Die nationalsozialistische
Judenverfolgung – Die Verfolgung
in der Zeit von 1933 – 1938.*
Via: www.hagalil.com/deutschland/
ost/judentum/nsverfolgung.htm
Stekelenburg, Henk van,
Kamp Vught en de Vughtenaren.
 (Vught 1984)
Ternede, Maarten,
*De Ordedienst van kamp Westerbork
1939-1943. Over de grens van
slachtofferschap.* (Scriptie Amsterdam
2005)
Trunk, Isaiah,
*Judenrat. The Jewisch councils in
Eastern Europe under Nazi occupation.*
(Lincol USA 1972)

Veen, Harm van der,
Westerbork 1939-1945.
(Westerbork 2008)
Veldman, Guusta,
*Knackers achter prikkeldraad: kamp
Erika bij Ommen 1941-1945.*
(Utrecht 1993)
Vintcent, Sjra,
75 verhalen uit Reuver.
(Panningen 1998)
Weinmann, Martin,
*Das nationalsozialistische
Lagersystem.*
(Frankfurt am Main 1999)
Werf, Folkert van der,
*Mijn oorlogsverhaal, politieman op het
platteland tijdens de Duitse Bezetting.*
(manuscript, Den Over 1999)
Wijbenga, P.,
*Bezettingstijd in Friesland. Deel ii,
Met de rug tegen de muur.*
(Leeuwarden 1995)
Willing, Willem,
*Afdrukken van indrukken. Dagboek en
brieven uit Kamp Westerbork, barak
67.* (Waalwijk 2006)
Winter-Levy, R. de,
Aan de gaskamer ontsnapt.
(Doetinchem 1945)
Zee, Nanda van der,
De Trein. (Soesterberg 2003)
Zwaluw Jean-Philippe van der, en Hor,
Joop van der,
Heijplaat in verzet.
(Hilversum, 2010)
Zwarte-Walvisch, Klaartje de,
Alles ging aan flarden.
(Amsterdam 2009)

Names Index

Photo credits

Wikimedia Commons CC 3.0. Attribution I, Dennis Nilsson Map: 4

Archief familie Pellinkhof (Pellinkhof family archives): 115, 116

Beeldbank wo2: 44, 120, 162

Author collection: 174, 174, 177, 177

Coen Cornelissen collection: 169

Drents Museum collection: 38

Collectie Herinneringscentrum kamp Westerbork (Collection Westerbork Memorial Center): 8, 17, 18, 25, 27, 30, 31, 32, 32, 36, 36, 37, 38, 39, 40, 42, 44, 45, 48, 48, 49, 52, 55, 61, 73, 30, 92, 99, 103 (Archive Rode Kruis), 105, 106, 107, 119, 125, 127, 129, 129, 136, 136, 137, 139, 139, 139, 152, 153, 191

Collection Libbe T. Henstra: 29

Collection Ulrich Bauhaus: 167

File Arthur Pisk, CABR, via Ministry of Justice: 108

File Hendrik van Dam, CABR, via Ministry of Justice: 67

Nationaal Archief (National Archives): 262

Polak: Stichting Oranjehotel, Doodenboeken (Foundation, Books of the Dead): 147

Systeemkaarten van verzetsbetrokkenen (System cards of those involved in the resistance), no. 218, :150

Stichting Oorlogs- en Verzetscentrum Groningen (Groningen War and Resistance Center Foundation): 150

www.delpher.nl: 217

Mechelen: Credits: Kazerne Dossin – Fonds Kummer, Mechelen : 231

Drancy: Credits: Wikimedia Commons. Attribution: Bundesarchiv, Bild 183-B10919 / Wisch / CC-BY-SA 3.0: 233

Abbreviations

ANWB
Algemeene Nederlandsche Wielrijders Bond

BdS
Befehlshaber der Sipo und SD

BRvC
Bijzondere Raad van Cassatie

BS
Binnenlandse Strijdkrachten

CABR
Centraal Archief Bijzondere Rechtspleging

DGvP
Directorate General of the Police

FK
Fliegende Kolonne

GESTAPO
Geheime Staatspolizei

HCKW
Herinneringscentrum kamp Westerbork

JHM
Joods Historisch Museum (Amsterdam)

JPA
Jüdische Presse Agentur

MS
Membres de la Surveillance

NA
Nationaal Archief (Den Haag)

NAD
Nederlandse Arbeidsdienst

NB
Notbereitschaft

NIOD
Instituut voor Oorlogs-, Holocaust- en Genocidestudies

NSB
Nationaalsocialistische Beweging

OD
Ordedienst

OT
Organisation Todt

PBA
Police Battalion Amsterdam

PF
Procureur-Fiscaal

POB
Police Training Battalion

POD
Politieke Opsporingsdienst

POS
Police Officers School

PRA
Politieke Rechercheafdeling

SA
Sturmabteilung

Sipo und SD
Sicherheitspolizei und des Sicherheitsdienst

SS
Schutzstaffel

VOP
Verordening Organisatie Politie

About the author

Dr. Frank van Riet (1964) is a Historian, Researcher and Policeman from the Netherlands. This book (*De bewakers van Westerbork*) was published in Dutch in 2016. Frank is specialized in the Dutch police during World War II as well as the Resistance. His dissertation about the Rotterdam Police in the war (*Handhaven onder de Nieuwe Orde*, 2008) was nominated for the mr. J. Dultilh prize. In 2022 his extensive research into a hidden part of history of persecution, resistance and betrayal in and around the city of Dordrecht (*De Dordtse Affaire*) was published.

About Nedvision Publishing
Nedvision Publishing is a publishing house of unique books on history, especially World War II in Dutch, English and German.

Other (English) books published by Nedvision:
Journey to the Horizon, escape and evasion in World War 2
by Hans Onderwater and Brian Lissette
American Saint-Nick
by Peter Lion
A winged gunner; the life and times of Air Cdre Andrew James Wray Geddes CBE DSO RAF,
by Hans Onderwater MBE

To be published in the course of 2023:
Blackout, Bombs and Sugar Beets
by Elisabeth Breslav
Merg
By Peter Lion
Stripes of a Zebra
by Andries van der Wal & Dick van der Zee

If you would like to receive the latest news about our publications, please subscribe to our newsletter or contact us.

Nedvision Publishing
Wagenmakerstraat 9
9403 VC Assen
The Netherlands
T +31 (0)592-749333
E info@nedvision.com
www.nedvision.com